AF560089

MEDIEVAL INDIA 2

MEDIEVAL INDIA 2

Essays in Medieval Indian History and Culture

Edited by

SHAHABUDDIN IRAQI

CENTRE OF ADVANCED STUDY
Department of History
Aligarh Muslim University

MANOHAR
2008

First published 2008

ISBN 81-7304-786-3

Published by
Ajay Kumar Jain *for*
Manohar Publishers & Distributors
4753/23 Ansari Road, Daryaganj
New Delhi 110 002

Printed at
Lordson Publishers Pvt Ltd
Delhi 110 007

Contents

Preface

In 1950, the Department of History, Aligarh Muslim University, decided to bring out a quarterly journal, *Medieval India Quarterly*, devoted to Indian history of medieval period. The aim was to promote research on different aspects of medieval Indian history—political, social, economic and cultural, and to discover the element of change and continuity. Effort was also made to publish or introduce the unpublished and newly discovered source material in the journal. It was received as a welcome addition to the historical literature on medieval Indian history.

After the publication of *Medieval India Quarterly*, vol. 5 in 1963, it was found difficult to get a quarterly journal printed on time, and then it was changed to *Medieval India—A Miscellany* and Asia Publishing House, Bombay, undertook its publication. After the publication of its fourth volume in 1977, the project had to be discontinued on account of litigation with the publishers. In 1990, it was decided to begin a new series under the title *Medieval India*. In 1992, Oxford University Press brought out its first volume under the title *Medieval India 1: Researches in the History of India 1200–1750*, on behalf of the Centre of Advanced Study, Department of History, Aligarh Muslim University.

The present volume, *Medieval India 2: Essays in Medieval Indian History and Culture*, contains articles and reviews of the scholars from Aligarh as well as outside. The Centre acknowledges their valuable contributions and hopes that in future also, the scholars interested in research on medieval Indian history would extend cooperation in this regard.

The Centre is grateful to Manohar Publishers & Distributors, New Delhi for undertaking the publication of this volume and to colleagues and staff for their help at various levels during the process of its publication.

SHAHABUDDIN IRAQI

PART I

HISTORY AND CULTURE

Social Changes under the Imperial Cholas and its Reflections in Later Ages: A Study

S. CHANDNI BI

The Cholas ruled south India between AD 850 and 1279. The society under the Cholas has been thoroughly studied by K.A. Neelakantha Sastri in his seminal work *Colas*. However, not much research has come out in the last fifty years in this field. Historians of repute have written a lot on the 'economy' of the Cholas but study of society under the Cholas remains untapped. True, scholars like Kathleen Gough (1950), Burton Stein (1960–70), and Noboru Karashima (1984) have made studies on the social life of this period but mainly focusing on, mainly the notion of the Asiatic mode of production, feudal production, and the chronology of such changes, and with reference to very small areas.[1]

A more or less similar pattern has been followed by Y. Subbarayalu in his analysis of land sales.[2] When Champaklakshmi writes about urbanization during the Chola period, again, her limits are set in time and space.[3] Hence, research on the society under the Cholas remains unexplored. An attempt is being made in this paper to overcome this limitation and to stress that changes were taking place in the Chola society and that it was not static: change as a result of the struggle between the Aryanized system of birth-based caste hierarchy and economy-based social status. The struggle seemed to be between the foreign and native cultures in the soil of south India. At the end of it seems native culture and economy based social status could derive the benefits. But a study on the nature of the benefits and its effect with time and space remains untapped.

For a study of the changes emerging in Chola society, many phenomena like landholdings, land sales, bureaucracy and caste dominance, the emergence of new castes and sub-castes, their privileges and fights need to be studied. The changing roles of the different groups in the temples and temple-related affairs, the relation between the different caste-groups and the administrative bodies, changes in the idea of religion and religious institutions of the non-Brahmin castes are also relevant to changes in the society as a whole.

LANDHOLDINGS

Land was the chief wealth in the pre-industrial era when production depended on land and the economy on production. In the first half[4] of Chola rule, AD 850–985, individual landholding was noticeable in the Brahmadeya villages; but not so in other villages. Citing the examples of Isanamangalam and Allur, a Brahmadeya and a non-Brahmadeya village of the same region and time respectively, Karashima has concluded that individual landholding was common in the Brahmadeyas villages and communal landholding in the non-Brahmadeya villages in the first half of the period.[5] Though individual landholding was marginal in the period, it increased thereafter,[6] leading to changes in the social order, and these changes in landholding closely reveal the change in the social order. When communal landholding existed, there was only one class of cultivators—the owners were the cultivators too. But as individuals began to hold large tracts of land, there came a new social order of landlords and cultivators separately. This marked division became significant with the passing of time and in the last and fourth period of Chola rule, landowners were influential people who held important positions in the local and central administration and held titles such as *Araiyan* and *Muvendavelan*. Thus appeared two distinct strata in rural society—owners and cultivators. This also brought changes in their economic and social standards.

CHANGES IN GOVERNMENT OFFICE HOLDINGS

The state officer holders—the Olai, Kanakkus, Varippottagams, Naduvirukkais, Adhikaris, and Senapatis—were considered by the people of the village as the government itself. They commanded immense respect in public because of their association with the king. Certain castes appear to dominate a particular office during the focus period.

Table 1 adapted from Y. Subbarayalu's studies, gives the overall picture of office holders during the Chola dynasty, and their titles.[7]

Brahmarayan and Bhattan are titles which clearly show they were from the Brahmin caste. The landholding and cultivating caste, the Vellalas, had titles such as Velan, Kilan, Muvendavelan and Udaiyar. Table 1 shows that the Vellalas occupied a leading role in all important government offices except one, i.e. Naduvirukkai. Similarly, the absence of Brahmin titles is noticeable in the revenue department. The Naduvirukkai seems to be the monopoly of the Brahmin community. The majority of the class 'bureaucrats' seems to have been dominated by the Udaiyar and Muvendavelan community. These bureaucrats were also landlords.

The Chola rulers granted certain concessions to some communities for their military and other services with political considerations in mind. The Pallis for instance, were granted the privilege of tying, silk cloth on their forehead during festive occasions.[8] Pallis, Kanmalas, weavers, smiths, and military men were given concessions ranging from royal titles to trivial social practices like wearing sandals. The concessions were granted either to a few families or to the whole community in a particular region.

TABLE 1: CORRELATION OF OFFICES AND TITLES
(ALL PERIODS TOGETHER)

Name of the Officer	No. of Officers	Udaiyar	Muvend-avelan	Brahma-rayan	Aryan Group	Nadu Group	Kings Titles
Adhikari	227	89	125	8	50	7	183
Senapati	24	4	–	6	11	2	16
Dandanayagam	15	3	4	2	11	1	12
Olai	85	24	27	10	29	7	48
Naduvirukkai	29	–	–	27	–	–	1
Srikariyam	56	26	9	8	7	5	14
Naduvagai	25	18	1	2	4	–	6
Puruvari Top	159	91	55	1	10	5	45
Middle	126	90	17	1	7	2	19
Lower	62	33	1	–	3	1	4

Surplus agricultural produce, the growth of large temples with multipurpose activities leading to a 'temple culture', and the promotion of trade activities in medieval south India made the new social changes inevitable among the artisan and trading communities. These new circumstances and developments resulted in the social elevation of skilled and semi-skilled groups. For instance, among the goldsmiths a prominent section grew to meet the needs of the court and temples, who in turn received special royal titles and tax-free lands as concession.[9] From the weaver community a section became privileged to weave royal robes and attend to the needs of temples and Brahminical ceremonies.[10] Some carpenters, stone-masons, and smiths also became privileged for the same kind of services.[11] These people were sometimes allowed to live in groups and establish their colonies (*cherry*) near the temples.[12] They migrated in groups from other places and began their establishments in these tax-free lands as colonies in the hamlets of the Brahmadeyams[13] and in the later period in the precincts of the temple (temple *vilagam*).[14]

These skilled, semi-skilled, concessioned, and privileged sections experienced a sort of unrest, which reflected in the entire society, as leading to confusion and chaos in the long run. They did not want to be placed in the fourth category, but could not be called the twice born of Manu. Hence, they craved a new label that would suit their elevated status.

Thus changes became noticeable among landholders, government officers, artisans, craftsmen, and traders. In these groups there emerged two strata—one with privileges and concessions and new titles and a better standard of living, the other with no remarkable change in their lives. R. Thirumalai brings out the fact that wages remained constant for most of the period under study.[15] Hence it appears as if a major contradiction had emerged between the caste principle and actual economy-based social standards.

GROUPINGS AND SUB-GROUPINGS

To establish their specialized new social status these sections adopted many dynamic steps. In the first instance they emerged as separate occupational groups since they felt strength in unity.

All these minor groups allied themselves either with the Right Hand or Left Hand.[16] The tussle for social concessions is a well-known fact. Many theories have come up regarding the origin, development, and history of these factions. But the inevitable growth of the artisans and traders caused further splits in these factions and formed many sub-groups, some quite powerful. In the sixteenth century, the Panchalas got separated by a social legislation.[17] Saurastrians, Saliyars, Kaikolas, Pattinattars, Pattunulkarars, and Devangars were all weavers with different specializations and therefore formed separate unions. Later they emerged as separate castes with changed food habits and customs.[18] Likewise many examples can be cited among the Chettis, Vyaparis, Vaniyas, Naidus, Vellalas, and others.

Invariably, these groups claimed a genealogy dating back to the Smriti Age. The different groups of smiths traced their roots to the Panchalas, and the Panchalas in turn called themselves the ancient Rathakaras and associated themselves with Anuloma and Pratiloma sections as defined by the Smritis.[19] The stonemasons and sculptors claimed their origin from the sacred architect Vishvakarma.[20] The Left Hand faction associated itself as slaves of the Brahmin families who had migrated to south India on royal request and claimed colonies next to Brahmin residences (*agraharas*).[21] Such identification with Brahmins, prompted a change in food habits. Many occupational groups, split into vegetarians and non-vegetarians.[22] This is how perhaps a vegetarian section among all castes emerged and they added a prefix Shaiva, meaning vegetarian, to their caste names in the later centuries.

TEMPLE-ASSOCIATED ACTIVITIES

Every section of society, aware of the growth of the new temple culture, felt the necessity to associate itself with temple activities and establish its identity in society. Donating to the temple became a symbol of prestige. The Manradins, a special group of shepherds who maintained the temple cattle, made cattle donations,[23] the Kanmalas were privileged to construct temple *gopuras* (towers) and *mandapas* (halls) the inner halls of the temple, and it was only they who could construct icons of gods and goddesses. They levied a tax on their community (*inavari*) and constructed a hall in the temple as donation.[24] The Pattinattar weaver's group who enjoyed the privilege of supplying cloth to temples and Brahmins, placed themselves as temple servants pledged to provide the needed cloth for temple festivities and a certain amount of gold annually.[25] The Sankarapadin oil-pressers also donated to the maintenance of perpetual lamps in the temples.[26] Those who were given service tenures and allowed to stay in and around the temple precincts claimed supra-status among their community in the society.

CONCESSION FOR LUXURIES

Social movements among Brahmins and temple groups and their privilege of enjoying certain royal concessions and economic benefits made the demand rise for certain luxuries that had hitherto been the privilege of the 'twice born'. The use of palanquins, wearing of sandals, sounding of horns and conch-shell to mark sad and happy occasions, certain hairstyles and headgears with birds' feathers, construction of double-storeyed houses, whitewashing the walls, floral decorations on houses, and a double-door were some of the luxuries for which these groups fought at times.

Thus we have many examples in medieval south India to show that these groups sometimes fought viciously, [27] citing precedents from other regions to claim a right to luxuries.[28] Some tried to obtain such privileges by bribing corrupt officials[29] and some even by forging inscriptions.[30] Sometimes the authorities who were burdened with these problems worked out other ways. They too cited examples from other regions to deny privileges.[31] There were awkward incidents of group clashes, murders,[32] and threats of mass evacuation. Some even went to the extent of asking for separate halls and hours of worship in the temples and separate dancing girls.[33] On one occasion a place of worship was even burnt and destroyed.[34] The idea of superiority by virtue of birth, and the purity attached to certain castes were questioned, and the question of equality on the basis of economic status sprang up. But this did not percolate to the lower castes and slavery and untouchability in society continued. The economically advanced sections of the society wanted to climb to higher positions in the caste ladder but wished the lower groups to remain where they were. Communal disputes occurred every now and then and drew the attention of the authorities. The issues were settled by referring to the rules and regulations written in the Smritis,[35] or according to traditional practice and custom.[36] Most of the time to settle such disputes the authorities and the Brahmins sat together.[37] Old copper-plates from Kanchipuram were brought to check the authenticity of the inscriptions that provided concessions, and new ones were inscribed.[38] In settlement of disputes between groups there was often loss of life,[39] with orders to 'kill a person on the spot with spears',[40] if he happened to cause a disturbance in public.

The rift, started among the artisans for certain petty social privileges, however did not stop there. They never ended fights among themselves but carried them further. I agree with many historians who have worked on the origin, growth, and theories of Right and Left Hand factions that the fight was over trivial issues but the spirit and vigour behind that was different. I submit these groups were successful to certain extent in gaining equal social status with other castes.

The concessions as stated above were specifically meant for the service of an individual or a group of a particular area for a particular purpose. In the long run, the purpose of the privilege was defeated as the whole community began to claim the privileges as their right. As a next step, the same community in different regions across southern India, wanted to enjoy that status, just because they belonged to that particular community. Thus the personal titles and concessions first became hereditary, then regional, and finally communal. The Kanmalas could bend the *nattar* (administrative body of the *nadu*) of Tiruvamattur village (South Arcot district, Tamil Nadu) to give an undertaking to the royal official (*rajakaryabhandara*) that they would no more be ill-treated or deprived of their privileges and rights hitherto enjoyed by their community in other areas (Padaivedu, Senji, Tiruvannamalai and Kanchipuram) and in the case of a violation of the promise, the *nattar* would pay a fine.[41]

After establishing success among themselves, Brahmins became their targets. For instance, the Pattunulkarar or silk-thread weavers, who had assumed Brahmin caste names and spread certain legends (that they were originally Brahmins but had lost their status but now wished to renew the practice of wearing the sacred thread) which resulted in disputes with Brahmins. The state was forced to interfere and the case was decided in favour of the defendants.[42] The Kaikola and Devanga weavers who lived around the temple precincts began to have a share in the temple administration. In earlier instances, when these two groups of weavers had shown their protest to the *ilaivaniyār* (betel-leaf sellers), by leaving the place, the state had settled the dispute in favour of the weavers, and the inscription was inscribed again. Gradually these communities could establish their place in the social dynamics. Ultimately they asked for separate times and halls of worship. The grant of such a demand concerning the daily routine of the temple is amazing and brings home their unchallenging position in society. It also indicates the silent degenerate position of the Brahmins, the so-called unquestionable authorities as specified by the Smritis and the Agamas.

The powerful artisan groups continued to exist even after the sixteenth century and carried on their disputes. The clash that they started for trivial social concessions like wearing sandals or to wear their hair loose and long, ended with demands for social equality. Even in this century, especially in Tamil Nadu, these groups have emerged as the bastion of caste-based political parties.

CONCLUSION

The changes in land holding meant a change in the social order. Rural society became divided into two classes—the landlords and the cultivators. The idea of government officers and offices tabled by Y. Subbarayalu has given us a picture of social strata and the caste dominance in bureaucracy that existed under the imperial Cholas. Two different classes of artisans and craftsmen that survived in this period have been discussed. One supra-class among them would get elevated due to the various concessions and privileges shown in the beginning by the royal authorities.

Later many communities would demand the same, and gain them by prolonged fights. The changed trade-based economy and temple-oriented culture had brought them benefits. Hence it is concluded that Chola society saw transformations at many levels, which were reflected in the ages that followed.

ABBREVIATIONS

ARE : *Annual Reports on India Epigraphy*
EC : *Epigraphia Carnatica*
EI : *Epigraphia Indica*
QJMS : *The Quarterly Journal of the Mystic Society*
SII : *South India Inscriptions*
SITI : *South India Temple Inscriptions*

NOTES

1. Kathleen Gough, 'Mode of Production in Southern India', *Economic and Political Weekly,* Annual Number, February 1980; Burton Stein, *Peasant State and Society in Medieval South India,* Delhi: Oxford University Press, 1980; Noboru Karashima, *South Indian History and Society, Studies from Inscriptions* AD *850–1800,* Delhi: Oxford University Press, 1984.
2. Y. Subbarayalu, *Studies in Chola History,* Chennai: Koodal Publishers, 2001.
3. R. Champakalakshmi, 'Growth of Urban Centres in South India: Kudamukku-Palayarai, the Twin-cities of the Cholas', *Studies in History,* vol. I, no. I, Delhi: Sage Publications, 1979.
4. The period of the imperial Cholas has been divided for convenience into four periods, AD 850–985, 986–1070, 1071–1178 and 1179–1279.
5. Karashima, op. cit., p. 74.
6. Y. Subbarayalu, *Studies in Chola History,* Table 1, p. 47.
7. Ibid.
8. K.A. Neelakantha Sastri, *The Colas,* Chennai: Madras University, 1984.
9. 'Introduction', *SII,* vol. 2, *Mysore,* Delhi: Archaeological Survey of India, 1913, pp. 10–11.
10. *ARE* 396 of 1922.
11. *ARE* 479 of 1908.
12. *ARE* 319 of 1911.
13. *ARE* 162 of 1918.
14. Ibid.
15. R. Tirumalai, 'Land Reclamation under Kulottunga', *Journal of the Epigraphical Society of India,* vol. XI, 1984, pp. 82-3.

16. T.V. Mahalingam, *Administration and Social Life under Vijayanagar*, Chennai: Madras University, p. 25.
17. *ARE* 44 of 1916.
18. *Madras Gazetteer*, Chennai: Tamil Nadu Govt., 1952, p. 111.
19. *ARE* 473 of 1921. For that matter, the goldsmiths were referred to as Pattar and Achary, which remains in vogue even today as corruptions of Bhattar and Acharyar, terms which generally denote Brahmins.
20. *ARE* 1913, para 39. Burton Stein, op. cit., p. 198, n. 81.
21. *ARE* 1913 para 39, summarized by K.A. Neelakantha Sastri, op. cit., pp. 551–2.
22. This section is present even today among Tamil communities such as the Mudaliyars, Vellalas, Pillais, Naidus and Chettis.
23. Many examples are available throughout the social history of the Cholas and Vijayanagar.
24. Discussed by K.V. Subramanya Aiyar, 'Largest Provincial Organization in Ancient India', *QJMS*, vol. 45, no. 2, 1954, pp. 77ff.
25. *ARE* 274 of 1910.
26. Many inscriptions do mention the donation.
27. Arjun Appadurai, *Right and Left Hand Castes in South India*, Chennai: Madras University, 1985.
28. *ARE* 293 of 1928–9, para 66.
29. *SII*, vol. VII, no. 865, Delhi, 1990.
30. *ARE* 201 of 1936–7, para 61, *ARE* 237 of 1920.
31. *ARE* 273 of 1939–40, para 101.
32. *ARE* 185 of 1921.
33. *ARE* 1921, part II, p. 47.
34. Ibid.
35. Sastri, op. cit., pp. 550–1.
36. Ibid.
37. *ARE* 1909, para 45, 479 of 1908.
38. *SII*, vol. VII, no. 865, Delhi, 1990, *ARE* 237 of 1902.
39. *ARE* 185 of 1921.
40. Taylor, *Cat. Kais*, III, p. 305.
41. *ARE* 65 of 1992, para 54.
42. Mahalingam, op. cit., vol. II, pp. 29–30.

Jahangir's Relations with the Contemporary Ulama and Sufis

IQBAL SABIR

From a very early age Jahangir, was deeply attracted towards religion and sincerely believed in Islam. He writes in his *Tuzuk-i-Jahangiri*, 'I am hopeful that my whole life would be spent in accordance with the Divine Will and even a single moment will not be passed without His remembrance.'[1] In his boyhood Jahangir had been placed under the care of Shaikh Salim Chishti, and as a result he developed deep interest in Sufism and immense respect for Sufis. He was taught to read and write by Shaikh Salim Chishti's son, Shaikh Ahmad.[2] Later on, Maulana Mir Kalan Harwi,[3] Abdur Rahim Khan-i-Khanan[4] and Saiyid Sadr Jahan Pihani[5] also instructed him in the basic tenets of Islamic theology and in the popular sciences. Likewise, his personal association with Nawab Murtaza Khan, commonly called Shaikh Farid Bukhari, especially on account of the latter's role at the time of his accession to the throne—whom he also continued as the Mir Bakhshi under his rule[6]—created in Jahangir a deep love for Islam and religious personalities.[7] The sources inform us of several saints and scholars who were on close terms with him. The present paper seeks to analyse Jahangir's relations with some of the Ulama and Sufis (*mashaikhs*) of his time.

Shaikh Abdul Haq Muhaddith Dehlawi was a leading religious scholar during Jahangir's reign.[8] The latter's association with him started when the Shaikh, on the occasion of Jahangir's accession to the throne, his requested friend Shaikh Farid Bukhari[9] to place a letter before Jahangir unploring the Emperor to understand the need to implement the *Shariah* and show respect to the *Sunnah*.[10] This letter refused Jahangir, the fortunate successor of Akbar and wished that the new emperor maintain peace, ensure justice, and exert himself to create conditions for the welfare and prosperity of his subjects.

As the Shaikh had closely observed religious activities and experiments at Akbar's court before his journey to Hejaz,[11] he tried through this letter to bring to Jahangir's notice the importance of the Prophet of Islam and his mission. He also desired to check the tendency initiated in Akbar's time, of seeking spiritual solace from the teachings of other religions and schools of thought. Though the letter was couched in polite and academic language, it did not leave out any point that the Shaikh wanted Jahangir to bear in mind.[12]

Owing to lack of information in this regard, it is difficult to say anything about the relationship between Jahangir and Shaikh Abdul Haq during the early years of Jahangir's reign. It was only in his fourteenth regnal year that Shaikh Abdul Haq's famous work, *Akhbar-ul-Akhyar*[13] was brought to Jahangir's notice. The emperor was so impressed by the book that he invited the Shaikh to his court. Jahangir writes in his *Tuzuk-i-Jahangiri*:

> Shaikh Abdul Haq Dehlawi, who belongs to the class of learned and pious people, had the good fortune of paying respects to me. He has compiled an account of the *mashaikh* of India. He produced the book before me, He had put great labour in its preparation. He has been leading a life of resignation and seclusion in a corner of Delhi for a long time. He is a revered personality and his company is not devoid of mystic delight.[14]

The emperor is also reported to have granted village Bakrwala near Delhi to the Shaikh. At first the Shaikh declined to accept, but on Jahangir's insistence he reluctantly accepted it.[15]

Shaikh Abdul Haq generally spent his time in prayer, instructing scholars in science, or writing on various aspects of Islamic theology, history, etc. Unfortunately Jahangir's relations with him could not remain permanently cordial. The reasons for this is not known.[16] Anyhow, Jahangir summoned him to Kashmir in 1627.[17] But, as Prince Dara Shikoh, in his *Sakinat-ul-Auliya*, says,

> When Shaikh Abdul Haq reached Lahore, he visited Miyan Mir to obtain his blessings. The latter assured the Shaikh that he would return to his native place without meeting the Emperor and join his family. It so happened that four days after Shaikh Abdul Haq's visit to Miyan Mir news of the death of Jahangir was received.[18]

According to relevant sources, in the last decade of his life Jahangir also maintained relations with the famous Naqshbandi saint of the early seventeenth century Shaikh Ahmad Sirhindi, popularly known as 'Mujaddid-i Alf-i-Thani' or 'Renovator' of the second millennium of Islam.[19] The latter had shown a lot of interest in Jahangir's accession to the throne,[20] but personal contacts started somewhat late. In the beginning the relations between them were not very cordial. Jahangir had been annoyed by the Shaikh's condemnation of his father's religious policy.[21]

It was in AH 1028/AD 1619, when Mujaddid-i Alf-i-Thani, in his process of organizing the Naqshbandi order in India and abroad, deputed one of his followers Maulana Badiuddin, as his representative in Agra. Sources say Badiuddin achieved remarkable success in a short span of time. A large number of soldiers and officials are also reported to have joined the circle of the Shaikh through the mediation of Badiuddin.[22] But the opponents of the saint poisoned Jahangir's ears by saying that the activities of the Shaikh and his Khalifa could lead to political disturbance.[23] These people also brought to Jahangir's notice a letter written by Mujaddid-i Alf-i-Thani,[24] to his spiritual mentor Khwaja Baqi Billah[25] ten years earlier. Shaikh Ahmad had described his spiritual experience in this letter. But his opponents at the Mughal court explained to Jahangir that the Shaikh had claimed to be superior to the first Pious Caliph, Hazrat Abu Bakr Siddique (held by Muslims as Afzal-il Bashar Ba'd Al-Ambiya—the most spiritually distinguished and the most excellent of the human beings after the chain of prophets of God). This annoyed the emperor and Sirhindi was summoned to the royal court in Agra to explain.[26] Shaikh Ahmad defended himself by saying that his status was not above the first Pious Caliph. It is what happened in the course of his spiritual journey for a moment and was actually meant to show him the most-elevated spiritual station occupied by Hazrat Abu Bakr Siddique after the Prophet of Islam. Illustrating his point, the Shaikh further explained, addressing Jahangir, 'If you, in your royal court, summon some inferior servant of yours in the presence of all your courtiers to speak to him, he will have to reach you by passing through all of the high and superior nobles, and momentarily he will be nearer to you than your great nobles. But that does not mean that he (the servant) is greater than them or permanently occupies a place in closer proximity to you'.[27] This was a fair enough and reasonable argument but since Shaikh Ahmad had not made the customary obeisance to Jahangir, the latter regarded him as arrogant. When commended to observe the usual court etiquette by performing *sijda-i-tazimi* (prostrating in respect), according to *Hazarat-ul-Quds*, the Shaikh replied, 'I have never bowed my head to any of God's creatures and I never will'.[28] As was expected, the Shaikh's reply once again incurred the wrath of Jahangir. He ordered to a Rajput official, Ani Rai Singh Dalan, to imprison the Shaikh in Gwalior fort.[29]

Jahangir's memoirs bear evidence that subsequently the emperor changed his mind about Shaikh Ahmad Sirhindi and ordered his release after a year in AD 1620. On the latter's arrival at the court in Agra, Jahangir honoured him by giving him a robe and a present of a thousand rupees. Jahangir writes in his *Tuzuk-i-Jahangiri*, 'I summoned Shaikh Ahmad who had been in prison for some time . . . I released him, giving him a robe and one thousand rupees. I also authorized him either to go home or to remain with me. And he expressed his desire to remain in my service.'[30]

Contemporary and later sources say that the Shaikh remained in the royal camp for three years. Wherever the royal army and the emperor encamped, Shaikh Ahmad accompanied them. In the course of this time he visited several cities and towns in northern India.[31] First he seems to have journeyed to Kashmir: According to the *Majma'-ul-Auliya*,

The great Emperor Abul Muzaffar Nuruddin Muhammad Jahangir, on his departure from Kashmir, fell seriously ill. Physicians treated him but he did not recover. His personal and private servants advised him to turn to pious people. Shaikh Ahmad Sirhindi, who was accompanying the royal caravan, was therefore approached for spiritual benedictions. He went to the royal palace and invoked God for the Emperor's recovery and good health. The Shaikh also exhorted Jahangir to popularize Islamic teachings. The latter said to the Shaikh, 'It is for you to say, and it is for me to do.' The Emperor recovered in the same night. Subsequently the royal army left for Sirhind. While encamped at Sirhind the Emperor desired to have his meal at the Shaikh's residence. The saint next day sent him a variety of dishes prepared in his house. It is said that all the items were so delicious that Jahangir took only half of it and the saved the rest for the next day.

It was during Jahangir's stay in Sirhind that he asked Asaf Khan to request Shaikh Ahmad to accept an annual or monthly grant, either in cash or in kind, for the expenses of his *khanqah*. But the Shaikh declined.[32]

It appears that the Shaikh could not stay with his family members, disciples and khalifas in Sirhind for long as the royal caravan left for another destination. Afterwards he seems to have reached Delhi and then Agra. His presence in the royal camp provided him with frequent meetings with the emperor. He never missed an opportunity to persuade Jahangir to follow Islam and the *Shariah*. Once he wrote to his son Muhammad Masum from the royal camp,

> Thanks to God that everything is all right here. I am keeping good company with the Emperor. By Divine Grace, I do not lose a single moment without describing the theological points and the principles of Islam to him (Jahangir). If I start to write only about one meeting, it would require a whole volume, especially the conversation of this night, the 17th of Ramazan. Many points were discussed such as the creation of the prophets, the faith in hereafter, the concept of reward and punishment, the Divine Appearance, the seal of the prophecy of the last of the prophets (the Prophet of Islam), the *mujaddid* of every century, the following (*taqlid*) of the Pious Caliphs, the lawfulness of *tarawih*, the falsehood of the concept of transmigration, jinns and their affairs etc. The Emperor listens to me with full attention. In this connection the *aqtab*, the *abdal*, the *autad* and their affairs of spirituality were also explained. Thanks to God that the Emperor completely participated in the discussion. I am thankful to God who guided me to do so. Undoubtedly our Holy Prophet came to this world with Truth.[33]

In 1620 Jahangir sent an expedition to Kangra under the command of Sunder Das *alias* Raja Bikramajit.[34] The author of *Hazrat-ul-Quds* says that when Bikramajit was ordered to lead the expedition he approached the Shaikh in all humility and requested his blessings. Finding him persistent in his request, the Shaikh meditated for a while and said, 'Victory is certainly yours, you need not worry, go without any fear.' Bikramajit departed and without much difficulty conquered the fort.[35] When Jahangir visited Kangra, the Shaikh also accompanied him.

The third volume of the letters of the Shaikh, the *Maktubat-i-Imam-i-Rabbani*, contains an epistle addressed to Jahangir. The concluding remarks of this letter are, 'Though this humble person does not find himself capable to be counted in the *lashkar-i-dua* (the group of saints), he is not at all free from invoking God's blessings for you. He regards himself as one of the well-wishers of your Empire and prays for your prosperity.'[36] Anyhow, the Shaikh continued his sojourns to different places along with the royal army.[37] Finally, they encamped in Ajmer where he seems to have stayed for several months.[38] It was in 1623, that, on account of his failing health, the Shaikh, along with his sons Khwaja Muhammad Said and Khwaja Muhammad Masum left for Sirhind.[39] He died therein AH 1034/AD 1624.

Miyan Mir of Lahore,[40] a saint of the Qadiri order was another prominent spiritual figure during Jahangir's period. The latter came to know of him in January 1620 while travelling from Sirhind and Lahore to Kashmir. He says in his *Tuzuk-i-Jahangiri*,

> It was reported to me that in Lahore that a saint, Miyan Shaikh Muhammad Mir, a lord of ecstasy, had seated himself in the corner with reliance upon God. He was rich in his poverty and indifferent to the material world. My truth-seeking mind was not at rest without meeting him and my desire to see him increased. I wrote to him explaining my desire to meet him. Notwithstanding his old age and weakness he took the trouble to come to me. I sat with him for a long time alone and enjoyed a thorough interview with him. Truly he is a man of noble qualities. The existence of such people is exceedingly rare. I heard him speak sublime words on truth and gnosis. Although I desired to make him some gift, I found that his spirit was too high for this and I did not press my wish. I left him the skin of a white antelope to pray upon, and he immediately bade me farewell and went back to Lahore.[41]

Dara Shikoh writes that when Jahangir requested the saint to ask for something from him, Miyan Mir replied, 'Would you be prepared to give me whatever I ask for from you?' The emperor said, 'Certainly, you may take it for granted.' The Mir, thereupon, said, 'I then ask you to allow me to depart'.[42]

According to the *Sakinat-ul-Auliya*, after some ume, Jahangir, again wished to meet Miyan Mir and it appears that a second meeting took place. There are two letters in which Jahangir wrote to the saint in his own handwriting. Jahangir addresses Miyan Mir as 'Hazrat Pir Dastgir' and seeks his blessings and favours so that he and his people may gain success against the ruler of Iran.

Emperor Jahangir hoped that with Miyan Mir's blessings and benedictions the cruel Shah Abbas of Iran (who had besieged Qandhar in those days), would be punished with divine wrath.[43]

The sources also shed light on Jahangir's relations with Amir Saiyid Abul Ula Akbarabadi.[44] A descendant of the renowned Naqshbandi of Central Asia, Khwaja Ubaid Ullah Ahrar, he had been in the service of Akbar as a *mansabdar* to Raja Man Singh. It appears from his biographical accounts that Abul Ula also held the *mansab* of 3000 *zat* and *sawars,* and resided at Burdwan in Bengal. At the time of his accession Jahangir asked the nobles and officials of the empire to be present before him in Agra. Amir Abul Ula, in compliance with the orders, also called on him. The emperor had already come to know of this noble saint's administrative and personal career, scholarship, and piety.[45] Jahangir is said to have been so deeply impressed by Abul Ula that he allowed him to visit his court, and even his private chambers, at any time without prior permission. It is also said that Jahangir always asked the saint to sit beside him.[46] Once Abul Ula visited Jahangir on the occasion of a royal festival and found him drinking wine. The emperor offered him a cup with great affection but Abul Ula declined. When Jahangir insisted, Abul Ula took the cup of wine and threw it on the ground before the emperor. Thereupon, Jahangir looking at the saint with fury, asked him, 'Are you not afraid of the Imperial wrath?' Amir replied boldly and confidently, 'I am only afraid of the Divine wrath, the *Qahr-i-Ilahi.*'[47] Soon after he renounced the world and after distributing his wealth and property among the poor and needy, left Agra for Ajmer.

In Ajmer Abul Ula is said to have stayed for a long time in the shrine of Khwaja Muinuddin Chishti so as to benefit from his spiritual blessings. The Amir also received *Uwaisiyat,* to directly benefit from anybody's spirituality without the mediation of a *pir,* from the spirit of the Khwaja. It was on the Khwaja's mystical instruction that Abul Ula later joined the Naqshbandi mystic discipline and married the daughter of his uncle, Amir Abdullah.[48] After a while, he settled down in Agra and seems to have led a retired life.

Jahangir is also reported to have maintained cordial relations with the famous *alim* of his time, Mulla Abdul Hakim Siyalkoti.[49] Unique in his age in so far as his knowledge of the rational and traditional sciences of Islam was concerned and as an author of scholarly works, Abdul Hakim occupied a respectable place in Jahangir's time.[50] It was on the latter's desire that he started teaching the Quran and Islamic sciences in Lahore.[51]

It may, therefore, be concluded that, though sometimes misled by others, Jahangir, had deep respect for Islam and held its Ulama and Sufis in great esteem. Whenever he heard of a pious *alim* or Sufi, he desired to meet him and obtain his blessings. The beginning of his relations with Shaikh Abdul Haq of Delhi and Shaikh Miyan Mir of Lahore bear testimony to this fact. In the case of Shaikh Ahmad Sirhindi, initially he treated him shabbily, but later on he not only changed his opinion, but also evinced profound interest in his spiritual mission. Jahangir's relations with other Ulama and Sufis also reflect the same attitude.

NOTES

1. *Tuzuk-i-Jahangiri*, ed. Sir Syed Ahmad Khan, Aligarh: Private Press, 1864, p. 223.
2. Afzal Husain, *The Nobility under Akbar and Jahangir*, Delhi, 1999, p. 117. It may be mentioned that Shaikh Salim Chishti's daughter-in-law (the wife of Shaikh Ahmad, who had been Jahangir's *ataliq* as well) had acted as Jahangir's foster mother. (See *Tuzuk-i-Jahangiri*, p. 14.) It was, therefore, on account of his deep attachment to the saint's family that after ascending the throne, Jahangir gave high ranks and assignments to its different members (see *Tuzuk-i-Jahangiri*, pp. 13, 14, 55. See also, Afzal Husain, op. cit., pp. 118, 120–6).
3. Abdur Rahman Sabahuddin, *Bazm-i-Taimuria*, Azamgarh: Darul Musannifin, 1948, p. 128; Abdul Haiy, *Nuzhat-ul-Khawatir*, vol. 5, Hyderabad: Idarah Dairat-ul Ma'arif, 1976, p. 122.
4. Ibid.
5. Ghulam Ali Azad Bilgirami, *Maathir-ul-Kiram*, vol. II, Agra: Mufid-i A'am Press, 1910, p. 93; *Nuzhat-ul-khawatir*, vol. 5, p. 181; see also *Bazm-i-Taimuria*, op. cit., p. 128.
6. *Tuzuk-i-Jahangiri*, p. 6.
7. Ibid., pp. 149–50. For Jahangir's devotion to Khwaja Muinuddin Chishti of Ajmer and his *dargah*, see, *Tuzuk-i-Jahangiri*, pp. 125–6, 132.
8. Born in AH 958/AD 1551 in Delhi, Shaikh Abdul Haq Muhaddith belonged to a spiritual and scholarly family of high repute. His father

Maulana Saifuddin and grandfather S'ad Ullah were held as great Ulama of their times. The famous historian, Rizq Ullah Mushtaqi was Shaikh Abdul Haq's uncle. The Shaikh received his education from his father and then proceeded to Hejaz. On his way to Mecca and Madina he stayed for a year at Ahmedabad and benefited from the scholarship and spirituality of the famous saint Shaikh Wajihuddin Alavi. In Mecca, Shaikh Abdul Haq remained at the feet of the great scholar of sciences and renowned mystic of the Qadiri order, Maulana Abdul Wahab Muttaqi. During his stay at Hejaz he visited the mausoleum of the Prophet of Islam at Madina. Shaikh Abdul Haq produced a number of valuable works on different religious sciences. His work on the life of the Prophet of Islam, *Madarij-un-Nabuwwah,* in Persian, earned him great fame. He was a disciple of the famous Shaikh Musa Gilani. As a member of the Qadiri order, the Shaikh was keenly devoted to its founder Shaikh Abdul Qadir Jilani of Baghdad, and begins his *Akhbar-ul-Akhyar* with a description of *Ghauth-ul-Azam,* the title with which Shaikh Abdul Qadir Jilani is addressed. Shaikh Abdul Haq, during the reign of Akbar, had been in close contact with Abul Faiz Faizi. His various visits to the latter in Agra had provided him with opportunities to observe the religious condition of Akbar's court. The Shaikh was spiritually affiliated to the Chishtiya and Naqshbandiya orders as well. He had been closely associated with Khwaja Baqi Billah, the founder of the Naqshbandi order in India. Shaikh Abdul Haq died in 1642 during the reign of Shahjahan. For a detailed biography of him see K.A. Nizami, *Hayat-i-Shaikh Abdul Haq Muhaddith Dehlawi,* Delhi: Nadwat-ul-Musannifin, 1964.

9. For Shaikh Abdul Haq's friendship with Shaikh Farid Bukhari, see Muhammad Umar's article 'Shaikh Farid Bukhari's Relations with the Contemporary Ulama and Sufis', in a cyclostyled volume for IHC Session, 1977, Research Library, Centre of Advanced Study, Dept. of History, AMU, Aligarh.
10. K.A. Nizami has included this letter in his *Hiyat-i-Shaikh Abdul Haq Muhaddith,* pp. 378–85.
11. As mentioned above, Shaikh Abdul Haq through his association with Faizi (Shaikh Muhammad Ikram, *Rud-i-Kausar,* rpt., Delhi: Taj Company, 1984, pp. 358–61), and Farid Bukhari, had the opportunity to have lived in Fatehpur Sikri for ten or twelve years. He must therefore, have, got to know the religious conditions in Akbar's court. See Nizami, op. cit., p. 145; Ikram, op. cit., pp. 348–9).
12. Modern scholars have interpreted Shaikh Abdul Haq's actions in different ways and with different viewpoints. See Ishtiaq Husain Quraishi, *Ulema in Politics,* Delhi: Renaissance Pub. House, 1985, p. 84; Nizami, op. cit., pp. 145–6; Ikram, *Rud-i-Kausar,* pp. 381–2; S.A.A.

Rizvi, *Muslim Revivalist Movements in Northern India in the Sixteenth and Seventeenth Centuries*, Agra: Agra University Publication, 1965, p. 161.

13. As stated earlier, this comprises biographical as well as mystical accounts of the Sufis of different orders that flourished in the close of the sixteenth century. Nizami's view is that this work was finally completed in 1591–2. It starts with the biographical accounts and teachings of the founder of the Chishti order in India, Khwaja Muinuddin Chishti of Ajmer. In order to express his deep devotion, the author first gives details about the life, teachings and spiritual attainments of the great saint of Islamic world and founder of the Qadiri order, Shaikh Abdul Qadir Jilani Baghdadi. The *Akbar-ul-Akhyar* was published in 1866–7 by Matba-i-Muhammadi. It also published two later editions, one in 1892 and another in 1914. The first Urdu translation of the *Akhbar-ul-Akhyar* appeared in 1910. The manuscripts of *Akhbar-ul-Akhyar* are found in the Asiatic Society, British Museum, Cambridge University Library and Khuda Bakhsh Library.
14. *Tuzuk-i-Jahangiri*, op. cit., p. 282.
15. Nizami, op. cit., p. 148.
16. Dara Shikoh remarked that some people had wrongly attributed things and events that never occurred to Shaikh Abdul Haq, with the intention of annoying the Emperor. See *Sakinat-ul-Auliya*, Tehran: Matbu'at-i Ilmi, 1965, p. 115. But the author of *Mirat-ul-Haqaiq* says that Nurjahan was not on good terms with Shaikh Abdul Haq and always wanted to harm him. He suspects that she created misunderstanding in Jahangir's mind. See: *Hayat-i-Shaikh Abdul Haq Mahaddith*, p. 149.
17. Nizami, op. cit., p. 148; Rizvi, op. cit., p. 161; *Rud-i-Kausar*, p. 382.
18. *Sakinat-ul-Auliya*, op. cit., p. 115.
19. Shaikh Abdul Ahad Faruqi's son Shaikh Badruddin Ahmad Sirhindi, who was held as one of the greatest exponents of the mystical philosophy of Ibn Arabi, was born in 1563 in Sirhind. Having received his formal and traditional education from his father, he proceeded to Sialkot, a famous seat of learning in those days, and studied advanced Islamic sciences especially the science of *hadith*, under eminent scholars Shaikh Yaqub Sarfi Kubrawi and Maulana Kamal Kashmiri. Later he started teaching at his ancestral seminary in Sirhind and his reputation spread. Shaikh Ahmad later lived in Agra for about nine years, where he met eminent personalities of the royal circle particularly Shaikh Farid Bukhari, Abdul Rahim Khan-i-Khanan, Miran Sadr-i-Jahan, Mirza Aziz Koka, Abul Faiz Faizi and Abul Fazl. The latter had played a prominent role in Akbar's deviation from Islam. Shaikh Ahmad held several polemical discussions with him at his residence and he guided Faizi in the completion of his exegesis of the Quran *Sawati-ul-Ilham*.

    Initiated into the Chishtiya, Suhrawardiya and Qadiriya Silsilahs,

Ahmad Sirhindi (in later 1599) joined the mystic discipline of Khwaja Baqi Billah of Delhi and received Khilafat in the Naqshbandi order as well. He organized the order across the Islamic world in a systematic way. Jahangir recognized that his followers were to be found in every city and town of the Mughal empire (*Tuzuk-i-Jahangiri*, p. 272).

Shaikh Ahmad produced brochures and treatises on various aspects of Islamic learning. The collection of letters entitled *Maktubat-i-Imam-i-Rabbani*, which runs into three volumes, has been held as his contribution to Islamic literature. On account of his significant contribution to the revival of Islam in India he is popularly known as the Mujaddid-i Alf-i-Thani, the Renovator of the Second Millennium of Islam. For details see Muhammad Hashim Kishmi, *Zubdat-ul-Maqamat*, Kanpur: Nawal Kishore Press, 1885; Also, Badruddin Sirhindi, *Hazarat-ul-Quds*, vol. II, Lahore: Punjab Waqf Board, 1971. For his thought and ideology, see his letters *Maktubat-i-Imam-i-Rabbani*, 3 vols., Turkish edn., Istanbul: Isik Kitabvi, 1977; B.A. Faruqi, *The Mujaddid's Conception of Tawhid*, Aligarh: Deptt. of Philosophy, A.M.U., 1940; Yohanann Friedman, *Shaikh Ahmad Sirhindi*, Montreal: McGill University, 1971; Abul Hasan Zaid Faruqi, *Hazrat Mujaddid and his Critics*, Lahore: Progressive Books, 1982; Nasim Ahmad Faridi, *Tajalliyat-i-Rabbani*, Lucknow: Al-Furqan Press, 1985; Muhammad Manzur Numani, ed., *Al-Furqan* (Mujaddid-i Alf-i-Thani Number), Bareilly: Al-Furqan Press, AH 357.

20. Shaikh Ahmad's contribution to the accession of Jahangir to the throne lies in his convincing and motivating some important Mughal nobles, particularly Shaikh Farid Bukhari. The latter's role in Jahangir's accession is an established fact. Most historians agree on this point. Besides, Shaikh Farid had taken a promise from Saleem to defend Islam. See R.P. Tripathi, *The Rise and Fall of the Mughal Empire*, Allahabad: Central Book Depot, 1985, p. 340; Also I.H. Quraishi, *Akbar: The Architect of the Mughal Empire*, rpt. Delhi: Idarah-i Adabiyat-i Delhi, 1985, pp. 66–7; also Beni Prasad, *History of Jahangir*, Allahabad: Indian Press, 1962.

Shaikh Ahmad Sirhindi exerted his influence on Shaikh Farid Bukhari. His *Maktubat-i-Imam-i-Rabbani*, contains many letters addressed to the latter. These epistles give a clear impression that the Mujaddid looked upon this great Mughal noble as an ardent supporter of Islam. These letters also show that there had been previous consultations and that mutual understanding had been reached between Ahmad Sirhindi and Shaikh Farid, and also between Shaikh Farid and Prince Saleem. The saint could not have written to such a high dignity so frankly unless he had found his ideas acceptable, For detailed study, see K.A. Nizami, 'The Naqshbandi Influence on Mughal Rulers and Politics', *Islamic Culture*, vol. 39, no. 1, January 1965, pp. 41–52; S.

Nurul Hasan, 'Shaikh Ahmad Sirhindi and Mughal Politics', *Proceedings of the Indian History Congress,* Annamalai Session, 1945, pp. 248–57; Muhammad Aslam, 'Jahangir and Shaikh Ahmad Sirhindi', *Journal of the Asiatic Society of Pakistan,* vol. X, pp. 135–48. For Shaikh Farid Bukhari's relations with Shaikh Ahmad Sirhindi, see Muhammad Umar, 'Shaikh Farid Bukhari's Relations with his Contemporary Ulama and Saints', Cyclostyled IHC volume of 1977, Research Library, Centre of Advanced Study, Department of History, AMU, Aligarh.

21. For Shaikh Ahmad's views in regard to condemnation of Akbar's religious ideas and policy, see *Maktubat-i-Imam-i-Rabbani,* vol. I, Istanbul: Isikkitabvi, 1977, Letters 17, 51, 53, and 54. Also Shaikh Ahmad Sirhindi's *Ithbat-un-Nabuwah,* Karachi: Aa'la Kutub Khana, 1963.
22. *Zubdat-ul-Maqamat,* op. cit., p. 348.
23. Ibid.
24. *Maktubat-i-Imam-i-Rabbani,* vol. 1, letter 1, op. cit.
25. Born in 1564 in Kabul, Baqi Billah travelled to many cities and towns of northern India, Afghanistan, and Central Asia with the intention to meet and benefit from Sufis and *mashaikhs,* and finally joined the mystic fold of Maulana Khwaji Amkangi at Amkana near Bukhara. The latter authorised Baqi Billah into the Naqshbandi order as his khalifa and then asked him to go to Delhi and spread the Naqshbandi teachings there. Baqi Billah founded the Naqshbandi order on his arrival in Delhi in 1599 but died a few years later. In this short period he attracted not only a large multitude of common people but also many important nobles of the Mughal empire and eminent Ulamas and Sufis of the time. Khwaja Baqi Billah's greatest achievement was to produce a famous disciple and Khalifa, Shaikh Ahmad Sirhindi. *Zubdat-ul-Maqamat,* pp. 5–61; Badruddin Sirhindi, *Hazarat-ul-Quds,* vol. I (Urdu trans), Lahore: Allah Walon ki Dukan, 1914, pp. 213–60.
26. According to Badruddin Sirhindi, Prince Khurram (Shahjahan) was devoted to the Shaikh. Due to the situation in the court and the emperor's summons, he was anxious and worried, and tried his best to save Ahmad Sirhindi from the wrath of his father, Emperor Jahangir. He sent Maulana Afzal Khan and Mufti Abdur Rahman, eminent *alims,* to Sirhind to convince the Shaikh to observe the customary obeisance to Jahangir. These Ulama conveyed Prince Khurram's message to the Shaikh that prostrating in respect (*sajda-i-tazimi*), before the king was lawful in some conditions, and if he (Shaikh Ahmad) did so, he (Prince Khurram) assured and guaranteed him full protection. Though the Shaikh, who had much affection for Prince Khurram (Shahjahan), declined saying that his (Khurram's) proposal was an 'act of departure from the "Divine Laws"' (known in the terminology of *Shariah* as *rukhsat*); prostration is only for God. *Hazarat-ul-Quds,* vol. II, p. 116.

27. Ibid., pp. 115–16.
28. Ibid., p. 115.
29. *Tuzuk-i-Jahangiri*, pp. 272–3.
30. Ibid., p. 308. Shaikh Ahmad Sirhindi's stay in the royal camp with Jahangir has been a point of controversy among the scholars. Was his presence there really voluntary, as Jahangir has said in his *Tuzuk-i-Jahangiri*, or was he forced to remain with the emperor? Muhammad Masud Ahmad, *Sirat Mujaddid-i alf-i-Thani*, Karachi: Madina Publishing Company, 1976, p. 198; S.M. Ikram, *Rud-i-Kausar*, p. 273. It may also be noted in this connection that the author of the *Zubdat-ul-Maqamat*, the first biography of Shaikh Ahmad Sirhindi, completed in 1627, writes, 'In his old age for three years on account of the opposition of the Emperor of the time, the Shaikh had to go to several cities along with the royal army'. Similarly Shaikh Ahmad Sirhindi, in a letter to his son, Muhammad Masum, also expresses his disappointment and helplessness (*Maktubat-i-Imam-i-Rabbani*, vol. III, Letter 83). In another letter the Shaikh says, 'I consider it a good-fortune to live in the royal camp though with disappointment and helplessness' (ibid., Letter 87).
31. *Zubdat-ul-Maqamat*, p. 159.
32. Ali Akbar Husaini Ardistani, *Maja-ul-Auliya*, (MS) (India Office Library, no. 145), f. 442.
33. *Maktubat-i-Imam-i-Rabbani*, vol. III, Letter 43.
34. When in March 1615 Jahangir appointed Shaikh Farid Bukhari, then governor of Punjab, to lead an expedition to the Kangra fort, the latter too had approached Shaikh Ahmad for a blessing. In one of his letters to Shaikh Farid, the saint not only prays to God for his success (in the Kangra expedition) but excuses himself from not taking part in the expedition. Sirhindi writes, 'I am unable to come to you on account of my physical weakness, otherwise I would have come to persuade you personally to do this act' (*Maktubat*, vol. I, Letter 269). The author of the *Hazarat-ul-Quds* has also mentioned Shaikh Farid's request to the saint on this occasion (p. 178).
35. *Hazarat-ul-Quds*, vol. II, pp. 178–9.
36. *Maktubat-i-Imam-i-Rabbani*, vol. III, Letter 47.
37. Ibid., Letter 72.
38. Ibid., Letters 78, 85.
39. *Zubdat-ul-Maqamat*, pp. 283–4.
40. Born in 1550 in Swistan near Thatta (Sindh), Shaikh Muhammad Mir, popularly known as Miyan Mir or Miyan Jeo, was a descendant of the second caliph, Umar al-Faruq al-Azam. At the age of twenty he shifted to Lahore for higher education and settled there. He spent most of his time in gardens and in the wilderness, engaged in prayer and meditation and hard spiritual exercises, mostly keeping night vigils.

On account of his poor health he returned to Lahore after a year and died there in 1635. His famous Khalifa Mulla Shah was the spiritual mentor of Prince Dara Shikoh. For his biographical account see: Dara Shikoh, *Sakinat-ul-Auliya,* Tehran, 1965.

41. *Tuzuk-i-Jahangiri,* pp. 286–7.
42. *Sakinat-ul-Auliya,* p. 47.
43. Ibid., pp. 47–8.
44. Born in 1582, he belonged to an aristocratic scholar family. His grandfather Amir Abdus Salam, who earlier lived in Narela near Delhi, had subsequently shifted to Fatehpur Sikri on the request of Akbar. Abul Ula passed his early boyhood in Fatehpur Sikri where in the meantime his father Amir Abul Wafa passed away. After his grandfather's death in Mecca, Amir Abul Ula came under the care and guidance of his maternal grandfather Khwaja Muhammad Faiz, popularly known as Khwaja Faizi, who used to live in Burdwan in Bengal. There he gained mastery in the art of warfare and other crafts. Meanwhile Khwaja Faizi died fighting in a battle under the command of Raja Man Singh against the Afghans in 1592. As Man Singh is said to have had a deep affection for Abul Ula, he recruited the latter in his maternal grandfather's place. A murid and Khalifa of his uncle Saiyid Amir Abdullah, Abul Ula was basically a Sufi of the Naqshbandi *silsilah,* but adopted various customs and traditions of the Chishti order. His own *silsilah* came to be known after him as the Abul Ulaiya *silsilah.* Amir Abul Ula was succeeded by his younger son Amir Nurul Ula. His shrine, popularly known as the *dargah* of Saiyidna, has been an important Sufi centre through the centuries. For a detailed biography, see *Azkar-ul-Ahrar, Asrar-i-Abul Ula.*
45. *Asrar-i-Abul Ula* (MS) f. 11a. But the sources of the political history of the time are totally silent in this regard.
46. Abdul Haiy, *Nuzhat-ul-Khawatir,* vol. V, p. 22.
47. Ibid. Also *Asrar-i-Abul Ula* (MS), f. 16.
48. *Nuzhat-ul-Khawatir,* p. 22.
49. He was a renowned scholar of the seventeenth century. A pupil of Maulana Kamaluddin Kashmiri and Shaikh Yaqub Sarfi, Mulla Abdul Hakim had been a classmate of Shaikh Ahmad Sirhindi during his studies in Siyalkot. It was Abdul Hakim who first addressed the latter as Mujaddid Alf-i-Thani. He died in AH 1068/AD 1658. For details, *see* Ghulam Sarwar, *Khazinat-ul-Asfia* (Urdu trans.), Lahore, 1983, pp. 338–9.
50. Ibid., p. 338.
51. Ibid.

Dadu's Relations with the Rulers of His Time

SHAHABUDDIN IRAQI

The foundation of the Delhi Sultanate in the beginning of the thirteenth century, led to the co-mingling of the followers of the cosmocentric and the anthropocentric traditions in the towns and cities. Both seem to have been influenced by each other's practices and thought. The Hindu yogic practice of breath-control gained popularity among Muslim mystics of different Sufi orders. The Sufi concept of love that embraces all mankind regardless of birth or creed influenced sensitive Hindu minds. The Hindu concept of renunciation that meant the severing of all relationship with the mundane world and single-minded devotion to the deity underwent change in many cases. Like the Sufis, they too considered the service of man the best form of worship, and catered to the spiritual needs of people, irrespective of caste and community. Such teachings and ways of life gave rise to the bhakti cult. The leaders of the bhakti cult belonged to high as well as low castes, but attached no value to rituals or caste. Their teachings made low-caste people, who were debarred from places of worship, conscious of being as people like everyone else. They gained confidence in themselves as worthy of receiving divine grace without the help of an intermediary. Amongst the great leaders of the bhakti movement, Kabir and Guru Nanak do not appear to have been interested in having relation with the contemporary rulers, but Dadu's attitude was different. Like the Sufis of his time, he maintained good relation with the king and the members of the ruling elite. The aim of this article is to analyse the relevant evidences available from miscellaneous sources about Dadu's relations with Emperor Akbar and the members of the ruling elite.

Dadu (1544–1603),[1] who was Akbar's contemporary and a Nirguni Bhakti saint, is said to have willingly interacted with men of the ruling class. Though previously associated with Sambhar from 1568 to 1579, he left for Amber (capital of Jaipur), where he received a warm welcome on the shores of the Maota lake from the ruler, Raja Bhagwandas, then a commander in Akbar's army.[2] This was the time Dadu also attracted the attention of Akbar who in a conversation with Bhagwandas expressed his desire to see and talk to him. Jan Gopal of the Dadupanth gives a detailed account of Dadu's visit on an invitation from Akbar and the subsequent meetings and discourses with Akbar at Fatehpur Sikri in 1584. Abul Fazl, Birbal and Raja Bhagwat Singh [?Bhagwandas] also participated in these discussions.[3]

It is true that there is no reference of this meeting in any of the Persian chronicles but the same has happened with many other such cases of discourses with Akbar, like that with Swami Bithalnath (1515–85), Swami Haridas, and Kumbhandas (d. 1583),[4] obviously because they did not belong to the elite. But Jan Gopal's *Dadu Parichaya* explicitly narrates in its eight chapters the whole process as to how a meeting was arranged at the instance of Birbal and by the efforts of Raja Bhagwandas and one of his faithful retainers named Suja Kinchi specifically in AD 1584 (VS 1642).[5] Moreover, the meeting is also mentioned by Dadu himself in one of his verses.

अकबर साह बुलाईया। गुर दादू को आप।।
सांच झूठ ब्योरौ हुवो। तब रहयो नांव प्रताप।।[6]

Contemporary historical accounts record the presence of Akbar and the above nobles at Fatehpur Sikri from February 1584 to August 1585, when Prince Salim was married to Man Bai, daughter of Bhagwandas, who played a vital role in the meeting between Akbar and Dadu. Besides, the preliminary interview with Abul Fazl and Birbal gives a realistic touch to the meeting. In the case of a distinguished Jain saint and scholar named Hiravijay Suri, who visited Akbar's court in 1582, Abul Fazl was 'made over to his care until the sovereign found leisure to converse with him'.[7]

This meeting also reconciles with the development of Akbar's religious policy at that time, when the Ibadat Khana had started and the Tauhid-i Ilahi was taking its shape. Cow slaughter was prohibited, and abstinence from meat on certain days was enjoined. Under these circumstances, Jan Gopal's claim that the emperor's order prohibiting animal slaughter was issued under the influence of Dadu seems to be also well justified.

On the basis of the traditional biographies, Narayandas mentions Dadu's frequent contacts with the royal figures of the time.[8] Even before Akbar, Dadu had impressed Raja Bhagwandas, the ruler of Amber, and later made some local Rajput rulers his disciples, such as Sundardas the Elder, Hapaji, etc., as will be discussed subsequently. Thus, while in Rajasthan, Dadu enjoyed the patronage of local rulers and nobles, he was also extended due respect outside, particularly at the Mughal court.

Like the unity of God at the spiritual level, Dadu emphasized the need of a single political authority at the worldly level:

> There would be peace only if there is unity of political authority; if there is duality (i.e. double authority), no one can remain happy due to the ensuing conflicts. With one political authority there is tranquility in the city (state); the king and the subjects are happy and there is light everywhere.[9]

Secondly, while for Dadu it was a matter of pride in being a subject of Raja Ram, he advises him self-restraint in order to govern the state effectively: 'Dadu, Rawat (*rayat*) of Raja Ram, never forsakes (His) name; take care of your soul and you can control the village (state) very well.'[10] Such references and symbolic expressions show that Dadu accepted the ideals and the institutions of government.

On the other hand, it also appears from Jan Gopal's account that Dadu had to face opposition from the religious leaders of the Hindu and Muslim communities on the one hand, and Raja Man Singh's dislike for him on the other. On the death of Bhagwandas, his successor Raja Man Singh came to Amber. The whole populace arrived to meet him but not Dadu, which was taken as discourtesy. There were other complaints also against him: 'he disregards caste rules, and makes no difference between the Hindus and the Muslims'.[11] This complaint is very similar to that made against Kabir to Sikandar Lodi by the religious leaders of both communities. Thus there was a prolonged ideological conflict between Dadu and his opponents and he was forced to leave Amber and to wander from place to place for about ten years.

Dadu at first went to Marwar, where he made some new disciples, among whom there were two Rathor noblemen, Rao Man Singh of Bhawadi and Kishan Singh of Merta. From Marwar, Dadu went to Bikaner, where the Rao of Bhuratiya met him and invited him to settle permanently in his village. Dadu declined, but during this visit a very important incident took place: Sundardas, known as the Elder, became his disciple. Sundardas's life is not given in Jan Gopal's account, but Raghava's *Bhaktmala* narrates a story according to which he was a Rajput prince of Bikaner and had served in the imperial military force at Kabul.[12] Having lost his throne in a battle, Sundardas along with his family priest Prahladdas renounced the world, and both came to Dadu. Sundardas became Dadu's disciple and Prahladdas, the disciple of Sundardas.[13] Both are said to have been associated with the Thambha of Ghatra (now in Alwar state) to which the Dadu-panthi Nagas trace their origin.

Prince Hapaji, the youngest son of Bhagwandas of Amber was another Rajput disciple of Dadu, who also renounced the world after meeting him. Narayandas tells of him that he had left a spiritual lineage as a prince, which was recognized at the court.[14] However, there was such an adverse effect of Dadu's conflict with Man Singh on his mind that he himself refrained from any contact with the ruling family of Amber. During his journey, when Dadu passed on from Sambhar, though he accepted the invitation of Rathorani, queen of Amber, to meet her, he left the place soon afterwards without even informing her.[15] Dadu finally settled at Naraina in 1602, where he soon died.

To conclude, it may be stated that, in spite of being a man of low caste, a cotton carder, Dadu's selfless devotion to God and respect for all human being brought popularity to him. Free from all prejudices, he felt love for all, no matter whether a prince or a low-born. For a man like Dadu, the universe was his family.

NOTES

1. For details of Dadu's life and teachings, see W.G. Orr, *A Sixteenth Century Indian Mystic*, London and Redhill: Lutterworth Press, 1947; also P.R. Chaturvedi, *Uttari Bharat ki Sant Parampara*, 2nd edn., Allahabad, 1964, pp. 488–501.

2. Orr, op. cit., Chap. 3, p. 30. Of the gifts presented to Dadu, he kept nothing for himself, asking for himself only simple food and shelter.
3. Jan Gopal, *Dadu Janma Lila Parichaya* (Life Story of Dadu), Jaipur: Mangal Press, 1949, *vishrams* (chapters) 4–11. This is a very important Dadupanthi work which was written some time in the early seventeenth century. The work not only provides a complete and consistent history of Dadu's life and career, but also refers to the socio-religious condition and some political events of Akbar's time. It also speaks of the conflicting trend between the Hindus and the Muslims, on the one hand, and between the qazis and the saints of Sambhar (near Amber), on the other; and a prolonged ideological conflict between Dadu and Man Singh during the closing years of the sixteenth century. The work ends with the narrative of the installation of Dadu's eldest son, Gharibdas, as spiritual head of the order.
4. For details about Akbar's meetings with these saints, see Shahabuddin Iraqi, 'Akbar's Relations with Non-Sufi Saints of India', *Islamic Heritage in South Asian Subcontinent*, vol. II, ed. Nazir Ahmad and I.H. Siddiqui, Jaipur: Publication Scheme, 2000, pp. 124–5 and 128–9.
5. According to Jan Gopal, Dadu along with some of his disciples including Jan Gopal, set out for Fatehpur Sikri in 1584 under the escort of Suja Kinchi. The company was received near the city by Raja Bhagwandas and was brought to the Raja's house. Then the emperor was informed, and by his orders Dadu was brought to the palace where Abul Fazl and Birbal took a preliminary interview of him. Being impressed by Dadu's spiritual thoughts, both the nobles reported to the emperor about the worth of the saint who was then called into the royal presence accompanied by Abul Fazl, Birbal, and Bhagwandas. A long discussion took place on spiritual matters. The emperor was greatly impressed and wanted him to stay on. Abul Fazl suggested Dadu to be his guest; the same proposal was also extended by Birbal, and finally it was agreed that Dadu should stay for a few days at the latter's house. Meanwhile, at the Raja's request, Dadu visited the *zanana* apartments and the ladies of the house were delighted to meet him. Before leaving the palace, however, another meeting was arranged between Dadu and Akbar, and conversation took place in the presence of many other courtiers. Next morning Dadu was brought to the house of Raja Bhagwandas, where he was persuaded to stay for more than one day. Then with his company of disciples Dadu set out for Amber, and Bhagwandas accompanied him to the outskirts of the city.
6. Quoted from *The Sarbangi of Rajjabdas*, ed. S. Iraqi, Aligarh: Granthayan, 1985, *anga* (chapter) 40, hymn no. 6, p. 247.
7. V.A. Smith, *Akbar, The Great Mughal (1542–1605)*, rpt., Delhi: S. Chand & Co., 1966, p. 119.

8. Narayandas, *Shri Dadupanth Parichaya*, published in three volumes from Dadu Mahasabha, Jaipur, 1978–9. For present reference, see vol. I, pp. 98–104.
9. *Dadu Dayal Granthawali* (based on a MS dated vs 1710/AD 1653), ed. P.R. Chaturvedi, Varanasi: Nagiri Pracharini Sabha, vs 2003/AD 1966, pp. 130–2.
10. Ibid., pp. 19, 36.
11. Orr, op. cit., p. 37.
12. Narayandas, op. cit., vol. 1, pp. 378–86.
13. Ibid., p. 396.

    Another story is that Sundardas was serving with the imperial forces at Kabul when a false rumour of his death reached his home. His wife committed sati. Recovering from his wounds and knowing this tragedy, the Rajput prince resolved not to return to Bikaner but to renounce the world by adopting the life of an ascetic. Laying his weapons at Dadu's feet, he became his disciple, though Dadu asked him to retain his arms and still remain his disciple. See, W.G. Orr, op. cit., chapter IX, p. 189.

    But the story, similar to that of Rajjabdas, is comparatively of a late origin. There is no reference of it in Jan Gopal's *Dadu Janma Lila Parichaya*. The story first appears in Raghava's *Bhaktimala* which was written about a century later. It seems to have been designed to explain the later development of a branch of the Dadupanth into a body of armed ascetics. The Rajput warrior retaining his arms on his Guru's instructions formed a link with the fighting Nagas who flourished under him and became prominent during Raghava's time.

    However, Sundardas the younger (1596–1689) was another saint who returned from Kashi to Fatehpur in 1625. His father, Parmananda was a Khandelwal Mahajan of the Busar clan. The then nawab of Fatehpur, a descendant of the famous Qayam Khan, a Chauhan Rajput converted to Islam some time in the fourteenth century, became a close friend of the saint. The local Mahajans built a house for his use with an underground 'gufa' or cave.

    See *Sundar Granthawali*, ed. Purohit Hari Narayan Sharma, Calcutta: Rajasthan Research Society, 1939, p. 65.
14. It is said that after twelve years when Hapaji returned to visit his native place and encamped with his followers outside the city, his ruler brother invited him to the court where he impressed the members of the thirteen Noble houses of Amber to such an extent that they declared him as the founder of the 'Thirteen Noble Houses'. Though requested by all to stay, the saint left Amber leaving behind a few disciples to be there.

    For details about Hapaji, see Narayandas, op. cit., vol. I, pp. 416–23.
15. Orr, op. cit., p. 41.

Life and Culture in the Katehar Region under the Rohilla Chiefs During the Eighteenth Century

IQTIDAR HUSAIN SIDDIQUI

The dissolution of the Mughal empire in the eighteenth century was paradoxically paralleled by the expansion of intellectual and material culture which had developed under the patronage of the imperial court in Delhi and Agra in the preceding centuries. The high *mansabdars* and hereditary *zamindars*, the erstwhile *subehdars*, *faujdars* and vassals of the emperor became practically independent of the centre, and developed their territories economically and culturally with a view to enhancing their limited sources on one hand and the grandeur of their administrative headquarters on the other. As a result, new cities and towns were founded or old villages and small towns expanded. The towns of Katehar (later Rohilkhand) being part of the imperial *suba* of Delhi and in close proximity to the metropolis (Delhi), were in an advantageous position to receive those scholars, poets, artists, merchants and craftsmen who were forced to leave Delhi. With settlement in different towns of Katehar, the progress of arts and crafts, learning and culture started. The Rohilla chiefs extended their full patronage to them.

This paper seeks first to explain the circumstances that helped Rohilla adventurers who came to India from Roh (the hill region between Ghazna and Peshawar) to India in search of fortune, and then to discuss their relations with the Mughal emperor, the chiefs in the neighbouring region, and the Marathas and Ahmad Shah Abdali. Last, it discusses the socio-economic growth and progress of culture that ensued.

The rapid decline of Mughal power resulting from Nadir Shah's invasion of India in AD 1739 encouraged fissiparous tendencies among the powerful *zamindars* everywhere in the empire. The Rajput and the Jat *zamindars* started fighting one another for booty and territory. The Rohilla Pathans who served in the Mughal army were also able to carve out principalities under the leadership of Nawab Muhammad Khan Bangash, Ali Muhammad Khan Rohilla, and Najib-ud-Daula in the *doab*, and in each principality the Pathan rulers created conditions conducive to economic development and cultural progress. It is worth emphasizing that the Rohillas in Katehar were fresh immigrants, having no pretensions to a cultural literary background yet, because they had adopted the best of the Mughal culture and polity, they became patrons of learning and the learned. They emulated Mughal standards in literature, architecture, and in dress. In fact, the traditions of the imperial court continued to provide a cultural reference for long. Like others, the Rohilla chiefs of Katehar too were heirs to the cultural legacy of the empire.

According to Rustam Ali Bijnori's contemporary account of the rise and fall of the Rohillas,[1] Katehar, extending from the *tarai* of Kumaon and the Garhwal mountains, included within its boundaries, the modern districts of Saharanpur, Muzaffarnagar, the entire commissionary division of Rohilkhand of the British time, i.e. the districts of Bareilly, Pilibhit, Rampur, Moradabad, Bijnor, Badaun and Shahjahanpur.[2]

The man who paved the way for the rise of Rohilla power in Katehar was Daud Khan, originally a slave of a Sufi Shaikh of Roh named Hassan Khan Bharech. In his youth he had fled and, having served under Nasir Jung, the Mughal administrator of Peshawar, for two years, came to Delhi with a few Tatari horses for sale during the reign of Emperor Muhammad Shah (AD 1719–48). He proceeded from Delhi to Katehar where the Rajput *zamindars* had started employing Rohillas in their army. Daud Khan joined the service of the Rajput *zamindars*, Madar Shah of Madhkar. The latter utilized his services against his rivals, one of them being the *muqaddam* of Bankuli, known for his predatory activities. In Bankuli, Daud Khan seized a huge booty, besides thirty prisoners amongst whom was included a ten or eleven years-old Jat boy, Prem Singh. Impressed by the intelligence and behaviour of the boy, Daud Khan adopted him as his son and made arrangements for his education and training in the art of warfare. He was named Ali Muhammad Khan. The boy learnt Persian and the tenets of Islam and also become an excellent equestrian within a few years. Later he was nominated by Daud Khan to be his heir in preference to his own son, Muhammad Khan. Upon Madar Shah's death in AD 1733, Daud Khan joined the service of Dip Singh, the Raja of Almora (in the Kumaon hills). The Raja entrusted him with the charge of the *tarai*. Some time later, Daud Khan attacked the recalcitrant *zamindars* in the territorial units of Bareilly and Badaun and returned loaded with booty. Many Rohillas joined his service. His fame and resourcefulness and the favourable inclination of Nawab Azmatullah Khan, the *nazim* of Moradabad, made the courtiers of the raja very envious. They advised their ruler to have Daud Khan eliminated before he became too powerful. Raja Dip Singh invited Daud Khan to his court and on his arrival had him arrested and tortured to death.[3] Thereupon, Daud Khan's adopted son, Ali Muhammad Khan, went with a few Rohilla followers to Nawab Azmatullah Khan who sympathized with him and took him in his service. He was posted in Rampur with the permission to employ the followers of Daud Khan who would return to him. Ali Muhammad Khan re-organized his force within a short time and led military campaigns against the *zamindars* hostile to his master. With the wealth that he acquired as booty, he purchased the *zamindari* rights of a number of villages around Rampur. Upon the death of Nawab Azmatullah Khan in 1736, his son Nawab Muinuddin Khan was allowed by the imperial court to succeed his father as the *nazim* of Moradabad. The new *nazim* also showed favour to Ali Muhammad Khan.[4]

The most important military achievement of Ali Muhammad Khan in the early period was his victory over Danish Khan Mahli, a Mughal *mansàbdar*, and Raja Jagat Singh of Aonla. The latter had usurped the revenue of a village held by Ali Muhammad Khan in *zamindari* right. Taking advantage of the rivalry between the leading nobles at the royal court in Delhi, Ali Muhammad Khan advanced against the raja of Aonla and laid siege to that fortress, demolishing it in two days. Aonla was made the headquarters of the Rohilla army and Ali Muhammad Khan developed it into an important township.[5] It was in Aonla at this time that many Rohilla chiefs joined Ali Muhammad Khan. The Rohilla army now comprised 10,000 intrepid *sawars* and footmen. With their support, Ali Muhammad Khan seized the *tarai* territory, including Kashipur, from the Raja of Kumaon. The annual revenue from all the territory under his control by own amounted to Rs. 20 lakh.[6]

The death of Danish Khan Mahli provided Amir Khan an opportunity to persuade the emperor to appoint a competent man, *nazim* of Moradabad to deal with the Rohilla rebels. The emperor, in consultation with the leading nobles, appointed Raja Harnand and sent him with a large army. But the Rohillas under Ali Muhammad Khan were more than a match for the effete Mughal generals and their soldiers. When the two armies came face to face near Chandausi, the Rohillas won, killing several nobles including Raja Harnand. The entire artillery and belongings of the vanquished army fell into the hands of the victors.[7] About the same time the news of Nadir Shah's invasion prevented the Mughals from sending another punitive expedition against the Rohillas. The defeat by Nadir Shah of the Mughal army in 1739 and his return to Iran with treasures and every costly thing found in the Red Fort was a severe blow to the emperor.

Encouraged by the changed circumstances, Ali Muhammad Khan invaded Kumaon, overcame the resistance of the raja, and reached Almora town. The raja and its residents fled leaving their belongings behind. The Rohillas plundered the town of money and idols of gold. Every soldier got enough booty.[8] Thereafter, Ali Muhammad Khan cleaned Katehar of corrupt officials, streamlined the administration, and ensured impartial justice to all.

In 1744, Safdar Jung, the *subedar* of Awadh, was appointed *mir-i-atish* (minister in-charge of artillery). His arrival streng-thened the position of Umdat-ul-Mulk Amir Khan, the leader of the Irani faction, hostile to the Turani faction led by the wazir, Qamaruddin Khan. Safdar Jung persuaded the emperor to take action against the Rohillas. When the emperor expressed his inability to meet the expenses of organising an expedition, Safdar Jung undertook the responsibility of providing necessary funds. As a result, preparations were made without taking the Wazir into confidence. The Emperor started for Katehar on 25 February 1745 at the head of a large army supported by artillery and war elephants. The wazir had to join against his wishes. Upon the approach of the emperor, the Rohillas withdrew from Aonla to Bangarh Fort, 10 miles south of Badaun and surrounded by dense bamboo forests. The emperor also reached Bangarh and surrounded it. The Rohillas continued to inflict losses on the royal army by sallying out at night for a few months. The imperial army was not able to assault the fort, owing to internal dissensions caused due to infighting. After a few month's struggle, the wazir persuaded Ali Muhammad Khan to pay a visit to the emperor and seek his forgiveness. He also assured him of his safety and the grant of a royal *mansab*. When Ali Muhammad Khan visited the emperor, he was ordered to be taken to Delhi.[9] There, Ali Muhammad Khan was treated by the wazir as his guest. A thousand Rohillas stayed with him for one year. In 1746, the emperor appointed him the *faujdar* of the *sarkar* of Sirhind (Eastern Panjab) and also conferred the title of *yar-i-wafadar* on him. He then proceeded to Sirhind with 10,000 Rohillas. Forcing the rebel Jat *zamindars,* including Alah Singh of Patiala into submission, he reorganized the administration of Sirhind. But in 1748, when Ahmad Shah Abdali invaded India, Ali Muhammad Khan entered into alliance with him and left Sirhind for Katehar without royal permission.[10]

Thereupon Chhatar Bhoj Khatri, the *nazim,* fled to Delhi. The Rohillas re-established their control over entire Katehar. They came from different places to join this army, which increased to 30,000 within a short time. In the changed situation of Delhi, Ali Muhammad Khan only allowed the agent of Safdar Jung to manage his *jagir,* comprising the *parganas* of Sherkot, etc., because he had been elevated to the post of wazir after the death of Nawab Qamaruddin Khan in the battle of Sirhind fought against Ahmad Shah Abdali (1748). Moreover, the son and suc-cessor of Emperor Muhammad Shah was under his influence and the Turani nobles had also accepted his leadership. But Safdar Jung was the sworn enemy of the Pathans as he wanted to destroy their power and annex both the Bangash territory of Farrukhabad and Katehar to his *suba* of Awadh. The Turani nobles whose support Ali Muhammad Khan enjoyed were also antagonized because the *jagir* of Nawab Qamaruddin Khan had been seized by the Rohillas. Qamaruddin Khan's son, whom the emperor had assigned his father's *jagir*, got nothing from it.[11]

As regards the distribution of territorial units among his followers, Ali Muhammad Khan assigned each unit to a Rohilla commander as *jaidad* instead of *jagir*, charging the assignee with the duty of maintaining law and order therein along with the right to collect revenue for the maintenance of his family and the military contingent. It may be pointed out here that the Mughal *jagir* was transferable, while *jaidad*, meaning property owned by an individual or a family, was given in perpetuity to be inherited by the descendants of the assignee.[12]

With the pressures of affairs of his territory, Ali Muhammad Khan fell ill, and died on 16 September 1748. Upon his death, the Rohilla chiefs assembled in *jirga* and unanimously accepted Sadullah Khan, the ten-year-old son of Ali Muhammad Khan, as their leader. Sadullah's brothers, Abdullah Khan and Faizullah Khan were at that time with Ahmad Shah Abdali in Qandhar as their father's representatives. Hafiz Rahmat Khan assumed for himself the role of the regent, and as other Rohilla chiefs co-operated with him, their unity remained intact.[13]

Taking opportunity of the death of Ali Muhammad Khan, Safdar Jung and Intizam-ul-Daula had Nawab Qutbuddin Khan appointed by the Emperor Ahmad Shah (1748–54) the *nazim* of Moradabad and sent him out with a strong force. Being the grandson of Nawab Azmatullah Khan, Qutbuddin Khan had local support in Moradabad. Yet he too failed to gain success on account of indiscipline among the Mughal soldiers and their ignorance of the changed tactics of warfare. Faced by the intrepid Rohillas near Kiratpur, they fled, leaving their leader behind. Qutbuddin Khan died in the battlefield fighting valiantly, although he was requested by the Rohillas to retreat. Upon his fall, the Rohilla chiefs met his mother to offer condolence, and not only restored their *zamindari* villages but also assigned a few more villages for her dependants.[14]

On the fall of Qutbuddin Khan, the *jagirdars* of the region and Nawab Qayam Khan Bangash of Farrukhabad, one of the leading *mansabdars* were sent the *farman* by the Emperor to bring Katehar under control. Qayam Khan was also killed. This event is important as it resulted in the ultimate humiliation and expulsion of Safdar Jung from Delhi. Now Najib Khan emerged as an important and powerful man with the title of Nawab Najib-ud-Daula. The treachery of Safdar Jung against the Bangash Pathans after the death of Nawab Qayam Khan Bangash led the Rohilla chiefs of Katehar to unite with the fellow Pathans of Farrukhabad against the common enemy. Safdar Jung plotted to seize the Bangash territory of Farrukhabad through treachery. He took the Emperor Ahmad Shah to Aligarh and invited the relatives of Qayam Khan Bangash to visit the royal court, offer *peshkash* (gifts and money), and receive a *farman* regarding the confirmation of Qayam Khan Banghash's successor as a royal *mansabdar.* Qayam Khan's mother came with rich *peshkash* but she was placed under arrest along with her relatives, her property confiscated, and the Bangash territory seized. Nawal Rai, the deputy of Safdar Jung, was posted in Kanauj to keep the Pathans under suppression. Subjected to alien tyranny, the Pathans made Ahmad Khan, son of Nawab Muhammad Khan Bangash, their leader and rose in arms. They gave battle to Nawal Rai and killed him in 1750.[15]

The defeat and death of Nawal Rai and the heavy losses suffered by his army men at the hands of Bangash Pathans filled Safdar Jung with rage. He decided to destroy the Pathans at all costs. With his ally Suraj Mal Jat he marched towards Farrukhabad. The Pathans were able to defeat this army also.[16] On his return to Delhi Safdar Jung spent the treasure bequeathed by his predecessor Saadat Khan Burhan-ul-Mulk on preparations for war and he hired the Maratha chiefs, Jai Appa Sindia and Malhar Rao Holkar to assist him. For his part Nawab Ahmad Khan Bangash appealed to the Rohilla chiefs of Katehar for help. They responded and joined him with their army. When Hafiz Rahmat Khan found it difficult to gain success against the combined forces of Safdar Jung and the Maratha chiefs, he advised Ahmad Khan Bangash to retreat to Chilkiya in the Kumaon hills and continue the war from there. Thereupon the region of Katehar was ravaged by Safdar Jung and his allies. After several months' struggle, the Pathans won over Malhar Rao Holkar and Nawab Javed Khan Mahli (the royal eunuch, elevated to the status of a high *mansabdar*) by bribing them. Both of them pressed Safdar Jung to make peace with the Rohillas. In the meantime, on hearing about Ahmad Shah Abdali's invasion, Emperor Ahmad Shah recalled the *wazir* to Delhi. Now Safdar Jung had to stop fighting. A peace treaty between him and the Pathans was concluded in 1754.[17]

On his return to Delhi, the Wazir Safdar Jung had Nawab Javed Khan assassinated. This caused estrangement between him and the emperor.[18] The emperor invited the nobles and chiefs, including the Rohillas of Katehar to assist him against Safdar Jung. Of the Rohillas, Najib Khan, the son-in-law of Dundey Khan, agreed to proceed to Delhi with 5,000–6,000 *sawars* and footmen. An experienced soldier and tactician, Najib Khan inflicted defeat on Safdar Jung and his ally Suraj Mal Jat. They were forced to free to Awadh and Bharatpur respectively. In reward for this Najib Khan was conferred the title of Nawab Najib-ud-Daula and assigned the *jagir* of Safdar Jung in Katehar, including the entire modern district of Bijnor. He was also entrusted the *faujdari* of the *sarkar* of Saharanpur in which was included, besides the *parganas* of modern Saharanpur district, the region of Muzaffarnagar district.[19] Thereafter, Najib-ud-Daula built-up a strong army and became the most distinguished chief in north India. He outshone the fellow Hindu and Muslim chiefs in diplomacy and statesmanship as well. The interest evinced by him in the economic development in his newly-carved out principality created immense goodwill among the people in the region.

Let us now discuss the process of urbanization, started under the fostering care of the Rohilla chiefs in Katehar. The beautiful monuments erected in Aonla, the headquarters of Nawab Ali Muhammad Khan, were demolished by Shuja-ud-Daula after the defeat of Hafiz Rahmat Khan in 1774. Only mosques and tombs were spared. The ruins of the monuments tend to reveal that Aonla had developed into an important city under the Rohilla chief. References contained in Qayam Chandpuri's Urdu verses to the palatial buildings in different towns supplement the relevant information available in the contemporary historical works. They show how the members of the ruling elite vied with one another for having beautiful palaces constructed, the poets attached to their establishment composed chronograms about the date of their completion and in praise of their grandeur. One of the short *mathnavis* composed by Qayam Chandpuri casts light upon the hardship faced by the residents of Bisauli,[20] a village developed into an important township under Nawab Dundey Khan (d. 1771) who held Moradabad and Bisauli as his *jaidad.*[21] The nawab made Bisauli his headquarters and his officers and scholars had to take up residence here. The artisans, craftsmen, and masons came and settled down in large numbers. But the construction of roads and streets was not taken into consideration, with the result that the area got inundated during the monsoon season. The employees of Nawab Dundey Khan who went to attend his *darbar* on horseback or in palanquins got their clothes spoilt with mud or dirty water, so common everywhere in the town. In this poem we find references to the *rath* (chariot), bullock carts, horses, elephant and palanquins that were used as means of transportation.[22]

Likewise, the city of Moradabad which served as the administrative headquarters of an extensive territorial unit since its foundation during the reign of Emperor Shah Jahan was further beautified through the constructions of new buildings and laying out of gardens. As regards Hafiz Rahmat Khan, the chief Rohilla leader, he made Bareilly his headquarters and developed it into a mart to attract merchants. The town of Pilibhit received a more favoured treatment from him. It was not only fortified with strong walls and gates but also beautified with splendid buildings. The Jama Mosque in Pilibhit was constructed with the same architectural features as that of Shah Jahan's grand mosque in Delhi. Besides, beautiful gardens were laid out. Another town named Hafiz Gunj was founded between Bareilly and Pilibhit.[23] Another Rohilla chief, Amir Khan, a subordinate of Hafiz Rahmat Khan, founded Amir Gunj (now in the district of Bareilly) that soon developed into an important township.[24] The towns named with the suffix Gunj had arrangements for weekly bazaars for cattle and other commodities. They played an important role in socio-economic growth.

Of all the Rohilla rulers, Najib-ud-Daula was the most successful in leaving his mark as a great builder. Foster gives a description of Najibabad, founded by Najib-ud-Daula, on a swamp but at a point that would 'facilitate the commerce of Kashmir, which having been diverted from its former channel of Lahore and Delhi, by the inroads of Siques (Sikhs), Marathas, and Afghans, took a course through the mountains at the head of the Panjab, and was introduced into the Rohilla country through the Lall Dong Pass.' According to Foster, merchant caravans travelled from Rohilkhand to Jammu through Srinagar town, situated in the Garhwal hills. This new route linked Rohilkhand with Kashmir, Kabul, and Central Asia for overland trade.[25] There are also references contained in *Forsters' Travels* to the towns and forts constructed by Najib-ud-Daula in other districts. For instance, he mentions the famous fort of Pathargarh, built within a mile's distance from Najibabad. The town of Gauthgarh was founded 35 miles south-east of Saharanpur, and Shukrtal Fort near an area of ravines and ridges, 17 miles east of Muzaffarnagar. Moreover, *serais* were built around important towns for the convenience of travellers and traders. The author of *Tarikh-i-Balda-i-Nijbabad* adds to this information. The main bazaar constructed by Najib-ud-Daula was square, containing the beautiful Jama Mosque. Besides, several Gunj were established and named after Najib-ud-Daula's sons, such as Zabita Gunj, Kalu Gunj, Munir Gunj, and Nawab Gunj. Najib-ud-Daula also had a beautiful tomb constructed for his burial. Lakhs of rupees were spent on its construction because its interior, particularly the ceiling, was studded with precious stones (taken out by the Marathas in 1772).

Najib-ud-Daula planted Pathan colonies at strategic places such as Basihi Kotla, 9 miles from Najibabad. His officers and relations too are credited with the construction of towns and beautiful buildings. For instance, Nawab Afzal Khan, his brother, founded Afzalgarh, an important town in the district of Bijnor.[26] The relevant evidence contained in the *Kuliyat* of Qayam Chandpuri also tends to show that other civil and army officers of Najib-ud-Daula had beautiful buildings constructed in different towns. Raja Ram Prasad of Chandpur had a beautiful palace built in the midst of a garden setting in 1758. The tank and flower-beds inside the garden made the *diwan khana* so fascinating that it looked like paradise.[27]

A word may be added about the reorganization of the extensive *sarkars* into smaller units, called *zila* for administrative convenience and economic development both in towns and the countryside in north India during this period.[28] This reorganization was also politically necessary because a large number of military officers had to be entrusted with the charge of administration independent of each other. So the *zila* (or district) is not the creation of British rule.

As for the socio-economic life and culture, the odd bits pieced together from literary works written in Persian and Urdu in the eighteenth century help us reconstruct socio-economic history. The *tazkira* and the poems contained in the *Kulliyat* of Qayam Chandpuri[29] yield interesting source material. The *qasidas* (panegyrics), *ruba'is* (quartrains), *qitas* (short poems), and *mathnavis* (long poems) provide insights into the life and conditions in the region. The Rohilla nobles and *zamindars*, Hindu and Muslim, helped the men of learning and talent who had to face hardship after the decline of Mughal power. Several *ruba'is* composed either in their praise or in condemnation of the government officers tell us about generosity as well as corruption.[30] The *qadi* of Sambhal has been condemned as a corrupt man notorious for taking bribe.[31]

In the *qitas* we find small bits of information about the celebration of Hindu and Muslim festivals. Muslim aristocrats arranged grand banquets to celebrate Id-ul-Fitr. One of the patrons of Qayam Chandpuri spent a huge amount in charity and on a banquet on this occasion. The *nauroz* (spring) festival was also celebrated by him in the same way.[32] Hindu *zamindars* and nobles spent lavishly on Holi celebrations—as one *mathnavi* describes. Muslims visited the houses of Hindus on this day. The rich people sprinkled colour all around while the poor used all sorts of things, including mud and dirty water. The poet glows with pride when he praises a certain Kunwar (a Hindu *zamindar*), his friend in Chandpur, who used to invite his friends over on this occasion.[33]

Certain poems shed light on the means of recreation available in the cities and towns. Nobles and chiefs patronized musicians and dancers and thus helped the survival of classical art. Some of the ruling elite appear to have spent a lot on the training of dancing girls. The girls were trained in different classical dances, particularly the popular *akhara.*[34] Boys and young men in every town and city were fond of kite flying. Likewise, people enjoyed fireworks on occasions such as the birth of a child or a wedding etc.[35] Marriage ceremonies of the rich were opulent affairs. Besides the distribution of money and other gifts among servants, money was thrown from above the palanquin of the bride at the time of her arrival at her father-in-law's residence.[36] Shows staged by magicians, mimics, and buffoons (called *nats* and *naqals*) were enjoyed equally by the rich and the poor. A long *mathnavi* on the art of a certain *nat* and his wife shows that some of them could hypnotize the spectators. Such artists were richly rewarded by the rajas and nawabs.[37]

Of the weapons mentioned in the verses, the poet attaches great importance to the European gun (*bandooq*). He tells us that the gun imported from Europe was a most coveted possession.[38]

A poem on the severity of winter provides information about the conditions of people of different strata in the towns and cities. The wealthy heated the rooms in their houses with *kangris* (fire vessels of clay) and covered the windows and doors with heavy curtains of costly cloth whereas the artisans and daily wage-earners suffered from the want of sufficient clothing. They would be unable to go out when it was extremely cold and could not earn their daily wages. Even the craftsman did not have sufficient clothing.[39]

The development of the Hindawi dialect into a literary language, later called Urdu, is also worth mentioning. Rustam Ali Bijnori's work *Qissa-o-Ahvali-Rohila* provides us with an example of the refined Urdu prose of the elite in Katehar.[40] Qayam Chandpuri in his *Tazkira-i-Makhzan-i-Nikat* about Hindu and Muslim poets writing in Urdu casts light on social relationships among the Hindu and Muslim elite in the urban centres and reveals how powerful a vehicle of thought and expression this language had become in the north during the eighteenth century. Moreover, this *tazkira* furnishes information on scholars of Persian literature who composed verses in Urdu. They belonged to the *shaykhzadas* or *zamindar* families. Among the leading poets were Mir Saadat Ali Saadat of Amroha, Shihabuddin Saqib of Seohara (District Bijnor), Muhammad Ali Hashmat Kashmiri who had settled in Moradabad, Mir Abdul Rasul of Amroha, Lala Khushvaqt Rai Shadab of Chandpur and Lala Nawal Rai Wafa.[41]

This *tazkira* also provides insights into the polity under the Rohilla chiefs. The Rohillas had stepped into the shoes of the Mughals and employed people on the basis of merit irrespective of creed. Finances under Ali Muhammad Khan and his immediate successors was managed by the Hindus. The Revenue collectors were also Hindus. For instance, Qayam makes mention of Gulab Rai and his nephew, Lala Nawal Rai Wafa. The former was the *diwan* (finance minister) of Nawab Najib-ud-Daula, while the latter held the charge of a few *parganas* across the river Ganges in Saharanpur district.[42] Likewise, Raja Hilas Rai Rangin, the Resident of Bareilly, served as *Diwan* under Hafiz Rahmat Khan.

The region of Katehar remained undisturbed, enjoying peace and prosperity until Shah Alam Badshah's return from Allahabad to Delhi with the support of the Maratha army in 1772. On arrival in Delhi, Shah Alam sent Zabita Khan, who had succeeded his father, Nawab Najib-ud-Daula (d. 1770), the robe of investiture with the *farman* regarding his appointment as *Mir Bakhshi.* In return the king demanded the customary fee of succession and also urged him to settle the account for the Khalsa *parganas* controlled by his father for several years. Zabita Khan put on the robe but refused to pay any money, although he was the richest man after the death of his father who had bequeathed huge treasures.

Annoyed by Zabita Khan's defiance, Shah Alam asked the Marathas for help against the Rohillas and Zabita Khan was defeated and driven away, his treasures and property looted by the Marathas. Having settled scores with Zabita Khan, the king and his Maratha allies marched against other Rohilla chiefs, who withdrew to the Kumaon hills. The Maratha army looted the undefended towns and cities. Aonla, Bareilly and Rampur were ransacked. Only Amroha was spared because its *saiyids* had purchased peace by paying Rs. 60,000. Qayam Chandpuri's poem *Shahar-i-Ashob* sheds light on the tyranny to which people were subjected. According to it, the return of Shah Alam from Allahabad to Delhi (on 6 January 1772) filled both the Hindus and Muslims everywhere with hopes for a better future. But soon people were disillusioned on account of the misery that his invasion of Katehar (Rohilkhand) caused all around. Since the poet belonged to the region of Katehar and was associated with the Rohilla chiefs, he laments the loss of life and property and condemns in severe terms both Shah Alam and his allies, the Marathas. He calls Shah Alam a tyrant unworthy of kingship, 'a scoundrel moving at the head of an army of plunderers'. Likewise, the Marathas were condemned as freebooters. Shah Alam's grandfather and father, Jahandar Shah and Alamgir Thani (1754–60) are called fools and then the poet would have us believe that their descendants were known for their stupidity. We are also told that Shah Alam brought Marathas into Katehar for the destruction of the Pathan race but could not achieve his end. The Pathans fled, but innocent people were killed and pillaged. The whole region was laid waste. Left without food, people faced starvation in every town and city. Those rich people who thought it derogatory to wear fine cotton clothes, could not afford to have even coarse cloth for a turban. Those who maintained large kitchens and a number of people, had no food for themselves. Stables emptied of horses and fodder. Beautiful cities that could be compared with Cairo had been denuded of everything worth mentioning. The markets were left without any commodity, even medicines could not be found there. The moneylenders disappeared. The lanes were full of corpses. The beautiful buildings were raised to the ground and noblemen like Raja Gulab Rai who was the *hakim* of a *zila* and maintained more than a thousand servants, became penniless.[13] The kaisthas, the *ulama*, comprising *qadis* and *muftis* (judges and jurists), also were on the verge of starvation. The revenue collectors were also ruined. Those who survived the carnage found it difficult to keep body and soul together. After the withdrawal of Shah Alam and his Maratha allies from Katehar in 1772, chaos and anarchy continued till the time the Rohilla chiefs could again restore law and order. The Pathan soldiers who had returned from their hideouts looted people of whatever was left with them.[44]

The *qasidas* in the *Kuliyat* also give vital insights into the cultural life. Even minor chiefs associated with the Rampur court went out of their way after the fall of Rohilla power in 1774, to support poets and scholars.

Last, we may make a brief allusion to a long *mathnavi* relating to the platonic love between a recluse, Shah Ladha, and a newly-married girl of the Panjab. Apparently the poet has successfully versified in Urdu a sixteenth-century romance; it is important as it helps us measure the depth to which popular Sufism had sunk. It also shows that in consequence of the ontological philosophy of *Wahdat-ul-Wujud* (unity in essence of the creator and the created), platonic love had become a common vice among the Sufis. No doubt, the educated Sufis among the followers of Ibn Arabi continued to adhere to orthodox Islam and tried to gain spirituality through self-purification, but they had also, since the fifteenth century considered *ishq-i-majazi* (platonic love) a means to spiritual progress.[45] As a result, the less educated or unlettered Sufis became negligent of the *Shari'at.* They did not attach importance to the daily rituals and lived in isolation from people. By chance if they cast their eye on a beautiful girl or boy, they fell in love with him or her. In the literature, the departure of the beloved causes severe grief to the lover. Ultimately the lover dies and is followed by the beloved to the grave: union is possible only in death. Qayam as a Sufi also believed in the *ishq-i-majazi* as a means to the path of real love and gnosis.[46]

To conclude, it may be stated that the discovery of fresh historical evidence contained in contemporary documents is of historical significance for it may either substantiate a fact or serve as a corrective to the known sources. The works of Rustam Ali Bijnori, Qayam Chandpuri and Tahmasp Beg provide us with insights into the socio-political changes that took place in north India during the eighteenth century. The information in them enables us to reconstruct life and culture in different colours.

In fact, the decline of the Mughal power was paradoxically paralleled by the expansion of the Mughal imperial culture because the new regional rulers emulated Mughal cultural norms and practices. The literature produced under their patronage in Persian and Urdu languages bears testimony to the fact that the Mughal court continued to provide a cultural reference point even after the establishment of the British supremacy in India.

NOTES

1. Rustam Ali, a resident of the town of Bijnore, belonged to a non-Pathan family. He compiled the history of the rise and fall of the Rohillas in Katehar in 1774, two years after the fall of Hafiz Rahmat Khan and at the instance of an English general posted at Daranagar to assist the administration of Nawab Shuja-ud-Daula of Awadh. It is written in a non-partisan way, giving due credit to different Rohilla chiefs for their attainments in different fields. It serves as a corrective to the accounts compiled by the writers associated with the Awadh court or by the son and grandson of Hafiz Rahmat Khan. Note that not only is this the first major historical work in Urdu prose but it also provides us with an example of how Urdu was spoken and written by the elite in Delhi and Katehar during the eighteenth century.

   The rare manuscript copy of the work, entitled *Qissa-o-Ahval-i-Rohila* is stored in the library of The Anjuman-i-Taraqi-i-Urdu, Karachi. In view of its literary value, I have edited the text and published it with notes and introduction in Urdu and English both. See *An Eighteenth Century History of North India*, ed. Iqtidar Husain Siddiqui, Delhi: Manohar, 2005, hereafter cited as Rustam Ali Bijnori.
2. Rustam Ali Bijnori, pp. 26, 38, 45–6.
3. Ibid., pp. 29–30.
4. Ibid., p. 31.
5. Ibid., pp. 32–3.
6. Ibid.
7. Ibid., p. 34.
8. Ibid., pp. 35–6.
9. Ibid., p. 40.
10. Ibid., pp. 41–2.
11. Ibid., p. 48.
12. Ibid., p. 46.
13. Ibid., p. 47.
14. Ibid., pp. 48–52.
15. Ibid., pp. 54–8.

16. Ibid., pp. 59-62.
17. Ibid., pp. 62-4.
18. Ibid., p. 65.
19. Ibid., p. 69.
20. Bisauli is now a *tahsil* headquarters in the district of Badaun.
21. Rustam Ali Bijnori, p. 46.
22. Qayam Chandpuri, *Kuliyat-i-Qa'im Chandpuri*, vol. 2, ed. Iqtida Hasan, Lahore, 1965, pp. 181–4 (hereafter cited as *Kuliyat*).
23. Mustajab Khan, *Gulistan-i-Rahmat*, Aligarh MS no. 180/46, ff. 77a–b.
24. Ibid., ff. 1450b.
25. G. Foster, 'A Journey from Bengal to England through the Northern Part of India, Kashmir, Afganistan and Persia into Russia, by Caspian Sea', *Forster's Travels*, London, 1798, vol. I, p. 190.
26. Nawab Saidullah Khan, *Tarikh-i Balda-i-Najibabad*, MS, Abdul Salam Collection, Maulana Azad Library, Aligarh, no. Urdu (2) 2 10/76, ff. 3b–4b, 42b. This work was written by the descendant of Najib-ud-Daula, soon after the Revolt of 1857 had been suppressed.
27. *Kuliyat*, pp. 43–4; also Rustam Ali Bijnori, pp. 145, 206.
28. *Kuliyat*, pp. 49, 71; Rustam Ali Bijnori, p. 81; also Makhdum-ud-Daula 'I'tiqad Jung Tahmas Beg Khan Rumi, *Tahmasnama*, ed. Muhammad Aslam, Lahore: University of the Punjab, 1986, pp. 283–4.
29. *Kuliyat*.
30. *Kuliyat*, pp. 14, 16, 78.
31. Ibid., pp. 32–4.
32. Ibid.
33. Ibid., pp. 197, 202, *mathnavi* no. 10.
34. The *akhara* was a group dance in which a group of dancing girls turned up, decked in jewels, and embroidered silk clothes. They made quick movements with lit earthen lamps on their palms. *Qasida* no. 11 in the *Kuliyat* shows that Nawab Muhammad Yar Khan, the brother of Nawab Faiz Ullah Khan of Rampur, maintained such a group. It was very popular in medieval times.
35. *Kuliyat*, pp. 158–64, Short *mathnavi*, no. 2.
36. Ibid., pp. 255–7.
37. Ibid., p. 316.
38. Ibid., pp. 255–7; also *Tarikh-i-Balda-i-Najibabad*, f.4a, for the display of fireworks.
39. *Kuliyat*, p. 168, line 8.
40. Cf. the Urdu text in *An Eighteenth Century History of North India*, op. cit.
41. Ibid., pp. 188–9, *Mathnavi*, no. 7; Idem, *Makhzan-i-Nikat*, ed. Maulvi Abdul Haque, Aurangabad: Anjuman Taraqi-i-Urdu Hind, undated, pp. 7, 18, 24, 26, 66, etc.
42. *Makhzan-i-Nikat*, p. 72.

43. *Kuliyat*, pp. 57–64.
44. Ibid., pp. 57–64, 119, 130, 131.
45. Sayyid Muhammad Akbar Husaini, *Jawami-ul-Kilem*, Kanpur, 1356 H, pp. 13–14.
46. Cf. Iqtidar Husain Siddiqui, 'Sufis and Sufism in the Territorial Unit of Kalpi, 15th and 16th Centuries', *Pakistan Journal of History and Culture*, vol. V, no. 1, 1984, p. 68.

Some Muslim Patron Saints of Hindu Chiefs in North India and the Impact of their Interactions

Z.U. MALIK

Studies in Islamic mysticism (*tasawwuf*) have come to occupy a special space in the fast-growing literature on Islam. The range and depth of available studies is considerable. They have discussed subjects spanning the genesis, evolution, ideology, role and impact of mysticism from diverse perspectives and in a variety of ways. Inevitably, the interpretations, identifications, and classification, formulated historically and epistemically have differed widely. Some controversial issues such as the shrine-cult, *pir-murid* relations, rituals and practices, have created a sharp divide between two school of thought, with one side swearing by its theoretical constructs rooted in the Koran and *Hadis,* and the other rejecting these outright, being a 'foreign plant in the sandy desert of Islam'.

As part of a design to denigrate mysticism the detractors have incorporated all sorts of hybrid groups of *qalandars, malangs, madaris* and pretenders into the category of the great Sufi saints or *mashaikhs,* the true representatives of this fine spiritual movement in the religious history of Islam. As far back as the eleventh century, Shaikh Ali Hujwari (d. 1077) had succinctly distinguished perfect spiritualists from pseudo Sufis in the following statement: 'Today Sufism is a name without reality, but formerly it was reality without a name, and this frock (patched garment) must have been sewn in pre-eternity'.[1]

Nevertheless, mysticism is a living tradition in a religion-dominated society, and its influence on the religious consciousness of common folks is deep and enduring. Every year seminars are held in South Asia, at national and international levels, on this subject attended by opponents and exponents.

The shrines of the celebrated Sufis are still popular centres of pilgrimage for thousands of devotees, credulous and ignorant as they may be characterized.

One subject on which recent scholarship has focused is the nature of the relationship that existed between many a mystic order (*silsilahs*) and contemporary rulers and ruling establishments. The monarchs and nobles, by and large, showed reverence to reputed saints of almost of every order and sect, and sought their blessings and benediction for military success or for political success. They protected and patronized mystic institutions—*khanqahs, langer, madrasas,* and *dargah*—through land grants and cash subsidies. They oriented their patronage, not necessarily out of altruism or mystic inclination, but in order to broaden their social base and legitimacy. Mystics of the Naqsbandiyya, Qadriyya and Suharwardiyya orders normally maintained intimate relations with the elites of the day, treated them with indulgence, and graciously accepted their land grants and gifts. They believed that a close association with the royal court would enable them to exert a moderating influence on despotic ways of governance. To what extent such aspirations were fulfilled, or appeals to alleviate the sufferings of poor masses received a response, is a question that has been thoroughly debated by the modern scholars.

For their part, the Chishtiyya Sufis resolutely opposed contact with kings and political leaders, denounced acceptance of land grants and accumulation of wealth, and expressed an aversion to state service; for these involvements would surely afflict the souls of mystics and lead seekers of the truth astray. The early great Chishti saints, therefore, kept away not only from the corridors of power but also from the currents of politics.[2]

What has not been dealt with so extensively is the range, scope and effects of contacts established by the Hindu chiefs with local Muslim saints in their dominions. Originating in certain incidents in the life of a particular raja, the early casual connection with a saint developed into a personal intimacy that eventually gained permanent footing and went a long way to promote inter-communal harmony and partnership. This essay is an attempt to fill in the needed gap, to set straight the record of incidents and explain aspects of the relationship between the rajas, satraps and their patron saints in a historical context. Here we shall inquire about Shaikh Burhan al-Din, revered by Raja Mukal of Shaikhawati (r. 1430–45), and Shah Mansur, closely associated with Mahadji Sindia (1727–94), the ruler of Gwalior. Both saints lived in the rural interior, cut-off from political centres, with no traditions of historical or *tazkirah* writings as a genre, no hagiographies could be compiled of them: if any, these are not extant. Reliance has thus to be placed on the available record, scanty and fragmentary, to pursue our theme.

An important source of information on Shaikh Burhan al-Din Chishti is *Karnama i-Rajputana*[3] written in Urdu by Maulvi Hakim Muhammad Najm al-Ghani, who had for long served as Head Maulvi in Maharana High School, Udaipur. His grandfather, Haji Muhammad Saeed, was a disciple of Shah Waliullah (1703–63). Similar evidence with different points is *Waqa'i Rajputana*[4] composed in Urdu by Babu Juwala Sahey during the last decades of the nineteenth century. Both authors have depended on local traditions and statements to portray Shaikh Burhan al-Din, but neither could explore any original source material. Ranbir Sinh in his *History of Shekhawats*[5] has also described the life and career of this saint and his links with the Rajput princes, but along the path usually trodden. However, the identity, spiritual status, and social standing of Burhan al-Din are unquestionably established on firmer grounds. Again, with regard to the information about the early life, antecedents, and spiritual genealogy of Shah Mansur, the Sufi *tazkiras* of the period are silent. There are only two contemporary political chronicles which have briefly described how Mahadji Sindia came into contact with this obscure saint and throw some light on their relationship which lasted for long. The *Ibrat Nama*[6] was written by Khair al-Din Allahabadi (1751–1827), who had served James Anderson (the British Resident at Sindia's court as his Secretary), and stayed at Gwalior from 1780 to 1787. The second is *Tarikh-i-Muzaffari*[7] composed in 1791 by Muhammad Ali Khan Ansari,[8] son of Hidayatulla Khan. Recently Daniel Gold has contributed an extensively researched article on the Sufi shrines of Gwalior, including a brief note about Shah Mansur, based on fables and popular sayings, mainly details of ceremonies in which the relics of the patron saint of the princely dynasty are brought out and worshipped by the raja. One such ceremony that was attended by Daniel Gold took place in 1997.[9] I now attempt to collect and piece together the scattered factual information into a reasonable shape for coherent, comprehensive analysis.

What was the message of these saints to people with whom they lived? It may be briefly stated that Shaikh Burhan al-Din and Shah Mansur had fearlessly worked to spread their moral and ethical message amongst common people independently of any state patronage or military support. Shah Mansur and Dariya Saheb flourished in a period when the Mughal central authority had declined and the Muslim ruling classes had disintegrated. The old balance of power between Muslim political dominance and Hindu majority, conceptualized as an 'equilibrium between power and religion',[10] supposedly a determining factor for inter-communal peaceful co-existence in the previous centuries, had been upset.[11] Yet a Hindu–Muslim symbiosis subsisted in the midst of continuous warfare and political upheaval, mainly because of the strenuous efforts of the Muslim and Hindu leaders. While these Muslim saints taught spiritual doctrines, mysticism, and austere exercises to a restricted circle of disciples, their discourse to the public in general mentioned non-violence, patience, charity, and social service to fellow beings. In consonance with the socio-cultural ethos of the region, these ideas appealed to the people. Their piety, spiritual qualities, mystical ways of life, acculturation with local customs and conditions, and tireless espousal of the cause of the deprived and downtrodden attracted people to their fold. 'The Chishti Khanqahs did offer consolation, peace and nourishment to thousands of Muslims who crowded the towns.'[12] The divine light that the purified soul of a Sufi receives is reflected in radiance, and the highest reflection of this radiance is selfless service, to console and help suffering people. 'The inner feeling of the relation between God and man is bound to issue in the service of humanity.'[13]

SHAIKH BURHAN AL-DIN CHISHTI

According to Najmul Ghani, Shaikh Burhan al-Din was an immigrant from Khurasan who wandered from place to place, from the wilderness of Shaikhawati to the north-west of Jaipur.[14]

In this desert land only one crop of coarse grain (*jawar, bajra*) was cultivated in the rainy season; it was under the sway of Qa'in Khani Chauhan Rajputs before Udey Karan, Raja of Amber, subjugated them and established his ascendancy over it.[15] Juwala Sahey informs us that Shaikh Burhan al-Din Chishti had come here from Delhi at the time of Timur's invasion, 1398, and had engaged in reforming moral, by enjoining people to perform noble and virtuous deeds, eschew violence, and live together in peace and amity.[16] These messages were easily understood and appreciated by the people and his reform agenda made the Sufi popular in the area. When Shaikh Burhan al-Din visited Amarsar, Raja Mukal (1430–45), a grandson of Udey Karan, come to meet him, and, inspired by his devotion to God and his liberal outlook, solicited him to reside in the town and carry on his mission.[17]

Shaikh Burhan al-Din accepted the invitation of the raja and in due course of time an intimate relationship developed between them. Once, in a meeting, the raja requested him to pray to God to bless him with a son because the question of succession perpetually bothered him. The Shaikh prayed for him, and a son was born to the raja's youngest wife, Nirabanji. The father, attributing the happy event to the efficacy of the Shaikh's prayers named the child Shaikha or Shaikhaji in gratitude. The descendants of this Shaikha were called Shaikhawatis, and because of their vast progeny that grew over the period, the entire region came to be known as Shaikhawati. Compared to other families of Kachhawa Rajputs, writes Najmul Ghani, the Shaikhawatis were more sturdy and hardworking.[18] Shaikh Burhan al-Din Chishti asked Raja Mukal Singh that a thread (perhaps given by him) should be tied round the head of the child, and on its removal it should be bound to the dome of a *dargah*. When the child was grown up he should wear a *kurta* and cap of blue colour. He also advised the raja to give up eating pork, and on the occasion of the birth of his son a goat should be sacrificed to celebrate the event. The raja should adopt the policy of tolerance and benevolence in the conduct of administration, and act on principles of equity and justice in dealing with diverse ethnic groups and religious communities in his kingdom. Raja Mukal died in 1445, and was succeeded by Shaikha, his only son, under the title Rao Shaikha.[19]

Soon after his accession, Rao Shaikha set out to extend the frontiers of his ancestral territory to the farthest limits, and through wars and annexation he ultimately succeeded in liberating himself from the bondage of his former overlord, Chandra Sen, the Kachhawa raja of Amber. A valiant soldier and tactful commander, Rao Shaikha fought 52 battles, but at the end (1488), he lost his life, leaving behind six wives and twelve sons. He had built the fort of Sikargarh and temple of Jagdishpur in Amarsar. He had established his supremacy over vast areas in Shaikhawati region, united the clansmen, and worked for the well-being and security of his subjects. He was liberal in religious matters, generous in his treatment on the general public, and judicious in the processes of governance. He had permitted the Pathans of the Panni tribe to settle in the villages of his newly built principality. For him Ram and Rahim were same and he saw no difference between a temple and a mosque. He respected Islam and provided protection to its followers living within his territorial jurisdiction.[20] Such tolerance and social harmony, generated in the reign of Rao Shaikha, were reinforced by the political alliances which his successors formed with the Mughal government in the following century. By means of conciliation and patronage the Mughal emperors succeeded in winning the allegiance of their Shaikhawati satraps and building—a relationship founded on mutual interest, trust, and respect. The sardars among them who were honoured and raised to high positions by Akbar and Jahangir were Raja Loon Karan (1548–84), Raja Manohar (1584–1616), Raja Raisal Darbari (1538–1614). With their gallantry, spirit of loyalty, and hereditary leadership, they rose to the opportunities created by imperial service. Moreover, the affirmation and legitimization of local autonomy and religious liberty helped them sustain the relationship to the end of mid-eighteenth century. How such process of reciprocity unfolded may be illustrated by the manner in which Manohar Singh was educated and trained at the court-palace of Akbar. The emperor had met the Rajput prince on his way to Ajmer, and, pleased with his intelligence and personality, he took him to the royal palace. He entrusted his education to Prince Salim. Manohar mastered Persian in a short time and began to compose verses in that language. His exposure to the cosmopolitan atmosphere at the court and his interaction with nobles like Abul Fazal, Todar Mal, and Birbal broadened his intellectual horizon and added to his knowledge of politics.[21]

Thus we may conclude that Haji Najim al-Din Shaikhawati (1818–70) of Jhunjhunu brought about a visible change in the social life and moral behaviour of people.

SHAH MANSUR

It was in 1760 that the grand Maratha army, under Sadashiv Rao Bhau,[22] embarked on its long journey from Patdur near Jalna into north India to drive Ahmad Shah Durrani (1722–72) out of the Panjab.[23] The army eventually encamped at Mathura.[24] Mahadji Sindia held a high position as a captain of a special contingent. During his sojourn in Gwalior he went out, accompanied by a few comrades-in-arms, on some sight-seeing. In an adjoining town he passed by the hermitage of Shah Mansur. At that moment the saint was standing outside his humble hut, and was in a state of ecstasy, deep in love of God.

Seeing Mahadji Sindia, he uttered, 'Timur comes', and picking up a piece of wood threw it towards Sindia, saying, 'Go, get a leg broken and come.' Mahadji Sindia took no notice of the Sufi; nor could he understand the significance of his utterings. He went away.[25] Here Khair al-Din ends the episode of Sindia's first contact with Shah Mansur.

But the report given by Maulavi Khair al-Din about Sindia's first meeting with Shah Mansur in the vicinity of Ujjain can not be credited, simply because the Maratha army did not pass through that place on its northward march.[26] Nor does Bheel in Maharashtra seems to be the abode of Shah Mansur as has been identified by Daniel Gold, for this location is not corroborated by historical works in Persian or Marathi,[27] and is not traceable on the available modern maps.[28] The identification made by G.S. Sardesai may help to trace the exact location of the place of the Sufi's dwelling. According to him Shah Mansur died at Bind where, on his grave, a tomb was constructed by Mahadji Sindia. In spite of the persistence requests of the raja to come to Gwalior and reside there, the Shah, true to the mystic principle did not oblige him. He continued to live in that town, and instead sent his son Shah Habib to the raja's court.[29] This Bind may be taken for Bhind in the northern part of Madhya Pradesh, north-east of Gwalior. It lies in the valleys of Chambal and Sind, between the Kunwari and Pahuj rivers.[30]

What happened to Mahadji Sindia in the third battle of Panipat, 14 January 1761, and how he escaped from that terrible battlefield, form an important part of this fascinating tale, omitted by Maulavi Khair al-Din but narrated briefly by Muhammad Khan Ansari, the author of *Tarikh-i-Muzaffari*. The latter narrates that when Mahadji fled and arrived in Farrukhnagar, 12 *kos* from Delhi, he was overtaken by the enemy and stopped an arrow that wounded one of his legs and made him unconscious. The assailant seized his horse and all his belongings, and ran away. At this critical moment a water-career (*saqqa*), named Rana Khan, a citizen of Delhi, spotted Mahadji Sindia lying on the ground. He gave him water, placed him on his pony, and carried him to Delhi. There he arranged for his treatment, probably keeping him in his own house for security reasons. When Sindia was cured and felt fit to move, Rana Khan took him by bullock cart to Gwalior, and then returned to Delhi.[31]

At Gwalior Mahadji Sindia organized a new force, which was trained and equipped it with artillery, and strove to collect funds from various sources to meet its expenses. He then travelled to Poona in December 1762, joined the new Peshwa Madhavrao (1761–3) in the siege of Miraj, and pressed his claim to the kingdom of Malwa in the absence of any other legitimate contestant. His brother, Jankoji Sindia had been captured at Panipat and was put to death along with Ibrahim Gardi by the orders of Ahmad Shah Durrani. His other brother, Jayappy Sindia, was murdered at Nagore in July 1755. Balaji Baji Rao died in (1761), and his elder son Vishwas Rao was killed in the battle of Panipat. His second son, Madhavrao had assumed the charge of Peshwaship. But the real power was wielded by Raghunath Rao, the director of affairs and maker of policy, in the Maratha government at Poona during this period. Raghunath Rao demanded from Mahadji Sindia an enormous sum of money as succession fee. This he could not pay, and he failed to obtain possession of Gwalior legally and peacefully. Raghunath Rao appointed Kedarji and afterwards Mahadji Sindia succeeded to the territory left by Ranoji.[32]

Mahadji was an experienced military general, courageous and daring, endowed with uncommon patience under adversity. While the Peshwa was engaged in the affairs of Karnatak in 1764, he silently left Poona, arrived in Ujjain, and took the manage-ment of his patrimony into his own hands. 'Thus', writes Sardesai, 'the period of some eight years from 1761 to the end of 1768 marks the tutelage of Mahadji's life, and in the beginning of 1769 he emerges as a man of destiny in the pages of history'.[33]

From a perusal of historical texts it is not clear whether Mahadji Sindia met Shah Mansur a second time on his way from Gwalior to Poona or on his return journey from that capital city to Ujjain. It may, however, be conjectured that Sindia would have now remembered the prediction made by the saint to the effect of his becoming lame like Timur, the great conqueror, and the piece of wood as he had thrown towards him the symbol of an arrow that would cut his leg. The memory of the incident naturally inspired in him a desire to meet the Sufi, to know what lay in store for him. Mahadji Sindia decided to pay a visit to Shah Mansur. The meeting between the two has been graphically described by Maulavi Khair al-Din. This time the Shah was in a normal, stable condition, and recognizing him, politely welcomed Sindia, bringing out an old dusty carpet from the house. He spread it and asked the guest to sit on it. Mahadji paid homage to the saint who blessed him by placing his hand on his back. He prayed for his success in his struggle for power, and remarked, '*Din* (religious faith) is for the world (*duniya*) and the world is for religion (*Din*)'. In consequence Mahadji Sindia attained power, prestige, and fame as master of a principality and *Wakil-i-Mutlaq* of the Mughal empire under Shah Alam. Mahadji Sindia developed faith in the spiritual virtues of Shah Mansur and consulted him at all times. After his death the Raja constructed magnificent buildings in the compound of the saint's shrine, comprising a *khanqah*, tomb, mosque, and rest house, and sent costly goods worth of lakhs of rupees for their decoration and upkeep.[34]

Whenever Mahadji Sindia was doubtful about the outcome of a plan regarding war or diplomacy, he resorted to omens, in public. Khair al-Din was present on one such occasion and a summary of his eye-witness account of the process of observance is given below:[35]

The Maharaja issued instructions to his servants to gather flowers of all varieties and colours from far and near. Wreaths were made of these flowers. One big room in the palace was cleaned by a chosen few courtiers, a throne made of silver was brought in and on a small pillar were fixed the wreaths strung in twisted shapes, leaving space on the top of for more flowers. Maharaja Sindia prostrated before the pillar as the drum was beaten. A sheet of cloth was spread near that pillar decorated with wreaths of flower. If the agenda was to be successful, the flowers placed on the top of the pillar would fall on the sheet, and the pillar itself would bend a little. This happened, and the Maharaja stood and bowed before the pillar. Musicians and singers waiting outside to hear the happy news appeared on the scene and began to entertain the audience with songs; drums were beaten, guns were fired, and sweets were distributed to all present. At the end of the ceremony Maharaja moved to Shah Habib, son of Shah Mansur, and exchanged greetings with him. Looking on Maulavi Khair al-Din, he asked, 'Did you observe the miracle (*khawariq*) of the *pir*?' The Maulavi praised the Maharaja, and acknowledged his firm belief in the omnipotence of Almighty God, reflecting in his liberal and tolerant attitude to religious faiths other than his own.[36]

Mahadji Sindia was a man of devout temperament who regularly prayed and worshipped, composed devotional songs, heard daily recitations of the sacred *Bhagavat Puran* and led a chaste life. He held in high regard Dattanath, a Hindu saint, and invited him to reside in his camp. He had established his headquarters at Mathura from where he could easily visit Vrindavan, both cities being under his control. He secured an imperial order prohibiting cow slaughter throughout India. He had learnt both Sanskrit and Persian and had a colloquial knowledge of Urdu. A patron of poets, scholars, musicians, and astrologers, he built a library at Gwalior. Though a strict and sincere adherent of his religion he employed in his army and administration Hindus of all different castes and also Muslims. He was respected by both communities.[37] About a change in the perceptions of Muslims in north India with regard to Maratha hegemony Sardesai comments, 'If any hostile feeling of Muslim rulers existed towards Shivaji and his mission, it had entirely died down after Aurangzeb's death, giving place to mutual trust and cordiality, as is evidenced by Mahadji's management of the Emperor's affairs.'[38]

Mahadji maintained all the Mughal administrative insti-tutions, especially the judicial system, and retained the services of Muslim jurists *(muftis)*, judges (*qazis*) and other subordinate officers in the courts of towns and cities. His steadfast devotion to true ascetics, Sufi and bakht, was unusual and exemplary. In the course of military operations against Ghulam Qadir Khan Rohilla (1788–9), it was reported to Rana Khan, commander of operations, that Maulavi Ibrahim (son of the spiritual mentor of the rebel) had placed the jewels and money of the rebel in the custody of a saint, Shah Abdullah Baghdadi. Rana Khan immediately sent a military force to seize the treasure. The soldiers surrounded the house, took possession of the treasure, and brought Shah Abdullah to the camp of Rana Khan. On hearing of this incident, Mahadji Sindia was angry and chided his brother, urging him to return the plunder to the victim as he was a saint, respect by both Hindus and Muslims. They kept their money in his custody in the belief that no one in the world would lay hands on it in those days of turbulence and violence. He wrote, 'Arresting saints and confiscating their properties is not approved in any religion.' Without delay Rana Khan gave back whatever had been plundered by his soldiers to the saint and himself went to his camp, tendered unconditional apologies, and stayed for some time with him. Then Shah Abdullah Baghdadi was taken in a palanquin in a procession attended by captains and chiefs of the army to his house, and having obtained the deed of agreement (*razinama*) from the saint, Rana Khan submitted it to Mahadji Sindia.[39]

This Rana Khan was the same water-carrier who had saved the life of Mahadji Sindia after the third battle of Panipat, 1761. He lived in Delhi, and though a water carrier by profession he had received military training, for reasons of self-defence in these times in his early youth like every other person. When Mahadji

Sindia became secure in his seat of power, he had called Rana Khan from Delhi, and in the open darbar embraced him and declared him his own brother. A ceremonial exchange of turbans as a mark of brotherhood took place. Moreover, the raja rewarded his saviour by raising him to the first command in his army comprising non-Muslim majority, Marathas and others, and always called him Bhai.[40] Rana Khan proved a competent, brave general, loyal to the raja, and he considered the interests of the Maratha state over and above every other motive. No decision was considered final in the council of Mahadji unless Rana was consulted.

CONCLUSION

From the foregoing account of Shaikh Burhan al-Din Chishti and Shah Mansur it may be concluded that their teachings were primarily aimed at reforming the moral and social behaviour of common people in the peripheral areas where they had spent most of their lives. Politically disengaged as they were, the Sufis endeavoured to bring about a change in the prevalent ways and attitudes of life, and the relationships between diverse classes of the local population. In the matter of dietary habits they stressed vegetarianism, and forbade the use of intoxicants like wine and smoking. They urged people to eschew violence, and set aside parochialism or, chauvinism, and to help their neighbours and fellow beings. Dariya Saheb (1700–90) of Dumraon in the Shahabad district (Bihar) denounced religious bias, caste barriers and sectarian dissent. He insisted on the inner freedom of spirit as a key to salvation and union with God whom he called Satyanam (true name). Throughout his life he lived in Shahabad, which was dominated by Ujjainiya Rajput *zamindars* who held him in reverence. In his preachings he would recite a couplet of Kabir, indicating the influence of that renowned monotheist on his mind. His followers refrained from drinking, eating meat, smoking, or using any intoxicating substance, worshipping idols, and molesting fellow beings. Bikramajit, the Ujjainiya chief of Dumraon, a devotee of the Sufi Haider Shah, built a *khanqah* and mosque for him after his return from Calcutta in January 1782.[41]

Through such sermons the saints rekindled the spirit of generous tolerance and cosmopolitanism, and played a part in the process of transformation of the social order, without trying to replace with a new one. There was no effort to indoctrinate laymen in mystic ideology, spell out concepts and theories of spiritualism, or train them in rigorous austerities—these were for the small circle of a few chosen disciples.

They maintained a unique kind of contact with the Hindu chiefs built on a code of mutual respect, trust, and understanding. Their relations affirmed the truth that any religion if sincerely practised leads to the same Supreme Reality, and there was no unbridgeable divide between Hindus and Muslims. The Sufis projected Islam as a religion of peace, moderation, and tolerance. Under the impact of these ideals, the rajas, landlords and other givers of jobs and work transcended the limitations of any and all particularism and economic communalism. They provided opportunities of employment for Muslims on their estates and gave them access to material advancement and social mobility. The historical records of the eighteenth century pertaining to the regions of Shaikhawati, Gwalior state and Shahabad (Bihar) show that they enjoyed economic security, social justice, and freedom of worship under the benevolent rule of their Hindu masters.

NOTES

1. Shaikh Ali bin Usman al-Jullabi al-Hujwari, *Kashful Mahjub*, Urdu translation Mufti Ghulam al-Din Naimi, Karachi: Madina Publishing Company, pp. 63–72. English translation R.A. Nicholson, London: 1939; Persian text printed at Gulzar-i-Hind Stream Press, Lahore.
2. In this area of study K.A. Nizami has outdistanced early Urdu writers, and his contribution to the modern history of Islamic mysticism in South Asia is immense. On a canvas stretching from the thirteenth to the nineteenth century he has drawn portraits of Chishti saints. See his—*The Life and Times of Shaikh Farid-ud-din Ganji-Shakr,* Bombay: British India Press, 1955, and *Tarikh Mashaikh i-Chisht*, 5 vols., Delhi: Nadwat-ul Musannifin, 1954. There are many others scholarly studies of value published in the nineteenth century; only some of these can be mentioned here: Annemarie Schimmel, *Mystical Dimensions of Islam*, North Carolina: Chapell Hill, 1975; S.A.A. Rizvi, *A History of Sufism in*

India, 2 vols., Delhi: Munshiram Manoharlal, 1978; Mir Valiuddin, *The Quranic Sufism,* Delhi: Motilal Banarsidass, 1976; Christian W. Trolp (ed.), *Muslim Shrines in India,* Delhi: Oxford University Press, 1989; Carl W. Ernst and Bruce Lawrence, *The Chishti Sufi Order in South Asia and Beyond,* London: Curzon Press, 2000; Carl W. Ernst, *Eternal Garden,* Albany: State University of New York Press, 1992; P. Jackson (tr. Sharfuddin Maneri), *The Hundred Letters,* Bombay: Better Yourself Books, 1985; Bruce Lawrence, tr. and annotated, *Fawa'id al Fuad,* Amir Hasan Sijzi, New Jersey: Paulist Press, 1992; J. Spencer Trimingam, *The Sufi Orders in India,* London: Oxford University Press, 1971; Richard M. Eaton, *Sufis of Bijapur,* Princeton: Princeton University Press, 1978; Liyaqat H. Moini, *The Chishti Shrine of Ajmer,* Jaipur: Publication Scheme, 2004; Ghulam Gadir Lone, *Muta'la i-Tasawwuf* (Urdu), Delhi, 1994; Mohammed Khadim Hasan, *The Path of Tasawwuf,* The Hague: East-West Publications, 1978.

3. Muhammad Najmul Ghani, *Karnama i-Rajputana* (Urdu), Bareilly: Gazat, Rozana Akbar Panjabi (Undated).
4. Babu Juwala Sahey, *Waqa'i-Rajputana* (Urdu), Agra: Mufeed 'Am Press, 1978–9.
5. Ranbir Sinh, *History of Shekhawats,* Jaipur: Sheetal Offset Printers, 2001.
6. There is ample information about Shaikh Burhan al-Din Chishti available in Rajasthan sources. The author of *Muhnot Nainsi ri Khyat* has identified this saint as Pir Brhan Chishti. He states that the dwelling place of the saint (*takiya*) was situated on the top of a hill near Masharpur. This famous work was edited by Badri Prasad Sakriya, and published by Rajasthan Oriental Research Institute, Jodhpur, 1984, vol. I, p. 304. Some other important sources containing information about the saint may be mentioned here. Thakur Ishwar Sinh Madadh, *Rajput Vanshavalee,* Delhi: Chetna Publisher, p. 110; Girja Shanker Sharma (ed.), *Kavi, Koormi Vilas,* Bikaner: Rajasthan State Archives, 1991, pp. 105–6; Ratan Lal Mishra, *Kayam Khani Vansha Ka Itihas* (Hindi), Jhunjhunu: Kuteer Prakashan, 1994).
7. Khair al-Din Allahabadi, *Ibrat Nama,* MS, A.M.U., Central Library, Aligarh.
8. Muhammad Ali Khan Ansari, *Tarikh-i-Muzaffari,* MS, A.M.U., Central Library, Aligarh.
9. Daniel Gold, 'Sufi Shrines of Gwalior City: Communal Sensibilities and the Accessible Exotic under Hindu Rule', *Journal of Asian Studies,* The Association for Asian Studies, I.N.C. Wisconsin-Madison, vol. 64, no. I, 2005, pp. 127–50.
10. Louis Dumont, *Nationalism and Communalism: In Religion, Politics and History in India,* London, 1970, p. 97.
11. S.A.A. Rizvi, *History of Sufism,* op. cit., vol. I, p. 398.

12. S. Radhakrishnan, *An Idealist View of Life*, London: Unwin Books, 1961, pp. 56–7.
13. *Karnama Rajputana*, op. cit., pp. 35, 49.
14. It was a separate branch of Chauhan Rajputs found in the Bawal Nizamat and in Jaipur state and descended from Ga'in Khan, a famous convert to Islam. Denzil Ibbetson, *A Glossary of the Tribes and Castes of the Panjab and North-West Frontier Province*, Delhi: Lal Publishers, 1985, vol. III, p. 257. The Rajput chiefs of Sadul suppressed the power of Ga'in Khani Nawab and seized Jhunjhunu. *Karnama Rajputana*, p. 49; Savitri Gupta (ed.), *Rajasthan District Gazetteers*, Jhunjhunu, Jaipur: Mahavir Printing Press, 1984, p. 20; S.C. Bhatt (ed.), *The Encyclopaedic District Gazetteers of India*, Delhi, 1998, vol. I, p. 945.
15. Babu Juwala Sahey, *Waqa'i-Rajputana*, op. cit., vol. I, p. 660.
16. Ibid., pp. 662–5; *Karnama Rajputana*, pp. 322–4.
17. Ibid.
18. Ranbir Sinh, *History of Shekhawats*, pp. 5–8, 20–6.
19. *Waqa-i Rajputana*, p. 665; *History of Shekhawats*, pp. 42–3, 44–9.
20. For details see A.L. Srivastava, *Akbar the Great*, Agra: Shiva Lal Agarwala & Company, 1962, vol. I, pp. 75, 186, 191, 200; S.P. Gupta, *The Agrarian Systems of Rajasthan*, Delhi: Manohar, 1986, p. 231. *History of Shekhawats*, pp. 42, 43, 20–6, 44–9; *Tuzuk-i-Jahangiri*, English tr. Alexander Rogers & Henry Beveridge, Delhi: Munshiram Manoharlal, 1978, pp. 25, 42–3.
21. He was the son of Chinnaji Appa, and nephew of Peshwa Balaji Baji Rao (1740–61).
22. For details of Ahmad Shah Durrani's invasion of India in 1759–61 (fifth in series), and the third battle of Panipat, 14 January 1761, Ganda Singh, *Ahmad Shah Durrani*, Delhi: Asia Publishing House, 1959, pp. 225–48, 250–67.
23. G.S. Sardesai, *The New History of the Marathas*, Bombay: D.B. Dhawale Bombay: Phoenix Publications, 1948, vol. II, p. 417. 'Sadashiv Bhau arrived at Gwalior on 30 May, and in the neighbourhood of Dholpur (crossing the river Chambal about ten miles to the south-west) on 8 June. It was here on the northern bank of Chambal that Malhar Rao Holkar and Suraj Mal Jat joined him. He stayed here for about five weeks and then marched to Agra.'
24. Khair al-Din, *Ibrat Nama*, f. 198.
25. Ibid.
26. *Isufi Shrines of Gwalior*, p. 132.
27. Irfan Habib, *An Atlas of the Mughal Empire*, Delhi: Oxford University Press, 1982, 8A, 8B, 26+80, 6A, 26+74, pp. 82–3; see also the map of Bhansaheb's route, *New History of the Marathas*, II, p. 435.
28. *Ibrat Nama*, MS. University Farsiya Akbar, no. 47, Central Library, A.M.U., Aligarh, f. 199a.

29. A.M. Sinha (ed.), *District Gazetteer of Bhind*, Bhopal: Nirmal Publication, 1996, pp. 23–8.
30. *Tarikh-i-Muzaffari*, f. 297.
31. *New History of the Marathas*, vol. II, pp. 443–5.
32. Ranoji Sindia, the father of Mahadji Sindia and founder of Gwalior state, died in 1745 at Shujalpur near Bhopal. He left behind four sons, equally valiant and capable. Jayappy Sindia was murdered at Nagore in 1755; Dattaji Sindia fell fighting at Barari Ghat in 1760; and Jankoji was killed at Panipat. Mahadji Sindia survived to inherit the principality of Gwalior. Mahadji Sindia died at Poona in 1794 at the age of 67. He had no son, and after his death, his adopted son Daulat Rao Sindia, son of his cousin Anand Rao, fourteen-years-old, succeeded as ruler of Gwalior. For details see *New History of the Marathas*, pp. 495, 481, 495, 514, 578.
33. *Ibrat Nama*, f. 198b.
34. Ibid., f. 199a.
35. Ibid., f. 199a.
36. *New History of the Marathas*, p. 267.
37. Ibid.
38. *Ibrat Nama*, ff. 165–6, 173, 175.
39. *Tarikh-i-Muzaffari*, f. 298.
40. K.K. Dutta, *Survey of India's Social Life and Economic Condition in the Eighteenth Century*, Calcutta, 1961, pp. 5–6.
41. Munshi Binayak Prasad, *Tawarikh-i-Ujjainiya*, Lucknow: Newal Kishore Press, 4 vols. (undated), vol. II, p. 154.

PART II

POLITICS, STATE ADMINISTRATION

Royal Patronage of Artisans of Kashmir under Sultan Zain-ul-Abidin (1420–1470)

JIGAR MOHAMMAD

The artisans of India by their arts and crafts formd a noticeable section of Indian society during the ancient and medieval period. Even the invaders were impressed with the work of the Indian artisans. It is well known that Mahmud Ghaznavi and Timur not only spared the lives of artisans during their invasions of India, they also carried their work back and utilized their skills for the promotion of architectural activities. During his invasions of India (1398–9), Timur captured a large number of artisans and took them to Samarqand. He used the services of these artisans for the construction of a huge mosque there. Artisanal skills contributed to the cultural development of various regions of India during the medieval period. Some regions even came to be identified with special kinds of arts and crafts. Kashmir was one of them.

Both the topography and climate of Kashmir suited indoor art and crafts. Moreover, Kashmir had established cultural contacts with China, Tibet, Central Asia, and Persia during the ancient and medieval periods, particularly in the field of art and architecture.

With the establishment of the Sultanate in Kashmir in 1339 by Shah Mir or Sultan Shamsuddin (1339–42), cultural contact with Central Asia and Persia was strengthened. Sultan Zain-ul-Abidin created a revolution in Kashmir in terms of cultural development. He not only exploited the local potential but also welcomed new techniques, arts and crafts from elsewhere. He honoured skilled persons generously. Contemporary historians of Kashmir call Zain-ul-Abidin a promoter of merit. Jonaraja, the Sanskrit historian and a courtier of the sultan, was impressed by the policies of the sultan. He writes, 'appreciating merit in others, the king encouraged learning and the stream of learning which had run downward, like a canal which breaks through a gap, now began to flow smoothly once more'.[1]

Although most of the rulers of ancient and medieval Kashmir extended support to artisans for the promotion of various crafts, Sultan Zain-ul-Abidin added a new and long chapter to this history. He acted as the patron of all types of artisans and professionals of Kashmir. Under his rule the artisans received both financial support and opportunities to exhibit their skills. According to Srivara, a Sanskrit historian and a favourite courtier of the Sultan, artisans gave Zain-ul-Abidin the status of Vishwakarma.[2] Mirza Haider Dughlat gives all credit to Zain-ul-Abidin for the origin of the growth of different kinds of arts in Kashmir. According to him,

> In Kashmir one meets with all those arts and crafts which are, in most cities, uncommon, such as stone polishing, stone cutting, bottle making, window cutting (*tabdan turash*), gold beating, etc. In the whole of Mavaru-un-Nahr, except in Samarqand and Bokhara, these are nowhere to be met with, while in Kashmir they are abundant. This is all due to Sultan Zain-ul-Abidin.[3]

For the first time Zain-ul-Abidin provided wood carvers were provided so much opportunities. During his reign, a number of wooden tombs, palaces, mosques and bridges were constructed. Mirza Haidar Dughlat, impressed by a wooden structure built during the period observes,

> In the middle of this lake (Wulur) Sultan Zain-ul-Abidin erected a palace. First of all he emptied a quantity of stones into the lake, and on those constructed a foundation of closely-fitting stones measuring two hundred square *gaz* in extent and ten *gaz* in height. Hereupon, he built a charming palace and planted pleasant groves of trees, so that there can be but few more agreeable palaces in the world. Finally, this same Sultan Zain-ul-Abidin built himself a palace in the town, which in the dialect of Kashmir is called Rajdan. It has twelve stories, some of which contain fifty rooms, halls and corridors. The whole of this lofty structure is built of wood.[4]

Syed Muhammad Madani's mosque built by Zain-ul-Abidin, is the earliest specimen of a wood construction in Kashmir. It was built by Zain-ul-Abidin in 1444.

Zain-ul-Abidin also encouraged the costruction of wooden bridges and the first permanent wooden bridge constructed over the Jhelum was built by him. Srivara provides the architectural details of this bridge, 'In the midst of the city (Srinagar) with four piers made of pine wood and stones struck deep down into the depths of the Vitasta, having a span covering rows of ten horses walking abreast to cross-over.'[5] It was named Zainakadal after the sultan. (In Kashmiri bridges are known as *kadal.*) The wooden structures built by Zain-ul-Abidin lasted for centuries. For example the Zainakadal bridge survived until the 1930s.[6]

Zain-ul-Abidin is also credited with the introduction of shawl manufacturing in Kashmir. Though local traditions also give credit to the Sufi saint Ali Hamdani along with Zain-ul-Abidin,[7] but Zain-ul-Abidin certainly deserves the credit for it. He invited shawl weavers from Turkistan.[8] It is important to mention here that during the sixteenth century shawl weaving had become the one of the most famous crafts of Kashmir. Impressed with the enormous scope of the industry, Akbar (1556–1605) encouraged it.[9] Jahangir too was impressed by the different varieties of shawls. According to him, his father Akbar had given a new term—*parm narm*—to the shawls of Kashmir.[10] During the seventeenth century the shawl industry had become the largest employment-generating sector. According to the French traveller Francois Bernier, the demand for Kashmiri shawls was so high that the manufacturers employed small children also.[11] According to Srivara, *pashmina* quality wool was made available to the shawl weavers by the sultan.[12] Thus the establishment of shawl industry under Zain-ul-Abidin became the source of livelihood of the weavers of Kashmir for generations to come.

Zain-ul-Abidin also introduced embroidery in Kashmir. Srivara writes in detail about the multi-coloured threads used for embroidery: 'On seeing various embroidered patterns (*nanachitralatakriti*) woven of creepers and other images in diverse colours, the art of drawing pictures became dumb-founded.'[13] With the introduction of embroidery, shawls of Kashmir also started to be designed differently. It is important to mention that from the fourteenth century onwards embroidered textiles of Kashmir were in huge demand in Central Asia, Europe, and in other parts of India. A large number of craftsmen were employed in the embroidery profession. Various types of craftsmen such as *naqash* (designers), *khandwao* (weavers) and *raffoogar* (darners) displayed their skills on the Pashmina shawls of Kashmir.[14] Kashmiri embroidery from Zain-ul-Abidin's period onwards became famous all over the world and established a distinct identity of its own.

Zain-ul-Abidin imported the technique of carpet making from Samarqand and introduced this industry in Kashmir. It is said that he was sent to Samarqand by his father Sultan Sikander (1389–1413) and there he realized the significance and potential of the carpet industry. When he became sultan, he introduced it in Kashmir. This industry too survived for a long time. But with the passage of time the industry declined. Under the Mughal Emperor Jahangir it was again revived by one Akhun Rahnuma.[15]

Zain-ul-Abidin also made a contribution to the emergence and growth of Kashmiri silk weaving. An important craft since ancient times it relied on local sericulture from the fifteenth century. When Mirza Haider Dughlat came to Kashmir he discovered that the cultivation of mulberry trees for the rearing of silkworms to be a highly profitable business. He writes, 'among the wonders of Kashmir are the quantities of mulberry trees [cultivated] for their leaves, [from which] silk is obtained. The people make a practice of eating the fruit, but rather regard it was wrong'.[16] The introduction of sericulture meant increased production of silk cloth and improvement in weaving technology. According to Srivara, '[by the induction of such craftsmen] Kashmiris could skillfully operate the shuttle and the loom and thus weave precious and attractive silk cloth.'[17] To encourage the manufacture of silk cloth Zain-ul-Abidin started using silk for his royal robes. He also introduced silk printing, using geometric designs. Srivara appreciates that Zain-ul-Abidin paid special attention to the printing of silk cloth in terms of colour combinations and designs. He writes

> The illustrious Sultan loudly resplendent with his incomparable qualities [of head and heart] made silken robes printed with accurate pictures of bracelets and designs of other ornaments, in specially various colour combinations, taken to kindly by the elite, providing comfort, very popular,

inasmuch as by his intelligence (the sultan) got these woven from the finest pick of possible yarn thus gave name and fame to his dress, as also to the country.[18]

With the expansion of the silk industry in Kashmir, job opportunities for different artisans vastly increased.

To the credit of Zain-ul-Abidin also goes the introduction of both fireworks and firearms, particularly artillery. Srivara gives an interesting description of the fireworks. According to him, for the manufacture of fireworks artisans had to use different ingredients. The manufacture of fire arms was a source of wonder for the people of Kashmir. From Zain-ul-Abidin's period onwards fireworks became an important source of both income and amusement for the different segments of Kashmiri society. Srivara writes,

The display (of fireworks) of myriad hues manufactured by the artisans by assembling charcoal, saltpetre, lime, sulphur, and other chemicals, draped the venue with multi-coloured brilliance. A solidified discharge of sparks dashed out of the (hollow) reed filled with combustible chemicals creating the delusion of a golden creeper in full bloom. Flames of fire in the shape of (crawling) snakes released within the water, struck-terror and fright (mingled with) amazement in the minds of the audience.[19]

Srivara hints at the use of remote control for the lighting of the fireworks. According to Srivara, fireworks were one of the wonders of Kashmir. He writes,

The rows of flaming balls rising up to the sky from the red with silvery sheen shone like the planets Jupiter and Venus (*jivashukropma*). The flaming reed containing chemicals, fastened to a string covered a good distance and in the same way many such (reeds) were released, and it appeared as if they had gone to call back the earlier ones. These reeds were like very loudly blazing meteors, going to and fro, and stole the gaze of the spectators.[20]

Srivara's account also shows that Zain-ul-Abidin had appointed an expert by the name of Habib, to take charge of these shows for the enjoyment of the common people.[21] For the progress of the fireworks industry in the state the sultan ensured the availability of saltpetre. According to Srivara, saltpetre was not available in Kashmir before Zain-ul-Abidin's time. A manual on fireworks was prepared under Zain-ul-Abidin. Regarding the preparation of the manual, Srivara writes, 'The conversation in question and answers indulged in [by the sultan] with Habib was [later] composed in Persian verse [by the sultan]. On going through it, [I feel] that none could reach (to that excellence of form and content) of those days.'[22]

Besides fireworks, Zain-ul-Abidin also introduced artillery in Kashmir. Though it is generally believed that artillery was introduced in India by the Mughal Emperor Zahir-ud-din Muhammad Babur (1526–30), Srivara's *Zaina Rajatarangini* shows that it was introduced in Kashmir in the fifteenth century under Zain-ul-Abidin. At first he imported cannons, but later manufactured them in Kashmir. Srivara does not mention from which country the cannons were imported but it seems that he imported them from Central Asia.[23] As far as the year of the first manufacture of cannon is concerned, it was 1460–1. For the cannon Srivara has used two terms—*topa* and *kandu.* According to Srivara, 'he [the sultan] got this cannon made in the forty-first year which came to be known as Topa in the Muslim language and Khandu in local language'.[24] Srivara also speaks very highly of the effectiveness of cannons in the battlefield. They could destroy forts and it was impossible for the rival forces to comprehend these cannons.[25] Since they were very heavy, they were transported by mules.[26] Srivara wrote a panegyric to celebrate the use of cannons by Zain-ul-Abidin.[27] There is also mention that under Zain-ul-Abidin the artisans manufactured a special type of arrow which were most effective and deadly. According to Srivara, '. . . on hearing the thunder of these [missiles], the hearts of the most courageous began to tremble'.[28]

Zain-ul-Abidin also brought a revolution in the field of writing materials. He was the first to introduce paper in Kashmir and opened the door's of Kashmir for the artisans of Central Asia for the foundation and development of the paper industry. He invited papermaking experts from Samarqand.[29] He also sent two persons from Kashmir to Samarqand to receive training in the art of papermaking and bookbinding. According to the author of *Baharistan-i-Shahi*, nobody in Kashmir knew the art of papermaking and bookbinding before Zain-ul-Abidin.[30] It is important to mention here that Sanskrit, Persian and Kashmiri literature also made tremendous progress under Zain-ul-Abidin. A large number of books were written in all these languages in his time.[31] With the introduction of bookbinding, a culture of book collection and preservation also developed. According to Srivara, 'The Sultan, beloved of the noble mind, got all these books prepared anew, like the spring does the bees, and adorned the land with these.'[32]

Papermaché, one of the most famous and beautiful craft products of Kashmir, took birth in the region under the patronage of Zain-ul-Abidin. He imported the technique of the use of paper pulp as a base to manufacture painted and lacquered ware. The first object in the form of papier mâché was the *kalamdan* (a pen/brush-holder and inkpot).[33] The manufacturing of *kalamdan* became famous and expert artisans contributed to the development of this craft.

Zain-ul-Abidin also provided large job opportunities to builders. He founded a large number of cities in Srinagar. Both Jonaraja and Srivara are full of praise for the foundation of cities by the Sultan.[34] He also encouraged the digging of canals. He is known to have worked for the improvement in the quality of boats and houseboats.[35] Since both the building and transport industries were maintained by the state in an efficient way, the artisans realized a degree of economic security.

The introduction of the various crafts and techniques by Zain-ul-Abidin led to the establishment of a distinct identity of Kashmiri artisans. Kashmir not only became a special region for the various crafts, the artisans both local and foreign felt proud to work in Kashmir. Craftsmen flocked to Kashmir for better opportunities from different areas. According to Srivara, 'Hosts of craftsmen from afar, thronged to him (the Sultan) the wish . . . with the idea of introducing new crafts.'[36]

Most of the crafts introduced by Zain-ul-Abidin survive till today. Under the Mughals these became the source of cultural contact between Kashmir and other parts of the world. Artisans became some of the most famous social groups of Kashmir. Sujan Rai Bhandari found Kashmir to be an abode of all classes of artisans.[37] The French traveller Bernier was also impressed by the skills of the artisans of Kashmir. He writes, 'The workmanship and beauty of their *palkeys*, bedsteads, trunks, inkstands, boxes, spoons and various other things are quite remarkable and are in use in every part of the Indies (India).'[38] Zain-ul-Abidin has been appreciated by all contemporary historians for his patronage of crafts and craftsmen.

NOTES

1. Jonaraja, *Rajatarangini*, Eng. tr. R.C. Dutt, in *The Kings of Kashmira*, 2nd series, Delhi, 1986, p. 78. Jonaraja was a Kashmiri Brahmin. Sultan Zain-ul-Abidin was impressed by his scholarship in Sanskrit and appointed him to revive the tradition of Sanskrit historiography in his court. History had been introduced by Kalhana in the twelfth century. Jonaraja thus wrote a second *Rajatarangini*.
2. Srivara, *Zaina Rajatarangini*, Eng. tr. with text Kashi Nath Dhar, Delhi, 1944, p. 14. Srivara was a Kashmiri Brahmin and a reputed Sanskrit scholar of the fifteenth century. He was a disciple of Jonaraja. Srivara was also appointed as a courtier and scholar by Zain-ul-Abidin. After the death of Jonaraja in 1459, Zain-ul-Abidin asked Srivara to carry on writing the *Rajatarangini*. Srivara wrote *Zaina Rajatarangini* and dedicated it to the sultan.
3. Mirza Haider Dughlat, *Tarikh-i-Rashidi*, Eng. tr. N. Elias, ed. Dennis Ross, Delhi, 1986, p. 434.
4. Ibid., pp. 429–30.
5. Srivara, op. cit., p. 140.
6. N.K. Zutshi, *Sultan Zain-ul-Abidin of Kashmir: An Age of Enlightenment*, Jammu, 1976, p. 141.
7. Jaya Jaitley (ed.), *Crafts of Jammu, Kashmir and Ladakh*, Ahmedabad, 1990, p. 48.
8. Zutshi, op. cit., p. 203.
9. Abul Fazal, *Ain-i-Akbari*, vol. I, Eng. tr. H. Blochmann, ed. D.C. Phillott, Delhi, 1994, p. 48.
10. Jahangir, *Tuzuk-i-Jahangiri*, vol. II, Eng. tr. Alexander Rogers, Delhi, 1944, pp. 147–8
11. Francois Bernier, *Travels in the Mogul Empire, 1656–68*, Eng. tr. A. Constable, Delhi, 1968, p. 402.
12. Srivara, op. cit., p. 237.
13. Ibid., p. 237.
14. Jaitley, op. cit., p. 61.
15. G.M.D. Sufi, *Islamic Culture of Kashmir*, Jammu, 1999, p. 236.
16. *Tarikh-i-Rashidi*, p. 425.
17. Srivara, op. cit., p. 237.

18. Ibid., p. 238.
19. Ibid., pp. 166–7.
20. Ibid., pp. 167–8. Srivara has compared the flames of the fireworks with the rays of sun in terms of their shining. Ibid., p. 168.
21. Ibid., p. 169.
22. Ibid., p. 169.
23. Ibid., p. 37.
24. Ibid., p. 39.
25. Ibid., p. 40.
26. Ibid., p. 38.
27. Ibid., p. 38.
28. Ibid., p. 37.
29. Zutshi, op. cit., p. 203.
30. *Baharistan-i-Shahi,* Eng tr. K.N. Pandit, Calcutta, 1981, p. 64. The *Baharistan-i Shahi* is written by an anonymous Kashmiri writer during the seventeenth century.
31. Zutshi, op. cit., pp. 188–92.
32. Srivara, op. cit., p. 214.
33. P.N. Kachru, 'Paper-Mache', in Jaya Jaitly, op. cit., p. 131.
34. Jonaraja, op. cit., pp. 87–8, Srivara, op. cit., pp. 118–19, 182–5, 251.
35. Ibid., p. 195.
36. Ibid., p. 236.
37. Sujan Rai Bhandari, *Khulasat-ut-Twarikh,* Eng. tr. Sir J.N. Sarkar, in *India of Aurangzeb,* Calcutta, 1901, p. 111.
38. *Travels,* p. 402.

The Concept of Equality and the State and Society in Sixteenth-Century Orissa

AMAL KUMAR MISHRA

Inequal treatment leads to violation of basic human rights by sheer discrimination. No doubt, it occurs in every society in many ways and forms. It amounts to exclusion, restriction or preference on grounds such as race, religion, caste, descent, ethnic origin, gender, colour of skin and creed which has the effect of impairing the performance, exercise or enjoyment by any person of his/her rights as human beings on an equal footing. Discrimination can thus never be justified on any ground or situation as human beings are to be treated equally since that is the mandate of equality.

Utkal, as Orissa was known and in medieval times, shockingly promoted a group of people with vested interests coming under the impact of centuries old social traditions.[1] They were the *Sanatanists* or traditional conservatives who in the name of religion, completely blocked the path of social progress and intercourse among people of various segments, particularly those belonging to the lower strata of society. A true religion never pushes anybody or any class of people to the abyss and abominable depths of social ostracism. But the puritan Brahmins conniving with the Kshatriya ruling class and Kayastha officials of the sixteenth century let loose a hell for ordinary mortals, especially the Shudras, who turned fatalists under the extreme pressure of circumstances. The situation had almost gone out of hand when there appeared in the scene five daring men—Balarama Dasa, Jagannatha Dasa, Achyutananda Dasa, Jasobanta Dasa and Ananta Dasa, who by sheer dint of their daring, fearless writings and selfless leadership came to the forefront of Oriya society to redeem the innocent masses from their horrible plight.

The hallmark of these five comrades or Panchasakhas,[2] as they are called and remembered, had been their Shudrabhava leading to Shudrabhakti,[3] considered a unique feature not only in medieval society of Orissa but in India as well.

The moot question is, what was the type of state and society that existed in Orissa or medieval Utkal during the sixteenth century? The state and society was completely dominated by priests. King Kapilendra Deva bowed and prostrated himself before at least two Brahmins at the break of the day. He expressed a wish to donate the whole world to Brahmins. Successive rulers like Purusottama Deva and Prataprudra Deva bore almost the same attitude and temperament. Emphasis on Sanskrit studies[4] and making it the official and religious *lingua franca* had completely alienated the masses from the mainstream. The non-Brahmins mostly the Shudras felt disenchanted and became mute spectators and victims under the circumstances. An outlet to speak out their minds and feeling was felt very much necessary, which the Panchasakhas came forward to take up diligently. They guided the suffering masses, risking their own lives, at this time of social crisis. They held Sanskrit as the language of the elite class and championed the cause of the newly introduced Oriya, which was the language of the common people. Moreover, they felt that Sanskrit, called the *Deba bhasha*, had in reality snapped the link between the masses and God. Now people brought out their innumerable writings in simple Oriya dialect, which could develop their inner self and spiritual urge in a grand way. They also held out that God can never be appeased by mere rituals or recitations of mere *shlokas* or *mantras*, but by self-purification coupled with unstinted devotion by freeing the mind from the body. Before God, there no one is high or low—all are equal. The concept of equality thus developed by them in sixteenth-century Orissa, has few parallels in history. It was a protest movement launched against social tyranny, oppression and stigma attached particularly to the lower classes or stratas of society for centuries.

In actuality the Panchasakhas were born with different titles or surnames, such as Mohapatra, Khuntia, Mallick and Mohanty, and most of them were non-Brahmins with the exception of Jagannatha Dasa, who was a Brahmin. But in their egalitarian spirit they dropped these titles and suffixes to their names as meaningless and adopted instead a significant surname Dasa uniformly. It was in order to justify their humility as well as servility in words and action both, that they preferred it as a kind of suffix to their original names.[5]

Balarama Dasa,[6] the eldest among the five, was a Kayastha by caste. He entered a state of ecstasy for which he came to be called *matta* or the 'most infatuated' or 'mad one' in *bhakti.* Balarama Dasa founded a *math* at the mouth of the river Banki in Puri, known as Gandharva Math. His philosophy is found in many treatises and writings, notable among them being *Dandi* or *Jagamohana Ramayan, Bata Abakasha, Baula Bata, Bhava Samudra, Vedantasara Gupta Gita, Amarakosa Gita, Bedha Parikrama, Panasa Chori, Laxmi Purana, Brahmanda Bhugola, Gupta Tika.* His aim in life was to bring about a change in the socio-religious outlook of the people towards the deprived and dispossessed sections of society, especially the Shudras and womenfolk. While in *Bhava Samudra* and *Panasa Chori* he tried to uphold the dignity of a real *bhakta* or a devoted soul in union with God for whom the God even appeared in person to chastise the king; in *Laxmi Purana* he at once upheld the dignity, a Shudra women, Sriya Chandaluni, for whom Goddess Laxmi even chastized both Lord Balarama and Lord Jagannatha. Even to this day a pious Oriya follows this tradition of reciting *Laxmi Purana* of Balarama Dasa on the Thursdays of the month Margashirsha. The manner in which he was admonished and mistreated for taking part in the learned discourses on Vedanta held at Mukti Mandapa of Lord Jagannatha temple and finally, the way King Prataprudra had to release him from prison on listening to his erudite scholarship and knowledge, is a pointer to the social taboos put on the lower class people learning the religious literatures and also how Balarama Dasa fought for social justice and equality.

Jagannatha Dasa,[7] the next in the category of the saint-poets, was originally a *Purana Pdnda* in the temple of Lord Jagannatha. Among his followers were many pious women devotees who regularly attended his discourses in the temple precincts. It was something which created jealousy in the hearts and minds of the priestly class for which the king was approached and Jagannatha

Dasa was put behind the bars for some time. But he braved this humiliation and overcame it because of his sacred self and saw remained no distinction between a man and woman at all, particularly in the fields of knowledge, scholarship and religion. All were equal before him. King Prataparudra got convinced by his erudition and set him free. Sri Chaitanya conferred on him honorifics like *atibadi* for his notable achievements, among which, *Bhagabata* in Oriya, *Tulavina, Rasakrida, Bhavisya Malika, Pramoda Chintamani, Dutibodha, Gupta Bhagabata, Brahma Gita, Mruguni Stuti, Gundicha Vije, Rukmuni Malika* and *Gaja Stuti* were considered significant contributions. Soon the masses in the villages of Orissa organized and set up *Bhagabata Tungis*, a kind of socio-religious institution, in the remote mofussil areas where the recitation of *Bhagabata* in Oriya was held in the evenings. It was hitherto only available in Sanskrit and therefore, in a way forbidden for their hearing and understanding. In course of time, these innumerable *Bhagabata Tungis* in the remote villages acted also as centres of unity and rejuvenation of the Oriya masses besides playing a good societal role of disposing of petty village disputes in front of the *Bhagabata pothis*. Thus, Jagannatha Dasa is long remembered for instilling a common cause among the Oriya populace. Bada Odiya Math in Puri was from where he preached.

Achyutananda Dasa,[8] yet another vibrant social revolutionary, was the third in the line of this Panchasakha tradition. He became very prominent for such landmark writings like *Harivamsa, Gopal Ugala, Bipra Chalaka, Chaurasi Yantra, Nitya Rahasya, Sunnya Samhita, Anakara Samhita, Bhavanabara, Amara-Jumara Samhita, Gurubhakti Gita, Tattvabodhini* and *Barana Charita Gita*. Expressing the theory of void he incurred the displeasure of the conservative priestly class and suffered a lot of tribulations because of his unorthodox radical views on society and religion. Becoming the patron saint of the cowherd community he founded a *math* at Puri and even dared to launch his invectives against the ruthlessness of the state machinery. He could make daring comparisons of the king as a vulture sitting over the corpses who were his hapless subjects. He adopted an anti-feudal and anti-establishment stand for giving his ideals of social reform a concrete shape and footing. Among his disciples Naran and Nanda were blacksmiths, while Ramadasa was to be a potter. Through his *Sunnya Purana* and *Mahamantra* he expounded innovative and lofty ideas to the depressed classes of the society on the proper way to attain Godhead and salvation. He was a much-travelled personality in those times who had gone round many of the parts of the country like Kashi, Mathura, Vrindavan, Ayodhya, Gaya, Magadha, Mayapuri, and Mithila in the north; Madurai, Dhanushkoti, Rameshwaram in the south; Kamakhya in the east and Dwaraka in the west. He condemned the growing number of frauds who usually masqueraded in the guise of *sadhus* and *fakirs* and held out that only by keeping beard and hairlocks and putting up attire of a saint, one cannot aspire or claim to be a real *sannyasi.* It was a great eye-opener in those times in the country. He at once transformed the disqualification of the Shudras into a great qualification by merely announcing that in the true state of spirituality the more one became humble and the more he/she became free from ego it became easier to realize Godhead and attain salvation. The Shudrabhava must be taken up without any question or doubt in order to attain Shudrabhakti, that would alone become the pathfinder to know the concept of equality.

Yet another champion of the cause of spreading the message of equality among the masses was Jasobanta Dasa,[9] who founded a *math* at Adanga in Jagatsinghpur. Originally a Kshatriya he gave up his caste title Mallick and adopted the Dasa suffix as a mark of his humble disposition, like his other comrades. His innumerable writings include *Premabhakti Brahma Gita, Tika Govinda Chandra, Atma Parache Gita, Siva Svaradaya, Chaurasi Agna, Mantraboli, Bagha-leela, Yantraboli, Dhanachori,* and *Rasa.* A much travelled saint-philosopher he went round the country and dealt mainly on the performance of *yoga.* A community of *yogis* thus emerged who sang the hymns and songs composed by Jasobanta while moving from door-to-door collecting alms. In a simple and lucid manner he explained the *Nirakara, Anakara, Omkara,* forms of Brahma. In his *Tika Govinda Chandra* he espoused the social norms regarding noble and polite behaviour. He placed much importance on the *guru* or teacher/guide who is to be offered utmost reverence no matter to which class, caste or strata of the society he belonged. Here, he depicted Govinda Chandra, the king, paying his obeisance to Guru Hadippa; no matter if the latter happened to be a sweeper by caste. Thus, he held the knowledge or wisdom of the *guru* as far important and superior to his birth, position or status in the social hierarchy.

Ananta Das,[10] the last but not the least, among the Panchasakhas, is credited with works like *Garuda-Keshava Chautisa, Hetu Udaya Bhagabata, Bhavisya Purana, Agata-bhavisya Malika, Pinda Brahmanda Gita, Vaishnaba Purana, Bhakti-Juktidayaka Gita, Anakara Sabat,* etc., among others. Belonging to the Shishu order, he later became known as Shishu Ananta. He had a *math* at Tentuliapada where he described the importance of God remaining within the minds and hearts of the people and not in temples. Therefore, only by controlling the mind one could reach divinity. In other words, he did not appreciate the dominance of the priestly class and the system of worship prevalent then. He exemplified in his person the way to attain spirituality by submitting the mind and soul completely to God, who is *avarna* or has no colour.

Thus, the Panchasakhas became unique symbols of social leadership in sixteenth-century Orissa. Their thoughts and approaches as reflected in their typical actions and writings were revolutionary in nature. It is another matter that each one of them, when they came in contact with Sri Chaitanya, who made Orissa his own abode during the last eighteen years of his life, [11] got profoundly impressed by his personality and accepted him as a coreligionist. But certainly it was not at the cost of their own individual claims and distinct characteristics. While the Panchasakhas, as a whole, were preaching the Utkaliya form of Vaishnavism based on Jnana Bhakti, Sri Chaitanya's was a Gaudiya form of Vaishnavism based on Prema Bhakti.[12] The difference was only in the content but certainly not in so far as socio-religious objectives of both were concerned. The Shudrabhava and Shudrabhakti concepts[13] in fact led to the concept of equality in so many ways. Only by developing this type of mindset the society could attain equality in all spheres. Hardly in other *bhakti* movements of the period taking place in elsewhere in the country, one finds such a revolutionary idea. The supreme realization, that there is no distinction between the divinity and the universe, the divinity and humanity and the personal existence and cosmic existence, had dawned on them and it became their mission to preach it in so many ways to the masses of medieval Orissa. Thus, the concept of equality as developed by the Panchasakhas who came up as agents of social change in sixteenth century Orissa squarely attacked *varnadharma* long held sacred by the Sanatanists and certainly brought about a social upheaval, as marked in the rest of India[14] in no uncertain measure. They bewailed the marginalization and consequent degradation and insignificance of the Shudras since they had only been allotted duty without any position in the social ladder as other *varnas* had. They were expected and forced to render *seva* or service to the higher *varnas* or caste groups with all humility. If at all this was a disqualification, as held by the puritan society then, the Panchasakhas wished and tried hard to transform it into a great qualification by making this *seva* mindset an essential aspect and component of *bhakti* for all because that required complete surrender of one's ego and Self, leading to the development of the vision and concept of equality. The medieval state and society of Orissa gradually adjusted itself with this new and innovative approach and concept of equality to a great extent with the passage of time.

NOTES

1. A.C. Pradhan, *A Study of History of Orissa*, Bhubaneswar, 1996, pp. 134–6.
2. Ibid.
3. C.R. Das, *A Glimpse into Oriya Literature*, Bhubaneswar, 1982, pp. 82–4.
4. H. Panda, *History of Orissa*, Cuttack, 1997, pp. 160–1.
5. B.K. Mallik, *Medieval Orissa*, Bhubaneswar, 1996, p. 23.
6. For Pathani Pattanayak, Siddhakabi Balarama Dasa, see B.M. Mohanty (ed.), *Orissara Sadhu Santa*, 1, Cuttack, 1982, pp. 103–6.
7. S.N. Dash, *Atibadi Jagannatha Dasa*; Mohanty, ibid., pp. 116–20.
8. C.R. Das, *Achyutananda O Panchasakha Dharma*, Viswabharati, 1951, pp. 264–6.
9. B.M. Mohanty, *Mahapurusha Jasobanta Dasa*; Mohanty, op. cit., pp. 130–3.

10. D.S. Patnaik, *Mahapurusha Shishu Ananta Dasa*; Mohanty, op. cit., pp. 134–7.
11. A. Lahiri, *Chaitanya Movement in Eastern India*, Calcutta, 1993, pp. 281–9.
12. S.C. Panigrahi, *Bhima Bhoi and Mahima Darshana*, Cuttack, 1998, pp. 16–18.
13. C.R. Das, op. cit.
14. Irfan Habib, 'The Historical Background of the Popular Monotheistic Movement of the 15th–17th Centuries', in Bishweswar Prasad (ed.), *Ideas in History*, Bombay, 1969.

Change and Continuity in the Prices in Bikaner from the Close of the Seventeenth to the Early Nineteenth Century

K.L. MATHUR

The study of the general price index helps us to understand the economic condition of any region. As the economy of Bikaner state was basically an agrarian one and the area is a desert, it was mainly the agricultural prices which affected the general price level. An attempt has been made in this paper to study and put up a comparative analysis of the available prices of various commodities in Bikaner during the period from AD 1687 to AD 1820.

The official price data surviving in the *bahis* for the aforesaid period is of immense help in studying the economic history of the State. The State *bahis,* specially the *Byav Bahis*[1] provide us details of the purchases of different commodities in various years spread in a span of 133 years from 1687 to 1820 in Bikaner. The prices cover food grains, pulses, spices, metals, intoxicants, dry fruits, edible oil, *ghee,* meat, etc. These prices appear to be the retail prices[2] current in Bikaner in normal times. Hence, one can estimate the price level of commodities and its emerging trends.

But one difficulty in analysing the available raw data of prices is that they are available in the contemporary fractional value of *maunds, seers* and *chhatang* weights. The value of a rupee then also varied in *takka* and *dam.* Moreover, there was the prevalence of a *kachcha* and *pucca maund* in the state which too differed from place to place and village to village. Another significant limitation of price data, to which we are referring, pertains to different dates in different years and they do not belong to strictly comparable points each year for which they are available. This has to be kept in mind while examining the tables of prices for commodities we offer ahead.

To dispense with these difficulties and convert the available prices into per unit in rupees, the following methodology has been adopted to compare prices and also to show the trend, through price index number.

METHODOLOGY—ESTIMATION OF PRICES AND PRICE INDEX NUMBER

For imparting uniformity and a clear understanding of the comparison, the available raw data of prices of various commodities in these *bahis* of Bikaner State, have been converted into rupees per *maund* assuming a *maund* to be standard *maund* comprising 40 *seers* and a rupee equal to 100 paisa,[3] because there used to be variation in the *maunds* and value of rupee. To compare the prices and observe their trends, price indices are measured as per the categories of the commodities, with change in the base year. These indices show the percentage increase or decrease in the prices during the period under study. The formula for measuring the price index number is as follows:

$$P_{01} = \frac{P_1}{P_0} \times 100$$

where P_{01}, indicates price index number, P_1 is the current year price and P_0 is the base year price. With this methodology prices have been analysed as under. In the case of summation of prices the formula for price index number is as follows:

$$P_{01} = \frac{\sum P_1}{\sum P_0} \times 100$$

here, $\sum$ (Sigma) indicates summation.

Table 1 reveals the comparative prices of *gur*, sugar, *ghee* (edible oil), rice and red chilly. It is observed that prices of all commodities increased except edible oil and red chilly from 1687 to 1820. Price of edible oil reduced from Rs. 11.24 per *maund* in

TABLE 1: COMPARATIVE PRICES OF *GUR*, SUGAR, *GHEE*, RICE AND RED CHILLY IN BIKANER DURING AD 1687–1820

(*prices per maund in Rs.*)

Commodity	AD 1687[4] P_0	AD 1770[5] P_1	AD 1782[6] P_2	AD 1820[7] P_3
Gur	0.638*	2.758	4.210	–
Sugar (*khand*)	12.195	–	9.412	13.072
Ghee	2.031	7.797	8.888	14.545
Oil	11.235	–	3.404	2.500
Rice				
(a) Rajgarh quality	4.338	–	24.540	40.000
(b) Pali-thick	4.154	–	22.857	–
(c) Pali-thin	4.197	–	22.857	–
Red chilly	16.806	8.000	1.000	–

Note: *In case of two prices the average prices have been considered.

1687 to Rs. 2.5 per *maund* in 1820. There was a sharp decline in the prices of red chilly from Rs. 16.81 per *maund* to Re. 1 per *maund*. This decrease in prices indicates that gradually the supply of imported edible oil and red chilly was increased.

Table 2 shows the price index number of the prices quoted in Table 1 assuming as the base year. Index numbers indicate that during the period 1687 to 1820, there was a significant rise in the prices of various commodities, such as, prices of *gur* increased by more then six and a half times, and *ghee* by more then seven times; prices of different quality of rice showed a hike by 5.44 to 9.22 times. Price index number of sugar shows a more or less constant trend, which is Rs. 107.19 for the year 1820. The index numbers of oil (22.25) in 1820 and of red chilly (5.95) in 1782 indicate a significant decline in the prices of these commodities as stated above.

Likewise Table 3 includes comparative prices of flour, pulses and intoxicants from 1687 to 1820, and except for *besan* and tobacco, there is a general hike in prices of flour, pulses and opium during the period. Prices of *besan* reduced from Rs. 5 per *maund* in 1687 to half, i.e. Rs. 2.5 per *maund* in 1782; whereas prices of tobacco declined from Rs. 12.31 per *maund* in 1687 to Rs. 5 in 1770. The decline in the prices of *besan* seems to be the

TABLE 2: PRICE INDEX NUMBER OF *GUR* (SUGAR), *GHEE* (EDIBLE OIL), RICE AND RED CHILLY IN BIKANER DURING AD 1687–1820

Commodity	1687 P_0	1770 P_1	1782P_2	1820 P_3	(+) Increase (-) Decrease
Gur	100	432.28	659.87	–	(+) 659.87
Sugar (*khand*)	100	–	77.18	107.19	(+) 107.19
Ghee	100	383.90	437.62	716.15	(+) 716.15
Oil	100	–	30.298	22.25	(-) 22.25
Rice					
(d) Rajgarh quality	100	–	565.70	922.08	(+) 922.08
(e) Pali-thick	100	–	550.24	–	(+) 550.24
(f) Pali-thin	100	–	544.60	–	(+) 544.60
Red chilly	100	47.60	5.95	–	(-) 5.95

TABLE 3 : COMPARATIVE PRICES OF FLOUR, PULSES AND INTOXICANTS IN BIKANER DURING 1687–1820

(*prices per maund in Rs.*)

Commodity	AD 1687[8] P_0	AD 1770[9] P_1	AD 1782[10] P_2	AD 1820[11] P_3
Maida	5.000	–	2.286	5.714
Besan	5.000	–	2.500	–
Moong dal	4.672	–	11.834	–
Tobacco	12.307	5.00	–	–
Opium	170.940	–	–	634.920

outcome of a good supply of gram in[12] 1782. Tobacco, which was also produced at Rajgarh, Sujangarh and Bhadra area, was available in the market.[13] Besides, the improvement in supply of tobacco due to import from Malwa and Sindh led to the decline in prices.[14]

The relevant price index number shown in Table 4 for flour, pulses and intoxicants assuming base year 1687, records accordingly a general rise in *moong dal* (pulses) by about 2.5 times from Rs. 4.67 in 1687 to Rs. 11.83 in 1782; opium by more than 3.72 times from Rs. 170.94 in 1687 to Rs. 634.92 in 1820. *Besan* recorded a steep decline by 50 per cent from Rs. 5 per *maund* in 1687 to Rs. 2.5 in 1782, and tobacco by 60 per cent from Rs. 12.31 in 1687 to Rs. 5 in 1770. *Maida* showed more or

TABLE 4: PRICE INDEX NUMBER OF FLOUR, PULSES AND INTOXICANTS IN BIKANER DURING AD 1687–1820

Commodity	AD 1687 P_0	AD 1770 P_1	AD 1782 P_2	AD 1820 P_3	(+) Increase (-) Decrease
Maida	100	–	45.72	114.28	(+) 114.28
Besan	100	–	50.00	–	(-) 50.00
Moong dal	100	–	253.30	–	(+) 253.30
Tobacco	100	40.63	–	–	(-) 40.63
Opium	100	–	–	372.02	(+) 372.02

less a constant trend which was Rs. 114.28 for the year 1820, except a short fall by 45.72 per cent in 1782, the reasons are not clear for this eventual decrease. It can be mentioned that there was a negligible production of opium in the state and the overall demand was satisfied by importing it from Kota and Malwa.[15] Since, these places were the chief producers and suppliers of opium in the country there used to be a shortage in supply, which in turn, led to price escalation. *Moong* (for *moong dal*) was also produced in a very limited fertile part of the north-east and in the north of the state and the additional demand was met by the supply received from Marwar and Kota.[16] The imbalance in regular supply raised the prices.

Table 5 exhibits the prices of spices and food grain during 1770 to 1820. In the table, except for *saunth,* all other commodities like wheat, *bajra, moth, dhania* and turmeric showed a

TABLE 5: COMPARATIVE PRICES OF SPICES AND FOODGRAINS IN BIKANER DURING AD 1770–1820

(*prices per maund in Rs.*)

Commodity	AD 1770[17] P_1	AD 1782[18] P_2	1820[19] P_3
Dhania	2.254	3.077	–
Turmeric	4.332	7.273	6.563
Sunth	9.308	–	8.000
Wheat	6.416	10.322	–
Bajra	0.571	0.629	0.952
Moth	0.615	0.800	0.851

considerable increase in prices. The prices of *saunth* decreased from Rs. 9.31 per *maund* in 1770 to Rs. 8.00 per *maund* in AD 1820. In fact, this marginal decline in the prices of *saunth* in the span of some 50 years was because of the short supply of *saunth* through the import trade from Sindh and Multan in the state but is insignificant.[20]

The corresponding price index has been shown in Table 6 with assumed base year 1770. It also represents accordingly and registers a gradual increase in prices of spices like turmeric by 1.5 times (approximately 51 per cent) from Rs. 4.33 per *maund* in 1770 to Rs. 6.56 in 1820. Wheat, prices, increased by more than 1.5 times (60.88 per cent) from Rs. 6.42 per *maund* in 1770 to Rs. 10.32 in 1782, whereas *bajra* also followed the same trend and rose more then 1.5 times (66.72 per cent) from Rs. 0.57 per *maund* in 1770 to Rs. 0.95 in 1820. The price trend for *dhania* and *moth* also showed a moderate hike respectively by 36.51 per cent in 1782 and 38.37 per cent in 1820. The wheat production in the state was very low and there was a general shortage and often the state imposed restrictions upon its *nekal* (export) or transportation anywhere.[21] However, the necessary requirements of wheat was fulfilled by the supply from Sindh, Marwar and Kota which was often hampered for reasons like insecurity of routes.[22] This carried an adverse impact and the prices rose gradually. *Bajra* and *moth* were, though, the chief crops of the state but were the main ingredient of their staple diet also and were chiefly, grown for consumption. Since, the chiefs of Bikaner

TABLE 6: PRICE INDEX OF SPICES AND FOOD GRAIN IN BIKANER DURING AD 1770–1820

Commodity	AD 1770 P_0	AD 1782 P_1	AD 1820 P_2	(+) Increase (-) Decrease
Dhania	100	136.51	–	(+) 136.51
Turmeric	100	167.89	151.50	(+) 151.50
Saunth	100	–	85.95	(-) 85.95
Wheat	100	160.88	–	(+) 160.88
Bajra	100	110.16	166.73	(+) 166.72
Moth	100	130.08	138.37	(+) 138.37

during the period from 1770 to 1820 encouraged fresh settlements in the villages and towns, the populace also seems to have increased, whereas the crop was still dependent upon the natural rainfall. Therefore, this was one of the factors for the rise in the prices of *moth* and *bajra. Dhania* prices, which also increased moderately, was not produced in the state and was imported from Marwar and Nagaur, causing the price rise.[23]

Likewise, Table 7 enlists the prices of dry fruits in Bikaner from 1770 to 1816. The dry fruits listed in Table 7 have increased in prices in the period. Pistachio price increased from Rs. 8.45 per *maund* in 1770 to Rs. 22 in 1816; price of almond increased from Rs. 12.16 per *maund* 1770 to Rs. 22.00 in AD 1816, and price of currant from Rs. 8.45 per *maund* in 1770 to Rs. 16.12 in 1820. Accordingly, price of dry *gota* (dessicated coconut) also rose from Rs. 13.30 per *maund* in 1770 to Rs. 24.62 in 1782.

The related price index (Table 8) of the dry fruits with base year in 1770, shows a significant rise in 1816. Pistachio increased

TABLE 7: COMPARATIVE PRICES OF DRY FRUITS IN BIKANER DURING AD 1770–1816

(*prices per maund in Rs.*)

Commodity	AD 1770[24] P_0	AD 1782[25] P_1	AD 1816[26] P_2
Pistachio	8.45	13.51	22.00
Almond	12.16	11.84	22.00
Dry *gota* (coconut)	13.30	24.62	–
Currant	8.45	7.50	16.12

TABLE 8: PRICE INDEX OF DRY FRUITS IN BIKANER DURING 1770–1816

Commodity	AD 1770 P_0	AD 1782 P_1	AD 1816 P_2	(+) Increase (-) Decrease
Pistachio	100	159.76	260.36	(+) 260.36
Almond	100	97.37	182.98	(+) 182.98
Dry *gota*	100	185.11	–	(+) 185.11
Currant	100	88.76	192.31	(+) 192.31

by more than 2.5 times (260.36 per cent) in 1816, almond and *gota* by more than 1.75 times respectively (almond 82.98 per cent in 1816 and *gota* 85.11 per cent in 1782), whereas the prices for currant shot up by around 2 times (92.31 per cent) in 1816. The cause of this increase seems to be imminent as the supply of dry fruits was chiefly adjunct with the horse trade from Sindh and Multan, the chief suppliers. The demand for dry fruits and horses, rose during the period was because these two things were largely required by the ruling classes of Rajputana.[27] The supply from the north-west too was, often, hampered due to the disturbances and plundering activities on the trade routes in the north-west by the Raths, Bhattis and Johiyas. This also led to price hike of dry fruits.

The general phenomenon of price hike was not restricted to essential commodities alone. There was also hike in the prices of precious metals as well, i.e. gold and silver. The price of gold and silver also shot up significantly during the period which also bore a relative impact upon the purchasing power of the silver rupee. Table 9 shows the prices per 10 gram of gold and silver in rupees. The prices shown in the table evince that there was gradual rise in the price of gold prices from Rs. 11.5 per 10 gram in 1687 to Rs. 16.90 in 1852; also the bullion which was Rs. 0.86 per 10 gram in 1770 rose up to Rs. 1.93 in 1852.

The measured index number (Table 10) exhibits that gold prices shot up nearly 1.5 times (46.96 per cent) and the bullion 2.25 times (124.42 per cent). The rise in the prices was exclusively dependent upon the supply of these metals from the middle-east through the north-west[28] and like other commodities the prices of these also went up considerably.

Interestingly, we could have an access to the prices of some

TABLE 9: COMPARATIVE PRICES OF GOLD AND SILVER IN BIKANER DURING AD 1687–1852

(*prices per 10 gram in Rs.*)

Commodity	AD 1687[29] P_0	AD 1770[30] P_1	AD 1852[31] P_2
Gold	11.5	14.70	16.90
Silver	–	0.86 (P_0)	1.93 (P_1)

TABLE 10: PRICE INDEX OF GOLD AND SILVER IN BIKANER DURING 1687–1852

Commodity	AD 1687 P_0	AD 1770 P_1	AD 1852 P_2	(+) Increase (-) Decrease
Gold	100	127.83	146.96	(+) 146.96
Silver	–	100.00 (P_0)	224.42 (P_1)	(+) 224.42

essential commodities available in the *bahis* for different years, i.e. for Suratgarh in 1784[32] and for Anupgarh in 1817,[33] shown in Table 11. Despite the difference in weights and period, an attempt to match the prices of these two *qasbas* was ventured to ascertain the price level in these two *qasbas.* The prices available have been converted into rupees per *maund* first (considering the prevailing of actual *seers* in a *maund* at the places) and then to prices in rupees per 100 *seer.*

The results are interesting and do not show any drastic change in the price structure in different years in these two *qasbas.* Generally, the prices prevailing in Anupgarh in 1817 show a slight increase over the price level of 1787 in Suratgarh. The prices of wheat was cheaper at Suratgarh in comparison to Anupgarh. The reason is obvious. Suratgarh has a fertile zone that produces wheat more than Anupgarh. Further, there is a difference of about 30

TABLE 11: PRICE COMPARISON OF SURATGARH AND ANUPGARH OF *GHEE*, EDIBLE OIL, WHEAT, *MOTH* AND RED CHILLY

(*price per unit in Re.*)

Commodity	Suratgarh (1 *maund* =28 *seer*) AD 1787 price		Anupgarh (1 *maund* =32 *seer*) AD 1817 price	
	per *maund*	per 100 *seer*	per *maund*	per 100 *seer*
Ghee	3.830	13.679	5.016	15.675
Oil	2.871	10.254	3.200	10.000
Moth	0.553	1.975	0.717	2.243
Wheat	0.818	2.921	1.333	4.166
Red chilly	2.154	7.693	2.667	8.334

years for the margin of prices which seems justified for the difference in prices.

Thus, the prices, in general, show a gradual trend of increase in price level in a long span of time in Bikaner which witnessed earlier, as a part of the Mughal Empire and later in its detachment from it in the second half of the eighteenth century and its subordination to British East India Company in the year AD 1818. However, these prices have been of normal days, but during times of famine, war and political instability there was a hike in prices for which supply of the commodities was badly affected due to failure of crops and insecurity of routes.

NOTES

1. *Byav Bahis* of Bikaner State contain the details of marriages, ceremonies, income and expenditure pertaining to it and the details of the purchases of required items. The prices (per rupee) have been recorded therein of a variety of goods purchased from the *modikhana* and *karkhana*. The following *Byav Bahis* have been consulted which are available in the Rajasthan State Archives, Bikaner (RSAB). *Bai Ram Kanwar Ro Byav Anup Singh Ji Kiya Teri Bahi—Byav Bahi*, no. 143, VS 1744/AD 1687; *Bai Sardar Kanwarji Re Byav Wa Naler Melo Teri Bahi—Byav Bahi*, no. 159, VS 1827/AD 1770; *Baiji Shri Udai Kanwar Ji Re Byav Re Jeenus Ri Khata Bahi—Byav Bahi*, no. 167, VS 1839/AD 1782; *Bahi Maharaj Kanwar Shri Ratan Singh Ji Re Byav Ri—Byav Bahi*, no. 170, VS 1877/AD 1820.
2. The rates quoted in the *bahis* seems to be retail prices as the goods purchased were not in larger quantities.
3. The method adopted for converting 'per-rupee-prices' into 'per-*maund*-prices' (in rupees) is set out below for convenience:
   Gur purchased in AD 1687 for 1 rupee = 62 *seers* & 11 *chhatang*
   To convert 11 *chhatang* into *seers* subtract it with 16 = 0.69 *seers*
   62 *seers* + 0.69 *seers* = 62.69 *seers*
   To convert 62.69 *seers* into per *maund* prices in rupees = (100/62.69)× 40 *seers* = 63.80/100 = 0.638 paise per *maund*
4. *Byav Bahi*, no. 143, VS 1744/AD 1687, RSAB.
5. *Byav Bahi*, no. 159, VS 1827/AD 1770, RSAB.
6. *Byav Bahi*, no. 167, VS 1839/AD 1782, RSAB.
7. *Byav Bahi*, no. 170, VS 1877/AD 1820, RSAB.
8. *Byav Bahi*, no. 143, VS 1744/AD 1687, RSAB.
9. *Byav Bahi*, no. 159, VS 1827/AD 1770, RSAB.

10. *Byav Bahi,* no. 167, VS 1839/AD 1782, RSAB.
11. *Byav Bahi,* no. 170, VS 1877/AD 1820, RSAB.
12. *Sanad Parwana Bahi,* VS 1840/AD 1783, f. 65, Jodhpur Records, Bhandar no. 14, Basta no. 13, VS 1887, Kota Records, cf. B.L. Gupta, *Trade and Commerce in Rajasthan,* Jaipur, 1987, p. 44.
13. G.H. Ojha, *Bikaner Rajya ka Itihas,* Ajmer, 1939, pt. I, p. 13.
14. *Byav Bahi,* no. 159, VS 1827/AD 1770. Tobacco found way into the State in good quantity from Sindh, Multan, Ajmer, Kota and from eastern provinces of India. *Sawa Bahi Mandi Bikaner,* no. 11, VS 1822/AD 1765, ff. 1–2, *Jagat Bahi Bikaner,* no. 69, VS 1858/AD 1801, ff. 1–12.
15. *Byav Bahi,* no. 143, VS 1744/AD 1687; no. 170, 1877/AD 1820, RSAB, G.S. Sharma, *Marwari Vyapari,* Bikaner, 1988, p. 21.
16. *Sanad Parwana Bahi,* VS 1840/AD 1783, f. 65, Jodhpur Records, Bhandar no. 14, Basta no. 13, VS 1887, Kota Records, Cf. B.L. Gupta, op. cit., p. 46.
17. *Byav Bahi,* no. 159, VS 1827/AD 1770, RSAB.
18. *Byav Bahi,* no. 167, VS 1839/AD 1782, RSAB.
19. *Byav Bahi,* no. 170, VS 1877/AD 1820, RSAB.
20. *Sawa Bahi, Mandi Bikaner,* no. 16, VS 1827/AD 1770, f. 48(b); no. 22, VS 1837/AD 1780, f. 32 (b), RSAB.
21. *Kagad Bahi,* no. 12, VS 1859/AD 1802, RSAB.
22. The routes had become unsafe and the Bhattis, Raths and Johiyas used to plunder the caravans carrying goods on the routes passing from the north-west region. G.H. Ojha, op. cit., pt. I, pp. 21–2.
23. *Parwana Bhai,* Bikaner Records, no. 1, VS 1700–1800, f. 629(b); no. 4, VS 1800–1900/AD 1743–1843, *Chitti Diwani,* VS 1823, Phagun Badi 5, Camp, Chandasar Village, RSAB.
24. *Byav Bahi,* no. 159, VS 1827/AD 1770, RSAB.
25. *Byav Bahi,* no. 167, VS 1839/AD 1782, RSAB.
26. *Bikaner Mandi Re Jama Kharach Ri Bahi,* no. 117, VS 1872-3/AD 1815-16, RSAB.
27. *Sawa Bahi Mandi Bikaner,* no. 3, VS 1805/1748, ff. 2(a), 63(a); no. 21, VS 1835-6/AD 1778-9, f. 10(a); *Sawa Bahi Mandi Anupgarh,* no. 14, VS 1899/AD 1842, f. 154; *Sawa Bhai Mandi Suratgarh,* no. 1, VS 1847/AD 1790, f. 71, RSAB.
28. Aziza Hasan, Mints of the Mughal Empire, 'A Study in Comparative Output', *Essays in Medieval Economic History,* ed. Satish Chandra, vol. III, New Delhi, 1987.
29. *Byav Bahi,* no. 143, VS 1744/AD 1687, RSAB.
30. *Byav Bahi,* no. 159, VS 1827/AD 1770, RSAB.
31. *Byav Bahi,* no. 178, VS 1909/AD 1852, RSAB.
32. *Sawa Bhai Mandi Suratgarh,* no. 1, VS 1844/AD 1784, f. 33, RSAB.
33. *Sawa Bhai Mandi Anupgarh,* no. 143, VS 1874/AD 1817, f. 67, RSAB.

Indians in Iran in the Eighteenth Century

SURENDRA GOPAL

The rise of the Ottomans, the Safavids, the Shaibanids and the Mughals in Turkey, Iran, Central Asia and India respectively in the sixteenth century resulted in a political situation in which the Shi'ite Iranians were keen to have ties with their eastern neighbours—the Mughals—in order to escape the possibility of being simultaneously attacked from the front and the rear by the Sunni Ottomans and/or the Shaibanids. This led to a lively exchange of traders, scholars and artistes. Throughout the seventeenth century, Indians could be found in all the major cities of Iran, viz., Bandar Abbas, Isfahan, Shiraz, Teheran, Tabrez, Kum, Mashad, Yezd, etc. From Iran, Indians moved on to the trade centres in the Caucasus, such as Baku, Shirwan, Derbent, etc., and to the Russian river port of Astrakhan on the mouth of the Volga River where it falls into the Caspian Sea.[1]

In the eighteenth century the political situation in this vast area, extending from the Bay of Bengal to the Black Sea changed considerably. The Indians in Iran were faced with new challenges such as the decline and the eventual disappearance of the Safavids, the temporary Afghan occupation of Iran, the rise of Nadir Shah in Iran and the decline of the Mughals and the establishment of the political dominance of the English East India Company on the Indian subcontinent.

The political turmoil in Iran could not but affect the Indians, who, however, tenaciously carried on. How adverse were the circumstances can be gauged from the following example.

When the Afghans besieged Isfahan in 1722, French clerics tried to escape in the company of two Indian *banias* (traders), who were arrested by the invaders; while the French escaped, the Indians were killed.[2]

In 1729, the Indians residing in Shiraz were practically killed to the last man by the invading Afghans who were infuriated because of an attack by the local ruffians.[3]

The hostile situation however did not deter the Indians living here. The Indian presence could not be eliminated also because the new Afghan ruiers of Iran were aware of the importance of the Indians. The invading Afghan army was accompanied by Indians who were to look after their financial interests and manage their economic affairs. The usefulness of the Indians for the Afghanis was so much that when the Afghans divided the local population into seven categories, Indians were assigned the fourth place and placed ahead of the Zoroastrians, the Jews and the Persians.[4]

However, in view of the prevailing political instability some of the Indians in Iran decided to move to Russia where Indians had established themselves in the last century and where the Tsarist administration was sympathetic and was willing to extend patronage to them even on Iranian soil.[5] The Russian government affirmed its resolve again in 1735 and agreed to confer citizenship rights on them.[6]

The rise of Nadir Shah, who ended the Afghan occupation of Iran, did offer some temporary respite to the Indians. The Iranian Shah had extended the boundaries of the Iranian Empire from the Black Sea to the river Yamuna and looked favourably on inter-regional trade.

An Englishmen who visited Mashad in north-east Iran in 1741, reported the arrival of caravans from Bukhara, Balkh, Badakshan and India.[7] Also Nadir Shah after his return from India had brought back a large number of Indian craftsmen, masons, stone-cutters, goldsmiths, etc., who built buildings for him at Kelat, where the treasures brought from India were housed. These craftsmen also constructed a few buildings at Mashad, which Nadir Shah dearly loved and wanted to transform into a magnificent city.[8]

In fact, under the Afghan occupation and subsequently under Nadir Shah's dispensation, the Russian support was an important factor in keeping Indian trade alive. The Russian government even entered into a treaty with the Persians, which stipulated that Russians, Armenians and Indians residing in Russia be given free access to Iranian territory for purpose of trade.[9]

In 1739, the Indian passengers, Sularam Minimilov, Maram Nenicov Sanmukht and his brother Bankir and Ramgerpur who had travelled on Russian ships to Iran and had come back, were interrogated along with their co-passengers. This was because the Russian authorities wanted to make sure that they had neither visited nor purchased goods from plague-infected cities of Iran.[10]

The Indians based in Astrakhan were carrying on a lucrative trade with Iran. Even their agents were travelling to Iran. This is evident from the fact that the Russian Consul in Iran demanded a ban on Tartar agents of Indian merchants visiting Iran.[11]

The Indians in Iran were reciprocating these visits. In February 1741, eighteen Indians left for Baku aboard two ships owned by Russians.[12] Sometimes Indians carried goods on behalf of the Persian Shah. In April 1741, the Persian governor of Gilan forwarded the names of seventeen Indians along with a list of commodities they were carrying to the Russian Consul who sent it to the Russian ministry. Of these names, five had the prefix Marwari, one the prefix Lahori, and five the suffix Multani. Names such as Lahi, Mirdas, Simmides, Dilram, etc., show that they were either Hindus or Sikhs.[13]

The cordial relations between the Indian merchants and the Persian ruling family received a setback in the mid-1740s when Nadir Shah, became tyrannical. In 1746 he extorted huge sums of money from Indian and Armenian traders in and around Isfahan. Some Indians were accused of keeping back pearls from the ornaments of horses sent to Nadir Shah by Shah Hussain, a scion of the Safavid house.

In 1744 when the Persian general Muhammad Hussain Khan stationed in Shiraz, needed money for paying salary to his soldiers, he sent his officers to Bandar Abbas to collect it from the merchants. The Indian merchants who refused to comply were subjected to extreme cruelties.[14] His soldiers arrested the broker of the English East India Company who was released only after a bond of 3,000 Tomans was given.[15]

In 1746 when a suspect in the theft of a royal carpet revealed that the carpet had been sold to a group of merchants consisting of four Jews, four Armenians and an Indian, all of them were arrested. The merchants were blinded and thrown into fire.[16]

The harsh punishment meted out to the Indians was imposed because Nadir Shah thought some Indians were sending information on the state of affairs prevailing in Iran to their compatriots in Qandhar. Even when he went to Mashad in 1747, his tyranny remained unabated. It is said, 'all merchants, military men, Persian Armenian, had to lose one eye or both'.[17]

Nadir Shah's behaviour caused great consternation among the people of Iran. As a result there was a general exodus of both Iranian and foreigners including Indians. Some left for Arabia, others went to the dominion of the Mughals in India. Contemporary Russian documents also indicate a migration of Indians to the Caucasus and Russia.

However, before Nadir's capricious conduct became unbearable, Indian merchants enjoyed the support of both the Iranian Shah and the Russian Tsar. The Indians retained a significant share in Perso-Russian trade. The Persian authorities told the local Russian Consul that the Commander of Astrakhan be asked not to charge customs duties on goods being shipped by Indians for the Shah of Iran.[18] The Russian authorities also wanted certain privileges for the Indians residing in Astrakhan and carrying on trade with Iran.

As a result of the support extended by the two governments, the Indians in Iran had not only consolidated their position in Perso-Russian trade in 1730s and in 1740s but also increased their share in the above trade. In order to cope with the extra volume of trade they enlisted the services of other nationalities such as the Armenians, Tatars and of course, Persians.

Contemporary Russian documents attest to the enhanced role of the Indians in Perso-Russian trade. The Russian Consul informed the foreign ministry that eight Indian merchants were carrying goods on behalf of the Shah.[19] Among these Indians one bore the surname Marwari which confirms that Rajasthani traders had become an integral part of the Indian trading community which carried on trade between Iran and Russia.

The Russian government showed its appreciation of the contribution of the Indians to Russian treasury by granting them temporary citizenship; the Russian Senate issued a decree to this effect in 1744.[20]

In 1742, 1743 and 1744, Indians in Astrakhan imported more from Persia than they exported. This set alarm bells ringing in Russia and in 1745 the Russian government barred Indians from writing to their friends and relatives in Persia. The Indians immediately protested and the Tsar withdrew his order.[21]

This close ties of the Indians in Astrakhan with their compatriots residing in Persia is evident from the fact that in 1747, of the 45 Indians staying in Astrakhan, 32 had business connections with Iran. Many had relatives and friends and incidentally almost all of them hailed from Multan or its neighbourhood.[22]

Nadir's tyrannical conduct caused the outbreak of rebellions in different parts of the empire. In 1746 Fateh Ali Khan, a rebel, captured one of Nadir Shah's caravans coming from India.[23] Nadir Shah was assassinated in 1747 and the new political climate changed the pattern of the activities of Indians in Iran. The empire he had created disintegrated.

Soon after Nadir Shah's death, Afghanistan declared its Independence under Ahmad Shah Abdali.

All the Abdali rulers in the eighteenth century depended heavily on Hindu revenue officers to conduct the financial affairs of the state. As a result, Hindu revenue officers and Hindu traders now dotted Afghanistan. The land route from India to Iran which ran via Afghanistan had become much more hospitable. We do not have the data but the number of Indians going to Iran seemed to have increased. This spurt in the arrival of the Indians was facilitated by the new political scenario unfolding in India.

The English East India Company in the second half of the eighteenth century launched upon its career of conquest on the Indian subcontinent. The Indians residing in the North-Western Frontier, Sindh and the Punjab found hard to travel to other parts of India as the Mughal Empire was disintegrating and new kingdoms, such as Awadh, Bengal, etc., were emerging with their own laws and monetary systems. As a result of these two factors Indians in Iran became more interested in Perso-Russian and Perso-Caucasian trade. They were now joined by their compatriots from Sindh and Rajasthan in larger numbers.

Thus passengers on board the ship *Serafin* and *St. Peter* arriving in Astrakhan in April 1755 consisted of the Indians Chesu Dadleave, Uvna Ramchawav, Childeram Nagonleev and Dunichand Pervomandov. They carried Persian goods for their compatriots residing in Astrakhan.[24] These goods carried consisted of varieties of silk, cotton textiles, paper, dry fruits, copper, etc. Of course, Astrakhan Indians were also travelling to Persia. In 1765 some Indians in Astrakhan applied for Russian passport for visiting Iran.[25]

However, problems had begun to arise for Indians residing in Astrakhan and especially for those who were carrying on trade with Iran. The Russians had become jealous of their prosperity; they petitioned to their government to curtail their activities. In 1777, a proposal was mooted to restrict the stay of Indians, who lacking in any support by their home government could not take any counter measures.[26] They continued trading with Iran though the volume had decreased. In 1778, several Indians sent goods mainly of Russian origin to Iran.[27] Twenty years later, we find Magudas, an Indian resident in Astrakhan, seeking the permission of the governor to load his ship *St. Anna* with goods destined for Persia.[28] Obviously, this particular Indian had prospered and had become a ship-owner while his compatriots had fallen on bad days.

Nevertheless, the diminishing participation of Indians in Perso-Russian trade did not result in the elimination of Indian presence in Iranian cities since this was only one dimension of their activities. Also the political situation in Iran changed for better in the second half of the eighteenth century.

An era of comparative peace enabled Indians to carry on their business in several cities of the country despite the fact that one of the most important centres of their activities, Bandar Abbas was abandoned by Iranians in 1760 in favour of Abu Sehr.[29] India's sea-borne trade to Persia now shifted to the port of Abu Sehr and Indians began to settle down here.[30] Francklin, who had sailed from Surat, got down at Abu Sehr and then proceeded to Shiraz. He noted that there were a large number of passengers going to different ports on the Gulf frcm India.

In Shiraz he found a special caravanserai for Indian merchants who paid rent for the premises they hired and carried on their business from there.

At this point of time, a new group of Indians came to the forefront. Indians residing in the Iranian cities were joined in increasing numbers by their compatriots hailing from Shikarpur in Sindh. Probably the British control over a number of important port towns and the decline of some old commercial centres such as Surat, Cambay, Agra, Delhi, Ahmedabad, etc., had given a spurt to the overland trade between the two countries. Sindh, by virtue of its geographical location and political stability, was in a very good position to take advantage of the new situation. It was not subjected to attacks as the Panjab had been since the days of Ahmad Shah Abdali, which had adversely affected the economy of the Panjab.

Secondly, the Abdali rulers in Afghanistan had adopted a policy of religious tolerance.[31] Timur Shah in 1785 extended his patronage to Hindus and encouraged them to settle down in Afghanistan, promising 'that they should carry on trade without the dread of indefinite extortion'.[32] Timur Shah was probably prompted to make this declaration because the Indian involvement in the trade between Afghanistan and Iran had increased. This is evident from the statement of Moulai Shadai who had stated in 1783: 'The caravans of Kandahar and Khorasan in winter used to come up to Shikarpur... Shikarpur, Sukkur, Rori, Larkana, Kandiaro, Nararpur, Sehwan Thatta and Karachi were the centres of trade.'[33] In fact, the Shikarpuris now emerged as the most active and visible group among the Indian traders in Afghanistan, Iran and Central Asia. They had replaced the Multanis and Indians were now generally identified as Shikarpuris.

George Foster, who travelled overland from Calcutta to England via Persia and Russia noted two hundred Hindus living in two caravan serais in Herat,[34] at the junction of Iran, Afghanistan and Central Asia. It should be noted that Herat situated on the north-east borders of Iran and north-western Afghanistan was a frequent bone of contention between the two powers as Kandahar had been in southern Afghanistan in the preceding century.

On his way to Mazandran on the southern coast of the Caspian

Sea in Iran, Foster met a Kashmiri who was going there for business purposes.[35] Here he found one hundred Hindus, chiefly from Multan and Jaisalmer.[36] He writes

> . . . they (Hindus) occupy a quarter in which no Mahometan is permitted to reside, and where they conducted business without molestation or insult and I was not a little surprised to see those of the Brahman sect, distinguished by the appellation Peerzadeh, a title which Mahometans usually bestow on the descendants of their prophet.[37]

When Foster travelled to Baku (in Azerbaijan), he was accompanied by five Indians among whom was a *sannyasi* (a Hindu mendicant) travelling to Astrakhan.[38] In Baku, he found a caravan serai full of Indians, mostly belonging to Multan.

The English East India Company was fully conscious of the importance of Indians residing in Iran. In 1800 a commercial treaty was concluded between the Company and the Iranian prime minister. It expressly stated: '. . . English and Indian traders and merchants should be permitted to settle, free from taxes, in any Persian seaport, and should be protected in the exercise of commerce in the Shah's dominions'.[39]

At the down of nineteenth century, Indians were found residing in various cities of Iran, such as Isfahan, Shiraz, Tabriz, Yezd, Mashad, Kashan, etc. Both Indian and European travellers to Iran such Fazil Khan, Mohan Lal, Pottinger, Vigne, Fraser, etc., attest to their presence.[40]

A few words about the nature of the activities of Indians may also be mentioned.

These traders did not form a very homogeneous group: differences of language, region, religion or caste separated them; economically some were small, some were medium and some were big businessmen. The latter combined wholesale and long distance trade with moneylending, discounting of hundis, issuing of letters of credit, etc., they operated through a host of agents, both Indians and non-Indians. They collaborated with European trading companies at different levels. The medium-sized traders were affluent; they combined wholesale trade with retail business and moneylending. The small trader was the poorest; he eked out a living by retailing and/or acting on behalf of his rich compatriot and by petty moneylending.

It may be noted that moneylending was an integral part of the activity of the Indian merchants. The small Indian trader-cum-moneylender served the need of the poor citizens or artisans and his profile as a usurer was noted by foreign visitors to Iran. Father Krusinsky noted, 'The first Indians that dwelt in Persia, came from the city of Multan: they drive the principal trade at Ispahan, are great usurers and have almost all the money of the capital in their hand.'[41] As usurers, the Indians became an object of hatred; the common Iranian looked at him as an exploiter and as an unmitigated evil.

Finally, how do we describe the nature of the trading activities of the Indians. Meilink-Roelofosz and Van Leur have characterized business activities of Indians as 'pedlar's trade'. Niels Steensgaard concurred with them though he adds that it was carried out with great sophistication.[42] However, a look at the scenario suggests that the Eurocentric view while evaluating the nature of the business operations of the Indians fails to take into account the context in which they functioned.

Lacking in state patronage and facing religious, regional, linguistic and cultural diversity amongst themselves, the Indian merchant was basically forced to operate on his own. He was an individualist and a loner. This fact needs to be underlined since he survived two centuries of violent political upheavals in India, Afghanistan, Iran and the adjoining lands. The reason for his success or survival was that he acted as a 'pure and simple trader'. If he made good, he became a top-ranking trader of his times in the country in which he lived. Dale realized this fact when he wrote:

> The ability of Indians to accumulate capital from trade and moneylending gave them a similar position in Iranian society to which a smaller number of their compatriots occupied in the late seventeenth- and eighteenth-century Astrakhan. They became bankers in a society that possessed no formal institutions that accumulated capital and extended credit. Indians in most of Iran's major cities are known to have lent money to Iranian merchants; in Astrakhan it is virtually certain that most loans were given for this purpose.[43]

But the economic clout hardly gave him proportionate political influence or manoeuvrability. In Iran or Afghanistan, he was always at the mercy of the political masters.

NOTES

1. Sara Ashurbey, *Ekonomicheskiye I Kulturniye svyazi Azerbaijana s Indiyel v Sredniye Veka* (in Russian), Baku, 1990, Chapter II, pp. 145–50.
2. L. Lockhart, *The Fall of the Safavi Dynasty and the Afghan Occupation of Persia* (henceforth cited as Lockhart), Cambridge, 1958, pp. 164–5.
3. L. Lockhart, *Nadir Shah*, London, 1938, p. 46.
4. Father Krusinski, *The History of the Late Revolutions of Persia,* vol. II, London, 1834, p. 197.
5. Ovchinnikov and Sidorov (Compilers) Russko-Indiiskiye Otnosheniya v XVIII v. (hereafter cited as R-IO. v XVIII v.), Moskva, 1965, p. 170.
6. Ibid., p. 180.
7. *Nadir Shah,* p. 197.
8. Ibid., pp. 193–4.
9. R-IO. v. XVIII v., pp. 133–4 and doc. no. 80.
10. Ibid., pp. 153–4 and doc. no. 80.
11. Ibid., doc. no. 84.
12. Ibid., doc. no. 95.
13. Ibid., doc. no. 98.
14. *Nadir Shah,* p. 243.
15. Ibid.
16. Ibid., p. 258.
17. Ibid.
18. R-IO. v XVIII v, doc. no. 99.
19. Ibid., doc. no. 100–1.
20. Ibid., doc. nos. 108 and 111.
21. Ibid., doc. no. 125–6.
22. Ibid., doc. no. 134.
23. *Nadir Shah,* p. 174.
24. R-IO. v XVIII v., doc. no. 161.
25. Ibid., doc. no. 183.
26. Ibid., doc. no. 192–3.
27. Ibid., doc. no. 194.
28. Ibid., doc. no. 206.
29. John Malcolm, *History of Persia From The Most Early Period to the Present Time,* London, 1815, vol. II, p. 1787.
30. William Francklin, *Observations Made on a Tour From Bengal to Persia,* Calcutta, 1788, p. 51.
31. Ibid., p. 25.
32. Iqbal Ahmad Memon, 'Shikarpur the Eighteenth Century Commercial Emporium of Asia', in M. Yaqub Mughal (ed.), *Studies on Sindh,* Jamshoro, 1988, p. 7.
33. Ibid., p. 99.

34. George Foster, *A Journey from Bengal to England,* vol. II, Patiala, 1970, p. 151.
35. Ibid., p. 184.
36. Ibid., p. 186.
37. Ibid., p. 186.
38. Ibid., p. 291.
39. Malcolm, op. cit., vol. II, p. 127.
40. Hafiz Muhammad Fazil Khan, *Tarikh-i-Manazila-Bukhara,* Eng. tr. Iqtidar Hussain Siddiqui, Srinagar, 1981; Mohanlal, *Travel to Punjab, Afghanistan and Turkistan, to Bulkh, Bokhara and Herat and Visit to Great Britain and Germany,* Calcutta, 1977; Pottinger, *Travels in Baloochistan and Sinde,* London, 1876; Fraser, *Narrative of a Journey into Khorasan in the Years 1821 & 1822,* Delhi, 1984; G.T. Vigne, *A Personal Narrative of a Visit to Ghuzni, Kabul and Afghanistan,* Delhi, 1986.
41. Father Krusinski, op. cit., p. 197.
42. Niels Steensgaard, *The Asian Trade Revolution of the Seventeenth Century,* Chicago, 1973.
43. Stephen Frederic Dale, *Indian Merchants and Eurasian Trade 1600–1750,* Delhi, 1994, pp. 74–5.

Indo-Persian Elites' Perception of the Western Expansion in the East

GULFISHAN KHAN

INTRODUCTION

The eighteenth century in world history witnessed a new phenomenon—the 'decline of the East', accompanied by a simultaneous process of the 'rise of the West'. The Mughal empire declined and disintegrated: the Safavid empire collapsed, the Uzbek Khanate broke up into fragments, and the Ottoman empire began its career of slow, but inexorable decline. One of the common factors that underlined the dissolution of the once powerful eastern regimes was the economic, technological, and intellectual rise of Europe in the period 1500–1700 as a centre of world commerce. Rise in population and a greater degree of urbanization indicate that a clear shift in the economic balance between Europe and Asia had already occurred in the seventeenth century. Europe had emerged as the principal market for the luxurious craft manufactures of the world. It attracted high-value products from the traditional Eastern markets. The Western impact subverted the polity and society of the East even before Europe actually confronted the East with its superior military prowess. Understandably, it was only in the latter part of the century that the Eastern politic felt directly threatened by Western imperialism. The Eastern empires failed to absorb the Western scientific and technological developments, whereas the West forged ahead technologically and scientifically with the application of new ideas to the art of war and to economic and commercial activities. This 'cultural failure' to imbibe the new scientific spirit of the West accentuated the technological backwardness and economic deterioration. Lack of technical innovation adversely affected the military efficiency of the empires and their capacity to grapple with the agrarian crisis. In addition, the same technological and intellectual aridity did not allow towns to emerge as 'safety valves'.[1] Modern historians postulate similar factors in case of societies and states of the Middle East—'a region defined in terms of something other than itself, and specifically in the modern period by its relation with the growth and decline of European power'.[2] The process began with the establishment of the European trading companies in the Indian Ocean which dislocated the pattern of trade between the Ottoman empire and the outer world, both Asia and Europe. Secondly, the discovery of America had an even greater effect. It led to a flow of gold and silver into the Mediterranean countries and so to a rise of prices which dislocated the finances of the State. The result was an increase in taxation which brought hardship to the productive classes. These processes were accelerated by technological backwardness, or rather, lack of progress, in agriculture, industry, and transport within the countries of the Middle East.[3]

This new phenomenon of the rise of the West and growth of Western expansionism, very early became a serious issue of concern and comment of the intelligentsia. There were a number of Indo-Persian writers who sought to unravel the various aspects of the complex European diplomacy as employed upon the countries of the East. Prominent among them were Abu Talib ibn Muhammad Isfahani (1752–1806), an intellectual, poet, literary critic and a gifted writer. He toured the three continents Asia, Africa and Europe between 1799 and 1803, and wrote a well-informed and a highly articulate account in his travelogue *Masir i-talibi fi bilad i-afranji.* In addition, Abd al-Latif al-Shushtari al-Musawi (1758–1806), a scholar, diplomat, historian and writer, was born and educated at Shushtar in Persia, whence he migrated to India in 1789 and served as *wakil* or a diplomatic representative of the Hyderabad state posted at Calcutta. It was here at the administrative headquarters of the English East India Company that the latter compiled an autobiographical account of his rich experiences entitled *Tuhfat al-alam.* Thirdly, Ahmad bin Muhammad Ali Bihbihani (1777–1819), again a Persian émigré, an *alim*, a member of the well-known family of religious scholars in Iran who recorded his views and observations of India and Iran in his travelogue-cum-autobiographical memoir *Mirat-al-ahwal-i-jahannuma* (world-reflecting mirror).[4]

All three writers belonged to the same generation. They were eye-witnesses as well as participants in the complex processes of the growth, expansion and consolidation of British colonial power in India in particular, and the Western political expansion in Asia in general. All three writers observed the process of the gradual subjugation of regional Indian polities of Bengal, Hyderabad, and Awadh and that of the Marathas to the growing British paramountcy, which in turn led them to diagnose the malaise of the indigenous Indian states. The story of the extinction of the state of Mysore was fully known to them. These Indo-Persian writers were also witnesses to the phenomenon of the decline of the once great empires—the Safavids, the Mughals, and the Ottomans. Furthermore, in order to understand the causes of the Western expansion they sought to analyse contemporary Western events such as the War of American Revolution (1775–83), and the Wars of the French Revolution (1792–1800), and the emergence of Napoleon Bonaparte and the Revolutionary wars. The reason for these statesmen-scholars' concern with these contemporary European events was their acute awareness of the fact that the events happening on one side of the globe came to exercise a direct impact on the other side also. Such a seemingly remote happening as the War of Independence in America had ramifications on the contemporary Indian political scenario, as it renewed ongoing hostilities among European powers. Again, a series of wars in the South known as the Anglo-Carnatic Wars were the direct result of inter-European power-politics. Here in the South, the English and the French competed with each other for political, economic and the commercial supremacy over India. The French Revolution had more direct repercussions on the non-Western world and the Napoleonic wars that followed the Revolution had a worldwide impact. France under Napoleon Bonaparte invaded Egypt and Syria in 1799, and temporarily occupied Egypt. The French occupation of Egypt and subsequent siege of Syria was followed by hectic diplomatic activities, which in turn led to British, French and Russian alliances and counter-alliances. The Anglo-French conflicts and rivalries in Egypt and Syria, two Ottoman provinces, were directly connected with their desire for commercial and political ascendancy in India. This was the most obvious manifestation of the far-reaching consequences of European events in Asia.[5]

These writers sought to unfold the story of the burgeoning Western hegemony on Eastern nations at the turn of the eighteenth century, considered to be 'a bad time for the Islamic states and the awareness among Muslims of their changed position'.[6] It was the time when the French under Napoleon had invaded Egypt and Syria, provinces of the Ottoman empire, and the Russians were in Georgia, the richest province of Iran. The Khanate of Crimea, previously an Ottoman protectorate, had already been occupied by Russia. The British had already established their supremacy over large parts of the Indian subcontinent either through outright conquest or through alliances, and now they were in the process of consolidating their authority by eliminating other indigenous powers who posed a serious challenge to their claims as did the Marathas and Tipu Sultan. However, in this paper we are primarily concerned with the causes, course and consequences of the Egyptian expedition of Bonaparte and the indirect political consequences of the French invasion of Egypt on India and Persia. It seems these events should not be studied in isolation, as our authors' narratives suggest all these historical events were correlated and interlinked.[7]

It is no less significant that the works of our authors in the form of travelogues, memoirs and histo-geographical encyclopaedias were compiled on Indian soil as early as that of the well-known Arab chronicles of the French expedition such as by the Egyptian scholar, Abd al-Rahman al-Jabarti (1756–1825), Niqula al-Turk (d. 1828), the Syrian commentator, and that of the Lebanese writer Hayder al-Shihabi (d. 1835).[8] The Indo-Persian versions presented here can be favourably compared with the contemporary Arab narratives of this first direct European military intervention in the Near East. What follows is largely an exposition of the views, comments and analysis of these gentlemen-scholars.

ANGLO-FRENCH CONFLICT IN THE LEVANT AND THE FALL/CONQUEST (*FATH*) OF SERIRANGAPATNAM

Among the great Oriental empires the Mughal empire was the first to decline and disintegrate, consequently it was also the first to experience Western encounter and later on full colonial rule. Weakening of the central authority had become a characteristic of the Ottoman empire too, therefore Egypt and Syria, also became the scene of Western expansionism. The event was important, 'for the first time since the Crusades, a military invasion was launched against the heartlands of Middle Eastern Islam'.[9] Abu Talib, our first commentator, sought to describe the French Revolution, rise of Napoleon Bonaparte and the successive Revolutionary wars fought in Europe with immense interest, and utmost accuracy. According to the author these finally resulted in the French invasion of Egypt. His detailed and interesting narrative account of revolutionary Europe is prefaced with a brief description of the geo-political conditions of the Continent, various nation states, their respective systems of government, their mutual diplomatic relationships, treaties, alliances and counter-alliances. His knowledge of the wars of the First Coalition (1792–7) and the Second Coalition (1798–1800) was first hand as the latter lived in the British capital city during 1800–2 and also visited France at a time when Europe was experiencing the Napoleonic wars.[10]

Abu Talib wrote that it was under the control and direction of Napoleon Bonaparte (1769–1821) that the French invaded Egypt. Napoleon, a brave young man, seized power and authority after the Revolution due to his unique martial qualities, military abilities, and courage. Abu Talib specifically sought to inform his readers that the latter, not a French by birth but originally from Corsica, a tiny Mediterranean island and its inhabitants were notorious for theft and robbery. This disparaging comment of the author reflects the prevailing conservative British opinion for the French leader. Otherwise he was an ardent admirer of the French Consul.[11]

According to Abu Talib, the main motive of Napoleon for the invasion and subsequent occupation of this Ottoman province, was to seek an unhampered route to India. Abu Talib noted that the British seized the Cape of Good Hope from the Dutch in 1795 with similar motives that the route to India should remain unbarred.[12] The main object of Napoleon's Egyptian expedition was professedly to attack the British Indian empire and to replace it with a French empire in the East. Abu Talib specifically pointed out that the French avoided a direct invasion of Britain as it was an impractical enterprise. Moreover, the French clearly rated their naval strength inferior to the British, even though they dispatched an army to the aid of the Irish rebels.[13] Napoleon's decision to harass Britain by interrupting its Islamic thoroughway, was interpreted as an ultimate threat to the British possession in India. The British viewed it as almost equivalent to an attack on Britain. The French invaded Egypt with a 50,000 strong force and with powerful artillery. He wrote, for 'the English it meant an assault (*hamla*) on England or India (*mulk-i Hind*)'.[14] Napoleon planned to conquer Egypt and via Egypt he planned to invade India and to wrest the territories of Bengal and Deccan from the British with the aid of Tipu Sultan. The British were apprehensive that Bonaparte, once established in Egypt, might cooperate with the anti-British ruler of Mysore, Tipu Sultan, who had been a thorn in the side of the English East India Company. The English took all necessary steps to guard India, their highly treasured possession, against their most dangerous rival, the French. At the same time, the English were fully confident of their naval strength and thought that Napoleon's idea of the conquest of India was far from realistic. It was not a realizable goal. First, the British defeated the French army sent to aid the Irish rebels and then a fleet was dispatched in pursuit of Napoleon. At the same time, the English were confident of their naval supremacy and regarded designs of the French revolutionaries for political supremacy of India were far from realistic. Yet the British fears were not totally imaginary. The same happened. Having occupied Egypt, the French general opened negotiations with Tipu Sultan. The situation became complicated because Tipu's secret communications with Napoleon which contained details of the friendly alliance between the two were intercepted by the English. The secret negotiations confirmed that the proposed diplomatic alliance was aimed at ousting the British from the territories of Bengal and Deccan, and to give a final blow to the English power in India. The English got alarmed at this friendship and projected collaboration between their most formidable rivals. As a precautionary measure, the English compelled Tipu Sultan to hand over to them all important coastal forts and seaports that lay in his dominion until the time the perceived threat of the French invasion was over.[15] Clearly, Abu Talib's comments echoed what the British diplomatists considered the inherent perils in the permanent occupation of Egypt by the French.

Abu Talib felt that Tipu Sultan had underestimated the British power. In his opinion perhaps Tipu was not fully convinced of the power of the English as in the earlier wars he had successfully defeated them. He became proud of himself and refused to bow down. Rather he resolved to take an offensive. He decided to give an open battle and abandoned the earlier method of hit and run (*qazzaqi*). He fought alone against the British to save his honour and throne. He himself defended the fort of Srirangapatnam as his family and treasures were in the fort. Even more, he fought to defend his honour, self-respect and freedom. No French help could reach Tipu. He fought bravely till the end of his life and fell fighting defending his fort, to the last. His body was found amidst those of his brave warriors. The kingdom of Mysore fell to the soldiers of the East India Company. As soon as the news of his death was confirmed the English entered the fort, and the arsenal with entire store of arms and ammunitions, treasures, his family and his sons fell into the hands of the British soldiers. At last this renowned victory (*fath namdar*) was achieved.[16]

It is implied in our commentator's analysis that the English considered Tipu as their most formidable opponent, not simply due to the latter's intimate contacts with the French revolutionaries, rather, the main reason for English hostility to Tipu was that he, unlike the other Indian princes, refused to become a tributary of the Company. Tipu was too independent, too proud, too able and too energetic to accept vassalage of the British. Quite obviously the English viewed him as the greatest obstacle in the realization of their supremacy over the Indian subcontinent. Hence they desired his total destruction.

Our second major analyst, Abd al-Latif's also agreed with Abu Talib that the English rightly interpreted the French invasion of Egypt as a formidable threat to their Indian possessions. He elaborated further that the major cause behind French designs to occupy Egypt was the same, to threaten British territorial possessions in India. They viewed the French attempt as almost equivalent to an attack on Britain. It was an ultimate threat to the British possession in India. For the British, control of Egypt and exclusion of other European powers was of vital importance from the point of view of their British Indian possessions. By getting control of Egypt, Napoleon planned to use it as a base for further advance to drive the British from India. The French argued, wrote Abd al-Latif, that first the English should forego their claims over their newly acquired territorial possessions in India, in turn, the French, would evacuate Egypt. In short, the French attack and the subsequent occupation of Ottoman lands was not to occupy those provinces; rather the prime motive of the French was to secure a direct passage to reach India, to annihilate the British with the help of Tipu Sultan. The real bone of contention was India not Egypt.[17] Yet another reason was Egypt's prosperity and strategic significance. Egypt, known as the 'mother of countries' (*Umm al-bilad i Misr*) was one of the most flourishing countries of the world of Islam. In addition, the French desired an outright annexation of this prosperous Ottoman province. Alexandria, the port city, was situated on the Mediterranean Sea which connected Europe with Asia and Africa. Therefore, the French were planning to cut a maritime canal across the Isthmus of Suez to link the Mediterranean with the Red Sea and thus to facilitate communication with India. Then the French would enter India through the proposed short route, fight against the British and thus bring India under their possession. Alexandria had thus become a critical station on the route to India. What had dissuaded the French so far from embarking upon the project, even during the period when they occupied this country, was the fear that if they cut this passage between the Mediterranean and the Red Sea, even though it was not more than 17 or 18 *farasangs* in length,[18] the balance of water and land-mass would be lost. They thought that if not the whole of the globe, at least the neighbouring countries of Africa,

Maghrib, Yemen, Jeddah and a few cities of Sudan would be submerged in water.[19]

Thus both writers agreed that the reason why Napoleon Bonaparte, crossed the Mediterranean was not only to conquer and retain Egypt but to have a passage to India. Dreams of an eastern empire, of making himself a latter-day Alexander the Great, undoubtedly had considerable influence on Bonaparte. When he sailed for the conquest of Egypt he carried with him maps of Bengal and the Ganges valley. The main object of the attack, was to open communication with India: 'to combat the satellites of the English government there and stop that source of its corrupting wealth . . . drive the English from all their Oriental possessions which he can reach . . . to ensure the French Republic the free and exclusive possessions of the Red Sea'.[20] Napoleon's memoirs confirm that his grand vision of an Eastern empire also included India:

> Should the fortune of war be favourable, the French might, by the middle of the summer, reach the Euphrates with one hundred thousand auxiliaries, who would have as a reserve twenty-five thousand veteran Frenchmen of the best troops in the world, and numerous trains of artillery. Constantinople would then be menaced; and if the French could succeed in re-establishing friendly relations with the Porte, they might cross the desert and march upon India towards the end of autumn.[21]

Significantly it was also admitted by the British diplomat John Malcolm,

> The ambition of Bonaparte gave an eager attention to every plan, which offered the most distant prospect of augmenting his means of injuring the principal power that impeded his progress to universal dominion: and, however visionary his plans may appear to those acquainted with vast difficulties he had to encounter, he certainly cherished the project of invading the dominions of British nation in India.[22]

THE FRENCH EXPEDITION TO EGYPT AND SYRIA: A NARRATIVE DISCOURSE

All the three commentators mentioned above provided detailed and interesting descriptions of the various post-Revolutionary and Napoleonic wars fought on the continent of Europe. But these authors' special interest lay in Napoleon's expedition to Egypt and Syria. Abu Talib's narration of events begins with Napoleon Bonaparte's landing on the shore west of Alexandria with a magnificent fleet on 1 July 1798. The observer notes that this important port city, Alexandria, presented no insurmountable barrier to the French advance through the Upper Egypt. After describing the easy capture of Alexandria, the author goes on to recount the French victory over the Mamlukes at the battle of the Pyramids on 21 July, and the submission of Grand Cairo (*Qahira i-muazziya*) six days after that battle, followed by a detailed account of the Battle of the Nile. Abu Talib remarked that the French forces won an easy victory on land as the capital was defended only by a rabble, a confused multitude of people who had nothing but sticks and stones to combat the enemy attack. On the other hand, the invading armies of the French were well-equipped with muskets, bayonets and canons and thus possessed a good assortment of artillery. Hence, the Turks were utterly routed, unable to defend the fort, many Egyptians joined the French, while others fled and found refuge in Istanbul, the Ottoman capital city. The French forces were successful on land due to the weakness and incapacity of the Egyptians, but unfortunately for the French, the expedition was cut-off from France as the British admiral Horatio Nelson destroyed the French fleet in the harbour of Aboukir Bay, east of Alexandria, on August 1798. The British fleet rendered reinforcements and provisions from France almost impossible. Thus cut-off from France, Napoleon abandoned his scheme of striking at the British possessions in India, which has been nothing more than an idea, a mere dream, or fantasy. Now, Napoleon, instead of waiting in Egypt, crossed the desert to wage an offensive in Syria and laid siege to Acre, a town on the Palestinian seaboard, in March 1799. Abu Talib wrote that the port of Acre was the seat of the government of one of the Turkish Pashas known as Jazzar Pasha. Jazzar Pasha and his garrison were caught unaware by the French forces.[23] At this critical juncture, the Ottoman governor was assisted by a small British squadron under Sir Sydney Smith, the English Commodore (*kaptan*). Smith was cruising off Syria with three English ships holding a force of marines and gunners. In the course of this siege, Bonaparte made eleven attempts to take Acre, but each time his forces were repulsed with heavy losses. Thus al-Jazzar with the aid of British forces under Sydney Smith withstood the French siege of Acre for three months (March–May 1799). Finally the French soldiers were exhausted by street fighting, their numbers decimated, and after a final assault the siege was abandoned and Napoleon returned to Egypt.[24] The analyst felt relieved to inform his concerned readers that fortunately for the Ottomans and their British allies the French general retreated with the remains of his forces to Egypt, leaving successively his trusted generals Jean Baptise Kleber and Menou, although the latter a man of weak intellect, as his deputies in command of the army in the east. In fact, without communication with France, Napoleon could not sustain this campaign. Abu Talib sought to describe a new development in continental politics, the formation of a confederacy of Allied Powers against France; the Second Coalition which compelled Bonaparte to abandon his prospect of an imperial career beyond the Euphrates and the Indus. Abu Talib wrote that sailing secretly with ten select companions Napoleon eluded the British fleet and landed safely in Paris. Abu Talib made it clear that he returned to France in search of greater glory where he plunged into politics. He overthrew the existing government by force and set up a new one with himself as the First Consul of the Republic. Abu Talib alluded to the overthrow of Directory and the Coup d'etat of Brumaire in November 1799, without using these terms. He had no equivalent for the French terms 'Republic' and 'Consul' also, while 'Revolution' was obviously called *inqilab.* Thus Abu Talib visualized the fact that Napoleon like an adventurous despot exploited revolution to suit his own ends. He commanded the loyalty and respect of the military due to his martial and above all to his charismatic leadership qualities. Afterwards, the First Consul successfully defeated the Allied armies. Abu Talib remarked that Bonaparte was the absolute ruler of France without formally declaring himself emperor. Of late, he got his own picture engraved on the coins, which was a prerogative of sovereignty as Abu Talib knew. Napoleon had virtually usurped all powers as Abu Talib commented, 'Day by day, his prestige and authority was increasing while that of the Republic (*ripablik*)was waning.'[25]

Abu Talib completed the narrative that after the departure of Napoleon [Zia]Yusuf Pasha, the Ottoman prime minister, proceeded to Egypt and had several hard fought battles with the French forces, with the Ottomans suffering frequent defeats.[26] Abu Talib noted the Turks suffered several humiliating defeats in spite of the fact the Turks greatly outnumbered the enemy. According to the author, the Turks far exceeded the French army numerically; in some of these battles, approximately 50,000 Turks faced 1,000 French. These disastrous defeats gave a severe blow to the Ottoman prestige and power. In other words, French victories over the Mamluke soldiers of Egypt demonstrated beyond any doubt the weakness of a once invincible army. These encounters exposed the weakness and lack of energy of the Ottoman army, once the scourge of Christian Europe, to other European powers. In fact, these defeats, at the hands of ones subjects and fearful neighbours, exposed the military weaknesses of the Ottoman empire to the whole of the European world. Following the exposure of these weaknesses of the Ottoman empire, other European nations, particularly Austria and Germany, began to entertain similar territorial ambitions at the expense of the Ottoman empire, as the Russians, its closest neighbours had been exhibiting already. Abu Talib revealed that the Ottomans still followed their traditional Islamic practices (*dasturat i-qadeem Islami*) which were prevalent in the days of their empire's greatness, when its European opponents were weak. In fact, the memories of the past still reverberated in European minds and hence the latter sought to avenge these earlier reverses.[27]

At the same time, Abu Talib admitted that the Ottoman administrative machinery had lost its vigour and efficiency and its weaknesses were perceptible. Decline now beset a once vigorous and expansionist Islamic state. The causes of the decay were to be sought mainly within its body politic. Luxury and pomp pervaded all sections of Ottoman society, which indirectly led to bribery, blatant corruption and embezzlement. The bureaucrats, especially the medium-level officials, were very corrupt and they widely indulged in bribery to fulfil their desire for luxury. Almost all the departments of the government administration lacked proper organization and firmness of discipline. Abu Talib had to conclude that at present, corruption was widely prevalent in almost all departments of the government administration. In his criticism he specifically pointed out that the military establishment, including the imperial arsenal (*topkhana*) and the department of transport and communication (*yamkhana, manzil khana*), were in shambles. According to his prescription what was needed urgently was a firm hand to restore political morality, since the prevailing mismanagement was not due to lack of resources, but due to the desire for ease and luxury which led to inefficiency and corruption. Furthermore, the Ottoman lower bureaucracy had become narrow in outlook, as they saw their own selfish interest and not that of the state. Bribery had become such a national weakness that high offices could be bought in the imperial Ottoman government.[28]

While Abu Talib provided a full narrative of the story of the siege of Acre and its defence, Abd al-Latif, could also narrate some of the crucial events of the Syrian campaign such as the capitulation of al-Arish, the storming of Jaffa garrison on the beach, the cold-blooded massacre of several thousand Turkish prisoners in reprisal for the murder of French soldiers carrying flag-of-truce, and the systematic sack and devastation of Akka, a Syrian port city.[29] Abd al-Latif wrote that the Ottoman sultan ordered his entire standing forces including the Janissaries, the Pasha of Syria, the Sharif of the holy city Mecca, and the other Pashas and Beys to join the vizier. Abd al-Latif provides a brief but accurate account of the battle of Heliopolis on 20 March 1800, without naming it, in which he notes that the French routed the Ottoman army and managed to gain control of Upper Egypt. When the British came to know of the disastrous defeat of the Ottomans at the hands of the French they saw it as an opportunity they had waited for.[30] Furthermore, Abd al-Latif noted in astonishment that when the Ottoman armies approached Egypt, many Egyptians sided with the French and together they resolved to fight against the Ottomans. Abd al-Latif admired that the French, during their brief period of occupation of Egypt, had won the hearts of the native populace. He could also see the positive side of French colonialism in Egypt, in the French attempts to improve agriculture and irrigation facilities. He had an appreciation for French methodical administration in the direct assessment and collection of revenues, replacing the Ottoman system of indirect collection. He appreciated that the French promoted agriculture and industry. They exempted the peasants from the payment of taxes (*mal u-jihat*), which earlier were exorbitant. In addition, they helped the local populace in their agricultural activities by helping them in fixing the schedule of crops and digging new canals. Socially too, the French frankly intermixed with the Egyptian upper classes. Thus the analyst discovered the French tradition of local autonomy in the administration of justice and finance.[31] Abd al-Latif wrote that compelled by the French occupation of Egypt, the Ottoman sultan was left with no option but to seek help from the British, hereditary foes of the French. The British agreed to rescue the Ottoman emperor, but on a different pretext. Apparently, the British argued that the Ottoman Porte was also a European power due to the geographical proximity of Turkey with Europe. But in fact the British had their vested interest, revealed Abd al-Latif, and that was to block the route of Napoleon, to prevent him from proceeding towards India. In the words of Abd al-Latif the English thus argued:

> The Ottoman Sultan also belonged to the larger community of the kings of Europe. As such, it was incumbent upon us, European rulers, to assist him in times of distress as laid down in the traditional laws (*qanun*) and also in the ancient charter (*ahdnama*) [i.e. help to the Ottoman Sultan was embodied in *qanun*]. At the same time, the safety and security of India, which now formed part of the British dominion, was a matter of grave importance to us. In turn the French counter-argued that the whole of India was seeking help from us. If you would forego your claims for India, we would also evacuate Egypt and would leave it in the possession of Sultan. In fact, we have forcibly occupied Egypt to liberate India from your [French] yoke. But these assertions of the French in defence of India were wholly devoid of truth. As in India, there was not a single individual who could challenge the British power. The crazy, hot-headed Tipu, son of Haidar, was an exception, who opposed the British relentlessly and he too, at last met his end.[32]

Thus, Abd al-Latif revealed that the actual motives of the Anglo-

Turkish Alliance of 1799 were veiled under the showy pretext of rescuing the Ottomans from French aggression. The main object was expulsion of the French from Egypt as the British realized the strategic importance of Egypt from the point of view of British possessions further east.[33]

Abu Talib further noted that in accordance with the terms of the said Anglo-Turkish Alliance the British Parliament also decided to send military aid to the Ottoman Sultan, to wrest Egypt from the French. A strong force consisting of more than 15,000 soldiers was dispatched to Egypt under the command of Sir Ralph Abercrombie, the elder brother of General Abercrombie, the hero of the Rohilla War (1774). Forces were also dispatched from Bombay and Madras under General Sir David Baird by way of the Red Sea and Suez to assist Abercrombie in his arduous task.[34] Before the British Indian armies (*fauj i-Hind*) could reach their destination, the English general arrived in Egypt and in the very first attack, Aboukir was wrested from the control of enemy forces. The conquest of Aboukir was followed by several fiercely fought battles between the French forces, led by General Menou and the British under General Abercrombie. In these offensives and counter-offensives both sides suffered heavy losses. Abercrombie himself lost his life along with 4,000 English soldiers in the battle.[35] At this juncture, the command of the allied armies was taken over by the Ottoman Prime Minister Yusuf Pasha. These combined armies led by the prime minister soon forced the French to surrender Grand Cairo. On the other hand, the French now showed signs of exhaustion and fatigue. The position of the French in Cairo became hopeless as they were surrounded by the combined English, Turkish and Egyptian forces. The French laid down arms and obtained an armistice on 18 June 1801. They surrendered Cairo to the grand vizier on the condition that they would be allowed to return back to France. The reasons for the French defeat seem to have been two: Firstly, the disunity and discord that prevailed among the French military leaders, and secondly having lost communication with their mother country, no assistance could reach them. Meanwhile, the English got possession of the fort of Alexandria until the terms of the peace treaty were finalized. The armies sent from India were lodged in the fort of Cairo.[36] Egypt was restored to the Ottoman sultan following the peace [of Amiens] in March 1802. The main motive for the conclusion of the treaty was not pacification as such, rather both belligerents required time to recoup their losses. The French planned to improve upon their naval strength, the British government was forced by the demand of common populace to end the war, which they hoped would reduce the soaring prices of daily provisions. In a sense it was only a temporary truce as both intended to use the time to re-equip themselves for war.[37]

Abu Talib accurately noted the terms of the Treaty Amiens which was in favour of British commercial and strategic interests. He knew that it was negotiated by Cornwallis after two months of haggling in Paris. The French were left in possession of Italy (*Rum i-qadeem*), and Germany, Switzerland, and Holland. Britain got the island of Ceylon while Cape of Good Hope remained with the Dutch, and Malta was left with its owners. Egypt was restored to the Ottoman sultan.[38]

Like Abu Talib, Abd al-Latif, too, had immense appreciation for the British counter-Revolutionary role. At the same time both writers had personal admiration for Bonaparte and noted that the First Consul who later became the emperor of France was an able military commander, an admirable general, and a military genius. Both highlighted the fact that due to these qualities the French Consul was regarded as the foremost military and political figure of contemporary Europe.[39] Yet, the British were successful against so formidable a foe due to their naval strength and superior diplomacy. Moreover Abu Talib revealed that England could play a successful counter-revolutionary role combating first the Jacobins and then Napoleon due to its superior navy.

Both the writers understood that the colonial rivalries which engulfed the entire Eastern hemisphere began over the occupation of India (*taskhir*).[40] It is absolutely clear in their narration that for Britain as well as for France in the Near East, nothing was of direct political importance or even of economic significance. It was the vision of a fabulous India which excited Napoleon's imagination. Therefore, it was obvious that having failed in their motive to reach India via Egypt and Syria, the French began to seek support and collaboration of a new Eastern ally, Iran, against Britain. It obviously alarmed the British, as their hold on India was still uncertain. The British, through their unofficial agent Mehdi Ali Khurasani, and later through their official envoy John Malcolm, were successful in convincing the Persian monarch to attack Afghanistan with the dual purpose of keeping the nascent British empire safe from possible invasion by Zaman Shah, the grandson of Ahmad Shah Abdali, and by making Herat, one of the greatest cities of Khurasan, a bone of contention between Persia and Afghanistan in the future.[41]

Our third commentator Aqa Ahmad bin Muhammad Bihbahani, largely followed Abd al-Latif, and to a lesser extent Abu Talib, in his account of the Revolution in France and the consequent rise of Napoleon Bonaparte. Writing in the first decade of the nineteenth century, Aqa Ahmad took serious notice of the increasing European diplomatic activity in Iran. His comments and analysis of the increasing Anglo-French diplomatic activities in Iran following the evacuation of the French from Egypt is uniquely his own contribution. When these events took place Aqa Ahmad was writing his *Mirat al-Ahwal* at Patna (Azimabad) in 1808–9. His other two colleagues, Abu Talib and Abd al-Latif were no longer in this world to comment on these affairs. Aqa Ahmad informed the readers that the French as well as the English were competing to establish close diplomatic relations with the Persian monarch Fateh Ali Shah Qajar (1797–1834). The French requested His Majesty to allow them a free passage via land to invade India so that they could expel the British (*angrezan*) from the lands of Hindustan. This friendship with Iran was envisaged as a possible counter-measure against the British. But their competitor, the British, strove to frustrate every attempt of France to form an alliance with Iran, lest it endanger the security of India.[42]

RISE OF RUSSIA: CONFLICT WITH IRAN AND OTTOMAN EMPIRE

It was not only Britain and France which entertained imperialist motives against Iran, there was yet another power, the Russians (*Jamaat i-Rus*). Russia followed an overtly bold, expansionist and aggressive policies. Of late, it had come to acquire a great military potential and began to confront the Persian, as well as the Ottoman sultanate. Abd al-Latif explained that geographically, Russia was the greatest country in the northern quarter of the inhabited globe. No other country could be compared with it in territorial extent. It occupies well above four quarters of the northern hemisphere as it also included the countries of Tatars, Kalmyck Turks and Kazakhs. Yet its enormous size did not correspond with its population which is not more than 3 to 4 crore in all. Due to excessively cold weather, large areas lay desolate. Abd al-Latif exclaimed 'all powerful and Almighty God (*Subhan al-Qadir wal Muqtadir*) decreed that China, which was approximately only one-fifth of the inhabited globe contained a population of 35 crore, while Russia, he sarcastically remarks, which comprised one-fourth of the inhabited globe had a population of only 4 crore.[43] Abd al-Latif further pointed out that Russia's rise to power was a recent phenomenon: it became a great power following the reforms of Peter I, known as Peter the Great (1672–1725), who was a contemporary of the mighty Persian conqueror Nadir Shah. Otherwise, prior to the measures undertaken by Peter, Russians were totally backward and uncivilized. Peter went to England in order to receive training in the methods of modern warfare. The Russian monarch spent more than two decades travelling widely in Europe, along with a selected band of his countrymen. During his travels he made careful observations of whatever he deemed useful for his nation, and later adopted it for the benefit of his country. He spent years learning the art of shipbuilding himself, as an ordinary craftsman, and also sent his people abroad to receive training in the modern methods of warfare. Upon his return, he reorganized his country's system of government and administration, although Russia was also a monarchy like Iran. Peter also invited a number of foreign experts, craftsmen and engineers from Europe to Russia. It was the same monarch who founded a new capital city, which he named as St. Petersburg, after his own name. Thus Abd al-Latif came to know about Russia's Baltic window on the West. Abd al-Latif noted that Peter's reforms turned Russia into one of the most powerful nations of Europe, one that the other European nations clearly envied. Russia possessed a huge standing army consisting of both, cavalry and infantry, 4 to 5 lakh troops. Russian influence throughout Europe was wide ranging. At the moment, thus Abd al-Latif wrote, none of the European monarchs enjoyed such magnificence and pomp as the Russian sovereign did. All the European kings (*Salateen i-farang*) vied with each other in paying respect and honour to the Russian emperor, according to our source. It was excessively proud of its strength and often attempted to encroach (*dast andazi*) upon its neighbour's territories.[44]

Herein, Abd al-Latif highlighted recent Perso-Russian conflict over Georgia, one of the richest provinces of Iran. Aqa Ahmad was also aware of the Perso-Russian conflict over the question of Georgia and Russian advances in that Persian province. Abd al-Latif asserted that Georgia (*Gurjistan*) had been an integral part of the Persian empire, but the Georgian insurgents had always been disobedient and rebellious subjects even during the heydays of the Safavid rule. According to Abd al-Latif in 1797, Aqa Muhammad Khan Qajar (1794–7), founder of the Qajar dynasty, was forced to undertake a punitive expedition against these troublesome and rebellious inhabitants. Because Georgia was in a state of anarchy, the Qajar ruler laid siege to the strong fort of Tiflis, its capital city. The aim of the Persian monarch's expedition against Georgia was to punish its rebellious inhabitants. The Georgians were put to flight and the fort of Tiflis was captured. Georgia was sacked and after devastation and massacre, more than 80,000 Georgians, young as well as old, were made captives and deported to Iran, where they were sold as slaves. Iran's military victory was proclaimed and Iran's political power was restored in the region. The author boasted that the Georgian expedition was successful because the Persians had expertise in siege operations. Georgians were punished and Russia's prestige which incited revolt in the region and provided protection and active support, was also damaged. Many Georgians fled to Russian territories where they sought the refuge and protection of Catherine II due to their common faith. In fact, giving shelter to the Georgian refugees was a mere pretext for the Russian empress what Russia was planning was to attack and occupy Iran by force of arms because it had an unconcealed drive for the territorial expansion.[45] Abd al-Latif recalled the heroic traditions of the Iranians in facing other powers that threatened Iran's sovereignty. He asserted that Iran's monarchy had enjoyed unquestioned supremacy in the past, and its sovereignty was acknowledged throughout the world, as powerful kings paid tribute to the Persian monarch. Here the author invoked Persia's second mythical dynasty, the Kiyanyans. He further claimed that Iranians were famous for their typical tradition of heroism, bravery, valour and courage. The Persians had been valiant warriors, as well as the strongest and wisest in the world was acknowledged by the British as well. The author wrote, 'I heard from an intelligent English gentleman those who could rule Iran, could rule the entire world.'[46] Abd al-Latif was aware that the question of Georgia could not be solved in the lifetime of Muhammad Khan Qajar. The results of the first expedition did not prove permanent. Indecisive war with Russia continued in Gilan and Erivan, and the Russians continued to threaten Iran's north-western provinces. For Abd al-Latif, Georgia was a province of Iran like Khurasan. Its secession was inconceivable and had to be resisted in the same way as the Persians would resist an attempt at the separation of Fars and Gilan. In January 1801, Georgia was claimed by Russian ruler, which perhaps Abd al-Latif did not know. Nonetheless his regretful tone indicates that he was aware of the loss of the rich Caucasian province to the Russians. The author lamented deeply that Iran was a mismanaged country as its political turmoil had left it without any active foreign policy. It was in dire necessity of capable hands to restore strong and efficient administration. Abd al-Latif regretted: 'Alas! In this kingdom (*saltanat*), nothing but mismanagement and anarchy prevailed otherwise if the rules of governance (*amr i-riyasat*) had been laid down firmly, the Iranian sovereign (*Padshah qizilbash*) would command supreme position amongst the monarchs of the world.'[47] Furthermore, Abd al-Latif revealed that Russian ambitions of territorial aggrandizement were not confined to Iran alone. The author commented that Russian policy and attitudes towards others was not without religious bias. It had entertained similar designs at the expense of the Ottoman empire. Abd al-Latif commented that if other

European kings had not exercised a counter-weighting force, the Russians would have seized the entire dominions of the Ottomans, including Constantinople, its proud capital.[48] Evidently Abd al-Latif's remark echoed what he would have heard from his British informants in Calcutta. The idea that the Ottoman empire was doomed, and Dar al-Islam would be swallowed up by the Muscovites, spread throughout the empire after defeat by Russia in 1770.[49]

The rise of Russia, and its imperialistic designs against Ottoman Turkey as well as against Iran were known to the Indian intelligentsia through various sources. Shaikh Itisam al-Din, a Muslim from Nadia district in Bengal who visited Great Britain in 1767–9, expressed a deep concern over Russian aggression against the Ottoman empire. He regretted the loss of Crimea, an Ottoman province, to the Russians. Itisam al-Din interpreted it as an expression of Russia's growing military strength, he saw the Ottoman defeat in conventional terms. The Ottomans were defeated because of their minister's treachery. Finally, a treaty was concluded so that the Russians could not wholly threaten the empire.[50] Similarly, Murtaza Husain Bilgrami (1719–95), a member of *qasbah* service gentry, employed as *munshi* by the British official Jonathan Scott (1754–1829), was informed by his patron about the Russian encroachments on Turkey. Murtaza noted that a female sovereign ruled Russia and the latter had seized a number of territories belonging to the Ottoman ruler, Sultan Salim.[51]

In the early medieval period, Amin Ahmad Razi, author of *Haft Iqlim* (Seven Climes), the famous geographical and biographical work provided, a significant account of political and dynastic history of the empire. He attempted remarkably accurate account of the rise, expansion and consolidation of the Ottoman power beginning with the founder Ertoghral in the thirteenth century to the accession of the thirteenth Ottoman Sultan Mehemed III (1595–1603). 'At present, Sultan Muhammad bin Sultan Murad was a powerful sovereign who ruled Turkey and Europe (*Rum wa Farang*), cities and kingdoms, lands and oceans with full authority. He possessed great magnificence and grandeur.'[52] He sought to describe the landmark events of the

Ottoman history. His description included major events of reigns of different Sultans (*ahwal i-Salatin i-Usmaniya*) and their main achievements. Expansion of the empire in the Balkan and Anatolia under Orkhan and Murad I, expedition to Hungary, Bosnia and Greece under Bayazid I, defeat of Hungary under Murad II and the conquest of Constantinople in 1453 by Mehemed II, the conqueror, are described with absorbing interest. The author was aware of the Ottoman conflict with the Christians (*nasara*) of Europe (*farang*).[53] The political narrative is prefaced with a fascinating portrait of the newly founded Ottoman capital Constantinople (Qustuntuniya) with its magnificent mosques, *madrasas,* coffee-houses and public fountains which dotted the landscape of the brilliant Ottoman capital. The capital city alone had 400 mosques where 'congregational prayers were offered on Fridays'.[54]

However, Abu Talib's analysis of the causes of the Ottoman administrative weakness was based upon his first-hand observations and experiences when the latter stayed in the Ottoman capital of Constantinople for four weeks on his return journey to India in November 1802. It is not unlikely that Abd al-Latif's up to date and well-informed account of Napoleon's invasion was based upon Abu Talib's letters as the two were in regular correspondence. The intelligent traveller sought to provide a refreshing and delightful description of the social life of the imperial metropolis. It is a lively portrait of the city with a graphic description of its geographical features, the topography of the city, its inhabitants, religious minorities, composition of its population, weather, roads, means of transport, water-transport, market-places coffee-houses, bath-houses, eating habits, social life of the Ottoman Turks, dress of the ruling classes, buildings, historical monuments, mosques, *madrasas*. He describes his visit to the sacred tomb of Abu Ayyub al-Ansari, the Companion, the magnificent Aya Sophia, the great mosque *par excellence* with its impressive grand courtyard, in his characteristic detailed lively manner. The traveller also offered his views about the position of women in Ottoman society along with some insightful comparative comments with their Indian and European counterparts.[55]

Abu Talib discovered that Istanbul was still a brilliant capital of the once powerful empire, where the court of Sultan Salim III set an example of luxurious life. Nonetheless, signs of decay were apparent. This principal city of the empire was no longer a centre of world commerce. He paid several visits to the 'La Porte sublima', the Sublime Porte (*diwan-i ali*) where he was admitted to private gatherings at the court of the young and reforming Sultan Salim III, one of the most enlightened members of the house of Osman. In the royal court he found welcome as a learned guest, respected scholar and man of letters. He presented the sultan (*Padshah Islam panah*) with a two-volume Persian dictionary, *Qamus*, being a translation from Arabic into Persian.[56] The visitor presented it to sultan with a specific request: that the manuscript should be printed and published under the auspices of the Ottoman government. And that it should be distributed throughout the Turkish realms for the propagation and dissemination of Persian language and literature. Abu Talib also requested that his name should be included in the Preface of the printed edition. As he reminded the sultan that the lexicon was a rare piece of scholarship which he obtained after many efforts. He also had to spend a fortune in preparing the manuscript for publication. Thus Abu Talib presented the lexicon with a definite aim in view that the valuable learning-aid 'would see the light of the day and would not remain confined in the four walls of the royal library'.[57] Although the cultural orientation of the Ottoman court had changed a lot since the sixteenth century, Persian was no more patronized as the language of historical writings, it was Ottoman Turkish which was the language of literature and learned composition.[58] Yet, Arabic remained the language of law and religion while Persian was considered a language of prestige and polite letters. The educated Turkish nobility possessed basic communicative skills in it. As the visitor had a long conversation in Persian with the Ottoman Prime Minister Yusuf Pasha in the latter's private apartment. Abu Talib was also introduced to the other Turkish notables such as Reis Effendi, the Ottoman foreign minister.[59] He also enjoyed an audience with Ahmad Effendi also called Kahya Bey (*Kahya Beg*) and in-charge of home affairs. Ahmad Effendi's elegant manners and polite conversation left a deep impression on the visitor and the meeting with Kahya Bey became a memorable event.[60] The sultan lavishly allowed a sum of 600 kurush as the travelling expenses of the esteemed guest. According to the established protocol and Ottoman diplomatic practice, a special official called *mihmandar* was appointed to escort him from the capital to Baghdad where the author intended to visit the holy places, the tomb of Hazrat Ali, the fourth Orthdox caliph and of his martyred son Imam Husain. This official, a mounted messenger (*chapar*) was to look after his wants and security, to arrange for transport as required. Special royal orders (*farmans*) were issued directing the district and provincial officials *en route* to provide every facility to the honoured guest.[61]

Abu Talib noted that the Ottoman empire was a dynastic state, and one of the longest living dynasty of the Islamic world, which had completed full six centuries, as Abu Talib noted. The sultan was a despot but not a tyrant autocrat. The Ottoman sovereign gave rulings with full regard to the wishes of his nobles (*umara*).[62] The ruling elite as well as the common populace of the empire were law-abiding citizens who obeyed Islamic law (*shariat*) as well as the state regulations called *qanun.* The sultan ruled over a vast polyglot empire composed of Muslims, Christians, Jews, Turks, Arabs, Armenians and a host of other population. The other religious communities were an integral but subordinate part of the empire. It accommodated religious differences. He found Armenians a rich and prosperous community of the city, while Greeks played an important intermediary role in the diplomatic affair of the empire with other European states as interpreters. It seems that in spite of his short stay, as Abu Talib himself complained, he had some notions about the Ottoman political culture. He also enjoyed the hospitality of the British envoy (*Ilchi Angrez*) Lord and Lady Elgin.[63] On the advice of the British envoy and also due to closeness to the British diplomat he preferred to stay in a rented house in the Galata quarters, 'one of the three cities of Constantinople and where the European ambassador (*Ilchiyan-i-Salatin-i-Farang*) resided'.[64] Signs of increasing European political influence were apparent to him. As he observed about Elgin that 'Beginning with the land of Constantinople (*Zamin Qustuntuniya*) up to Baghdad and Basrah, the port town, all British representatives (*wakilan*) obeyed his commands.'[65]

There, at Constantinople he also met Austrian Orientalist Joseph von Hammer-Purgstall (1774–1856) then serving as dragoman in the Austrian embassy. Abu Talib appreciated that Hammer, though a German by birth, but he was well-versed in a number of European as well as Oriental languages. His proficiency in languages included French, English, Greek, Arabic and Persian. Abu Talib knew that during the siege of Acre, he had acted as an interpreter of Sydney Smith. In Constantinople he was serving as a dragoman (*tarjuman*, literally, interpreter) of the German ambassador.[66] Abu Talib also presented his Persian compositions to the young orientalist who got these Persian lyrics (*ghazal*) translated into French and English and published them in a number of leading periodicals being published from the leading European cities such as London, Paris and Vienna.[67] Hammer, a very prolific writer, studied Turkish, Persian and Arabic at the Oriental Academy of Vienna (Dolmetscher-akademie). His knowledge of Oriental languages was extensive but not thorough. His version of the Persian poems of Hafiz inspired Goethe's 'Westöstliche Divan' (1815–19); Fredrick Ruckert and Platen were also indebted to him.[68]

Abu Talib was fairly conscious of his Persian identity as distinct from the Turkish.[69] Yet, unlike the numerous European visitors who had left their eye-witness accounts of the socio-cultural life of the Ottoman Empire in the form of travelogues and reports, our observer had to overcome no built-in barriers of language and culture.[70] There was no veil as he came from the same cultural world which Bausani has aptly described as 'un identico mondo culturale musulmano', an identical Muslim world of culture.[71] The formation of modern Iranian identity through the re-configuration of its national history, and restyling of the Persian language has not yet started. The process of crafting of distinct national identity and sodality based on pre-Islamic past of Iran was in oblivion. The programme of de-differentiated *milli* and *vatani* identity linked to ancient history and Persian language and consequent complete dissociation of Iran from Islam, and the total exclusion of Arab Islamic world from its history was yet to begin.[72] But the germs of such ideas are present in embryonic form as one could see in the comments of Abd al-Latif in recalling the pre-Islamic past of Iran. Most of all, Abu Talib was a product of the composite culture of eighteenth-century India. Born and educated in Lucknow, the cosmopolitan city of north India and the capital of nawabi Awadh, he had experienced and absorbed the best of Indo-Persian traditions and cultural values.[73]

Despite all political vicissitudes, Abu Talib's short stay in the Ottoman capital testifies that India continued to enjoy active social and cultural relations with this near Eastern imperial state, as the learned author was informed that many Indian students especially from the Punjab and Sindh were studying in Ottoman *madrasas*.[74]

CONCLUSION

Here we presented perhaps some of the earliest perceptions and interpretations of the worldwide phenomena of European imperialism and colonialism by Indo-Persian commentators. Our writers had neither a clear and articulated definition nor any equivalents for the two terms. Obviously these terms were not coined until the second half of the nineteenth century. European imperialism was only partly developed, and it was not yet fully recognizable. But their narratives clearly implied that the emergence of new forces conveyed notions of domination as well as political and economic control. Moreover the use of such Persian words as *taskhir*, which meant forceful occupation and subjugation, in their discourses, also suggested that it was the beginning of awareness of the coercion of the weaker societies by stronger geopolitical systems. The term was applied to describe British conquest of India, as well as Western political expansion in the Islamic East. They fully realized and admitted that these eastern polities suffered from crucial internal political and administrative weaknesses and inefficiencies, which undermined their capacity to resist European powers. For instance, the Turkish armies could not defeat the French; the expulsion of the French from Egypt was only possible with an active British military aid. Hence they saw an urgent need for reform in the social and administrative institutions of the Eastern empires. Paradoxically, neither the idea of nationalism nor of a national identity in the modern sense of the term was present. Yet, the Western aggression was clearly perceived as an intrusion, a potential threat to the sovereignty so far enjoyed by these dynastic empires which were being encroached upon. Some other broad observations could also be made on the basis of the above account. For these contemporary historians, writers and observers, the modern geographical expressions such as Central Asia, West Asia, and Near East were irrelevant as well as unknown. What concerned them most were the issues of the territorial integrity and sovereignty of the great empires, the Safavids, the Ottomans and the Mughals. There existed a well-articulated consciousness of dynastic identity, but a consciousness/concern for a comprehensive composite national identity is absent. Yet there seems to be no reaction of fear and subordination rather an active opposition to the threat. In fact Ahmad Bibihani's writings demonstrate strong anti-Western sentiments and a wish for revenge, while Abu Talib's narrative displays a balanced approach towards the emerging problem. The scholar Abd al-Latif described the situation with sarcasm and cynical humour. All of the observers correctly concluded that British policy was dominated by one obsession: the defence of India. Egypt was a key to India, not an objective in itself, a stepping-stone to the grand visions of a future Indian Empire. The history of the British imperialism in the East began in India. It was in India, with the Battle of Plassey and with Robert Clive that Britain began to collect its empire, and Britain began the process of its own imperial refashioning, from a mercantile Atlantic based, colonial power to a global territorial ruler and an imperial nation state.[75] It was solely due to their intense desire to safeguard their Indian empire that the British provided active military assistance to the Ottoman sultans against Napoleon. The British policy with regard to Iran was also motivated with the same objective—defence of India from the possible invasion of Napoleon. The question of Georgia did not form part of the British diplomatic considerations. It was the same motive, the protection of Indian territories, which led the British to explore the military and strategic positions of Persia and Afghanistan, and their decision to use the dispute over Herat for their own purposes. Thus Britain came to have diplomatic and strategic interests in Iran not due to its perceptions of a Russian but due to a perceived French threat.[76]

In spite of such a detailed, up to date and well-informed

account of the Napoleonic invasion of Egypt and Syria, and its impact on the Indian political scenario and the consequent intensification of the British political activities in Persia, our authors seemed to be unaware of the far-reaching consequences of this first direct European military intervention in the Near East. They were fully aware of its adverse impact on Indian political horizons particularly the total annihilation of Tipu Sultan in the Fourth Anglo-Mysore War, and the formulation and successful application of Subsidiary Alliances by Wellesley, on the independent regional states of Hyderabad, Awadh and the Maratha principalities. They could hardly imagine that this temporary occupation would create what came to be known as the Eastern Question of nineteenth-century international diplomacy. In case of Iran also they could not visualize that it was the beginning of the decline of Iran as an independent state, and that Iran was to become a pawn in the great game of European imperial power diplomacy. India, their major concern, had already passed under British subjugation. The writers seem to have had little consciousness of the possibility of the changing balance of power in the region, not to think of the kaleidoscopic shifts of power. Our writers could hardly visualize that it was the beginning of the Western hegemony over the Eastern world, a phenomenon, in which England and France would dominate the Islamic East for more than two hundred years as representatives of the West. Soon the colonial goods, the sugar, coffee and indigo of the West Indies would replace local products in the Near Eastern market: the Syrians would drink West Indian coffee, not Southern Arabian. The time was not far distant when Indians would wear machine-made cottons of Manchester instead of their home-spun Dacca muslin.[77]

NOTES

1. M. Athar Ali, 'The Passing of Empire: The Mughal Case', *Modern Asian Studies*, vol. 9, no. 3, 1975, pp. 385–96; M. Athar Ali, 'The Eighteenth Century: An Interpretation', *Indian Historical Review*, vol. 5, nos. 1-2, 1978–9, pp. 175–86.
2. Albert Habib Hourani, 'Islamic History, Middle Eastern History, Modern History', *Islam in European Thought*, Cambridge: Cambridge University Press, 1991, p. 98.

3. For an analysis of the causes of the decline of the Ottoman empire cf. Bernard Lewis, *Emergence of Modern Turkey*, New York: Oxford University Press, 1961, chapter 3. For an overview of the problem also see, B. Lewis, *The Muslim Discovery of Europe*, London: W.W. Norton & Company, 1983, pp. 45–57.
4. For the biographies of the above-discussed three writers Cf. Gulfishan Khan, *Indian Muslim Perceptions of the West during the Eighteenth Century*, Karachi: Oxford University Press, 1998, chapter 2 'The Observers', pp. 71–119 (hereafter *Indian Muslim Perceptions*). The study seeks to analyse these writers' perceptions of Western society and culture, social and political ideas and institutions, education, scientific and technological advances along with the life-stories of the perceivers.
5. For an analysis of the political expansion of Europe in the east cf. *Indian Muslim Perceptions*, pp. 45–65.
6. Cf. *Muslim Discovery of Europe*, p. 47.
7. Cf. *Indian Muslim Perceptions*, pp. 47–53.
8. The accounts of these Arab writers represent the high degree of articulate awareness of the West that the Arab world had reached by that time. Cf. Ibrahim Abu-Lughod, *Arab Rediscovery of Europe: A Study in Cultural Encounters*, Princeton, Princeton University Press, 1963.
9. Lewis, *Muslim Discovery of Europe*, p. 51.
10. Cf. Abu Talib ibn Muhammad Isfahani, *Masir-i-talibi fi bilad i Afranji*, Persian MS Ouseley, 108, Oxford: Bodleian Library, folio 161 (hereafter *Masir-i-talibi*).
11. Ibid., folio, 162b.
12. Ibid., folio, 165.
13. Ibid., folio163b.
14. Ibid., folio 164.
15. Ibid., folio 166.
16. Ibid., folio, 166.
17. Abd al-Latif al-Musawi al-Shushtari, *Tuhfat al-alam*, Pers. MS. Elliott 382, Oxford: Bodleian Library, folios 122b–3 (hereafter *Tuhfat al-alam*).
18. Ibid., folio 122. The Persian term *farasakh* means a *parasang*, a league, about 18,000 ft in length.
19. Ibid., folio 122. Perhaps Abd al-Latif is referring to the arithmetical error of Napoleon's engineers which represented the Mediterrenean Sea as 30 ft below the Red Sea an error which was corrected finally in 1847.
20. J.F. Howard (ed.), *Letters and Documents of Napoleon*, London, 1961, vol. I, pp. 232–3. Quoted in M.S. Anderson, *The Eastern Question 1774-1923: A Study in International Relations*, London: Macmillan; New York: St. Martins, 1966, p. 26.
21. Montholon, *History of the Captivity of Napoleon*, iv, Quoted in Edward S. Creasy, *History of the Ottoman Turks from the Beginning of their Empire to the Present Time*, London: Constable, 1878, vol. II, p. 38.

22. Colonel Sir John Malcolm, K.C.B., K.L.S. Late Minister plenipotentiary to the court of Persia from the supreme government of India, *The History of Persia from the Most Early Period to the Present Times Containing an Account of the Religion, Government, Usages and Character of the Inhabitants of that Kingdom,* London: John Murray, Albemarle Street & Longman and Co., Paternoster-Row, 1815, vol. II, pp. 316–17 (hereafter *History of Persia*).
23. *Masir i-talibi* folio 166. Ahmad al-Jazzar (b.1722), a Bosnian by origin was a dominant political figure in southern Syria during the last quarter of the eighteenth century and the early years of nineteenth. In 1799, when General Bonaparte advanced northwards from Egypt to occupy Syria, Jazzar, assisted by a British fleet, successfully repelled his attack on Acre and forced him to retreat. He thereby set the seal on Bonaparte's eastern venture and paved the way for the final expulsion of the French from Egypt two years later. Cf. Al Djazzar Ahmad, *Encyclopaedia of Islam,* Supplement, pp. 268–9.
24. *Masir i-talibi,* folio, 166–7.
25. Ibid., folio 167.
26. Ibid., folio 168.
27. Ibid., folio 168.
28. Ibid., folios 196–7a. Abu Talib does not mention newly promulgated reforms of Sultan Salim III known as the Nizam i-jadid.
29. For a brief account of the Syrian campaign of Bonaparte, refer *Tuhfat al-alam,* folio 126.
30. *Tuhfat al-alam,* folio 123.
31. Ibid., folio 123.
32. Ibid., folio 122.
33. Ibid., folio 122–3.
34. *Masir i-talibi,* folio 168. These Indian troops disembarked at the Red Sea port of Qusayr. 'The troops proceeded by ship in March 1801 from Bombay to Mocha at the entrance of Red Sea. Thence they sailed to Jeddah on the eastern coast, near Mecca, where they were joined by a force from the Cape. They then proceeded to Kosseir on the western shore; in August they reached the Isle of Rhonda and thence marched over the desert to Rosetta, where these Indian troops gazed on the blue water of Mediterranean. There they found the end of their quest, for the French had already been vanquished by Sir Ralph Abercrombie and were in treaty to surrender. Baird's army re-embarked for India at Suez in June 1802. It is true they had achieved nothing except their long marches, but they had made a most effective proclamation to the world that the far-off Indian Empire, instead of being merely a burden to the war-worn Mother Country was able to react upon the European situation'. Cf. P.E. Roberts, *India under Wellesley,* London, 1929, rpt., Gorakhpur, 1961, p. 148.

35. For a description of the battle of Canopus, see *Masir i-talibi,* folio 168.
36. Ibid., folio 168.
37. Ibid., folios, 168.
38. Ibid., folios, 168–9.
39. *Tuhfat al-alam,* folio 126, *Masir i-talibi,* folios 162, 167.
40. *Tuhfat al-alam,* folio 121.
41. For an exposure of the views of Abu Talib and Abd al-Latif on the issue and role of Mehdi Ali Khan Khurasani, Cf. Gulfishan Khan, 'Eastern Perceptions of the Western Diplomacy', in A.D. Safavid (ed). *Indo-Iranian Relations,* Aligarh: AMU, 2004, pp. 108–22. For a comprehensive view of Iran's relations with Britain and British India cf. Rose Greaves, 'Iranian Relations with Britain and British India 1798–1921', *Cambridge History of Iran: From Nadir Shah to the Islamic Republic,* P. Avery, G. Hambly (eds.), Cambridge: Cambridge University Press, 1991, vol. 7, pp. 374–425.
42. Ahmad bin Muhammad Bihbahani, *Mir'at al-ahwal-i Jahan-numa,* University Collection, *Farsiya Akhbar,* no. 18/3, Aligarh: Aligarh Muslim University Maulana Azad Library, folios 117b–18a.
43. *Tuhfat al-Alam,* folio 182.
44. Ibid., folios 182–3.
45. Ibid.
46. Ibid., folio 184.
47. Ibid. In the opinion of Malcolm what caused the vengeance of the Persian monarch against the Georgians was that its governor, known as a *wali,* encouraged by the political instability of Persia, transferred his allegiance from the Persian monarch (whose supremacy Georgia had acknowledged for centuries) to the Empress Catherine II of Russia. A formal treaty was signed between Erekle II (1762–98) and the Russian empress, known as the Treaty of Georgievsk, in 1783, which made Georgia a Russian protectorate. The Qajar monarch attacked Georgia in 1795, the Georgians fought with great valour but they were overpowered by numbers. Fifteen thousand captives were taken into bondage and the army marched back laden with spoils. The assassination of the Persian sovereign on 15 June 1797 near Shusha ended a plan for a second expedition to Georgia. In 1800, Russia annexed Georgia when its last king George XII, son and successor of Erekle II, appealed to the Russian ruler Alexander I for support against Persia. For a historical account of Georgia, and expedition to Tiflis, cf. *History of Persia,* pp. 212–14, 279–86, 293–5.
48. *Tuhfat al-Alam,* folio 183.
49. Cf. Albert Habib Hourani, 'The Changing Face of Fertile Crescent in the XVIIIth Century,' *Studia Islamica,* VIII, 1957, p. 116.
50. Mirza Itisam al-Din, *Shigarfnamah-i-Wilayat,* Pers. MS Caps. OR, A-8, Oxford: Bodleian Library, folios 102–3. For an autobiography of Itisam, cf. *Indian Muslim Perceptions,* pp. 72–8. The Khanate of Crimea was,

after Kazan, Astrakhan and Sibir, the fourth Muslim State to fall under Russian domination. Ravaged in 1736 and in 1737–8 by Russian armies, Crimea was occupied for the first time in 1771. The Treaty of Kuchuk-Kainardji (1774) put an end to the Ottoman protectorate over Crimea and made the Khanate theoretically independent. The manifesto of Catherine II dated 9 April 1783 proclaimed simply the annexation of the Khanate to the Russian empire. Officially, Turkey did not recognize the annexation until the Treaty of Jassy, 6 January 1792. For details cf. Gavin Hambly (ed.), *Central Asia*, London, 1969, pp. 192–3.

51. Murtaza Husain Bilgrami, *Hadiqat al-aqalim*, Pers. Elliot 157, Oxford: Bodleian Library, folios 469a, 481–2. The terms employed to denote the Russian encroachments upon the Ottoman lands are *tasarruf* and *ghalba.* Both meant possession by force. For the biography of Murtaza Husain Bilgrami, cf. *Indian Muslim Perceptions,* pp. 78–84.
52. Amin Ahmad Razi, *Haft Iqlim*, Maulana Azad Library, Aligarh Muslim University, Qutubuddin Collection, *Farsiya Jughrafiya*, 100/20, folio 486.
53. *Haft Iqlim*, folio 481–6.
54. Ibid., folio 481.
55. For a remarkably detailed eye-witness and interesting portrayal of the social life of Ottoman ruling classes and description of the city, cf. *Masir-i-talibi*, folios 194a–206b.
56. *Masir i-talibi*, folio 203. Perhaps this is a reference to the celebrated Arabic dictionary *al Qamus al muhit* compiled by the famous fourteenth-century lexicographer Abu Tahir Muhammad Firuzabadi (1329–1415). It has been translated into Persian and also Turkish by Asim Effendi (d. 1819) and published from Istanbul. See, *Encyclopaedia of Islam*, New edn., Leiden: E.J. Brill, 1965, vol. II, pp. 926–7.
57. *Masir i-talibi*, folio 203.
58. Sara Nur Yildiz, 'Persian in the service of Sultan: Historical Writings in Persian under the Ottomans during the Fifteenth and Sixteenth Centuries', *Studies in Persianate Societies*, vol. 2, 2004, pp. 145–63; also see, Gerhard Doerfer, 'The Influence of Persian Language and Literature among Turks', in Richard G. Hovannisian and Georges Sabagh (eds.), *The Persian Presence in the Islamic World*, Cambridge: Cambridge University Press, 1998, pp. 237–49.
59. For the office of the Reis Efendi also known as Reis ul-Kuttab (chief of the secretaries), see, H.A.R. Gibb and Harold Bowen, *Islamic Society and the West: A Study of the Impact of the Western Civilization on Moslem Culture in the Near East Islamic Society in the Eighteenth Century*, vol. I, part I, London: Oxford University Press, 1950, pp. 123–4; 'Reform and the Conduct of Ottoman Diplomacy in the Reign of Selim III, 1789–1807', *Journal of the American Oriental Society*, vol. LXXXIII, 1963, pp. 296–7.
60. *Masir i-Talibi*, folio 203, Abu Talib described him as an important official, a minister just below the prime minister in rank and above all other

ministers. But in reality he was the grand vizier's general deputy in home and military affairs. For the position of the Kahya Bey in the Ottoman hierarchy see Gibb and Bowen, *Islamic Society and the West,* p. 120.

61. For the Ottoman practice of appointment of *mihmandar* and his duties see Thomas Naff, 'Reform and Conduct of Ottoman Diplomacy', pp. 306–7.
62. *Masir i-talibi,* folio 201.
63. Thomas Bruce (1766–1841), British diplomatist and art collector, famous for his acquisition of the Greek sculptures now known as the Elgin Marbles, deposited in the British Museum in 1816. He served as envoy extraordinary at Constantinople from 1799–1803. Leslie Stephen, Sidney Lee (eds.), *Dictionary of National Biography,* London: Smith Elder & Company, 1908, vol. III, pp. 130–1.
64. *Masir i-talibi,* folio 193.
65. Ibid.
66. For the position of dragoman see, Thomas Naff, 'Reform and Conduct of Ottoman Diplomacy,' pp. 299–301. Also see, G.R. Berridge, 'Dragoman and Oriental Secretaries in the British Embassy in Istanbul', in Nuri Yurdusev (ed.), *Ottoman Diplomacy Conventional or Unconventional?* Basingstoke, Hampshire: Palgrave Macmillan, 2004, pp. 151–66.
67. *Masir i-Talibi,* folio 206.
68. Cf. Annemarie Schimmel, 'The West-Eastern Divan: The Influence of Persian Poetry in East and West', in *The Persian Presence in the Islamic World,* pp. 161–4.
69. See his remarks *Masir i-talibi,* folio 205.
70. Ezel Kural Shaw, 'The Double Veil: Travelers' Views of the Ottoman Empire, Sixteenth through Eighteenth Centuries', cf. in Ezel Kural Shaw C.J. Heywood, *English and Continental Views of the Empire 1500–1800* (papers read at a Clark Library Seminar, 24 January 1970 with an Introduction by G.E. von Grunebaum), William Andrews Clark Memorial Library, Los Angeles, University of California, 1972, pp. 3–29.
71. Antonino Pagliaro and Alessandro Bausani, *Storia della letteratura persiana,* Milan, 1960, p. 752; quoted in Gerhard Doerfer, 'The Influence of Persian Language and Literature among the Turks'.
72. Mohamad Tavakoli-Targhi, *Refashioning Iran Orientalism, Occidentalism and Historiography,* St. Antony's Series, Hampshire and New York: Palgrave Macmillan, 2001, pp. 96–112.
73. For cultural atmosphere of the period, Zahir Uddin Malik, *The Reign of Muhammad Shah (1719-1748)*, Delhi: Icon Publication, 2006, pp. 313–69.

74. *Masir i-talibi,* folio 200.
75. For an imaginative treatment of the French and British imperialism cf. Maya Jasanoff, *Edge of Empire Conquest and Collecting on the Eastern Frontiers and the British Empire, 1750–1850,* New York: Alfred A. Knopf, 2005.
76. For a different perspective M.E. Yapp, *Strategies of British India Britain, Iran and Afghanistan 1798–1850,* Oxford: Clarendon Press, 1980. The author disputes the accepted view that the defence of British India was an important determinant of British foreign policy, arguing that strategic discussion served mainly to conceal fundamental differences between London and Calcutta.
77. Cf. J.K. Burkhardt, *Travels in Arabia,* London, 1829, p. 17; quoted in Hourani, 'The Changing Face of Fertile Crescent in the XVIIIth Century', p. 117.

Zoological Interest of the Mughals (With Special Reference to the Cheetah and the Rhinoceros)

M. EHSAN AKHTAR

Much has been written about the military campaigns and the social and economic condition under the Mughals but little attention has been paid to the portrayal of the Mughals' interest in flora and fauna. The Mughal's love of nature emerges best in their descriptions of various species of animals.[1] Contemporary chronicles and depiction in Mughal paintings reveal the curiosity of the Mughals in studying animal's behaviour and their habitat, which is worthy of scientific probe.

After the establishment of their rule the Mughal devoted their attention towards encountering the various zoological species from a close range in the form of hunting, preserving and experiment for freak species.[2]

The animals undertaken for study here, viz., the rhinoceros and cheetah have different characteristics, while the rhinoceros is herbivorus the cheetah is carnivorous. The rhinoceros (unicornis) was first noticed by the early medieval travellers and historians.[3]

Babur in his memoirs provides detailed description of the flora and fauna of India, which includes the larger mammals such as the elephant, rhinoceros, lion and tiger as well as the smallest of animal such as the monkey and the mouse.[4] He gives detailed physical descriptions of the rhinoceros with anatomical precision.[5] The rhinoceros, he writes is a huge animal, equal in size to perhaps three buffaloes. It has a single horn on its nose, more than 9 inches (*qarish*) long, one or two inches is not visible. A rhino's hide is very thick. An arrow shot from a stiff bow, drawn with full strength right up to the armpit, if it does pierce at all, might penetrate 4 inches into it.[6] But rhinos have a poor vision and are unable to detect a motionless person at a distance of more than 30 m (100 ft).[7]

The height of a male rhinoceros may reach over 6 ft (180 cm) at shoulder. But the average height is about 5.8 ft (170 cm), with a total length about 11 ft (335 cm).[8] The weight of a rhinoceros is around 2,000 kg (4,400 lb).[9] Rhinos are herbivorous animals,[10] dependent on plant foliage, and need a large daily intake of food. Though they have high digestive capacity, they prefer nutritious leafy material.[11] The rhinoceros inhabitat tall swampy grasslands.[12] Assam and Sindh have been the primitive home of the rhinoceros.[13]

Al-Beruni writes that the banks of river Ganga too have been the home of the rhinos.[14] Babur in his memoirs is more particular in identifying the region Chunnar as being the habitat of this species.[15] He further states that Hash Nagar jungle, Peshawar, river Sindh, the jungle of Bhira (Punjab) and banks of river Saru have been the habitat of rhinos.[16] Abul Fazl reports its presence in masses in the region of sarkar Sambhal.[17]

The geographical distribution of rhinos on the basis of the above-mentioned evidences shows that they are to be found from the north-western passes of India to eastwards along the Gangetic plain to Assam, through Bihar, Bengal and the Sundarbans. Their population can also be speculated on the basis of their large geographical distribution. At present the rhinoceros is restricted to a few reserves in Assam and West Bengal with a total number of about 1,500.[18]

The favourite sport of the Mughal emperors was hunting. Akbar and Jahangir took great interest in this game, but surprisingly, they have not recorded any rhinoceros hunt. It is quite otherwise with Babur.[19] He was keen to hunt rhinos. His interest in the rhinoceros clearly comes out from a passage in his memoirs.

> A person brought a news that there was a rhino, I ordered to form a ring around the jungle, made a noise and brought the rhino out, when it took its way across the plain; Humayun and those who came with him from that side, who had never seen one before, were much entertained, it was pursued for miles; many arrows were shot at it and it was brought down.[20]

Rhinoceros' hides and horns had been used to make military equipment. Abul Fazl informs us that shields from rhinoceros' skin were made, and as well finger-guards for bowstrings from the horns.[21]

The medicinal properties of the rhinoceros' horn is widely known. It is used as an aphrodisiac as well as for curing fever, headaches, hearts, and liver troubles in India and China and the Far East countries.[22]

The cheetah, is often confused with the leopard. But the Mughals were well aware of the difference between the two animals. The physical characteristics of the two species of animals have been shown with minute accuracy by Mughal painters.[23]

Akbar was very fond of hunting and took tamed cheetahs with him while hunting antelopes.[24]

His interest in cheetahs clearly comes out from a passage in Abul Fazl's *Akbarnama.* When Akbar was only 12 years old 'he conceived an inclination for hunting with the chita . . . . For Wali Beg the father of the Khan-i-jehan presented as *peshkash* a 'chita' which had come into his hands from the Afghans at the battle of Maciwara which was called Fatehbaz'.[25]

The physical characteristics of the cheetah is not mentioned in *Ain* and other chronicles, but the Mughal painters depicted a variety of animals with great anatomical accuracy. A fascinating study of cheetahs is ascribed to the famous painter Baswan of Akbar's time. The painting is titled 'A Family of Cheetahs in a Rocky Landscape'.[26] For its sheer beauty and accuracy the painting is remarkable. The female cheetah and its four cubs are drawn accurately, the scene in the wild is authentically depicted as if by a zoologist.

The cheetah (*Acinonya jubatus*) has certain characteristics which distinguish it from the rest of the cat family. It has semi-retractile claws, long legs, a round head and short ears. It is sandy yellow-brown with black spots. The spots are smaller and merge better with the ground colour. There are black stripes from the eyes to the mouth on both sides. It is also the only big cat which when in good mood purrs like the smaller species of this family.

The cheetah measures, head and body length, about 4.6 ft and tail length, 2.6 ft.[27] Its weight varies from 100 to 140 pounds.[28]

The cheetah prefers for its habitat grasslands and deserts, low rugged hills bordering on wastelands, and lands with tall grass, where it can hunt its prey. Abul Fazl writes that the cheetah selects three places. In one part of the country they hunt; they rest and sleep somewhere else; and choose some other place for amusing themselves. They mostly sleep on the top of hills. The shade of a tree is sufficient for the cheetah.[29]

The geographical distribution of the cheetah is evident from the different chronicles of the Mughal period. Irfan Habib in his *Atlas of the Mughal Empire* shows the various locations where cheetahs are to be found—in west Panjab in the Lakhi Forest on the northern banks of the Sutlej; and at Pattan, Bhatnair, Suman, Bhatinda, and Hissar where imperial hunting grounds were situated. The other areas where the cheetah was found is in Rajasthan in the scrublands in close proximity of the rocky regions of the deserts at Jodhpur, Merta, Nagpur, Jhunjunu and Amarsar. Cheetahs were also located in Gujarat, near Bhutadi and Nava Nagar (near Bagmati River), and within Madhya Pradesh in the Chambal ravines near Gwalior. They were also to be found in Uttar Pradesh at Bari (near Dholpur), Alapur, Samuli and Nurabad, Nibraro (near Fatehpur).[30]

The favourite sport of the Mughal emperors was hunting. Akbar took great interest in the trapping and training of cheetahs[31] and used them in his hunts. He employed novel methods to trap them which astonished even experienced hunters.[32]

The cheetah was trained by experts for hunting. A body of knowledge grew in the art of training and hunting with cheetah. No other beasts were used or trained for such work in pre-modern India.

Akbar took personal interest in the training of the cheetah.[33] Abul Fazl records that the duration of training of the cheetah is 3 to 12 months. Akbar could do it in just 18 days.[34] This is obviously a sign of Abul Fazl's flattery, as it normally took anything up to one year to train an animal.[35]

According to Abul Fazl, 'Formally a cheetah would not kill more than three deers at one and same chase, but now he will hunt as many as twelve'.[36] Abul Fazl records three methods of hunting by the cheetah.[37]

During Akbar's period cheetahs were classified into eight categories and food was allowed accordingly.[38] The first class cheetah received 5 *seers* (1 *seer* = 933.12 g) of meat everyday; likewise the second, $4^1/_2$ *seers*; third, 4 *seers*; fourth, $3^3/_4$ *seers*; and subsequently eighth, $2^3/_4$ *seers*. The meat was given in lumps; and on Sunday since no animals were slaughtered no meat was given; but double daily portion was given on Saturdays.[39]

The basics of classification has not been explained in the *Ain*. Abul Fazl further records; 'Formely every six months but now annually four *seers* of butter and $^1/_{10}$ of a *seer* of brimstone are given as ointment which prevents itch'.[40] Akbar appointed four persons to train and to look after each cheetah; later on the staff was reduced to three.[41] A similar distinction was made among the keepers of the cheetahs on different scales of salaries.[42]

The cheetah were organized in various groups. Ten of these formed a *misl* or *taraf* (set); they were also divided accordingly to their rank. The first set was called *khasa*; they were kept at the court, the other sets forming a total of 50 animals.

Akbar's interest in the cheetah cannot be doubted; he named all his favourite animals. Each *khasa* (royal) cheetah had a name. The names of two such animals, Madan Kali and Chitranjan are actually given. Two other special cheetahs were named Daulat Khan and Dilrang Khan.[43] Akbar's most favourite cheetah, named Samand Manik, was carried on a palanquin and proceeded with much pomp. Its attendants fully equipped, by its side; the *naqqara* (a large drum) was beaten in front. Sometimes he was carried by two men on horseback, the two ends of the pole of the palanquin resting on the necks of the horse.[44]

Other Mughal emperors did not appear to have been as Akbar was in naming as well as providing the special honour to their cheetahs. Jahangir tells: 'Raja Bir Singh Deo brought a Yuz-i Safid (white cheetah) to show me. I had never seen a white cheetah. Its spots, which are (usually) black, were of a blue colour and the whiteness of the body was inclined to the same colour.'[45]

This is the only recorded instance of a white cheetah from India. In fact, it is rather an accurate description of the animal and the uniqueness of it was not lost on Jehangir. He further records a rare event in his *Tuzuk-i-Jahangiri:*

It is an established fact that cheetahs in unaccustomed places do not pair off with a female, for my revered father once collected thousand cheetahs.[46] He was very desirous that he should pair but this no way came off. He had many times coupled male and female together in the gardens, but there too it did not come off. At this time a male cheetah, having slipped its collar, went to a female and paired with it and after $2^1/_2$ months three young ones were born and grew up.[47]

This was indeed a rare event. It is the only recorded instance of cheetah's breeding in captivity till 1956.[48]

The cheetah, a graceful swift and unique member of the cat family, survived so long in spite of its being taken into captivity in such large numbers, where it failed to breed and keep up its population.

In various localities of the Mughal empire cheetahs for imperial sports were caught to maintain a regular supply to the imperial court. This tradition was continued even after the decline of the Mughal empire. The growth of human population during the Mughal period is thus estimated by Irfan Habib: 'In 1600 the human population in the subcontinent was a little under 150 million, which grew to 200 million by 1800 achieving an increase of about 33 per cent in 200 hundred years'.[49]

Such growth of population implies the immense pressure on grassland and shrub lands (which is easy to convert into use for cultivation). But this was the natural habitat of cheetahs. When the land was converted for cultivation this greatly restricted the natural habitat of this species. This was probably the main cause for the extinction cheetahs.[50] The heavy drain to the Mughal court may have been a contributory factor, but the cheetah was prolific in breeding in its natural habitat.

Today, with the total disappearance of the cheetah in the wild, its failure to breed in captivity, the Indian cheetah has probably disappeared from the zoos also. What we see there now is his African cousin.

The rhinoceros is also on the verge of extinction. It suffered a great reduction in number and considerable contraction of their range in the nineteenth and twentieth century, not because of hunting and poaching. The reason behind the decline of its population is most probably the rapid of growth of human population that led to the clearing of the forest land for cultivation. This restricted the habitats of wild animals, including the rhinoceros.

NOTES

1. *Baburnama,* vol. II, tr A.N. Beveridge, rpt., Delhi, 1979, pp. 489–90; Abul Fazl, *Ain-i Akbari,* vol. I, tr. Blochmann, Delhi, 1977, pp. 296–7.
2. Abul Fazl, *Akbarnama,* vol. III, tr. Beveridge, Delhi, 1972, p. 408 *Tuzuk-i-Jahangiri,* tr. Alexander Rogers, ed. Henry Beveridge, Delhi, rpt., 1994, vol. I, p. 204, vol. II, pp. 16–17.
3. *Hudud-ul-Alam,* tr. V. Monorsky, London, 1937, p. 86; *Al-Biruni's India,* tr. Edward C. Sachau, vol. I, rpt., Delhi, 1983, p. 203; Ibn Battuta; *Travel in Asia and Africa,* tr. H.A.R. Gibbs, vol. II, Delhi, 1986, p. 185.
4. *Baburnama,* tr. A.N. Beveridge, rpt., Delhi, 1979, vol. II, pp. 408, 503.
5. Ibid., pp. 489–90.
6. Ibid. Al-Biruni also give physical feature of the rhinoceros. It (*Genda*) is of the build of a buffalo, has a black scaly skin and dewlaps hanging down under the chin. It has 3 yellow hooves on each foot, the biggest one forward, the other on both sides. The tail is not long, the eyes lie low, further down the cheek, on the top of the nose there is a single horn, which is bent upwards. *Al-Biruni's India,* p. 203.
7. David MacDonald (ed.), *The Encyclopedia of Mammals,* Oxford, 1984, vol. II, p. 490.
8. S.H. Prate, *The Book of Indian Animals,* 3rd edn., Bombay, 1998, p. 229.
9. B. Seshadri, *India's Wildlife and Wildlife Reserves,* Delhi, 1986, p. 42.
10. *Baburnama,* vol. II, p. 490.
11. Ibid., p. 491.
12. *The Encyclopedia of Mammals,* vol. II, p. 495. Francis Robinson (ed.), *The Cambridge Encyclopedia of India, Pakistan, Bangladesh, Sri Lanka,* Cambridge, 1989, p. 23.
13. Anonymous, *Hudud al-Alam,* Eng. tr. V. Minorsky, *The Regions of the World Persian Grography* (*372* A.H.*–982* A.H.), London, 1937, p. 86.
14. *Al-Biruni's India,* p. 86.
15. *Baburnama,* p. 393.
16. Ibid., p. 490.
17. *Ain-i-Akbari,* vol. II, tr. Col. H.S. Jarrett, 3rd edn, Calcutta, 1978, p. 285. Irfan Habib, *An Atlas of the Mughal Empire,* Delhi, 1980, sheet 8B.
18. *The Encyclopedia of Mammals,* p. 495. *The Cambridge Encyclopedia of India, Pakistan, Bangladesh, Sri Lanka,* p. 23.
19. *Baburnama,* vol. II, pp. 378, 657.
20. Ibid., p. 451
21. *Ain-i Akbari,* vol. II, p. 285. Babur records in his memoirs that 'one large horn was made a drinking-vessel and a dice-box.'

22. *The Encyclopedia of Mammals,* p. 494.
23. 'The Lion Killing the Bull' by Nanda Gwaliori from *Anwar-i-Suhaili,* Mughal Painting, 1596–7 and 'The Lion Holding Court' by Misikin from *Anwar-i-Suhaili,* Mughal Painting, 1596–7.
24. *Akbarnama,* vol. I, p. 629.
25. Ibid.
26. *Anwar-i-Suhaili,* Mughal painting.
27. William T. Couch (ed.), *Collier's Encyclopedia,* New York, 1956, vol. V, pp. 60–1.
28. R. Spies Joseph, *Big Cats and Other Animals, their Beauty, Dignity and Survival,* New York.
29. *Ain-i-Akbari,* vol. I, p. 296.
30. *Atlas of the Mughal Empire,* sheet 4B, 6B, 7B, 8B; Shireen Moosvi, 'Man and Nature in Mughal Era' (Thematic Symposium: Man and Environment in Indian History), Indian History Congress (Symposia Papers: 5), 54th Session, Mysore, 1993, pp. 5–6; *Ain-i Akbari,* vol. I, p. 297.
31. Abul Fazl records in the *Akbarnama* that Akbar was specially inclined to the hunting of cheetah and he had traps made for catching them. When news was brought of a cheetah 'he, having fallen into a trap, immediately mounted a swift horse and went off to the spot. By proper methods the 'cheetah' was brought out from the hole and made over to the skillful in the business' *Akbarnama,* vol. II, pp. 508–9.
32. The *Ain-i-Akbari* gives the following details: 'Earlier, hunters used to make deep holes and cover them with grass pits called odi. The cheetahs on coming on them fell down to the bottom; but they often broke their feet or legs, or managed by jumping to get out again. Nor could you catch more than one in each pit. His Majesty made a pit only two or three *gaz* deep, and constructed a peculier trapdoor which closes when the cheetah falls into the hole. The animal is thus never hurt. Sometimes more than one go into the trap on one occasion no less than 7 cheetahs were caught.' *Ain-i-Akbari,* pp. 296–7.
33. *Ain-i-Akbari,* vol. I, p. 297.
34. Ibid., vol. I, p. 297.
35. Abul Fazl writes, 'Once a cheetah had been caught and without previous training on a mere hint by Akbar, it brought in that prey like trained cheetah' or again, 'A cheetah once followed the imperial suite without collar and chains like a sensible human being' (*Ain-i-Akbari,* vol. I, p. 297).
36. *Ain-i-Akbari,* vol. I, p. 293.
37. (a) Uparghati: The hunters let off the cheetah to the right from the place where the deer was seen.

    (b) Righni: The cheetah lies concealed, and is shown the deer from a distance. The collar is taken off; the cheetah with a perfect skill catches the deer.

(c) Muhari: The cheetah is put in an ambush down wind. The cart is taken away in the opposite direction. This confuses the deer and to enable the cheetah to make his way close to the antelope and catch it (*Ain-i-Akbari,* vol. I, p. 299).

38. Ibid., vol. I, p. 297.
39. Ibid., p. 298.
40. Ibid.
41. Ibid. There were 200 keepers in-charge of the Khasa cheetah, ibid., p. 297.
42. Ibid., p. 298. The wage of keepers vary from Rs. 30 to Rs. 5 per month.
43. When Akbar was on an expedition to Bihar in 1574, one of the boats which contained the cheetah Daulat Khan and Dilrang Khan was drowned (*Akbarnama,* vol. III, p. 132).
44. *Ain-i Akbari,* vol. I, pp. 298–9.
45. *Tuzuk-i-Jahangiri,* vol. I, p. 140.
46. *Iqbalnama-i-Jahangiri,* gives a different figure. 'He (Akbar) had about 9,000 cheetah collected in his reign' (*Ain-i-Akbari,* p. 298, fn. 4).
47. *Tuzuk-i-Jahangiri,* vol. I, p. 240.
48. The African cheetahs were bred in Philadelphia zoo in 1956. From Divya Bhanu Singh, *The End of a Trail,* Delhi, 1995, p. 41. The gestation period recorded in *Tuzuk-i-Jahangiri* is over 75 days. In the twelve instance of cheetahs from Africa bred between 1966 and 1968, the period of gestation varied between 86 and 95 days. Twenty-six instances of births in captivity were recorded of cheetahs from Africa between 1956 and 1991; of these in only 14 cases a single cub was born; in six cases the litter was of three cubs each. Eaton Randall (1994) quoted in Divya Bhanu Singh, *The End of the Trail,* Delhi, 1995, p. 41.
49. T. Raychaudhuri and Irfan Habib (eds), *Cambridge Economic History of India,* Cambridge, 1982, vol. I, p. 167.
50. Shireen Moosvi, op. cit., p. 28.

Ethnic Character of the Army during the Delhi Sultanate (Thirteenth-Fourteenth Centuries)

ALI ATHAR

Modern historians have made valuable contributions to the study of the ethnicity of the ruling class during the Delhi sultanate[1] and suggested proportional ethnic followings in the army as well. The study of the composition of soldiers of the sultanate's army reveals quite interestingly, the contrary of the above asumptions. The motives of Indian campaigns, the consolidation of the empire and checking of the Mongol invasions brought in changes in the battle strategies, thereby, leading to recruitment of requisite soldiers which served the purpose.[2]

An attempt is made in this paper to identify chronologically the various ethnic groups who contributed towards the establishment, consolidation, and expansion of the Delhi sultanate.

The sultans of Delhi had recruited soldiers in their army who belonged to different ethnic groups and communities. The early campaigns of Sultan Muizzuddin bin Sam was viewed as an invasion of Central Asian forces comprising largely of Turks. *Minhaj-i Siraj* informs us of the various tribes of Central Asia who formed the backbone of the sultan's army, namely Khitai,[3] Qarakhita,[4] Qipchaq,[5] Gariji[6] and Ilbari.[7] Since the Indian terrain facilitated horsemen, Sultan Muizzuddin employed 10,000 Afghan cavalrymen in his last campaign of India.[8] With the establishment of the sultanate, *Fakhir-i Mudabbir* informs us that Sultan Qutab-ud-Din Aibak employed Hindu soldiers too in his army.[9] The political scenario in the early thirteenth-century northern India witnessed Sultan Iltutmish confronting Jalaluddin Mangbarni, pursued by Chenghis Khan. His diplomatic overtures towards the Mongol Chief saved India from the deadly Chenghis Khan, but not from constant immigrants. Iltutmish employed contingents of Afghan soldiers belonging to the fugitive Jalal-uddin Mangbarni and at the same time Turkish refugees who had come to India escaping the onslaught of the Mongols.[10] The non-Turks too were the new entrants in the sultanate's army and were called Tajiks. Initially they were a microscopic section of the army, but later they increased in number and consolidated their positions in the higher echelons of the sultanate's administration.[11]

The substantial increase in the number of Tajiks bore the wrath of the Turks who massacred many of them including notables like Bahauddin Hasan Ashari, and Karimuddin.

Zahid, Ziya-ul-Mulk son of Nizamuddin Junaidi, Nizam-ud-Din Sharqani, Khwaja Rashid-ud-Din Malikani and Amir Fakhr-ud-Din.[12] The Turks having the notion of belonging to the ruling class gave no opportunity to others to predominate the sultanate's army. Razia, however, recruited the Khokars, Jats and the Rajputs to attack Delhi along with the Altunias in 1240.[13]

During the reign of Sultan Balban, we do not have any reference to the recruitment of Hindus.[14] He, however, placed complete faith on the Afghans during his campaigns in the Kohpaya region against robbers who had 'plundered the Musalmans and desolated the village of Haryana, the Siwaliks and Bayana'.[15] They served him with ruthless courage and ravaged the plunderers. Minhaj mentions that they were 3,000 in number.[16] Balban garrisoned all the important forts of Gopalgir, Kampil, Patiali, Bhojpur and Jalali with Afghan soldiers and officers.[17] Foreigners were given due position by Balban. Barani writes that Balban employed Sistani soldiers as his bodyguards; whenever he went out the Sistani soldiers accompanied him with unsheathed swords. To these soldiers, he paid 67000 *jitals* a year.[18]

The Mongols under the leadership of Ulughu Khan came to India during the reign of Sultan Jalal-ud-Din Firoz Khalji. They were taken into service and were given high ranks.[19] Recruitment of the Mongols was continued by Sultan Ala-ud-Din Khalji. During the Gujarat campaign of 1299, the Mongol officers Muhammad Shah, Kabhru, Yalhaq and Burraq along with 2,000 to 3,000 horsemen rebelled against Ulughu Khan on account of inhuman tortures inflicted upon the soldiers to exact the plunder. The Mongols killed Malik Aziz-ud-Din, a brother of Nusrat Khan and attacked Ulughu Khan's camp. This was a very serious mutiny and Ala-ud-Din Khalji retaliated by inflicting corporal punishment on the families of the rebels.[20] Similarly, Akat Khan who attempted to kill Ala-ud-Din Khalji had Mongol followers to carry out his plan.[21]

Ala-ud-Din Khalji having lost faith in the foreigners provided opportunities for the Indians to seek service in the army. Recruitment of soldiers were open to all and whosoever passed the test of archery and horsemanship conducted by the Ariz, were enrolled in the army.[22] The number of foreigners declined during his period. The power of kingship when it passed into the hands of Khusrau Khan, the Muslims in general were antagonized by his deeds and it was left to Ghiyas-ud-Din Tughlaq to consolidate the disintegrating Sultanate.

Sultan Ghiyas-ud-Din Tughlaq when he attacked Delhi, his army was of a heterogeneous ethnic composition. There were Ghuzz, Turks, Mongols, Greeks, Russians, Persians, Tajiks and Hindu soldiers in the army.[23] The Hindus were in considerable number in the Delhi army under Nasir-ud-Din Khusrau.[24] The *Tughlaq Namah* reveals the composition of the Delhi army thus:

> It was half Muslim and half Hindu, mixed together like black and white clouds. The Musalmans in the service of the Hindus were as friendly to them as their own shadow; they were as closely bound to the Hindu as the charity of the Musalmans is bound up with their sins. The army was so full of Hindus and Musalmans that both Hindus and Musalmans were surprised.[25]

Sultan Muhammad bin Tughlaq in his early reign gave preference to the foreigners. He had seen how his predecessors failed by having a coterie of one racial group or by giving admission to the Indians. He, therefore, recruited foreigners on a large scale. Ibn Batuta gives detailed accounts of the sultan's benevolence towards them.[26] His army therefore, consisted of Turks, Khitais, Persians and Indians.[27] For the Khorasan expedition, Sultan Muhammad bin Tughlaq recruited 370,000 soldiers within one year.[28] The incentives offered were very tempting. Hence, soldiers from different parts of the country and outside joined the army. Barani informs us that Amir Nauroz (son-in-law of Tarmashirin) had come with his followers to enroll in the Delhi army.[29] Other foreigners like Ismail Afghan, Gul Afghan, Shahu Afghan and Halajun also came to India during this period.[30] While the Afghans consolidated their position in India, the other foreigners were not keen to stay. Muhammad bin Tughlaq therefore introduced the common people into administration and this plebianization led Barani to lament that, 'The Sultan talked as if he hated low-born people more than he hated idols. Nevertheless, I have seen him promoting the low-born son of a musician to such an extent that he rose higher in status than many maliks, for Gujarat, Multan and Badaun were put in his charge.'[31] Barani's statement is testified by Ibn Batuta who categorically says that Hindus were given high posts and were extensively recruited in the army. Ratan, for example, was appointed as the governor of Sind with the title of 'Azim us Sind', and was permitted to keep a drum and flag, which was an honour conferred upon great *amirs* only.[32]

Within this heterogeneous army, the Afghans were a dominant group. They had steadily rose in number from the time of the establishment of the sultanate. They were now a formidable force and Shahu Afghan even went to the extent of claiming kingship in AD 1344 after killing Behzad, the governor of Multan.[33] The territories of Cambay, Broach, Gujarat and Nahrwala became the home of Afghans and Barani sarcastically refers to the region as 'Afghanistan'.[34] Malik Khattab, an Afghan, showed defiance to the sultanate's authority and captured the fort of Rapri,[35] though he was later pardoned and restored to his original position,[36] Qazi Jalal with his Afghan followers put his claim to kingship over the territories of Gujarat,[37] but was defeated by Sultan Muhammad bin Tughlaq himself.[38] The Afghan rebellion or the rebellion of the *Amiran-i Sadah*[39] spread to Daulatabad were Malik Makh Afghan was proclaimed the king. This revolt was again crushed by the Imperial forces[40] but it could not stop the emergence of the independent Afghan kingdom or the Bahmani kingdom.

Sultan Firoz Shah Tughlaq who is considered incapable in

matters of military administration,[41] gave preference to Indians. It is for the first time in the history of the Delhi sultanate that we come across an Indian wazir, Khan-i Jahan. Firoz Shah Tughlaq also took interest in purchasing foreign slaves and the favourite amongst them were those who hailed from Hazara. They always accompanied the Sultan, whenever he went out. Afif writes that these thousand upon thousands slaves from Hazara were mounted on Arab and Turki-horses, bearing standards and axes.[42] Such a scene of royal procession accompanied by numerous foreign slaves was a custom adopted earlier by Muhammad bin Tughlaq who had 'two lakh slaves' writes al-Qalqashandi who wear weapons, accompanying him always and fight on foot in front of him.[43]

The sultan of Delhi in general (due to political exigencies) initially preferred soldiers from Central Asia. Being good mounted archers they helped in the expansion of the sultanate. With complete consolidation under Balban and later under the Khaljis, foreigners from other countries too were recruited in the army. Many came here as refugees, many with the sole aim of employment.[44] If they possessed the requisite skill of a soldier they were recruited. The broad-base in administration and democratization of military service by the Khaljis and the Tughlaqs paved way for the Indians and the common man to seek employment in the Delhi army. Service was open in the army to 'any one who had the strength to bear the strain of war'.[45]

The Central Asian politics forced many immigrants like the Afghan and Mongols to settle in India. The Afghans who swelled in course of the sultanate's period carved out a separate kingdom for themselves in the south. Later they were masters of north India under the Lodis and the Surs.

NOTES

1. S.B.P. Nigam, *Nobility under the Sultans of Delhi, AD 1206–1398*, Delhi: Munshiram Manoharlal, 1968; David Avlon, *Aspects of Mamluk Phenomenon*, vol. I: *The Importance of the Mamluk Institution*, Der Islam, vol. 53, 1976, pp. 196–225; Irfan Habib, *Formation of the Sultanate Ruling Class of the Thirteenth Century: Medieval India I: Researches in History of India 1200-1750*, Delhi: Oxford University Press, 1992, pp. 1–22; Andre

Wink, *Al-Hind, The Making of the Indo-Islamic World,* vol. II: *The Slave Kings and Islamic Conquests 11th–13th Centuries,* Oxford: Oxford University Press, 1999. For Attributes and Ethnicity of the Turks, see pp. 77–8 and their Intrusions in India, see pp. 88–9; Peter Jackson, *The Delhi Sultanate: A Political and Military History,* Cambridge: Cambridge University Press, 1999, pp. 11–13. For immigration of nobility see pp. 41–3, 66–85; J. Ross Sweeney, 'Spurred on by the Fear of Death: Refugees and Displaced Population during the Mongol Invasions of Hungary', in M. Gervers and W. Schlepp (eds.), *Nomadic Diplomacy, Destruction and Religions from the Pacific to the Adriatic,* Toronto: Blackwell, 1994, p. 35; Jos Gommans, *Mughal Welfare, Indian Frontiers and High Roads to Empire, 1500–1700,* London: Routledge, 2002, pp. 67–81.

2. Ali Athar, 'The Ministry of War in the Delhi Sultanate', *Journal of Asiatic Society,* vol. XXVIII, no. 3, Calcutta, 1995; 'The Invisibility in Disuse, The Case of Cavalry in the Army of the Delhi Sultans 13–14th Century', paper presented at the Indian History Congress, Calcutta, 2001. Aligarh papers on History, Centre of Advanced Study, Department of History, Aligarh Muslim University, Aligarh.
3. N. Less (ed.), *Minaj-us Siraj-Tabaqat-i Nasiri,* Calcutta: Bib. Indica, 1846, p. 238.
4. Ibid., pp. 242–9, 252.
5. Ibid., pp. 247, 256, 258, 262.
6. Ibid., p. 259.
7. Ibid., pp. 276–89.
8. *Makhzan-i Afghani,* Eng. tr. N.B. Roy, *Niamatullah History of the Afghans,* Shantiniketan: Shantiniketan Press, 1958, p. 11.
9. Fakhr-i Mudabbir, *Tarikh-i Fakhruddin Mubarakh Shah,* ed. Dennison Ross, London, 1927, p. 33.
10. *Tabaqat-i Nasiri,* p. 166. Displacement of vast number of people was the product of the Mongol expansion. J. Ross Sweeney, p. 35. Peter Jackson, 'The Mamluk Institution of Early Muslim India', *Journal of Asiatic Society,* 1990, pp. 340–58. He remarks that due to the Mongol invasions India had become a 'veritable reservoir of unattached warriors and officials in North Western India in the 1220s'. *The Delhi Sultanate: A Political and Military History,* p. 39.

    Wahid Mirza is of the opinion that the early immigrant refugees were Lachin Hazaras of Turkish origin, who moved into India because of the Mongol invasion. *Life and Works of Amir Khusro,* Delhi: Idarah-i-Adabiyat-i-Delhi, rpt., 1974, pp. 6, 8, 12.

    Also see, I.H. Siddiqui, 'The Afghan and Their Emergence in India as Ruling Elite During the Delhi Sultanate', *Central Asiatic Journal* 26, nos. 3-4, 1982 and *Perso-Arabic Sources of Information on Life and Tradition in the Sultanate of Delhi,* Delhi: Munshiram Manoharlal, 1992. Olaf Carroe, *The Pathans,* London: Macmillan, 1958, p. 135.

11. Zia-ud-Din Barani, *Tarikh-i-Firoz Shahi,* ed. Sir Syed Ahmad Khan, Calcutta: Bib. Indica, 1862, p. 27.
12. *Tabaqat-i-Nasiri,* p. 183.
13. M. Usha (ed.), *Isami-Futuh-us Salatin,* Madras, 1948, p. 139.
14. Amir Khusro however informs us that Muiz-uddin Kaiqubad had Hindu soldiers in his army. Maulvi Md. Ismail, ed., *Qiran-us Sadain,* Aligarh: Aligarh Muslim University Press, 1918, p. 36.
15. *Tabaqat-i Nasiri,* p. 315.
16. Ibid.
17. *Tarikh-i Firoz Shahi,* pp. 57–8.
18. Ibid., p. 30.
19. Ibid., p. 219 early presents of the Mongols as nobles, see p. 133; their political role, pp. 133–4, 171, 173, 181–4; *Isami Futuh-us-Salatin,* pp. 181–8. Their dominance in the sultanate's administration is echoed by Ferishta, who says that the Mongols during the reign of Muiz-uddin Kaiqubad constituted one-fifth in the services. *Tarikh-i Ferishta,* Lucknow: Newal Kishore Press, 1864, p. 85.
20. Ibid., p. 253; *Isami-Futuh-us-Salatin,* pp. 244–5.
21. Ibid., pp. 273–4; for Sultan Alauddin Khalji's complete volte face attitude towards the Mongols see *Isami Futuh-us-Salatin,* pp. 269–97, 298–9. Barani considers them treacherous people who were disloyal to the state and always attempted to overthrow the administration. *Tarikh-i Firoj Shahi,* p. 133. Muiz-uddin Kaiqubad got rid of them by killing them in large number. *Tarikh-i Ferishta,* p. 85. Yahya bin Ahmad bin Abdullah as Sirhindi, *Tarikh-i Mubarakshah,* ed. Hidayat Husain, Calcutta: Bib. Indica, 1931, pp. 53–4.
22. Ibid., p. 319 Afif states that Alauddin Khalji possessed 50,000 slaves consisting mostly of Indians. *Tarikh-i Firoz Shahi,* ed. Maulvi Wilayat Husain, Calcutta: Bib. Indica, 1890, p. 72. For recruitment of soldiers in the Sultanates army, see 'The Ministry of War in the Delhi Sultanate', *Journal of Asiatic Society,* Calcutta, vol. XXXVII, no. 3, 1995; I.H. Siddiqui, 'The Nobility under the Khalji Sultans', *Islamic Culture,* vol. 37, 1963, Peter Jackson, *The Delhi Sultanate,* pp. 171–7.
23. Amir Khusro, *Tughlaq Namah,* ed. Sayyid Hashimi Faridabadi, Aurangabad: Matba-i-Urdu, 1933, p. 84. The presence of such heterogeneous groups can also be testified by availability and use of various weapons of war. Different types of bows used were, viz., *chachi, khwarizami, parwanchi, ghaznichi, lahori, hindivi, kohi,* etc. Fakhr-i Mudabbir—*Adab-ul Harb Wa-Shujaah,* ed. A.S. Khwansari, Teheran, 1346 *shamsi,* p. 242. Likewise swords of various ethnic identities like *chini, rusi, khizri, kashmiri* and *hindi* also were in possession of such ethnic groups serving the Sultanate's army. *Adab-ul Harb,* p. 257. For details on weapons see, Ali Athar, 'Military Technology of the Delhi Sultanate (Thirteenth–Fourteenth Centuries)', *Proceedings of Indian History Congress,* Gorakhpur, 1990, pp. 166–81.

24. Ibid., pp. 128–31.
25. Ibid., pp. 112–19.
26. Ibn Battuta, *Rehla,* Eng. tr. A.M. Husain, Baroda: Oriental Institute, 1976, pp. 56, 67–78.
27. Al Umari, *Masalik-ul-Absar,* Eng. tr. I.H. Siddiqui and Q.M. Ahmad, Aligarh: Siddiqui Publishing House, 1971, p. 37.
28. *Tarikh-i-Firoz Shahi,* p. 477.
29. Ibid., p. 533.
30. Ibid., p. 505.
31. Ibid.
32. *Rehla,* Eng. tr., p. 8.
33. *Tarikh-i Firoz Shahi,* p. 482; *Rehla,* p. 113; I.H. Siddiqui, 'The Afghans and their Emergency in India as Ruling Elite during the Delhi Sultanate', *Center of Asiatic Journal,* Wiesbaden, vol. 26, nos. 3–4, 1982, pp. 144–8.
34. Ibid., pp. 482–3, *Rehla,* Eng. tr., p. 113.
35. *Rehla,* Eng. tr., p. 162.
36. Afif, op. cit., p. 50.
37. *Rehla,* Eng. tr., p. 114; *Tarikh-i Firoz Shahi,* p. 507.
38. Ibid., pp. 92, 114–15.
39. *Tarikh-i Firoz Shahi,* pp. 503–7.
40. Ibid., pp. 513–14.
41. Banerjee, J.M., *History of Firoz Shah Tughlaq,* Delhi: Munshiram Manoharlal, 1967, pp. 28–33; Reyaz-ul Islam, *Encyclopedia of Islam,* vol. II, p. 924.
42. Afif, p. 271.
43. Al Qalaqashandi, *Subh al-Asha,* Eng. tr. Otto Spies, S. Moin-ul-Haq, Aligarh: Aligarh Muslim University, n.d., p. 67.
44. *Tarikh-i Firoz Shahi,* pp. 27–8, Irfan Habib, *Formation of the Sultanate Ruling Class of the 13th Century,* pp. 15–16; Peter Jackson, *The Delhi Sultanate,* p. 66; J. Ross Sweeney, 'Spurred on by the Fear of Death: Refugees and Displaced Population during the Mongol Invasions of Hungary', in M. Gervers and W. Schlepp (eds), *Nomadic Diplomacy, Destruction and Religion from the Pacific to the Adriatic,* Toronto: Blackwell, 1994, p. 35; Jos Gommans observes that 'military labour' market consisted of a 'sheer mass of warriors from the highly professional war lord or Jamdar to the part-time armed peasant looking for mere subsistence'. *Mughal Warfare,* pp. 67–8. He further notices that 'military marketing' was also a factor for enticing these 'military labour' to enroll in the army. Ibid., pp. 88–9. Sultan Mohammad bin Tughlaq for his Khorasan project had offered lucrative stipends and incentives to those who were willing to join in this enterprise. *Tarikh-i-Firoz Shahi,* p. 477.
45. M. Habib and K.A. Nizami, *Comprehensive History of India,* vol. V, Delhi: People Publishing House, 1982, p. 188.

Military Strategy of the Rajputs during the Early Medieval Period

RASHMI UPADHYAYA

Eighth century AD is represented by a particular landmark in Indian history. One of the outstanding phenomena of this period is the rise of the Rajputs in northern India with highly exalted notions of Kshatriyahood and chivalry. The political organization of these Rajputs was strictly governed by the monarchies which were carved out independently by each clan under the fluid political situation marked by the existence of political chaos and personal disintegrity, which led to the occurrence of fratricidal wars among them. Feeling an outward danger of neighbouring invasions, they needed to safeguard their newly established clannish monarchies with an efficient and organized military system. With the employment of their huge armed forces they tried to retrieve in every circumstance by opposing tooth and nail the advance of Arabs and Turks, despite the occasional struggle among themselves for power. Their magnanimous forts and strongholds, being the great centre of military activity, proved as a bulwark against such invasions.

It has been conventionally remarked that war was a passion with the Rajputs. But as these passionate wars were the result of an organized effort, the stratagem cannot be ignored as their essential feature. Their strategy emphatically formed one of the important subjects of the contemporary Indian (Sanskrit) sources, though; they speak of it in a retrospective manner. The eye-witness narrations of the Muslim historians, even if, sometimes, safe-guarding their patrons and race, also provide some clues relating to it. Thus, a combined explanation of both indigenous and foreign (Persian) accounts will expectedly reveal a much transparent illustration of various aspects of the military strategy under the Rajputs, such as the modes and tactics to deal with the enemy's forces, creating harm to their troops with appliance of some unlawful apprehensions, arrangement of troops in a wise manner on the battlefield and various other manoeuvrable devices, practised for winning over the enemy in course of a war.

The idea of strategic wars did not evolve out at once. It may exactly be traced back to the period of the Mahabharata war.[1] An astute politician like Kautilya could assess the significance of a strategic device, while passing the eloquent statement that 'an arrow discharged by an archer may kill one person or may not kill (even one) but the intellect operated by a wise man could kill even children in the womb'.[2] He advises with great force to adopt strategical devices against the enemy during the course of war. Focusing on the strategic means, he advises the king

> to strike terror in the enemy with machines, by the employment of occult practices, through assassins, slaying those engaged in something else, by magical arts, by (a show of) association with divinities, through carts, by frightening with elephants, by rousing the treasonable, through herds of cattle, by setting fire to camps, by attacks on tips and in the rear, by creating dissensions through agents appearing as messengers (saying), 'your fort has been burnt down or captured, a revolt by a member of your family has broken out; or; your enemy or a forest chieftain has risen (against you).[3]

Kamandaka, a political writer of eighth century, was again a great believer of trickery in war. He laid down destruction of the enemy even by unfair and immoral means and instructs the king to adopt *mantra-yuddha* (secret war), avoiding open warfare and to conduct nocturnal raids against the enemy, as it will require limited efforts for success.[4] Somdeva Suri (tenth century), the author of *Nitivakyamrita,* believes in winning over the relatives of enemy for vanquishing him as the greatest secret formula.[5] These checkmated relatives should also be inspired to rebel against their king, in his view.[6] *Tilakamanjari* of Dhanpala (tenth century) also refers to *sauptika-yuddha* (secret war).[7] The *Agni Purana* lays down that a king should always endeavour to achieve success through all possible means, i.e. *sama* (use of friendly measures), *danam* (payment of money), *bheda* (creating dissensions among the allies of an adversary), *danda* (war), *maya* (stratagem or treachery), *upeksha* (indifference) and *indrajalam* (deceit).[8] *Vishnudharmottara Purana,* too, provides instructions for waging a treacherous battle to punish the sinful.[9] In the view of Shukra, stratagem is that tool by which even a strong enemy could easily be subdued.[10] In his words, 'a king, whose arrangements are not certain, looking out for the opportune time, should practise duplicity like the concealed eye of a crow, he should pretend one thing and seize another'.[11] Like Kamandaka, he also tries to animate the king to distract the enemy's ministers, generals, subjects and women from his side by sowing seeds of contrivance among them.[12] A king, according to him, should aim for victory by means of creating dissensions in enemy ranks through expensive gifts and deceiving the rest of the army at night, while they were asleep and tired by watches.[13]

However, almost, all these authorities besides referring about such tactics of *kuta-yuddha* did not forget to state a few words on the patrimonial wars of India (*dharma-yuddha*) as described earlier in the *Mahabharata.*[14] But it must be remembered that these and similar other references are just quoted by them from the earlier texts in the context of *dharma-yuddha*, which was practically never followed by the Indian kings.

Taking such references literally, scholars generally remark[15] that the Indian kings including the Rajputs of our age staunchly believed in righteous wars instead of strategical devices, which led to their ultimate defeat against the Arab and Turkish adversaries.

Again, in an age of internecine wars, imbued with personal hatred and jealousy among the Indian kings, it was not possible to follow the age-old maxim of *dharma-yuddha.* There is no dearth of instances in historical sources when treachery was used in wars. It is, for example, well known that Prithviraj III led a night attack on Dharavarsha Paramara of Abu, the description of which is found in *Parthaparakramavyayoga* of Dharavarsha's younger brother Prahladana.[16] Jayasimha Siddharaja, being unsuccessful after the continuous fight of twelve years against the Paramara kings, Yashovarman and Naravarman ultimately resorted to treachery and won the victory by breaking the southern gateway of Dhara city, which was the weakest point, avoiding an open warfare.[17] *Nitivakyamrita* of Somdeva Suri, too, refers to one Bhadra, who captured the city of Kanchi with the help of warriors holding swords in the guise of hunters.[18] It is further evident that Narasimha Chalukya, the commander of Rashtrakuta king, Indra III, in course of his battle against the Pratihara king, Mahipala secured victory by capturing his champion elephants, which marched in front and putting to flight the rest of the troops.[19]

In some rare cases, they also tried to play treacherous games with the Muslims. Ferishta accounts that when Mahmud Ghazni set out on an expedition in order to conquer the fort of Kalanjar, which was under the control of the Chandella king, Vidyadhara, the latter 'in order to put the bravery of the Sultan's troops to test, intoxicated the elephants with drugs, and let them loose into the camp'.[20] It seems quite appropriate to assume that what Ferishta had called the object of Vidyadhara, 'to test the bravery of the Sultan's troops' was certainly a treachery planned by him to create confusion in the enemy's camp, the failure of which as proved by the same account is another matter. Gardizi points out to the indecisiveness of Mahmud's battle with Vidyadhara on account of the latter's retreat under cover of night taking away the horses and elephants.[21] Mahmud, thereafter gave up all idea of further advance into Chandella territory and promptly returned back to Ghaznin.[22] Treachery was also not unknown throughout ancient India prior to our age. Such events are well known to us.[23]

Coming to the arrangement of troops on the battlefield, it may rightly be asserted that the old ideology of *vyuha* persisted as a tradition but certainly was not followed in practice. Though their various formations are mentioned by almost all the writers dealing with the political history of the period,[24] the practical existence of a complexed *vyuha* strategy[25] during early medieval period remains suspect. The period of the Rajputs is generally marked with such defensive wars, while the invaded king could not get a suitable opportunity for the efficient organization of their composite forces.

Besides the references of *vyuha* formations, some other implicit details about the battle formations are also furnished by our sources. In relation to it, Kamandaka advices the placement of a commander-in-chief in the midst of expert warriors (*pravira purusha*) fighting bravely and guarding one another. Ordinary, soldiers, according to him, should be placed in the middle or central division of a formation and the war machines in the rear.[26] He views that in case of disorder in dangerous circumstances, mighty elephants should be placed in front, which meant that the infantry and cavalry should take place behind the war elephants.[27] His advise as to a separate arrangement of infantry, cavalry and elephant forces, with a sufficient gap in between[28] to avoid a clash or obstruction at the time of their movement or retreat, most probably suggests the system of phalanxes of different wings of the army. The author of *Agni Purana* lays down the formation of swordsmen in front of the army followed by the bowmen, then cavalry, car warriors and lastly, the elephant-men.[29] The bravest of the footmen elephant-men, car warriors and cavalry soldiers, according to him, should command the front of their respective lines.[30] *Manasollasa*, giving an enumerative account of the arraying of soldiers on the battleground states that in the rear, centre and flanks should be stationed men with swords, in *prapaksha* (extremity of a wing) those armed with *kodanda* (rod bearers), in *paksha* (wings), those armoured men and cavalry, in *puratah* (vanguard) cavalry and infantry and in front the elephants.[31] Chandesvara, however, provides for the placement of horses on flanks, those of chariots by the side of the horses and then of elephants followed by infantry.[32] The author of *Nitivakyamrita*, on the other hand, holds high the significance of *pratigraha* (rear forces) in an army[33] and requires the place of the king in the rear of it with the royal emblem in front.[34]

The above details gleaned from various sources suggest that there was an absence of uniformity in adoption of strategy and the organization of troops in general. Different dynastic clans probably had the tendency to organize the various components of their army in war, in accordance with their own convenience.

However, it is important to know that to what extent the above laid down rules were being followed in practice. Therefore, in order to find out the real situation, one must go into the details of some important battles of the age, provided by the Persian sources.

Chachnamah (eighth century), in the above context portrays a very clear picture that Dahar, the ruler of Sind, while arranging his troops to fight with the Arabs, 'led out the whole of his army. Some elephants, he sent with the advance column. The central forces he collected round himself. He placed in his front armed foot-soldiers and archers and on his left, armed horsemen with naked swords.'[35] The same work also quotes the case of King Maharat of Chittor, who divided his army into the centre, the right wing, the left wing and the advance guard, while fighting against Rai Chach of Sind.[36] None of our sources adds any information regarding the maintenance of reserve forces (the 5th division) by the Rajputs like the Turks. Such a division of army into four wings was probably made in order to set tunes with the Arab and the Turkish forces, which usually had these four divisions on the ground of fighting, while a fifth division of reserve forces was kept secure by the latter for surprise attack on the harassed enemy or to assist the four fighting wings in critical circumstances.[37]

Generally, the elephants were placed on the advanced guard or frontline, while the king commanded the centre or front of the army, sitting on a lofty *howdah* with royal emblem.[38] Nevertheless, such a display of the king heavily cost his life as it helped the adversaries to pinpoint their target on the leader of the forces and thus dishearten the rest of the army. The Indian kings also committed a blunder by placing themselves and their best generals, in the front to counteract the frontal attack on enemy's forces. The Paramara king Rai Mahlak Deo was not going apart from this tradition, while fighting against the forces of Ain-ul-Mulk by rendering his dear son in front with enormous multitude of forces, which in the words of Amir Khusrau, 'contributed to his fall'.[39]

Still, appears that the Hindus had not revived the old system of their military organization. That they greatly renewed it after the arrival of the Muslims is very much clear from the following remarks of the Chinese traveller, Yuan Chwang on the Indian military organization in the first half of the seventh century. He states: 'A leader in car warrior gives the command. . . . The general of the forces remains in the chariot, he is surrounded by a file of guards, who keeps close to his chariot wheels. The cavalry spread themselves in front to resist an attack. . . . The infantry by their quick movement contributed to defence. They carry a long spear and advance to the front with impetuosity.'[40]

Such a reorganization of forces was an intense necessity probably to keep pace with the Muslim forces. It seems quite relevant that in the absence of practiced mounted archery, owing to the technological reluctantness, the Hindus did neither allow their cavalry charges nor to their foot soldiers to command the front of the army. Instead, they liked to place their unwieldy, cumbersome and hardest elephants on the front in order to bear the smashing blows of expert Turkish mounted archers. No other option was open to them in case of their handicap in mounted archery.

In the Indian context, the commencement of war had taken place in such a manner that foot soldiers dashed against foot soldiers, horsemen against horsemen, elephants against elephants.[41] Under some circumstances, the soldiers were found to take recourse to hand to hand fight, avoiding the weaponry war.[42]

The military camp was also established at a site taking into consideration its strategic importance. There was a provision regarding the encampment of an area with defensive height which is as high as the height of a man, with scarce habitation, having entrance and exit of a very few persons only and provided with a front space for a large tent.[43] Besides, the river banks were usually regarded as good camping grounds owing to the easy availability of water and the safety of the site against the enemy's attack from at least one or two sides.[44] Such a site would have required a lesser number of men to guard the camp at night. Simultaneously, it would have also led to the saving of a considerable labour-force for digging entrenchment.[45] The river also provided sufficient water for filling the ditches of moats around the camp.[46]

A sudden attack on an enemy taking advantage of his weak position was also a part of strategy. Significantly, our sources did not neglect such an important aspect. Throwing an immense light on it, Kamandaka advices the king 'to assail upon the enemy, when his troops are found to be affected by the scorching rays of the sun or by cyclonic storms'. He further continues to state that 'the enemy's troops wounded or exhausted (in serious combats) in the first half of the day should be attacked for annihilation in the second half (i.e. before they could recuperate), so also those troops compelled to keep awake due to nocturnal raids'.[47] Shukra also lays down for a king to 'subdue in time the enemy, whose various provisions are scattered, whose corn and fuel is destroyed and whose subjects are incensed'.[48]

The chief military weakness of the Rajput armies was the slowness of their movement, in contrast to the lightning speed of the Turkish militias led by the expert mounted archers. It is true that the Rajput military strategy gave greater importance to weight than to mobility. The absence of practised mounted archery did not allow their horsemen to move rapidly during their attack on the enemy's troops. Rather, the Rajput cavalrymen used to fight with weapons of close combat like swords, daggers and spears. Their armies aimed to crush the adversary's forces by making a frontal attack, which effected the alertness of the enemy and hence a more conspicuous attack from his side. The great Turkish mounted horsemen, on the other hand, could easily disperse the adversary's rank by repeated attacks on their flanks. They employed the device of feigned retreat to destroy the cohesion of the enemy's forces. They first harassed the enemy from all sides by light mounted archers, who pretended defeat and flight. This was followed by a charge of heavy armoured cavalry. A visible example of such a tactical manoeuvre may be noticed in the Second Battle of Tarain. In the words of Minhaj-us-Siraj, the Sultan left 'the centre division of the army, the baggage, the standards and banners, his canopy of state and elephants, were left several miles in the rear'. He then advanced in a leisurely manner with the more mobile section of his troops 'The light armed and unencumbered horsemen, he had directed, should be divided into four divisions'; and had appointed them to act against the infidels on four sides; and the Sultan had commanded saying: 'It is necessary that on the right and left and front and rear, 10,000 mounted archers should keep the infidel host in play; and when their elephants, horsemen and foot advance to the attack, you are to face about and keep a distance of a horse's course in front of them.'[49] Remaining at such a narrow distance they could effectively beat the direct breach of the enemy's blows.

The strategy of feigned retreat was also adopted by Sultan Firuz Shah Tughlaq during his campaign of Lakhnauti. It is evident that Haji Ilyas, the ruler of Bengal took shelter in the fort of Ikdala to avoid an open engagement with the sultan's forces. He was probably waiting for the rains to come down after which he thought that Firuz Shah will choose retreat. At this moment, Firuz applied the strategy of feigned retreat. He spread the rumour that his army had retreated; hearing this Haji Ilyas came out of the fort to attack the rear of Firuz's forces but was surprised to see the whole army of the enemy in battle formation and ultimately met the defeat.[50]

The strong reliance of the Turks in mobility of arms and troops, besides their remarkable skill in planning a campaign with strategic and tactical modes was indeed a great steward in their success. Unlike the Rajputs they could shoot arrows meticulously on the target from a moving horse without halting or dismounting. Their horsemen were celebrated for their skill and speed in both attack and retreat.[51] Their mobile capacity did not provide any opportunity to the enemy to neutralize a forceful attack on their forces. They did not believe in a concerted action and a united march, instead they often adopted the device to get scattered and then to return to the fights and face the enemy by turning away.[52] They thought it less creditable to retreat than to pursue.[53] They utilized their speed in attacking the flanks and rear of the enemy and surrounding him from all sides.[54] Their forces were generally arranged into five sections, i.e. right wing, left wing, centre, advance guard and reserve forces, on the battlefield.[55] *Masalikul Absar fi Mamalikul Amsar* of Shihabuddin-al-Umri accounts such a disposition of Mohd. bin Tughlaq's army on the battlefield.[56] The arrangement of these forces was further altered in accordance with the strategical disposition to be followed in the ground. In case of an offensive action the cavalry was placed in front. For breaking the enemy's line of defence and for protecting the armies from enemy's attack, the elephants were placed in vanguard.[57] Circumstantially, the elephants were also placed in front of the centre. Alauddin Khalji had placed them in front of every division.[58] Sultan Mohd. bin Tughlaq also kept the elephants covered with iron harnesses with *howdahs* on their backs carrying warriors in front of him.[59] Brave and vainglorious soldiers in most cases were posted on the right wing and the expert archers on the left.[60] The king rested in the centre surrounded by senior generals and other officials.[61] The reserve forces were kept away from the main army to be entered in battle at a suitable moment for providing a final blow to the enemy's forces or to assist any particular wing at a critical moment.[62] Though the Rajputs were not unaware with the methods of retreating attacks, they felt themselves handicapped in the field of mounted archery, which hindered them to mobilize their forces like their adversaries.

The wisdom of the Turks in the tactical war was indeed far ahead than the Rajputs, who believed in the open field warfare in most cases. The Rajputs violated the principals of strategy and made tactical blunders; while not trying to take the advantage of the enemy's weakness. For instance, after the first battle of Tarain, Prithviraj III allowed the defeated Muslim army to return unmolested to Ghor. 'Mohd. Ghori on his return to Ghor made sleep and rest unlawful to him and prepared with his whole strength for a second war'.[63] Prithviraj's forces on the other hand lost thirteen months in siege of Tabarhindah, remaining unalert to the enemy's second attack. Again, he had committed a great blunder by promising a safe excuse to Ghori on the condition that he will return to his own country. Ferishta informs us that on reaching Lahore, Muizuddin sent an officer calling upon Prithviraj to embrace Islam and acknowledge his supremacy.[64] Prithviraj who was already on the battlefield of Tarain with a force of '300,000 horses, 3,000 elephants and considerable infantry',[65] wrote back to sultan, offering to do him no harm if he chose to return to Ghor, but threatening him with a complete ruin otherwise. According to Ferishta, the letter of Prithviraj contained the following matter,

> To the bravery of our soldiers we know you are no stranger, and to our great superiority in number, which daily increases, your eyes bear testimony. . . . It were better, then, you would repent in time of the rash resolution you have taken, and we shall permit you to retreat in safety; but if you are determined to brave your evil destiny, we have sworn by our gods to advance

upon you with our rank breaking elephants, our plain-trampling horses, and blood thirsty soldiers, early in the morning, to crush the army which your ambition has led to ruin.[66]

At this sultan sent a strategic reply: 'I have marched into India at the command of my brother, whose general I am. Both honour and duty bind me to exert myself to the utmost . . . but I shall be glad to obtain a truce till he is informed of the situation of affairs, and till I have received his answer.'[67] The conditional proposal for peace was replied positively by Ghori in a strategic manner, which relaxed the Rajputs, ultimately, relinquishing all the fresh preparations for war. But the revelrous night became an eternal gloom for them as at the same night 'the Sultan made preparations for battle . . . and when the Rajputs had left their camp for the purpose of obeying the calls of nature, and for the purpose of performing their ablutions, he entered the plain with his ranks marshalled.'[68] The defeat of Prithviraj in a state of sudden night attack by Ghori's forces is also confirmed by both the contemporary Muslim and Hindu sources.[69] *Jami'ul Hikayat* of Mohd. Ufi states that the Ghori sultan in order to prevent any suspicion kept 'fires burning all the night, so that the enemy might suppose it to be their camping ground. The sultan then marched off in another direction with the main body of his army. The infidels saw the fires and felt assured of their adversaries being encamped there. The sultan marched all night and got in the rear of Kola. At dawn he made his onslaught. . . .'[70] The stratagem played by Mohd. Ghori on Prithviraj is also confirmed by *Prithviraja Prabhandha* which refers, 'Prithviraja had been asleep. . . . In the meantime, the Prime Minister had the Sultan sent for.'[71] *Prabandhacintamani* of Merutunga also affirms that 'Prithviraja was asleep at that time after breaking his Ekadasi fast'.[72] The sudden night attack on the enemy was certainly a part of the strategy of Turks as Fakhr-i-Mudabbir refers to the attack on an enemy in a state of unawareness, as one of the artful methods of war. He suggests the afternoon in the summer and early hours of morning in the winter as ideal time for surprise attack, during which period the guards are usually asleep and the security is disturbed and neglected.[73] Ibn Battuta writes of a surprise attack on the Hindus of Ma'bar when their soldiers were taking rest after lunch and their horses were left for grazing.

Remaining unconscious of the enemy's attack at that time, they guessed them to be thieves and came outside of the fort unprepared for war. Thus, the Hindus met a terrible defeat at the hands of the Turks.[74]

The system of fortification adopted by the Rajputs was also a severe pitfall in their strategy. They could use the forts for the purpose of defence and not for an offensive attack. The forts built by the sultans of Delhi on the other hand were offensive in nature. Unlike the Rajput fortresses constructed on the top of a hillocks, they were built at ground level to facilitate the movement of cavalry. The expansionist policy of Delhi sultans was greatly served by their forts, which were utilized by them as base-camps.[75] They succeeded to a great extent in their distant campaigns on account of the established chains of the fortified settlements from where the expeditions were organized and the communications were maintained. The offensive nature of the Turkish forts may clearly be seen in their gateways, which are found built at quick intervals to facilitate the movement of the troops.[76]

The Rajput fortresses, even on being insurmountable became the targets of the enemy's attack and ultimately conquered by his forces on account of their extensive isolation and target on one fort and to capture it by all possible means. It was the result of the maintained self-sufficiency of the Rajput forts that during an investment, the enemy could easily capture the whole fort by cutting of the convoy. When the provisions stored in the fort came to an end, the fort was ultimately surrendered to the enemy. The mighty fort of Ranthambhor could be captured by the enemy owing to the famine which prevailed inside.[77]

Further, the great indiscretion of the Rajputs could be noted during the hour of a forceful attack on Jalor by Alauddin's forces. As *Kanhadade Prabandha* accounts that when the combined forces of the Rajputs marched into action and encountered the enemy at the order of Kanhadade and when the Rajputs got the upper hand at the initial stage of the battle with the Muslims, the two generals, Jaita and Mahipa, who were commanding the war, left the detachment of 4,000 Rajputs and rushed to Jalor to inform their overlord the news of victory.[78] The Muslims at last opened the siege of the fort through a stratagem.[79]

It can be observed after the above survey that in most cases the war stratagem of the Turks was more practical and tactical. The Turks made strategic use of forts as long it was required. They had also taken the step to wage open field wars too whenever it suited them. Though it may be remarked that the Rajputs of the age were fully conversant with the principles of strategy. Yet because of lack of effective cavalry and mounted archers, they failed to apply it successfully on the highly expert Turkish strategists.

NOTES

1. *Mahabharata* for the first time gives a bewildering account of different battle-arrays (*vyuhas*) like *suchi* (needle shaped), *krauncha* (in the shape of a heron), *syena* (hawk array) *makara* (crocodile shaped), *mandala* (circular) *vajra* (thunderbolt), etc. (see the formation of *vyuhas* in Udyoga, Virata and Bhishma Parvas), which facilitated all the possible kinds of movements of the armies. The references of war music for rousing the spirit of combatants, striking terrors and wishing victories are also found extant in it. (*Samkshipta Mahabharatam* (text and tr.), part II, ed. Prabhunath Dwivedi, Lucknow: Uttar Pradesh Sanskrit Academy, 1994, p. 365 (v. 35) & 390 (v. 204).
2. R.P. Kangle, *Kautiliya Arthasastra,* part II, Delhi: Motilal Banarsidass, 1986, p. 453, v. 51.
3. Ibid., p. 453, vv. 48–50.
4. *Nitisara,* Eng. tr. Sisir Kumar Mitra, Calcutta: Asiatic Society, 1982, p. 393 (vv. 15–17) & 409 (vv. 66–7).
5. न दायादादपरःपरबलस्याकर्षणमन्त्रेऽस्ति। (*Nitivakyamrita,* Eng. tr. with text by Sudhir Kumar Gupta, Jaipur: Prakrit Bharati Academy, 1987, p. 305, ch. 30, v. 65.)
6. यमभिगच्छेत्तस्यावश्यंदायादानुत्थापयेत्।, ibid., v. 66.
7. *Tilakmanjari,* ed. Pt. Bhavadatta Shastri, Bombay: Nirnayasagar Press, 1938, p. 44.
8. *Agni Purana,* Eng. tr. M.N. Dutt Shastri, vol. II, Chaukhamba Sanskrit Series, Varanasi, 1967, pp. 808–9.
9. G.P. Sinha, *Post Gupta Polity,* Calcutta: Punthi Pustak, 1972, p. 163.
10. *Sukraniti,* Hindi tr. with text by Pt. Mihir Chandra, Bombay: Shri Venkateshvar Steam Press, p. 176, v. 28.
11. Gustav Oppert, *On Weapons, Army Organisation and Political Maxims of the Ancient Hindus,* Madras: Government Press, 1880, p. 122, cf. *Sukraniti,* p. 176, v. 23.
12. Ibid., p. 177, v. 30.

13. Ibid., p. 181, vv. 86–8.
14. The ethical code relates to the non-killing of a person, who is aligned on the ground, who is emasculated, who has joined his hands as suppliants, one who sits with dishevelled hair or one who submits by saying, 'I am thine', one who is asleep, one without a coat of mail, a naked, an unarmed, a combatant who is looking on, one who is fighting with another, one who is drinking or eating, one engaged in another matter, one who is frightened, or one who is running away, an old man, a child, a woman and a king. (*Mahabharata,* Shanti Parva, Pt. I, (Skt. text with Hindi tr.), ed. Pt. Sri Damodar Satvalekar, Pardi (Gujarat): Bharat Mudranalaya, 1979, p. 510 (vv. 12 and 13) and 533 (vv. 24–6), part II of the same edn., 1980, p. 700, vv. 13 and 14. Also see *Sukraniti,* pp. 180 (vv. 76–9) and the quotations of Manu in Laxmidhar's *Rajdharmakanda* of *Kritya Kalpataru,* ed. K.V. Rangaswami Aiyangar, Baroda: Gaekwad Oriental Series, 1943, p. 132).
15. B.N.S. Yadav, *Society and Culture in Northern India during the Twelfth Century,* Allahabad: Indian Universities Press, 1973, pp. 212, 220, B.P. Mazumdar, *Socio-Economic History of Northern India (AD 1030–1194),* Calcutta: K.L. Mukhopadhyay, 1960, pp. 64–5; B.K. Majumdar, *The Military System in Ancient India,* Calcutta: K.L. Mukhopadhyay, 1960, 1st edn., p. 150; Pratipal Bhatia, *The Paramaras* (*c. 800-1305 AD*), Delhi: Munshiram Manoharlal, 1970, p. 229.
16. Dashrath Sharma, *Rajasthan Through the Ages,* vol. I, Bikaner: Rajasthan State Archives, 1966, p. 291; *Early Chauhan Dynasties,* Delhi: S. Chand & Co., 1959, p. 76. Also see B.N.S. Yadav, op. cit., p. 212.
17. A.K. Forbes, *Rasmala,* Delhi: Heritage Publishers, 1973, pp. 86–7.
18. *Nitivakyamrita,* p. 174, v. 27.
19. Dashrath Sharma, *Rajasthan through the Ages,* p. 177, also see D.C. Ganguly, *Indian Historical Quarterly,* X, 1934, p. 619.
20. *Tarikh-i-Ferishta,* tr. John Briggs in *History of the Rise of Mohemedan Power in India,* vol. 1, Calcutta: S. Dey from Editions Indian, 1966, pp. 39–40.
21. R.G. Mishra, *Indian Resistance to Early Muslim Invaders up to AD 1206,* Meerut: G.T. Printers, 1983, p. 47.
22. Ibid.
23. It was also adopted by our ideal heroes, Rama, Krishna, Indra and others and Bali and Vaman were killed by unfair fights. It is widely known that Bhima killed his enemy Duryodhana in a duel, violating the rules of *Dharmasastra,* at the instance of Lord Krishna. That this trend continued throughout Mauryan period can be proved by many examples. Even, further, Chandragupta II is known to have disguised himself as Dhruvadevi, the queen of his elder brother Ramagupta, to get entry into the Saka camp in order to kill the Saka monarch. Similarly, Sasanka of Bengal, acting as an ally of Malava king enticed

Rajyavardhan, the king of Thanesar, by fair promise to a conference and assassinated him by treachery.

24. A detailed description of battle arrays is found for the first time in *Mahabharata* (see the Udyoga, Virata and Bhishma Parvas). Further Kautilya's treatment to the division of these battle arrays seems more rational and fuller (*Arthasastra*, Book 10, concerning war). Their validity is also confirmed by Kamandaka in his *Nitisara* (*Vyuhavikalpa*, p. 423, v. 24). Regarding the exigencies of situation necessitating the formations of different *vyuhas*, Shukra states that if the alarm rises in the front, the *senapati* should march in an array resembling a crocodile, a double winged hawk or a needle with a strong point, if alarm rises in the rear, what is called a cart, if on the flanks, a thunderbolt, if on all sides, a wheel. (*Sukraniti*, p. 174, vv. 96–7). A vivid description of these *vyuhas* is also found in *Manasollasa* of Somesvara, vol. I, ed. G.K. Shrigondekar, Gaekwad Oriental Series, no. 28, Baroda, 1925, *Vimsati* II, vv. 1184-89), *Agni Purana*, pp. 844, 876–9 and *Nitiprakasika* (B.P. Mazumdar, op. cit., p. 64).
25. *Agni Purana* refers to seven divisions of a *vyuha* (p. 876), while *Manasollasa* mentions about nine divisions, viz., *mukha*, *praurasyam*, *pratigraha*, *kakshau*, *prakakshau*, *pakshau*, *prapakshau* and *prastham* (vol. I, p. 135, *Vimsati* II, vv. 1178–81).
26. *Nitisara*, p. 426, vv. 32–4.
27. Ibid., p. 423, v. 26.
28. The particular distance, according to Kamandaka between each of the foot soldier should be one *sama* (14 *angulas*), with horses each at an interval of 3 *samas* and elephants and chariots at an interval of 5 *samas* each (ibid., p. 423, v. 23).
29. *Agni Purana*, p. 845. The translator has referred the term car warriors probably for charioteers or warriors in carts using same type of war machines like *munjaniqs*, *arra'das*, etc.
30. Ibid., Kautilya also suggests to the placement of best troops in the front, the next best at the ends, the rear and the weak troops in the centre (*Arthasastra*, p. 448, v. 46). In a mixed composition of horses, elephants and chariots, he prescribes the stationing of elephants at the end of army, horses on the flanks, chariots in the centre or front and foot-soldiers in the wings or sides (ibid., p. 448, vv. 38–46).
31. *Manasollasa*, vol. I, p. 135, *Vimsati* II, vv. 1184–9.
32. *Rajnitiratnakara*, ed. K.P. Jayaswal, Patna: Bihar and Orissa Research Society, 1936, Text, p. 40.

    A study of our sources in general reveals that the use of chariots had become obsolete in the contemporary wars. The account of chariots within the formation of troops provided by Chandesvara and the author of *Agni Purana*, thus, appears traditional (for details see Chapter 3).

33. *Nitivakyamrita,* pp. 297 (v. 19) and 298 (v. 21).
34. Ibid., p. 298, v. 20. *Agni Purana* also advices the king to remain in the rear for the safety of his life (p. 844).
35. *Chachnamah,* tr. Mirza Kalichbeg Fredunbeg, vol. I, Delhi: Jayyed Press, 1979, p. 136.
36. Ibid., p. 21.
37. *Tabaqat-i Nasiri,* tr. H.G. Raverty, vol. I, Delhi: Oriental Books Reprint Corporation, 1970, pp. 467–8, also see fn. 2.
38. In the battle of Waihind (AD 1008), the course of the battle had ultimately changed in the side of Mohmmedans, when the elephant of Anandpala due to the naphtha balls and flights of arrows directed against it, came to fury and created a havoc in Hindu army (*Tarikh-i-Ferishta,* p. 27). Similarly, in the battle of Chandwar, the face of victory had turned, while Jayachandra seated on a lofty *howdah* received a deadly wound from an arrow and fell from his exalted seat to the earth (*Tajul Maasir* in H.M. Elliot and J. Dowson, *History of India as Told by its Own Historians,* vol. II, Delhi: Low Price Publications, 2001, p. 223).
39. Amir Khusrau, *Khaza'inul Futuh,* tr. Mohd. Habib, Madras: D.B. Taraporewala Sons & Co., 1931, p. 45.
40. S. Beal, *Buddhist Records of the Western World,* vol. I, Delhi: Oriental Book Reprint Corporation, 1983, Book II, p. 83.
41. *Sisupalvadh* of Magh, Hindi tr. with text by Pt. Hargovind Shastri, Varanasi : Chaukhamba Vidyabhavan, Vidyabhavan Sanskrit Granthmala, 1962, p. 4501, v. 17, *Chachnamah,* p. 148, *Sukraniti,* p. 180, vv. 74–5, Padmanabha's *Kanhadde Prabandha,* tr. V.S. Bhatnagar, New Delhi: Aditya Prakashan, 1991, p. 22.
42. At once Visaldev Chauhan and Baluk Rao Chalukya are recorded to have fought a terrible duel. (*Indian Antiquary,* vol. I, Delhi : Indological Book Reprint Corporation, 1872, p. 276.) *Naisadhiyacharita* refers that 'the army of Nala, the repository of many a sword, both indeed, thrive with hand to hand fights' (B.N.S. Yadav, op. cit., p. 213). The similar references of hand to hand fight are found in *Sisupalvadh, Tilakmanjari, Kathasaritsagar* and *Dvasrayakavya* (ibid.). *Prabandha-cintamani* also accounts of the combats of duels and push (ibid., P.C. Chakravarti also notices the prevalence of this mode of fight throughout the ancient and early medieval period. (*The Art of War in Ancient India,* Delhi: Low Price Publications, 1993, pp. 118–19.)

    That hand to hand fight was also prevalent among the Turks is known from *Fakhr-i-Mudabbir,* who lays down a guideline for fighting such combats. (*Adab-ul-Harb-wa'sh-Shujja'at,* in A.A. Rizvi's *Adi Turk Kalin Bharat* [Hindi], Aligarh: Aligarh Muslim University, 1956, p. 272).
43. 'पुरुष प्रमाणोत्सेधम् अबहुजननिवेशं चरणापसरणयुक्तम् ।
    अग्रतोमहामण्डपावकाशं च तदेगमध्यस्य सर्वदा स्थानं दद्यात् ।।'
    (*Nitivakyamrita,* p. 315, Ch. 30, v. 118).

44. P.C. Chakravarti, op. cit., pp. 106–7, also see S.K. Bhakhari, *Indian Warfare*, Delhi: Munshiram Manoharlal, 1981, p. 148.
45. Ibid.
46. Ibid.
47. *Nitisara*, Ch. XIX, Prak 31, p. 410, v. 68.
48. Oppert Gustav, op. cit., p. 122, *Sukraniti*, op. cit., p. 176, vv. 17–20. An almost similar view of repelling the enemy in times of his weak position is also held by Kautilya (*Arthasastra*, p. 438 (v. 3), p. 439 (v. 22).
49. *Tabaqat-i Nasiri*, vol. I, pp. 467–8. Also see *Tarikh-i Ferishta*, pp. 99-100, fn. 2.
50. *Tarikh-i Firuzshahi*, in Elliot and Dowson, vol. III, Delhi: Low Price Publications, 2001, pp. 294–6.
51. Alluding to the significance of mobility as an adamant feature of the Turkish armed forces. R.C. Smail writes, 'It enables them to remain at a distance from their enemy and to choose the moment at which they could close with him. . . . If a change essayed against them, they were ready to retreat, if the attempts were given up, they themselves attacked once more', R.C. Smail, *Crusading Warfare*, Cambridge: Cambridge University Press, 1956, Cambridge Studies in Medieval Life and Thought, vol. 3, Ch. IV, p. 78.
52. *Adab-Harb-Wa-Shujjat*, p. 78.
53. Smail, op. cit., p. 78.
54. Ibid., p. 79.
55. See the account of the second battle of Tarain in *Tabaqat-i Nasiri*, vol. I, pp. 467–8 and *Adab-ul-Harb-Wa-Shujjat*, in A.A. Rizvi, *Adi Turk Kalin Bharat*, p. 259.
56. 'The Sultan stands in the centre and round him the religious men and men of letters. The archers are in the front and in the rear; the right and left wings were stretched so that the two wings of the army are joined. Before him are elephants covered with iron harness and carrying towers in which the soldiers are hidden. . . . In front of the elephants are slaves, who march in light armour with swords and weapons. They make way for the elephants . . ., while the horsemen are on the right and left wing. The flank of the army surrounds the enemies and fight round the elephants and behind them a fleeing man does not find a cave or an entrance. And, hardly can one escape from them because encircling troops surround them and arrows and naphtha come from the above, and the footmen snatch them from below. So death comes to them from every place and the misfortune surrounds them from every side.' *Masalikul Absar Fi Mamalikul Amsar*, tr. Otto Spies, Aligarh: Aligarh Muslim University, 1943, p. 48.
57. Ibid.
58. *Futuh-ut-Salatin* in A.A. Rizvi, *Khalzi Kalin Bharat*, Aligarh: Aligarh Muslim University, 1955, p. 199.

59. *Masalikul Absar Fi Mamalikul Amsar,* p. 48.
60. *Adab-ul-Harb,* Rizvi, *Adi Turk Kalin Bharat,* p. 263.
61. *Adab-ul-Harb-wa-Shujjat,* p. 263.
62. *Tabaqat-i Nasiri,* p. 12, fn. 57, *Adab ul Harb,* p. 265.
63. Hasan Nizami quoted by Raverty in *Tabaqat-i Nasiri,* vol. I, p. 466, fn. 1.
64. *Tarikh-i Ferishta,* vol. I, p. 98.
65. Ibid., p. 98.
66. Ibid., p. 99.
67. Ibid.
68. *Tarikh-i Ferishta,* quoted by Raverty, *Tabaqat-i Nasiri,* vol. I, p. 466, fn.1.
69. Ibid.
70. Ibid.
71. *Prithviraj Prabandha* in *Puratanaprabandhasangraha,* Calcutta: Singhi Jain Granthmala, no. 2, 1936, p. 87.
72. *Prabandhacintamani,* Bombay: Singhi Jain Granthmala, no. 1, 1933, p. 117.
73. *Adab-ul-Harb-Wa-Shujjat,* Rizvi, *Adi Turk Kalin Bharat,* p. 262.
74. *Rehla,* Rizvi, *Tughlaq Kalin Bharat,* I, Aligarh: Aligarh Muslim University, 1956, p. 296.
75. For details see Ali Athar, 'Army Organisation Under the Sultans of Delhi: 13th and 14th Century' (unpublished Ph.D thesis), Aligarh: Aligarh Muslim University, 1987, pp. 179–83, 200–1.
76. Ibid.
77. Amir Khusrau who was probably an eye-witness to the capitulation of the fort informs us that, 'Famine prevailed to such an extent within the fort that they would have purchased a grain of rice for two grains of gold but could not get it. The fire of hunger had roasted their hearts within their earthen bosoms and they wished to open their bosoms and eat up their roasted hearts. Man can bear all afflictions except that of a starving stomach.' *Khazainul Futuh,* op. cit., p. 40.
78. *Kanhadade Prabandh,* Canto, III, p. 53.
79. Ibid., Canto IV, p. 89.

Some Aspects of Persian Influence on Mughal Painting under Akbar

ASHOK KUMAR SRIVASTAVA

Mughal painting, in the beginning borrowed a lot from Persia. There were three main sources of influence on Mughal painting: first, the works of the artists of Persian origin at the Mughal court made a distinct impression on the art of painting as a whole;[1] second, the huge Imperial library of the Mughals,[2] which contained valuable Arabic and Persian illustrated manuscripts as well as the collected or compiled *muraqqas* (picture albums) for the study of the historic and contemporary example of painting; third, the dominance of Persian culture at the Mughal court, which affected both the style and subject matter of the painter's art.

The Mughal painters were inspired by the artists of Persia in the treatment of landscape. This particular aspect is apparent in the depiction of a high horizon in the earlier manuscripts of the Akbari studio, but in later works, the line of horizon was lowered, creating a sense of space within the picture plane. Sometimes, rich vegetation in the landscape, as for instance noticeable in *Hamza Nama,* reminds us of the Shiraz school of Persian painting. The Mughal artist's special preference for Persian flora such as the cypress, chinar, almond, the triangular shaped tree on the hillocks, flowering as well as grassy tufts, blossoming shrubs, grassy fields, etc., are all borrowed from Persian paintings to emphasize the decorative aspects of landscape compositions. But this very characteristic is dominating only at the formative stage of Mughal painting and it occurs only occasionally from the time of its maturity when the illustrations became more true to nature. The Persian landscape has almost disappeared from the end of Jahangir's reign and onwards.

In the depiction of rocks and hills the Mughal painters followed the Persian idiom. Sometimes, as is observed in the works of the celebrated Persian Bihzad, different colours have been used for each hill to differentiate it from the other, and to bring about the filling of space and the distance as well.[3] With the maturity of style, the Mughal painters tried to get rid of the Persian conventions with the modulation of contours of the rocks by the use of variations in colours, shading and toning.[4] This particular aspect is apparent in 'The Ape Outsmarts Thieves',[5] Shah Ardashir's 'Fate',[6] 'Pradyumna Destroys Sambara',[7] 'The Raven Addressing the Assembled Animals',[8] and the 'Fall of Babur from His Horse'.[9] This innovation was further continued during the time of Jahangir as is evident in 'A Prince with a Youth and a Sage',[10] and 'Peafowl'.[11]

Rocks and hills, which were often depicted in the form of animals and humans[12] in the Shiraz and early Safavid styles of Persia—a survival of Persian nomadic traditions—also inspired the artists of the Akbari studio. Some comparative Mughal works that share similar devices include: 'Slave Girls Sporting in a Stream',[13] 'An Old Shepherd and His Flock',[14] 'Babur and his two Chieftains Race during their Retreat from Samarqand',[15] and 'Akbar Watches an Animal Combat During a Hunt'.[16]

The representation of water stream in the paintings of Akbar's court is very much identical with the Persian idiom. The Persian painters of both the late fourteenth-century Mongol style and the fifteenth-century Timurid style had developed a craze for depicting water streams or ponds with floating fishes or ducks in the foreground almost touching the lower margin. The artists of Akbar and Jahangir acted likewise in accordance with the same Persian fashion without any change.

The technique of dividing the whole dramatic event into several planes (generally not more than two) by the use of hills and mountains, was a tradition of the Herat school of Persian painting. It was subsequently further developed by the artists of the early Safavid and the Bukhara styles of Persia.[17] A good number of Mughal works relating to the period of Akbar, e.g. 'Prithu Chases the Earth Cow',[18] 'A Man Carrying a Lion on his Back',[19] and 'Akbar Hunting with Cheetas'[20] reflect similar compositional arrangements. Furthermore, the painting 'Young Woman with a Guru'[21] a production of the Allahabad workshop, reveals the continuation of the aforesaid traditions in the Salim studio.

The representation of architecture in Persian painting is flat, i.e. two-dimensional, and the tendency is to emphasize its decorative as well as pictorial character. Though the Mughal artists, right from the beginning, favoured the third dimension for indicating depth to the buildings, it appears that the aforesaid Persian conventional scheme was often applied in the formative years of Mughal painting as is observed in some illustrations of *Tuti Nama,*[22] *Hamza Nama*[23] and the *Tilasm and Zodiac* manuscripts.[24] By the end of the sixteenth-century, as the style became matured under the artists of Persian origin migrated to the Mughal court and their Indian disciples, the Persian fashion of architectural expression, with a few exceptions, discontinued.[25]

With regard to the architectural setting, the Mughal artists from the time of Akbar to Shahjahan borrowed at least three Persian devices which are given as follows.

First, in a considerable number of Mughal illustrations the entire dramatic event is divided into two parts by depicting the main action inside of a building while the secondary events are handled outside the courtyard by cutting the figures in the foreground near the lower margin. This particular method of treatment was applied especially in the court scenes, as is frequently observed in the identical works executed by the Persian master Bihzad, where the emperor is seen seated in a pavilion inside the courtyard with his attendants and a doorkeeper posted at the gate of the courtyard outside the building.[26] In such compositions the spectator, who is imagined to be looking at the scene from a certain elevation for the purpose of representing a complete scene, observed both the inside and the outside of the building at the same time.

Second, several Mughals paintings, such as 'The Scene in a Mosque School',[27] 'Feast of the King of Yaman',[28] and 'Episode in a Bazaar',[29]depict persons conversing as the centre of the main action either inside or outside of an arched pavilion. Such a compositional arrangement was originally a Persian convention which repeatedly occurs in Persian painting of the fifteenth and sixteenth centuries.[30]

Third, paintings representing a variety of occupations in the mosque, especially scenes of sermon and school, seem to have been favoured by the early Mughal artists, for instance, Mir Sayyid Ali[31] of Persian origin. It would be pertinent to draw attention towards the fact that such mosque scenes were very popular in Persia from the last quarter of the fifteenth century to the first half of the sixteenth century,[32] and the same subsequently spread to the Mughal school in India.

The minute study of lower class people in regard to the building construction scene was for the first time taken up by Bihzad in Persian painting as is evident in one of his paintings entitled 'The Construction of the Castle of Khawarnaq'.[33] In this connection the painters of the Akbari atelier followed the Persian artist Bihzad and produced several identical works in the illustrated manuscripts of the *Babur Nama,* the *Akbar Nama,* the *Jami-al-Twarikh,* etc. An example of this conventional scheme may be studied in 'Sultan Ghazan Khan builds Charitable Institutions',[34] where the arrangement of figures—such as the brick layers, stone—masons, porters, carpenters, blacksmiths and supervisors—and their poses as well as groupings are all derived from the celebrated Bihzad. Moreover, like that of the similar works by Bihzad, here the Mughal artists' main attention is direction not on the facial expression but on the reciprocal interaction between the figures.[35]

The two most striking characteristics of Persian painting in the early fourteenth century, as observed in the *Shah Nama* (Demotte) of Firdausi (*c.* 1330–6), are the cutting of the figures on the margin to suggest an illusion of continuity in the scene,[36] and the representation of figures in the extreme foreground—sometimes even with his back turned towards the spectator or even seeming to come forward out of the picture—with the intention of depicting the eye into the picture to the point the artist wishes to be the centre of attention.[37] Both of these Persian devices were inherited by the artists of Akbar. An example of the former may be studied in the painting 'Mughal Troops Chase the Armies of Daud' by Manohar;[38] while the latter technique is evident in a good number of works such as 'Aemr Disguised as the Surgeon Nizzmuhil arrives Before the Fort at Antalya',[39] 'A

Chained Elephant',[40] and 'A Hunting Scene'.[41] Besides, as regards the technique of extending figures as well as landscape compositions beyond the margin, a traditional design of Persian painting which frequently occurs from the fourteenth to the sixteenth century, the Akbari artists[42] again combined the features taken over from the Persian models.

In the treatment of human figures, round faces with heavy cheeks as well as rouged cheeks[43] as often observed in the formative stage of Mughal illustrations, are identical with the Persian convention. Some specimens of early Mughal painting[44] show the employment of the Persian Safavid manner in the handling of faces where the red outline is stressed in the nose, lips, and ears; but it was a temporary phase and was soon discontinued with the dominance of the indigenous features by the third quarter of the sixteenth century. The depiction of human faces in Mughal painting, on the whole has been made either in three-quarter view or incomplete profile, the former being inspired from the Persian convention while the latter was a continuation of the Indian tradition. However, both the styles were applied, and progressed side by side in the Mughal studio ever since the formative years of Mughal art.[45] It would not be improper to suggest, on the basis of the early production of the Akbari atelier, that the three-quarter profile was somewhat dominant in the beginning and it was subsequently superseded by the complete profile. During the time of Akbar and Jahangir the three-quarter view was usually preferred in group compositions, especially in the battle scenes and court scenes while the affluence of complete or rigid profile is observed in single portraits. It seems that with the maturity of style by the time of Shahjahan, the method of three-quarter profile, which is rarely observed in the works relating to the period of Shahjahan, was completely replaced by the complete or strict profile tradition.

Taking the Persian school of painting as a whole, but with a few exceptions, it lacks the emotive expression to the human faces which is in fact made subordinate to the decorative aspect of the compositions. Thus, the Persian painters invented certain conventional gestures for the depiction of facial expression as well as mental attitude of the figures. One of these devices was the putting of a finger to the lips as a sign of astonishment. This very characteristic gesture is apparent in a good number of Mughal works produced in the royal ateliers of Akbar, Jahangir and Shahjahan. Furthermore, it is observed that this particular gesture has generally been preferred in the cases where the human figures related to the picture look at the scene with somewhat unconcerned and emotionless faces. But it would be unfair, however, to suggest that such conventional substitutes were often applied due to any lack ability in the expression of emotions on the part of the Mughal artists who, compared to the painters of Persia, usually showed a greater amount of proficiency in the treatment of human interrelationships, psychological interactions and increasing emphasis on naturalism.

The Mughal artists while illustrating the heroic deeds of their patrons combined the same with the exploits of the early Persian kings following the traditions of the Sassanian pictorial art of Persian painting in the thirteenth to sixteenth century. The adventures of the Persian heroes, viz., Rustam, Iskander and Bahram Gur inspired the Mughal painters in regard to the themes of battle, hunting and struggle against the forces of evil such as combats with dragons.

Paintings produced during the reign of Akbar show that the Mughal artists concerned themselves with such subject matter of warfare and battle as depicted in the pages of the Persian *Shah Nama*, and that examples of such Persian paintings were available to the illustrators of the royal atelier. The presence of the Persian tradition in some early Mughal works may be noticed where the warriors in the frenzy of battle deal blows and receive mortal wounds with apparent indifference.[46] Even a vigorous blow of a foe is regarded with indifference as exhibited in the facial expressions. Similarly, a soldier from whose body the blood is pouring in abundance refrains from exhibiting any outward sign of the agony that must accompany such a painful experience.

A page from the *Babur Nama* (1597–8), represents a battle scene where fighting dominates in the foreground and progressively weakens in the background.[47] This is again a Persian derivation especially that of the Shiraz style of the fifteenth and sixteenth century.[48]

In the representation of certain favourite incidents of hunting, the artists of Akbar and Jahangir followed the traditional manner of Persian painting when they depicted galloping horsemen and wild beasts fleeing from their arrows or exhibited skill in shooting the deer.[49] It is interesting to note the depiction of the scene of *qamargah* hunting[50] by the Mughal painters[51] is very much that by Persian painters.[52]

Themes of hunting with lion or tiger seem to be very fascinating for both the Persian and the Mughal painters as it carried the symbolic meaning of fighting with the evil forces of nature. A similar Mughal work 'Akbar Hunting Tigers near Narwar',[53] by Basawan, is directly inspired by a Persian painting entitled 'Mihar Cutting off a Lion's Head at One Blow'.[54] Several features are common in both the works, such as the hunter is mounted on a horse and the head is being severed by sword at one blow and consequently the beast resists the stroke with its claws.[55]

Persian paintings depicting combats with dragons,[56] usually associated with Rustam, Iskandar and Bahram Gur may be traced back to the Sassanian wall paintings of the seventh century.[57] The theme was taken up by the Akbari artists[58] with the philosophy that there is a struggle between the forces of good (i.e. Bahram Gur, etc.) and evil (i.e. dragon) prevalent in the nature. These paintings represent an imaginary world where the monster, very close to the Dinosaur, with its huge scaly body, sometimes round a tree on a mountain side, and with open jaws often emitting fire and smoke, appear quite unearthly. Furthermore, it seems that the popular lion hunting scenes of Jahangir's reign were influenced thematically by the dragon hunting exploits of Bahram Gur.

As to the animal drawings in Mughal paintings, the representations of horse, camel and deer have closer affinities with those of the Persian tradition. The treatment of horses with powerfully rounded quarter and narrow longish faces in the Akbari works, display inspirations from Persian paintings of the thirteenth and fourteenth century. The process of Indianization of the features of horses appears to have been attempted first under Jahangir[59] and as a result, the Persian mode of expression became completely obsolete subsequently as we observe in the works relating to the period of Shahjahan.

In the depiction of conflicts between animals, the Mughal artists followed the conventional manner of the earlier painters of Persia. The theme of the lion leaping on to the back of a deer and burying its teeth in the shoulder of the unfortunate beast[60] had a long history going back to a period much earlier than that of the Sassanians and these reappeared repeatedly not only on Persian carpets but also in the margins of illustrated Persian manuscripts. Another similar motif adopted by the artists of Akbar is that of a lion in combat with bull.[61]

It seems more feasible to suggest that no doubt the introduction of humour in Mughal painting came through Persian painting but in the Mughal painting comparatively more instances of caricatural element were dealt with.[62] A good number of Persian works depicting humour and caricature are known to us, e.g., some illustrations of the thirteenth century 'Kalila wa Dimnah', 'Salim Visiting Majnum in the Desert',[64] 'Sultan Sanjar and the old Woman',[65] 'A Scene of Drunkenness',[66] and 'Drinking Party in the Mountains'.[67] Of the above-mentioned examples the scene of drunkenness by Muhammadi has greatly influenced the Mughal artists from the time of Jahangir onwards. The Persian master Muhammadi displayed mastery in drawing pictures of lively bands of merrymaking dervishes who behaved rather like a troupe of buffoons than professed religious men. Paintings of such vagabond groups of dervishes frequently occur during the period of Jahangir and Shahjahan.

Miskin, a reputed artist of Akbari atelier, was a great painter of animals. He often introduced humorous animals in a number of works such as the figure of a semi-human lions gazing at the spectators. These include, 'Noah's art',[68] 'Raven Addressing the Assembled Animals',[69] 'The World of Animals',[70] and 'Laila and Majnu with the Animal Kingdom'.[71] It would be pertinent to draw attention towards the fact that humour of the kind which Miskin represented in the aforesaid illustrations was originally borrowed from an earlier Persian work entitled 'Salim Visiting Majnum in the Desert',[72] and where also a sense of caricature has been depicted through the humorous lion staring at the spectators.

The depiction of a visit to a saint seated at the entrance of a cave, where the landscape dominates and engulfs the human figures, seems to be a popular compositional device invented by the fifteenth-century Herat[73] and the sixteenth-century Safavid[74] who were the renowned painters of Persia. The conventional scheme subsequently reappears in a number of Mughal works, viz., 'Hermitage of a Saint',[75] 'Iskander Visiting a Hermit',[76] 'Encounter with a Hermit in the Wildernes',[77] 'The God Shiva Appears to the Sage Viswamitra,[78] and the Devotee'. [79]

In consideration of the lack of variety of emotive expression, with regard to the portrayal of deep grief in the mourning scenes, the Persian artists had to devise certain conventional modes of indicating emotion, e.g. the gnawing of the back of the hand, veiling of the face, tossing of the arms, hands stretched out in supplication, and tearing of clothes in an outburst of sorrow. These characteristics are apparent in several Persian works, as for instance 'The Bier of the Great Iskander'[80] and 'The Mourning for the Death of Laila's Husband'.[81] A series of comparative Mughal works which share similar subject, technique and compositional devices as in the aforesaid two Persian examples include 'Women Mourning beside the Coffin of Mangu Khan',[82] 'The Death of the Emperor Timur',[83] and 'A Princess on her Death-Bed'.[84]

The representation of spotted demons wearing a variety of horns with animal faces and clad in short skirts, in Mughal painting,[85] have been greatly influenced from the identical monsters depicted in the illustrations of the Persian *Shah Nama*.[86] These Persian demons,[87] observable as early as in the Sassanian frescoes of the seventh century[88] occur more frequently in the pages of the *Hamza Nama*, the *Harivamsa* and the *Ramayana* manuscripts of the Akbari studio. But, as a matter of fact, the appearances of the Mughal demons on the whole suggest inspiration of Hindu demonology which has been so prolific in the production of such monsters.

Mughal artists' preference for a gold sky,[89] laying of scenes in ravines between two mountains, representation of flames,[90] handling of night scenes where either there is no darkness and the star shine on a fully illuminated scene or despite darkness all around, the faces of the figures look as visible as by day light,[91] and themes depicting Majnu in the desert with wild beasts.[92] All of these also exhibit features taken over from Persian models.

Considering the fact that Persian influence counted for much during the formative years of Mughal painting under Akbar, it has often been termed as 'Indo-Persian'.[93] This particular explanation is neither logical nor acceptable. Mughal painting had never been merely a reflection or a colonial expression of Persian painting. Even the earliest productions of the atelier of Akbar reflect a variety of characteristics which distinguish them from those of the Persian style of miniature paintings. As the art progressed to its maturity by the last decade of the sixteenth century, the Mughal painters, especially those of Indian origin,[94] tried to get rid of the Persian mannerism and consequently the process of Indianization becomes apparent in regard to gesture, movement, emotive expression, dress, landscape composition, and architectural setting. In fact, the course of adoption and adaptation of the Persian element on the part of the Akbari artists, right from the beginning, resulted in the transformation of quite a good number of these features borrowed from Persia. This particular process gave Mughal painting an identity of its own as distinct from Persian painting which contributed to its origin. Thus, Mughal painting at any stage is in no sense Persian or a part of Persian art.

Taking the Akbari school of painting as a whole, we may observe a kind of synthesis between the Persian two-dimensional as well as the three-dimensional treatment more particularly at the close of the sixteenth century.

NOTES

1. The Persian masters like Mir Sayyid Ali, Abdus Samad, Aqa Riza, etc., as in-charge of the painting studio, would have been certainly in a position to impose their will on the artists working under their direction.
2. Cf. *Ain-i-Akbari,* tr. H. Blochman, Calcutta, 1977, vol. I, pp. 109–10.
3. S.P. Varma, *Art and Material Culture in the Paintings of Akbar's Court,* Delhi, 1978, p. 24.
4. N.R. Ray, *Mughal Court Painting,* Calcutta, 1975, p. 89.
5. Anwar-i-Suhaili, MS. 1570 School of Oriental and African Studies, London; S.C. Welch, *Imperial Mughal Painting,* New York, 1978, p. 4.

6. *Darab Nama* (Qr. 4615), folio 3v, *c.* 1580–5, British Library, London; Welch, op. cit., p. 5.
7. *Harivamsa, c.* 1585–90, Los Angeles County Museum of Art. P. Paul, *Indian Paintings in Los Angeles Museum,* Delhi, 1982, p. IV.
8. Attributed to Miskin, *Anwar-i Suhili, c.* 1590, British Museum, London (1920–9-17-05); Welch, op. cit., p. 11.
9. *Babur Nama,* 1597–8, Delhi: National Museum; Rai Krishna Das, *Mughal Miniatures,* Delhi, 1955, p. 3.
10. Attributed to Abul Hasan, Gulistan of Saadi (W. 668), folio 49, *c.* 1610–15, Baltimore: Walters Art Gallery; M.C. Beach, *The Grand Mongol: Imperial Painting in India (1600–60),* Mass.: Williamstown, 1978, cat. no.18.
11. Attribute to Mansur, *c.* 1610–20, from a private collection; Welch, op. cit., p. 26.
12. B. Gray, *Persian Painting,* London, 1977, pl. on p.143. Here the coral hills in the left are given the shape of flying cranes.
13. *Tilasm and Zodiac,* folio 18 Feb., *c.* 1565, Rampur: Raza Library; K. Khandalavala and J. Mittal, 'An Early Akbari Illustrated Manuscript of Tilasm and Zodiac', *Lalit Kala,* no. 14, 1969, pl. IV, fig. 16.
14. *Diwan-i Hafiz,* folio 177, *c.* 1588, Rampur: Raza Library; Varma, op. cit., pl. V.
15. *Babur Nama, c.* 1593, Moscow: State Museum of Oriental Cultures; S.I. Tyulayev, *Miniatures of Babur Nama,* Moscow, 1960, illust. 15.
16. From a private collection, *c.* 1595–1600; S.C. Welch, *The Art of Mughal India: Painting and Precious Objects,* New York, 1963, pl. 12.
17. B. Gray, op. cit., pls. on pp. 128, 135, 149; L. Binyon, J.V.S. Wilkinson and B. Gray, *Persian Miniature Painting,* Oxford, 1933, pl. CIA.
18. *Harivamsa* (Acc. no. 659. M.), *c.* 1585–90, Banaras: Bharat Kala Bhawan.
19. *Anwar-i Suhaili* (9069.M.8), 1596, Banaras: Bharat Kala Bhawan.
20. *Akbar Nama, c.* 1604, Dublin: Chester Beatty Library; T.W Arnold and J.V.S. Wilkinson, *The Library of A. Chester Beatty: A Catalogue of Indian Miniatures,* Oxford, 1936, vol. 11, pl. 25.
21. *Dvadasa Bhava, c.* 1600–5, Edwin Binney Collection; Edwin Binney, *Indian Miniature Painter from the Collection of Edwin Binney,* 3rd edn., I; *The Mughal and the Deccani Schools,* Portland, 1973, cat. no. 44.
22. Folios 20.r. 32.v. (Cleveland Museum of Art).
23. 'Mihrdukht Shoots Her Bow at the Ring', *Hamza Nama, c.* 1558–73, collection of Mrs. Maria Sarre-Hermann, Ascona (Switzerland); D. Barret and B. Gray, *Indian Painting,* New York, 1978, plate on p. 76.
24. Folio 28a (Raza Library, Rampur); K. Khandalavala and J. Mittal, op. cit., pl. VIII, fig. 30.
25. Cf. *The Feast of the King of Yaman, Anwar-i Suhaili* (add. 18579), folio 331a 1604-10, British Library, London; J.V.S. Wilkinson, *The Light of Canopus,* London, 1929. pl. XXIX.

26. Some identical Mughal works are: *Kublai Khan and His Empress Enthroned Jami al-Tawarikh* (54.31), 1596, Freer Gallery Art, Washington; reproduced in M.C. Beach, *The Imperial Image: Paintings for the Mughal Court,* Washington, 1981, cat. no. 11; 'Akbar Hears a Petition', *Akbar Nama* (60.28), *c.* 1604, Washington: Freer Gallery of Art, reproduced in ibid., cat. no. 12.g; 'Darbar of Jahangir', *Jahangir Nama* (14.654), *c.* 1620, Boston: Museum of Fine Arts; *Imperial Mughal Painting,* pl. 17; Darbar of Shah Jahan, *c.* 1645; School of Shah Jahan. Bharat Kala Bhawan, Banaras; Rai Krishna Das, op. cit., pl. 8.
27. Ascribed to Mir Sayid Ali, School of Akbar, *c.* third quarter of the sixteenth century; L. Binyon, J.V.S. Wilkinson and B. Gray, op. cit., pl. CIII A.
28. See Ibid., fn. 25.
29. Attributed to Bichitr School of Shah Jahan, *c.* 1650–60, from a private collection; *The Grand Mogul,* cat. no. 35.
30. Binyon, Wilkinson and Gray, op. cit., pls. LXXX A&B, LXXXIV A, LXXXVI B, XC II B.
31. Ibid., pl. CIII A.
32. The Persian master Bihzad employed this particular compositional device in several of his pictures; ibid., pl. LXXB; B. Gray, *Persian Paintings,* plate on p. 123. For some other closely related Persian example, vide Binyon, Wilkinson and Gray, op. cit., pls. LXX A, LXXXIV B, LXXXIX.
33. Khamsa of Nizami (Wr.6810), folio 154v, Herat, 1494, British Museum, London; B. Gray, *Persian Painting,* plate on p. 116.
34. *Jami al-Tawarikh,* 1596, Former Imperial Library, Tehran; J. Marek and H. Knizkova, *The Jenghiz Khan Miniatures from the Court of Akbar the Great,* tr. Olga Kuthanova, London, 1963, pl. 29.
35. Some other similar Mughal works include *Building Operation at Agra Fort,* by Miskin, *Akbar Nama* (I.S.2-6), 4589 &-46/11, *c.* 1590, Victoria and Albert Museum, London; Geeti Sen, *Paintings from the Akbar Nama,* Calcutta, 1984, pls. 31–2; *Building of Fatehpur Sikri, Akbar Nama,* Calcutta, 1984, pls. 31–2; *c.* 1604, Chester Beatty Library, Dublin; *The Library of Chester,* vol. II, pl. 24.
36. 'The Indian Army fleeing before the Iran Warriors of Iskander', *Shahj Nama* (Demotle) of Firdausei, Tabriz, (1330–6), Fogg Art Museum, Harvard Uiversity; Basil Gray, *Persian Painting,* plate on p. 29.
37. Ibid., plate on p. 28.
38. *Akbar Nama* (54.30), *c.* 1604, Freer Gallery of Art, Washington; *The Imperial Images,* cat. no.12d; Basil Gray, *Persian Painting,* plate on p. 29.
39. *Hamza Nama* (60.15), *c.* 1558–73, Freer Gallery of Art, Washington, *The Imperial Images,* cat. no. 5.b.
40. From the *Muraqqa Gulsan, c.* 1590, Former Imperial Library, Tehran; ibid. fig. 12.

41. From a *Diwan of Amir Hasan Dihlavi* (w. 650), folio 109v, 1602–3, Walters Art Gallery, Baltimore; *The Grand Mogul,* cat. no. 1.
42. E.g. 'Bears and Monkey', *Anwar-i Suhaili,* 1570, School of Oriental and African Studies, London; J.V.S. Wilkinson, *Mughal Painting,* London, 1948, pl. 3. in this particular Mughal illustration the artists has chosen to depict trees going beyond the margin.
43. Such rouged and heavy cheeks, for instance, may be frequently noticed in the pages of *Hamza Nama.*
44. E.g. 'A Banquet for Two Spies at Akinigar', *Hamza Nama* (52/1 8770/59), *c.* 1558–73, Museum of Applied Arts, Vienna; *Imperial Mughal Painting,* pl. 3.
45. Paintings of the *Hamza Nama* reflect a good combination of these two modes of facial representation.
46. 'A Battle Scene', *Hamza Nama* (acc. no. 5401.M), *c.* 1558–73, Bharat Kala Bhawan, Banaras.
47. For some other closely related Mughal works; vide M. Busagli, *Indian Miniatures,* Delhi, 1976, pls. 19–20; *The Grand Mogul,* cat. no. 1, illust. on p. 38.
48. Cf. B. Gray, *Persian Painting,* plates on pp. 74, 89, 128, 135.
49. 'A Hunting Scene', *Diwan of Amir Hassan Dihlavi* (w. 650), folio 109v. 1602–3, Walters Art Gallery, Baltimore; *The Grand Mogul,* cat. no. 1, illust. on p. 34; 'Bahram Gur Hunting Deers', by Nadim Khamsa of Nizami (1920-9-17-0258), *c.* 1610, British Museum, London: *The Imperial Image,* fig. 25.
50. Vide *Tazkereh al-Vakiat,* tr. Major Charles Stewart, Lucknow, 1971, p. 67.
51. 'Akbar Hunting in a Enclosure', *Akbar Nama, c.* 1590, Victoria and Albert Museum, London (I.S. 2-1896 56/117); *Imperial Mughal Painting,* pl. 14. For an identical example from Jahangir's reign, vide *The Library of Chester Beatty,* vol. III, pl. 87.
52. 'Hunting Scene', *Zafar Nama,* folio 484, 1529 Gulistan Palace Library, Tehran; reproduced in B. Gray, *Persian Painting,* plate on p. 133.
53. Design by Basawan, *Akbar Nama, c.* 1590, Victoria and Albert Museum, London (I.S. 2-1896 17/117); *The Art of Mughal India,* pl. 11a.
54. Mihr and Mushtari of Assar (no. 32. 6), Bukhara,1523, Freer Gallery of Art, Washington; B. Gray, *Persian Painting,* plate on p. 149.
55. Some other similar paintings were also executed by the artists of Akbar and Jahangir. Vide *Codices Selecti; Phototypice Imperssi, Fascimile Volume LII/2, Hamza Nama,* vol. II, Gray, op. cit., pl. v on p. 27; P. Paul, *Court Paintings of India (16th–19th Centuries),* Delhi, 1983, pl. M.44 (School of Jahangir).
56. For some identical Persian examples; B. Gray, *Persian Painting,* plates on pp. 63, 112, 162; Binyon, Wilkinson and Gray, op. cit., pl. XXXIIA, B.W. Robinson, *Persian Miniature Painting from Collections in the British Isles,* London, 1967, pls. 45, 51.

57. Gray, *Persian Painting*, p. 12.
58. Vide Ziyauddin Nakshabi's 'Tales of a Parrot' (The Cleveland Museum *Tuti Nama*), Graz, 1978, pl. 48; *Codices Selecti; Phototypice Impressi*, Fascimile Volume LII/1, *Hamza Nama*, vol. I, Graz, 1974, pl. v. 8; *Imperial Mughal Painting*, p. 5.
59. Ray, op. cit., p. 73.
60. The motif has been frequently applied in the decorative margins of the Jahangiri paintings.
61. Cf. Gray, *Persian Painting*, plate on p. 84 (Timurid School of Persia); *The Grand Mogul*, cat. no. 6 (School of Akbar); *The Art of Mughal India*, p. 12 (School of Akbar).
62. One of the earliest examples of humorous representation in Mughal Painting may be studied in a portrait of Mulla Du Piyaza reproduced on plate I of A.K. Coomarswamy's *Indian Drawings*, Delhi, 1979.
63. T.W. Arnold, *Painting in Islam*, New York, 1965, p. 80.
64. By a pupil of Bihzad, *Khamsa of Nizami* (Qr. 681D/12), folio 18, British Museum, London; Gray, *Persian Painting*, plate on p. 120.
65. Shah Tahmasp's *Khamsa of Nizami* (Qr. 2265), folio 18, British Museum, London.
66. By Sultan Muhamadi, *c.* 1517–40; Binyon, Wilkinson and Gray, op. cit., pl. LXXV.
67. Attributed to Muhammad, *c.* 1590, Museum of Fine Arts, Boston (no. 14.649); Gray, *Persian Painting*, plate on p. 157.
68. Attributed to Miskin, *Diwan of Hafiz*, *c.* 1590, Freer Gallery of Art, Washington (no. 48.8); *Imperial Mughal Painting*, pl. 9.
69. See ibid., fn. 8.
70. Inscribed to Miskin, *c.* 1590, Freer Gallery of Art, Washingon (45.29); *The Imperial Image*, cat. no. 19.
71. Attributed to Miskin, *c.* 1605, from a private collection; P. Paul, op. cit., pl. M. 38.
72. See ibid., fn. 64.
73. 'Courtier Visits a Hermit', attributed to Bihzad, *Khamsa of Amir Khusrau* (MS. p. 163), folio 23, 1485 Chester Beatty Library, Dublin; Norah Titley, 'Miniature Paintings Illustrating the Works of Amir Khusrau; 15th, 16th, 17th, Centuries', *Marg*, vol. XXVIII, no. 3, 1975, p. 26, fig. 21.
74. 'Iskandar Visiting a Hermit', *Khamsa of Nizami* (Add. 25900), folio 250, 1535–40, British Museum, London; Gray, *Persian Painting*, plate on p. 140.
75. *Anwar-i Suhaili* (9069.M.7), folio 32, 1596, Bharat Kala Bhawan, Banaras.
76. Designed by Basawan, *Khamsa of Amir Khusrau Dihlavi* (no. 13.228.30), 1597–8, Metropolitan Museum of Art, New York; S.C. Welch, 'The Paintings of Basawan', *Lalit Kala*, no.10, 1961, pl. IV, fig. 8.
77. *Ramayana* (07.271), 1587–98, Freer Gallery of Art, Washington; Busagli, op. cit., pl. 49.

78. *Jog Bashishta*, folio 230, 1602, Chester Beatty Library, Dublin; *The Library of Chester Beatty*, op. cit., vol. II, pl. 49b.
79. *Anwar-i Suhaili* (Add. 18579), 1604-10, British Library, London; *The Lights of Canopus*, op. cit., pl. II. See also pls. III and IV in ibid.
80. *Shah Nama* (Demotte) of Firdausi (no. 38.3), Tabriz, 1330–6, Freer Gallery of Art, Washington; Gray, *Persian Painting*, plate on p. 32.
81. *Khamsa of Nizami* (Or.6810), folio 135v. School of Bihzad, Herat, 1494, British Museum, London; ibid., plate on p. 122.
82. Designed by Basawan, *Jami al-Tawarikh*, 1596, Former Imperial Library, Tehran; J. Marek and H. Knizkova, op. cit., pl. 21.
83. *Tarikh-i Khandan-i Timuria*, folio 134, *c.* 1584, Khuda Baksh Oriental Public Library, Patna. For another identical painting, see folio 186 of the same MS.
84. By Manohar, *Anwar-i Suhaili* (9069.M.15), folio 100, 1596, Bharat Kala Bhawan, Banaras.
85. Vide 'Hamza's Supporter Landahur kidnapped in His Sleep by a Demon', *Hamza Nama*, *c.* 1558–73, Museum fur Angewand te Kunst, Vienna; *Codices Selection* I, op. cit., pl. V5; 'Pradyumna Destroys Sambara', *Harivamsa*, *c.* 1585–90, Los Angeles County Museum of Art; Indian Painting in Los Angeles Museum, op. cit., pl. IV; 'Rama and Lakshman Battle the Demon Rakshasas', by Mohan, *Ramayana*, folio 38v, 1587–98, Freer Gallery of Art, Washington (no. 07.271), *The Imperial Image*, no. 15.j. 'Rama and Lakshman fight the Demoness Taraka', by Mushfiq, *Ramayana* (07.271), folio 35v., 1587–98, Freer Gallery of Art, Washington; *The Imperial Image*, cat. no. 15.h.
86. Gray, *Persian Paintings*, plate on p. 90; B.W. Robinson, op. cit., pls. 23, 28; Binyan, Wilkinson and Gray, op. cit., pl. XCVIII.
87. For jinns, devils, and demons in Persian art, vide *Painting in Islam*, pp. 108–9.
88. Gray, *Persian Paintings*, p. 12.
89. It is more frequent in the earlier manuscripts than that of the later works, e.g. folios 51V.158V, 194V, 219V, 293V (Cleveland, *Tuti Nama*); folios 14a, 22b, 26a (Rampur, *Tilasm and Zodiac*). The Persian master Bihzad also preferred the old fashioned gold sky. Though the Mughal painters employed this particular characteristic, on the whole it seems to have been rarely used as against the blue sky which are comparatively more common in Mughal painting.
90. Cf. Gray, *Persian Painting*, plate on p. 79 (Timurid School of Persia); Rai Anand Krishna, 'The Snake and the Camel Rider', *Marg*, vol. XXXV, no. 2. Illust. facing p. 32 (School of Akbar).
91. Vide Shahid Suhrawardi, 'Introduction to the Study of Indo-Persian Painting', *Marg*, vol. XI, no. 3, p. 28; Sir Leigh Ashton (ed.), *The Art of India and Pakistan*, London, 1950, no. 652, pl. 124 (School of Akbar); Gray, *Persian Painting*, pp. 1115–18, 121.

92. The subject was very popular during the reign of Jahangir; vide *The Library of Chester Beatty,* vol. III, pl. 70; Paul, op. cit., pl. M38; R.H. Pinder Wilson, 'Three Illustrated Manuscripts of the Mughal Period', *Ars Orientalis,* vol. II, 1957, fig. 4. In the representation of this particular theme the Mughal artists seem to have been initated the whole compositional arrangement from the identical Persian works.
93. Vide L. Binyon and T.W. Arnolds, *The Court Painters of the Grand Moguls,* Oxford, 1921, pp. 37–8; Shahid Suhrawardi, 'Introduction to the Study of Indo-Persian Painting', *Marg,* vol. XI, no. 3, 1958. Ray, op. cit., pp. 14–15.
94. Abul Fazl remarks about the Hindu painters that 'their picture surpass our conception of things' (*Ain-i Akbari,* p. 144).

Shams Siraj Afif's *Tarikh-i-Feroz Shahi*: A Source for the Study of Monuments of Delhi Built during Feroz Shah Tughluq's Reign

S.M. AZIZUDDIN HUSAIN

With the establishment of the Delhi sultanate significant changes took place in various aspects of life, specially the cultural life of India. *Madrasas, dargahs, sarais, shifa khanas, baolis*, dams, etc., were constructed. Three sultans of Delhi could be considered as builders of Delhi. They are Sultan Alauddin Khalji (1296–1316), Ghiyasuddin Tughluq (1320–5) and Feroz Shah Tughluq (1351–88). But amongst the sultans of Delhi, Feroz Shah was the most prolific in construction because he was very fond of architecture. He also founded new towns. His new capital, called Ferozabad, was the fifth city of Delhi. Feroz Shah built several mosques, *madrasas, kaushaks, baolis*, pigeon towers, *khanqahs, dargahs, shifa khanas, sarais*, dams, etc. His nobles took keen interest in building monuments. Feroz Shah not only constructed new monuments but also took interest in the conservation of monuments constructed by the earlier Sultans of Delhi. He directed Malik Najjari, Shahna-i-Mir-i-imarat to prepare a report about the condition of old mosques, *khanqahs, dargahs* and tombs whose builders had either died or had become economically weak. Earlier historians like Minhaj (the author of *Tabaqat-i-Nasiri*) and Ziauddin Barani (the author of *Tarikh-i-Feroz Shahi*) do not provide us information related to monuments. Shams Siraj Afif, author of *Tarikh-i-Feroz Shahi*[1] provides us valuable information on monuments. In this paper those monuments are being discussed whose description is given by Afif.

The first contribution of Feroz Shah was that when he received the report regarding the status of old monuments he directed

Malik Najjari to identify those monuments and allocated a large sum of money for the beautification of old mosques under the stewardship of *Mir-i-Imarat.*[2] So we can say that the first listing of monuments took place in his reign and considerable money and resources were allocated for their restoration and preservation.

The following new monuments were constructed during his reign. Afif writes that these mosques could accommodate nearly 10,000 persons during prayers.

Masjid-i-Jama Ferozi: Feroz Shah constructed this mosque in his new capital in 755/1354. He also arranged the inscription of the summary of his book *Futuhat-i-Feroz Shahi* on stone but the entire dome has now collapsed. Mirza Sangin Beg who prepared a descriptive listing of the monuments of Delhi, entitled *Sairul Manazil*, in 1827, does not give the text of the inscription. Sir Syed's *Asarus Sanadid*, published in 1846, also does not have any description of this mosque.[3]

Kalan or Kali Masjid: This mosque was constructed on the eastern side of Basti Nizamuddin. Its eastern gate has an inscription which gives the date of its construction as 772/1370.[4]

Kalan Masjid: This mosque is located near Shahjahanabad's Turkman Gate. Its eastern gate has an inscription which gives the date of its construction as 772/1370.[5] The mosque has witnessed many crucial events in history. Today, the people using it have painted it and have made new additions to the old structure as per their need.

Begampuri Masjid: This is located on Sri Aurobindo Marg. It is a spacious mosque having 24 arches. The central arch is higher than the other arches.[6]

Kalu Sarai Mosque: It is located on the Mehrauli–Delhi Road and constructed around 789/1387.[7]

Khirki Masjid: A built on the northern side of Khirki village and is one-storeyed high. There are three entry gates. The pillared

Begampuri Masjid

courtyard is divided into 25 squares, five on each side, each square consisting of nine squares. The rest of the squares on the corners are left uncovered to allow light and air. This is the first covered mosque in India.[8]

Khirki Masjid

Madarsa-i-Hauz Khas: Located near Aurobindo Marg this three storeyed *madrasa* is 'L' shaped and is built on the north and south bank of Hauz-i-Khas. From north it starts with a campus *masjid*. It has gates on the northern and western side of the *madrasa*. It is a large complex which could accommodate a large number of students. Barani writes that this *madrasa* attracted the attention of people of Delhi and consequently, they also constructed houses in the vicinity of the *madrasa*.[9]

Hauz Khas

Dargah of Nasiruddin Chiragh-i-Delli: Feroz Shah also built this *dargah*. There is a inscription on the main gate of the *dargah* which gives the date of its construction as 772/1370.[10]

Kaushak-i-Ferozi: It is located in the campus of Teen Murti Library. Feroz Shah used this building as his hunting lodge. It was earlier situated on a *bund* (barrage), but now there are no remains of this barrage, only one nullah is running nearby.[11]

Wazirabad Bund: Feroz Shah built one mosque and a *bund*. Inside the mosque, there is also one small tomb but we do not have details about this.[12]

Qadam Sharif and the Tomb of Fath Khan: Feroz Shah built this tomb, mosque, *madrasa* and a *hauz* in 776/1374. Makhdum Jahanian Jahan Gasht had brought and presented the Qadam Sharif (Footstep of Prophet Muhammad), to Feroz Shah which he fixed on the grave of his son, Fath Khan. It is located in the locality known as Nabi Karim.[13]

Dargah of Hazrat Saiyid Mehmud Bahar: He was among the descendants of Hazrat Saiyid Nasiruddin Sonipati, who was the grandson of Imam Jafar Sadiq. Saiyid Mehmud Bahar died in 778/1376, and Feroz Shah constructed the tomb on his grave. It is now located in Kilokhari facing Maharani Bagh, where once upon a time Ziauddin Barani used to live.[14]

Pir Ghaib: It is situated in the campus of Hindu Rao Hospital. There is one *chillagah* (a place of meditation) of some Sufi who came to be known as Pir Ghaib (Vanished Saint). There is also the Kaushik-i-Jahan-Numa built by Feroz Shah, as his hunting lodge.[15]

Malcha Mahal: It is located on Sardar Patel Marg and is almost square, with three main arches on its northern side. Feroz Shah constructed a *bund* which retained the rain water of the area.[16]

Bhuli Bhatyari ka Mahal: It is located near Panchkuiyan Road. It was also a hunting lodge of Feroz Shah. On its northern side he also built a *bund* which was used as a water reservoir.[17]

In Delhi, Feroz Shah had constructed 120 *khanqahs* and one person could stay in one *kanqah* for three days. If one stayed in all 120 *khanqahs* by rotation he could stay for a period of 360 days in Delhi even if he did not have his own resources.[18] This was done by Feroz Shah for the cause of poor people. All expenses of these *khanqahs* were borne by the sultan. During Mohammad Bin Tughluq's reign (1325–51) the *khanqahi* system was shattered as Barani rightly pointed out that as a result of the policies of Mohammad Bin Tughluq, even birds were not coming to these *khanqahs.* Just to revive the Khanqahi Nizam, Feroz Shah Tughluq took personal interest.

The monuments of Feroz Shah Tughluq's reign have perfect arches and domes. But they had gradually evolved and were a long way from the first original Islamic structure made on the Indian soil in 1199 in the form of an arched screen seen in the Quwwatul Islam Mosque basically to separate the courtyard from the sanctuary. The arch made in the screen is a corbelled arch wherein stone courses were laid in corbelled style, gradually achieving a gentle curve. The ogee shaped arch has a little S curve at the apex. The dome in the mosque is also not a true dome. Its made on the simple principle of trabeate order wherein the beam and columns support the stone slabs and make cup-shaped domes.

The arch as well as the dome got more refined with the gaining of expertise in construction technique by the masons, and we find the first true arch in Balban's Tomb constructed in 1280. A true arch means an arch made of voussoirs laid in a manner that it can take the load by means of tension and compression of the load above it. From the stand point of technological achievement, we see a prolific contribution of arches and domes in the structures of the Khaljis and Tughluqs.[19]

In Alai Darwaza made by Alauddin Khalji in 1305, there is a great degree of refinement and use of indigenous style and Indian motifs in its decoration. The shape and inventiveness of arches, in the method of walling, in the support of the dome by means of squinches and surface decoration shows fresh influence and technological advancement. This expertise and innovation passed on from one ruler to the next with few modifications and creativity of the Indian masons.

The earlier implementation of the arch was a bit hesitant and so a lintel beam was used along with the arch till Tughluq's time. There is an influence of the Persian style of architecture in buildings in the Delhi region. But for Indian masons architecture and the construction was more like a heavy industry wherein each block of stone was quarried, worked upon with a chisel and hammer and hence called for a lot of hard labour. It was not a facile manipulation of plastic material in the form of brick or glazed tiles of brilliant colour, rather it was more structural. This was passed on to Firoz Shah Tughluq's period.[20]

During his long reign Feroz Shah Tughluq constructed various types of buildings in a peculiar style of his own. The architectural character is fundamentally different and is a reflection of the political conditions that prevailed at that time in the city. A scarcity of skilled stone-masons and experienced workmen was one of the factors when the building's construction had to be commenced, especially when technical expertise was to be sought.

Another important factor was the reduced finances, hence the buildings that were constructed were made with inexpensive locally available materials and put up in a manner which did not call for too much workmanship. Locally available stones was used in the form of building blocks and were laid in random rubble masonry instead of finely coursed and well finished sandstone fitted squarely in ashlar masonry. The surfaces were untrimmed and cement-coated. Hence the architectural style can be seen as plain yet very serviceable.[21]

In the random rubble masonry, additional measures were adapted to give it strength and stability by building portions thicker at the base than at the top. This gave an angle of batter to the structure. The effect of the slope is emphasized by the attachment of tapering turreted buttresses at the quoins and by projecting conical bastion-like towers crowned with low domes from the four corners of the building. In certain parts of the building, features like lintels, doorposts, and pillars were formed of roughly dressed monoliths. The decoration was negligible, and mostly moulded in plaster instead of any carving of the stone. The structures so formed looked somewhat dull and, sombre with a colour scheme of monochromes and half tones.

These monuments have stood the vagaries of time and a lot of damage has happened to the structures because of weathering, etc. It is sad to see them broken, decaying, dilapidated and vandalized today, where were once the corridors of power.

NOTES

1. Shams Siraj Afif, *Tarikh-i-Feroz Shahi,* Hyderabad, 1938; Mirza Sangin Beg, *Sairul Manazil,* Delhi, 1982.
2. Afif, p. 100.
3. Ibid., p. 101.

4. Ibid., p. 101. Sangin Beg., p. 84.
5. Ibid., p. 101. Sangin Beg., p. 24.
6. Afif, p. 100.
7. Ibid., p. 101.
8. Ibid., p. 101.
9. Ibid., p. 100.
10. Ibid., p. 100.
11. Ibid., p. 101. Sangin Beg., pp. 92–3.
12. Afif, p. 101.
13. Ibid., p. 100. Sangin Beg., pp. 55–9.
14. Afif., p. 100. Sangin Beg., p. 88.
15. Ibid., p. 101.
16. Ibid., p. 101.
17. Ibid., p. 101. Mirza Sangin Beg., 62–3.
18. Afif, p. 100.
19. Percy Brown, *Indian Architecture, Islamic Period,* rpt. Bombay, D.B. Taraporevala, 1997.
20. Lucy Peck, *Delhi: A Thousand Years of Building,* Delhi, 2005.
21. Bianca Maria Alfieri, *Islamic Architecture of the Indian Subcontinent,* London, 2000.

PART III

ECONOMY

Administration of *Jagirs* in Malwa in Mid-Seventeenth Century: The Dhar Documents

SYED BASHIR HASAN

While a considerable amount of documentation exists on revenue grants (*madad-i-maash*) and *zamindari* estates, we are not so fortunate in regard to the way the *jagirdars* managed their *jagirs*, which they owned only on a temporary basis. It must be counted as a piece of good luck that the Islamic Art Museum, Kuwait, has obtained a set of 43 documents that once belonged to a family of *chaudhuris* of *pargana* Dhar, *sarkar* Mandu of *suba* Malwa belonging mainly to the latter half of the seventeenth century.[1] These provide a great deal of information not only on the working of the office of the *chaudhuri* but also on the way the *jagirs* were held and administered. For this paper I have selected 24 documents[2] covering the period 1644 to 1653. The period is of some interest, since it includes the period of the War of Succession, 1658–9, and some documents shedding interesting light on what happened on the ground during that tumultuous civil war.

The town of Dhar was the headquarters of Malwa at the time Dilawar Khan laid the foundation of an independent sultanate of Malwa. It was his son Alp Khan also known as Hoshang Shah, who shifted the seat of government to Mandu.[3] Better known as the capital of Raja Bhoja and many ancient princes,[4] and an important centre of Sufi activities, the town of Dhar lies at some distance from the imperial Mughal route passing through Malwa via Ujjain.[5] Abul Fazl lists the *pargana* of Dhar in the *mahal* list of *sarkar* Mandu.[6] Presently Dhar is the headquarters of a district of the same name about 65 km from Indore.[7] The other *parganas* mentioned in the Dhar documents including Nalcha, Amjhera, Barod[i]a, Lawani[8] and Hindaula[9] were in *sarkar* Mandu and are recorded under it in the *Ain.*[10] *Pargana* Sanwer, included in the *jagir* of Dara Shukoh, was in *sarkar* Ujjain.[11]

A perusal of these documents enable us to trace the family lineage of the *chaudhuris* of *pargana* Dhar to whom these documents are addressed (see Appendix B). Of them Parsottam Das, the *chaudhuri* appointed by Prince Murad Bakhsh remained in office throughout the period unaffected by either the war or by transfers of *jagirs*.

From 1653 to 1685 Dhar appears to have been held as *jagir* by nine *jagirdars* and remained for some time under *khalisa* (see Appendix C). When our documents begin (omitting one stray from Akbar's time, 1576–7),[12] it was held in *jagir* by Prince Murad Bakhsh. He was appointed *subadar* of Malwa in 1650–1[13] and remained in-charge of that province till 1653–4 when he was transferred to Gujarat as its *subadar.*[14] Our documents show that on his appointment as *subadar* of Malwa he still retained Dhar in his *jagir* and continued to hold that till 1655–7. A *parwana* dated 27 Muharram 28 RY/18 December 1653 addressed to the *chaudhuri* of *pargana* Dhar under the charge of Diyanat Khan[15] who held the office of the *diwan* of Murad Bakhsh (not of Gujarat) in 1653–4.[16] We may assume that Diyanat Khan might also have been the Prince Murad Bakhsh's *diwan* when that prince was previously *subadar* of Malwa. The *parwana* of Diyanat Khan also reveals that Mir Ibrahim was the revenue collector of the *pargana.* In this *parwana* Diyanat Khan appreciates the exertions of the *chaudhuri* as reported by Mir Ibrahim in respect of *rabi* cultivation and assures him of due favour if he continues his work in the same way and contributes to the increase of revenue.

A *parwana* issued by Mir Ibrahim, dated Shawal, RY 30/July–August 1656 addressed to the officials of *pargana* Dhar informs them that Prince Murad Bakhsh has appointed Parsottam Das to the office of the *chaudhuri* of *pargana* Dhar, together with the *inam* villages (revenue-free villages) attached to the office, on which he was required to pay a fixed *peshkash* of Rs. 300.[17] This order probably accorded formal approval to the succession of Parsottam Das to the office of *chaudhuri* after his uncle's death. In fact, this had already taken place because a *parwana* of Diyanat Khan dated Rabi I, 29 RY/17 January 1655 is already addressed to Parsottam Das referring him as the *chaudhuri* of *pargana* Dhar.[18] What is interesting here is that perhaps because of Murad Bakhsh's position as a prince, his appointment was deemed sufficient, and orders from the imperial court were not sought, as was usual for *chaudhuris* in ordinary *jagirs.*[19]

In an order dated 4 Safar 29 RY/3 December 1655, we see Mir Ibrahim adjudicating in a dispute over the use of water from an old tank between the peasants of villages Nauganwa and Qilchipur on one side, and the peasants of village Tarnod on the other. The *parwana* is addressed to the *chaudhuris, qanungos, muqaddams* and peasants of *pargana* Dhar, informing them 'that a tank situated near the villages of Nauganwa and Qilchipur of the said *pargana* is attached to the land of these two villages since old times; now however the peasants of village Tarnod intend to use the water of the tank for their cultivation'. This being contrary to the existing rights of the two named villages, the *parwana* directs the addressees that no one should interfere with the water of the tank except the peasants of the said villages. The peasants of Nauganwa should not be harassed and no one should treat oneself 'as a partner with them' in that tank. Any one doing so was liable to being punished. Interestingly, this *parwana* also directs the peasants of Nauganwa, as a kind of return for the official favour, that an additional 10 *bighas* of land must be cultivated with sugar cane annually, to yield revenue over and above the *jama* (fixed annual assessment).[20] This shows that revenue was here imposed through measurement, otherwise it would not be known whether the villagers were adding 10 *bighas* to the land cultivated by them. Moreover, the specification of sugar cane suggests that the revenue rate varied according to the crop grown there, as was the case with Akbar's *dasturu'l amals.*

Another *parwana* issued by Diyanat Khan, an officer of Prince Murad Bakhsh dated 15 Safar 30 RY/3 December 1656 addressed to the *chaudhuris, zamindars,* etc., displays anxiety about land-revenue collection not being gathered according to the peasants' capacity. The *parwana* says that owing to good rainfall the crops have been excellent and so no one is entitled to demand any remission.[21] The document contains valuable information in terms of revenue terminology since it calls the year of good crops as *sal-i kamil* and *akmal,* the latter meaning one better than the previous best in terms of abundant harvest. Perhaps, this is the earliest document using the terms *sal-i kamil* and *sal-i akmal*, though it is hard to suppose that the term *sal-i kamil* was not used earlier.

Prince Murad Bakhsh's *jagirs* in Malwa, including *pargana* Dhar, were transferred to Prince Dara Shukoh, the eldest son of Shahjahan, on the eve of the war of succession. A *parwana* of an officer of Dara Shukoh dated 24 Safar 1068/1 December 1657 addressed to the *chaudhuris, qanungos*, etc., issued on receipt of Prince Dara Shukoh's *nishan*, informs them of this transfer and intimates them that until the time the *faujdars, karoris* and *amins* arrive from Prince Dara Shukoh's headquarters, he would manage the *pargana* previously held by Prince Murad Bakhsh. He strictly forbids them to pay anything to Prince Murad Bakhsh's officers.[22] Naturally, Diyanat Khan and Ibrahim being in the service of Murad Bakhsh are heard of no more. This was the time when the news of Shahjahan's illness and suspected death was surrounding the empire and Murad had early in November 1657 looted Surat city and finally crowned himself on 5 December.[23] However, the fact is that by the middle of November 1657 Shahjahan had overcome his illness and completely recovered.[24] It was essential to curb Murad Bakhsh's power and resources, and so the transfer of his *jagirs* in Malwa to Dara Shukoh was a natural, precautionary step. It was also the prelude to the dispatch of strong forces under Qasim Khan and Rathor Raja Jaswant Singh into Malwa (and, subsequently, into Gujarat).[25] These forces suffered a heavy reversal at Dharamatpur on 22 Rajab 1068/25 April 1658, whereafter Aurangzeb and Murad, the victors, proceeded to Agra.[26] Dara's administration in these *jagirs* must have collapsed upon the receipt of the news of Dharamatpur.

But we can see disturbances intruding even before that battle had been fought. Taking advantage of the confusion, the Girasias, a type of *zamindars* or local chiefs, more common in Gujarat than Central India, began to cause disturbances around Dhar. An undated *parwana* of Hakim Muzaffar, an officer of Dara Shukoh, refers to official action against the Girasias as reported by Parsottam Das, the *chaudhuri* and Parasram, the *qanungo*. He directs the *chaudhuri* and *qanungo* to ride out to every village, taking from the village headmen an undertaking for immediate dispatch of information of any intrusion.[27] The same document refers to an addition of Rs. 9,000 to the revenue demand, since the cultivation of the *rabi* had been good and unaffected by crop failure, as compared to the previous year when the crops were struck with heavy calamity. Yet that year Khwaja Bhagmal, the *karori* (of Prince Murad, apparently) had recommended the addition of Rs. 11,300 on the assessment. The last document of Dara Shukoh's *jagir* administration in Malwa is dated 24 Jumada II 32 RY/31 March 1658,[28] and is thus just anterior to the defeat at Dharamatpur.

The next *jagirdar* Nawazish Khan is mentioned in *Alamgirnama* as having been sent off from the Punjab to his posting in Malwa on 11 Zilhij 1068/9 September 1658 with the rank of 3000/1000.[29] He finds mention in the same work again as one of those posted (*kumakiyan*) to Malwa on 2 Sha'ban, RY2/13 April 1660 and 15 Rabi I RY4/8 November 1661; on both occasions he is reported as holding the rank of 3000/1200.[30] When he died, he was still in Malwa, holding charge as *faujdar* of Mandu; the news of his death was received at the court on 19 Muharram 8 RY/ 1 August 1665.[31] The dated documents attesting to Nawazish Khan's term of assignment run from 23 April 1659[32] to 8 May 1664,[33] suggesting that Dhar was assigned to him upon his positing to Malwa in late 1658 and he remained in his *jagir* till his death in 1665.

Nawazish Khan managed his *jagir* well and took keen interest in the increase of cultivation,[34] and the realization of arrears.[35] He took serious view of the repeated petitions or remissions without detailed justification sent by Parsottam, the *chaudhuri,* and Parasram, the *qanungo* of *pargana* Dhar. He informs them that in the ensuing harvest the *jama* of the *pargana* will be assessed as per inspection of the actual conditions, but a clerk of his officers Mirza Asadullah or Rai Narsingh or an *amin,* with whom they are satisfied, will be sent for the purpose.[36]

A *parwana* of Nawazish Khan, dated 12 Shawal 1074 RY 37/ May 1664 gives expression to anxiety regarding collection of revenues and arrears. He asks the *chaudhuri,* Parsottam Das, to come to the headquarters [Mandu] with horsemen and *piyadas,* leaving his son behind to carry on the duty of collecting revenue.

He cautions the *chaudhuri* that during his absence there should be no relaxation in exacting revenues and arrears.[37]

The maintenance of law and order and welfare of the people was also the part of *jagir* administration. A case of theft of a camel of theologian Khalifa Jiu in the town of Dhar was reported to an officer of Nawazish Khan and he took quick action by asking the *chaudhuri* and *qanungo* of *parwana* Dhar to make utmost exertions in tracing the animal.[38]

There is another *parwana* dated 1659–60 issued by Asadullah, a subordinate of Nawazish Khan, which says that the *muqaddam* of village Khanpur in *pargana* Jamli had left his home and taken residence elsewhere. Now that the *muqaddam* has come back but he is not allowed to bring back his cattle. Asadullah takes Parsottam Das to task for this, saying 'this is not proper'.[39]

A *parwana* of an officer of Nawazish Khan dated 5 January 1661 is an interesting document for revenue administration as it refers to *paimaish tafriq*, measurement of individual holdings, to be carried out in every village of *pargana* Dhar.[40] This confirms our impression from an earlier document that measurement operations for assessment purposes were still in vogue in this area.

A document of some interest is a *dastak* (permit) issued by an officer of the *jagirdar* certifying that Nayak Sengha (perhaps a *banjara* chief) and other *banjaras* were permitted to buy grain in *pargana* Dhar without any transit duty (*zakat*). This is dated 1 Ramazan 1073/9 April 1663.[41] A point to be noted is that the agent of the *jagirdar* is exercising such an authority on behalf of the *jagirdar*.

These documents are also valuable in giving us a glimpse of the working of the *chaudhuri* of *pargana* level in revenue administration. Interestingly they bear ample testimony to show how Parsottam Das, the *chaudhuri* of *pargana* Dhar, used his position in fiscal administration and his financial resources to expand his authority and jurisdiction. He obtained a remission of Rs. 4,000 in the *peshkash* due from his uncle Chandrabhan, who died in *c.* 1665.[42] His son Nathmal obtained the tax-farm (*ijara*) of *pargana* Jaili referred to in the document dated 21 January 1664;[43] then document dated 18 July 1662[44] shows Parsottam Das taking interest in protecting peasants of that *pargana* from raids by revenue officials. Nathmal might have been holding that *pargana* in *ijara* as well.

Within *pargana* Dhar, Parsottam Das tried to extend his tax-free *inam/nankar* holdings. In 1656 he was obliged to pay Rs. 300 annually as *peshkash* on each village thus held by him.[45] In 1659 the number of such villages was left to the local *qazi* to settle.[46] In 1663 Parsottam Das's total *inam* holdings in *pargana* Dhar were 10 whole villages, 550 *bighas* of land (in addition), 43 mango trees and one garden.[47] Parsottam's family also increased its holdings of gardens. His son Nathmal was allowed 25 *bighas* tax-free land to create a garden in a village of *pargana* Dhar[48] allegedly for the comfort of travellers. This is a fine example of tax evasion and an increase in personal holdings on the plea of public utility. Clearly, while the *jagirdar* and his officers were vigilant in collecting revenue, they were not vigilant enough!

NOTES

1. The original Dhar Documents are in Islamic Art Museum Dar al-Athar al-Islamiyyah, Kuwait, numbered as LNS 235 MS a–qq. The xerox copies were sent to Professor Shireen Moosvi by Mrs. Henrietta Sharp Cockrell. Hereafter referred to as the Dhar Documents, the number being the one given to each document by Kuwait museum.
2. A calendar of these documents is appended (Appendix A).
3. U.N. Day, *Medieval Malwa*, Delhi, 1965, pp. 8–62.
4. Abul Fazl, *Ain-i Akbari*, ed. H. Blochmann, vol. I, p. 468.
5. Irfan Habib, *An Atlas of the Mughal Empire*, rpt., Delhi: Oxford University Press, 1986, sheet 9B.
6. *Ain-i Akbari*, vol. I, p. 464.
7. *Madhya Pradesh District Gazetteers*, Dhar (Bhopal, 1984), p. 297.
8. Nawali in the *Ain* seems to be an error for Lawani. See Irfan Habib, op. cit., p. 34.
9. Neither recorded in the *Ain* nor shown in Irfan Habib's *Atlas*.
10. *Ain-i Akbari*, vol. I, pp. 464–5; Irfan Habib, op. cit., sheet 9A.
11. *Ain-i Akbari*, vol. I, p. 457; Irfan Habib, op. cit., sheet 9A.
12. Dhar Documents, no. (d).
13. M. Athar Ali, *The Apparatus of Empire*, Delhi, 1985, p. 262.
14. Ibid., p. 279.
15. Dhar Documents, no. (e).
16. Ali Muhammad Khan, *Mirat-i Ahmadi*, ed. Nawab Ali, 3 vols., Calcutta, 1928, vol. I, p. 231. Athar Ali, op. cit., p. 279 is inaccurate in treating Diyanat Khan as the *diwan* of Gujarat.

17. Dhar Documents, no. (k).
18. Ibid., no. (b).
19. Cf. Irfan Habib, *Agrarian System of Mughal India 1556–1707*, revised edn., Delhi, 1999, pp. 335–6.
20. Ibid., no.(j).
21. Ibid., no.(d).
22. Ibid., no.(1).
23. Jadunath Sarkar, *History of Aurangzeb*, vols. I & II (combined), rpt., Calcutta, 1973, p. 176.
24. Ibid., p. 175.
25. Muhammad Kazim, *Alamgirnama*, ed. Maulvis Khadim Husain and Abdul Hai, Calcutta, 1865-73, pp. 32–3.
26. Ibid., pp. 59–83
27. Dhar Documents, no.(i).
28. Ibid., no.(h).
29. Muhammad Kazim, *Alamgirnama*, 1865-73, p. 189.
30. Ibid., pp. 274, 593.
31. Ibid., p. 908.
32. Dhar Documents, no.(e).
33. Ibid., no.(dd).
34. Ibid., no.(g).
35. Ibid., no.(f).
36. Ibid., no.(y).
37. Ibid., no.(dd).
38. Ibid., no.(II).
39. Ibid., no.(pp).
40. Ibid., no.(mm).
41. Ibid., no.(nn).
42. Ibid., no.(b).
43. Ibid., no.(gg).
44. Ibid., no.(cc).
45. Ibid., no.(k).
46. Ibid., no.(e).
47. Ibid., no.(o).
48. Ibid., no.(s)

APPENDIX A

Calendar of Dhar Documents 1576–7 and 1653–64

1. Grant of 200 *bighas* of land in village Gadrawada in *pargana* Dhar to Chaitidas, Nahardas, etc. in *inam* in return for their services, the grants to be exempted from all taxes. Dated 984 AH/1576-77. *LNS 235 MS (d).*
2. Diyanat Khan's *Parwana*:
Chaudhuri of *pargana* Dhar, province Malwa, is informed that Mir Ibrahim, incharge of revenue collection of Prince Murad Bakhsh has reported about his exertions in respect of the Rabi cultivation; if he continues his exertions in the same way and contributes to the increase of the revenues, he will receive due favour. Dated 27 Muharram 28 RY/18 December 1653. *LNS 235 MS (c).*
3. Order issued by Ibrahim, servant of Prince Murad:
The *chaudhuris, qanungos, muqaddams* and peasants of *pargana* Dhar are informed that the tank near the villages Nauganwa and Qilchipur of that *pargana* are attached to these villages from old times till the present. Now the peasants of village Tarnod want that they should take water from the tank for their own fields. It is therefore ordered that no one except the peasants entitled to do so from old times should draw waters from the tank; otherwise they will be punished. Also ordered that an additional 10 *bighas* of land shall be cultivated with sugarcane every year, outside the fixed *jama* in village Nauganwa. Dated 4 Safar 29 RY/3 December 1655. *LNS 235 MS (j).*
4. Diyanat Khan's *Parwana*:
Parsottam Das (brother's son of Chandrabhan), *chaudhuri* of *pargana* Dhar, is informed that his petition has been received. He writes that after Chandrabhan's death his heirs are greatly distressed and if a recovery of 4000 rupees, that Mir Ibrahim has been ordered by headquarters to make, is made, they would have to abandon their homes in which case nothing would be collected. This plea has been put before the Prince and he has ordered that the arrears be waived. In return Parsottam Das is to make utmost exertions to carry out his duties as *chaudhuri* and pay the *peshkash* regularly. Dated 9 Rabi I 29 RY/17 January 1655. *LNS 235 MS(b).*
5. Ibrahim's *Parwana*:
Officials of *pargana* Dhar are informed that by Prince Murad Bakhsh's *nishan* and the *parwana* of the officials of his headquarters, the office of the *chaudhuri* of the said *pargana* is given over to Parsottam Das. On his *inam* villages (attached to the office) he is to pay a fixed *peshkash* of 300 rupees. Dated Shawal, RY. 30/July-August 1656. *LNS 235 MS (k).*

6. [Diyanat] Khan's *Parwana*:
Chaudhuris, zamindars, qanungos, muqaddams, peasants and cultivators are informed that owing to good rainfall the crops have been excellent and this year can be deemed *sal-i kamil,* even *akmal.* No one is therefore entitled to demand remission. Dated 15 Safar 30 RY/3 December 1656. *LNS 235 MS (d).*
7. *Parwana* of Officer of Dara Shukoh:
Chaudhuris, qanungos, muqaddams, peasants, cultivators, and all residents in general of *pargana* Dhar, *sarkar* Mandu, are informed that Prince Dara Shukoh's *nishan* has been received to the effect that *pargana* Sanwer etc. as listed on the reverse has been transferred from Prince Murad Bakhsh to the *jagir* of Prince Dara Shukoh with effect from the beginning of *Kharif,* Takhaqui Il. The Prince (Dara Shukoh) has ordered that the undersigned has been appointed to take charge of the said *parganas* until the time the *faujdars* (commandants), *karoris* (revenue-collectors) and *amins* (assessors) arrive from the headquarters. All should continue to cultivate the land and not pay any revenue to the former revenue collectors. Dated 24 Safar 1068/1 December 1657. *LNS 235 MS(l).*
8. *Parwana* of [Hakim Muzaffar] Officer of Dara Shukoh:
Notes that Parsottam Das, the *chaudhuri,* and Parasram, the *qanungo,* have written that the Girasias, Akhibhan and Udai Singh have been harassing the peasants with a group of 30 horsemen; and that the officer Muhammad Aqil and the captain Harnath Singh have ridden out with four companies and that Khwaja Nand Lal came across Udai Singh Girasia and that two Girasia horsemen have been killed while four horsemen of Harnath Singh have lost their lives; and that the intelligence of this has been sent to different places. It is certain that by now Muhammad Aqil and Harnath Singh have dealt with the problems of the Girasias. You should also ride out village to village and take undertakings from village headmen that they would inform immediately if anyone intrudes into their villages. Note has been taken of the cultivation of peas and cotton. Last year 11,300 rupees had been added at the recommendation of Khwaja Bhagmal Karori although the crops were struck by heavy calamity. This year when the cultivation of Rabi *int il* is good and unaffected by calamity, an addition of 9,000 rupees has been fixed. This should be collected from each village. The entire Rabi crop depends on wheat, barley and opium. *LNS 235 MS (i).*
9. *Parwana* of Hakim Muzaffar, the Officer of Prince Dara Shukoh:
Parsottam Chaudhuri and Parasram Qanungo of *pargana* Dhar are informed that their report has been received. The undersigned is coming personally and when he sees their good service, they will be

duly rewarded. Dated 26 Jumada II 32 RY/31 March 1658. *LNS 235 MS (h).*

10. *Parwana* of Nawazish Khan, the Officer of Shahjahan:
Parsottam Chaudhuri and Parasram Qanungo of *pargana* Dhar are informed that their petition has been received. Whatever they have written about their *nankar* villages had earlier been told to Qazi Jiu in my presence. He is going to arrive there and whatever he fixes will be accepted by us. The addressees are to apply themselves to their work. Dated 30 Rajab 1069/23 April 1659. *LNS 235 MS (e).*

11. *Parwana* of Nawazish Khan:
Parsottam Chaudhuri and Parasram Qanungo of *pargana* Dhar are informed that their petition about their arrears of 1065 (fasli) and the arrival of a person sent by [the Diwan] Kifayat Khan has been received. It is necessary that whatever arrears are due should be paid and whatever they have to say in this connection they should write to Kifayat Khan and act according to what he orders. Dated 7 Shaban 1069/30 April 1659.
PS: Qazi Jiu, who is there, should be consulted in matters of account. *LNS 235 MS (f).*

12. *Parwana* of Nawazish Khan:
Exhorts Parsottam Chaudhuri and Parasram Qanungo of *pargana* Dhar to increase cultivation by 100 per cent or 200 per cent. Dated 8 Ramazan 1069/30 May 1659. *LNS 235 MS (g).*

13. *Parwana* of Officer of Nawazish Khan:
Refers to the letter of Parsottam Chaudhuri and Parasram Qanungo of *pargana* Dhar about Talaotis. The Diwan (*Wakalat Panah*) has written a letter in this regard. Dated 28 shaban 1070/9 May 1660. *LNS 235 MS (100).*

14. *Parwana* of Asadullah, the Officer of Nawazish Khan:
Parsottam Chaudhuri is informed that the captain Shaikh Abdul Rasul has stated that the *muqaddam* of the village Khanpur in *pargana* Jamli had left his home and taken residence [elsewhere]. Now he has returned to his old village but he is not allowed to bring back his cattle etc. This is not proper. Dated 1070/1659-60. *LNS 235 MS (pp).*

15. *Parwana* of [Nawazish Khan]:
Parsottam Chaudhuri and Parasram Qanungo of *pargana* Dhar are informed that in the ensuing harvest a clerk (Mirza) of Mirza Asadullah or Rai Narsingh Das or an *amin* with whom they are satisfied will be sent and the *jama* of *pargana* Dhar will be assessed according to the actual conditions. Why they make repeated petitions for remissions without detailed justification is not clear. Let them devote themselves to their work. Dated 16 Zilhij 1070/23 August 1660.
PS: A *parwana* has been issued to Hashim Khan. You should accompany him to village Bajor so that no such quarrel occurs. *LNS 235 MS (y).*

16. *Parwana* of an Officer of Nawazish Khan:
The theologian Khalifa Jiu has complained that a camel of his has been stolen in *qasba* Dhar (the town of Dhar). Parsottam Chaudhuri and Parasram Qanungo of *pargana* Dhar are therefore required to make utmost exertion to trace the animal. Dated 27 Muharram 1071/ 2 October 1660. *LNS MS (ll).*
17. *Parwana* of an Officer of Nawazish Khan:
Parsottam Chaudhuri and Parasram Qanungo are informed that the *salami* (perquisite) arising out of the inspection of the measurement of land distribution in every village of the said *pargana* should be paid to Khwaja Jharnarayan so that he may send it to the headquarters. Dated 10 Jumada I 1071/5 January 1661. *LNS 235 MS (mm).*
18. *Parwana* of Nawazish Khan, the servant of Aurangzeb:
Trusted officer, Lal Muhammad, is informed that a complaint has been received from Parsottam, *chaudhuri* of *pargana* Dhar, that Lal Muhammad had gone to *pargana* Jaili and told the peasants that he would raid and plunder these villages and that has demoralized the peasants there. This is very improper on the part of Lal Muhammad and he is informed that he has nothing to do with the *pargana* Jaili of my *sarkar.* Dated 1 Zilhij 5 RY/18 July 1662. *LNS 235. MS (cc).*
19. *Parwana* of Saiyid Muhammad Husain, servant of Aurangzeb:
Officers of *pargana* Dhar, *sarkar* Mandu, *suba* Malwa are informed that since son of Nathmal, son of Chaudhuri Parsottam has established a garden on 25 *bighas* of *banjar* land in village Sandhauri for the comfort of travellers, no tax is to be taken from this garden. Dated Rabi I 1073/ October–November 1662. *LNS 235 MS (s).*
20. *Dastak* of Asadullah, the Officer of Nawazish Khan:
Nayak Sengha and other *banjaras* come to *pargana* Dhar to buy grain. Let no one levy *zakat* (transit duty) on them. Dated 1 Ramazan 1073/ 9 April 1663. *LNS 235 MS (nn).*
21. *Parwana* of Asadullah Nawazish Khani:
Refers to *qubuliyat* (Agreement) of revenue (*mal*) received from Parsottam Chaudhuri and Parasram Qanungo of *pargana* Dhar. Dated 13 Ziqad 1073/19 June 1663. *LNS 235 MS (kk).*
22. *Parwana* of Mir Khan Chela? of Alamgir:
Officers of *pargana* Dhar are informed that according to the *sanads* of previous *jagirdars* 10 whole villages and 550 *bighas* of land, 43 mango trees and one garden are assigned in *inam* to Parsottam Chaudhuri along with his sons. These should be allowed to him and no taxes is to be levied on them. Dated 21 Rabi I 6RY/23 October 1663. *LNS 235 MS (o).*
23. *Parwana* of (Asadullah) servant of Nawazish Khan:
Parsottam Chaudhuri and Parasram Qanungo are informed that their report about the removal of the villages from the jurisdiction of Abdul

Hamid, the *shahna*, has been received. Abdul Hamid and Khuda Dost have been directed in writing to immediately remove their *piyadas* from the said village. Now the addressees should be satisfied and more so since for their satisfaction a sum of 23,000 rupees has been remitted. It is surprising that they have not sent even a part of the revenue collected. [1660–63] *LNS 235 MS (qq).*

24. *Parwana* of Nawazish Khan, 'Slave' of Aurangzeb:
Chaudhuri Parsottam is required to come to headquarters with horsemen and *piyadas* leaving his son to collect the revenue but there should be no relaxation in collection of revenues and arrears. Dated 12 Shawal 1074 7 RY/3 May 1664. *LNS 235 MS (dd).*

APPENDIX B

Genealogy of the *Chaudhuris* of *Pargana* Dhar

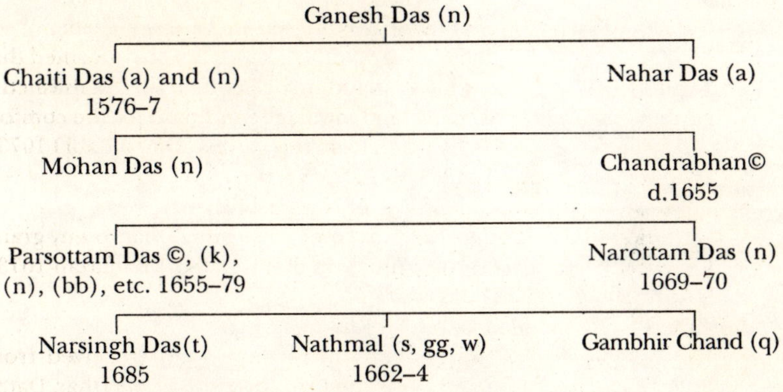

APPENDIX C

Jagirdars of *Pargana* Dhar

Jagirdar	Period	Reference (Dhar Documents)
Diyanat Khan (*diwan* of Murad Bakhsh)	1653–5	bc
Murad Bakhsh (Continues)	1655–7	j, k, l.
Dara Shukoh	1657–8	l, i, h.
Nawazish Khan	1659–64	e, f, g, pp, oo, ii, mm, cc, kk, qq, dd
Khalisa	1665 (?)	ee, z
Wazir Khan	1666–7	v, jj
Mahabat Khan	1671	P
Ali Beg Khan(?)	1674	U
Islam Khan	1675	hh
–Khan	1679	bb
Rahmat	1685	t

Sasan Grants under the Rathor Chiefs of Marwar: A Case Study of Maharaja Jaswant Singh (1638–1678)

R.S. SANGWAN

The Rathor chiefs of Marwar used to assign a part of their principality's tax-claim to the Charans (bards), Brahmins, the temple priests, Bhats, etc., by way of *sasan* or charity grants. Occasionally also termed as *punya-udik*, *udik*, and *doli*, these charity grants are broadly comparable to those given by the sultans of Delhi and the Mughal emperors (called *suyurghal*, *madad-i ma'ash*, *wazifa*, etc.). The Vijayanagara kings also made such grants and called them *manya* lands or villages. Historically, the Rathor chiefs seem to have been guided and inspired by the tradition or practice of the ancient Indian kings enshrined in the institutions like *brahmadeya*, *brahmotar* and *devadeya* charity land grants, enjoyed almost on hereditary basis in the line of the original grantees, and also those of their preceding Chauhan and Parihar rulers of Marwar in making *sasan* land grants.[1] In fact the tradition of offering charity or patronage, in some way or the other, to the priestly class and the learned men, etc., is such as no polity or ruling authority would normally afford to ignore, as such charity acts served as a powerful means in earning the goodwill, loyalty and support of the subjects in general, and its more vocal segments in particular, for the ruling dispensation. Another more important redeeming feature of such charity grants was in the form of promoting and sustaining the ideological and cultural heritage of a country. It may not be too much to assume that the enormous Dingle and Pingle literature of Rajasthan, the Marwar region specially boasts of, was produced by the Charans, Bhats and Brahmin scholars and owes a lot to such patronage.

Muhnot Nainsi provides us with *pargana*-wise detailed information about the *sasan* grants, their quantum, economic value as well as the beneficiaries and the distribution pattern, etc., pertaining to the seven *parganas* of Marwar, held by Maharaja Jaswant Singh at the time of the compilation of his *Vigat* (*c.* AD 1662).[2] It helps us in understanding the various facets of this institution. The present paper seeks to analyse this data for understanding the various aspects of *sasan* grants.

Under the Rathor chiefs of Marwar, there was no regular department meant for providing or managing the *sasan* grants comparable to that of *diwan-i sadarat* headed by *sadr-us sudar* in the Mughal imperial system which managed the *madad-i ma'ash* or *aimma* grants made to the *ulema* and *mashaikh* and the institutions run by them and, mainly from Akbar's period onwards, to the non-Muslim saints, scholars, priests, deities, etc.[3] However, as even after their accepting the Mughal suzerainty the autonomous Rajput chiefs were free to make revenue assignments in the form of *pattas* to their *sardars* and also revenue-free charitable land grants, the Rathor chiefs simply continued the practice they had already inherited from their preceding Chauhan and Parihar rulers of Marwar with regard to the *sasan* grants in their principality theoretically termed as their *watan* (homeland).

It is generally assumed that the Rathor rajas enjoyed the exclusive right of creating *sasan* grants. However, Muhnot Nainsi or for that matter any other available sources nowhere make it explicitly clear that such was the case from the very beginning of the Rathor rule in Marwar. In fact, Nainsi's *Vigat* contains several instances of the *sasan* grants made by Rathor *sardars* which tend to show that even they were free to make *sasan* grants from out of their rightful share of the land (*bant*), on the principle of *bhai-bant* (sharing among brothers). For instance, the sons of Rathor Jodha, Bar Singh and Duda were granted Merta territory when they and their descendants gave grants by way of *sasan.*[4] Even the Rathor *sardars* posted in the territory effectively controlled from Jodhpur, the nodal seat of Rathor authority, made the *sasan* grants.[5] However it may be presumed that from the time of Maldev, who asserted his supremacy over his clansmen treating them as mere clan-retainers (*bhai-band chakar* instead of *bhai-bands*) and in this bid began to grant *pattas* to those family members and other kinsmen who accepted his suzerainty, the rights of the *pattawats* might have began to be curtailed.[6] The *pattawats*, it can be safely assumed, might have to seek permission from the grantor, i.e. the raja, to make any charitable grant from out of such service *pattas*. Only few *sardars* enjoyed the right to make *sasan* grants. For example, Rao Maldev gave Akhairaj Randhirot Sonagara the *patta* of Pali. During his tenure he gave Aakelari, a village of Pali, by way of *sasan*.[7] Likewise Rathor Jaswant and Rathor Dungersi Udawat gave Karoliyo and Jana Wasni villages of Jaitaran by way of *sasan* during their respective *patta* tenure.[8] *Pattawats* who did not enjoy such rights yet desired to grant *sasan* to someone could request the raja to this effect. Thus Rathor *patta* Gangawat got the *sasan* grant of village Rincholi (*pargana* Siwana) for Barhat Hema from Maldev.[9]

After the re-establishment of the Jodhpur principality under Mota Raja Udai Singh in 1583, the Rathor chiefs came to exert greater control over their territory and the subordinate *sardars*. The *patta* system now tended to become practically a replica of the *jagir* system so much so that among other terms and conditions even the right to give *sasan* grants by the *pattawats* now begin to be clearly mentioned in the text of the *patta* grant itself.[10] Evidently only such *pattawats* could give *sasan* land as were authorized to do so, and as such charitable grants required confirmation by the raja following the resumption or transfer of the *patta* from the holder. Thus Rathor Karamsen Agrasenot who got Sojhat in 1607 (vs 1664), granted the village of Muliawas to Barhat Rajsi which 'continued only till he remained in possession of Sojhat'. Later on Raja Suraj Singh renewed the grant.[11] Thus now it was the raja who enjoyed the right to create *sasan* land grants and to decide to whom, to what extent, and where the *sasan* lands were to be given.

Sasan grants were mostly given to the Charans and Brahmins for their maintenance. Other recipients included the Jogis, Bhats, Leds, Pirzadas, etc. These grants were also made for the maintenance of the temples and the priests and the *bhopas* attached to them. Generally these grants were given to various persons as a reward for their contribution in the literary sphere as well as out of piety and religiosity of the grantors. Though *sasan* grants could be made any time, there were some specific occasions for the purpose. Thus at the time of pilgrimage *sasan* grants were also made by the rajas and their *sardars* with the object of absolving themselves from sinful acts of the past. For example, Rao Jodha gave a village of Jodhpur to Purohit Champa during his pilgrimage to Gaya. Maharaja Jaswant Singh and his son Prince Prithvi Singh gave a village of Sojhat by way of *sasan* on an occasion of a holy dip in the Ganges.[12] Similarly, on the occasion of solar or lunar eclipse, considered auspicious for giving alms and charity, *sasan* grants were made to the Brahmins. Thus we have a reference to *sasan* grants given by Rao Maldev and one of his *sardar*, Rathor Jaswant, on such an occasion.[13] Birth of a prince was yet another occasion for making such grants. Thus Maharaja Jaswant Singh is said to have granted a village of *pargana* Sojhat to Shrimali Triwadi by way of *sasan* on the occasion of Prince Prithvi Singh's birth.[14] Besides *sasan* grant could even be created for a person as a reward for some special service to the ruling house. Thus Charan Chandan Khariya was assigned *sasan* grant of four villages of Jodhpur and Sojhat for his showing a rare courage in performing the last rites of Rao Ranmall, killed by Rana Kumbha. Rao Ranmall's dead body was left on the battlefield. Chandan Khariya and his descendants were bestowed *sasan* grants by Rao Jodha and his sons and grandsons subsequently also.[15]

The *sasan* grants were made in the form of a *patta* (a written deed) or a copper plate.[16] Presumably the charity grant through *patta* was subject to renewal and even resumption, while that made through copper plate was a grant in perpetuity, as an available text of such grant suggests (see Appendix).[17] these grants were made in terms of a definite village or its portion, even some fields specifying the quantum of the land thus granted. The management of the distribution of *sasan* grants to the grantees at the specified place or in a village was the concern of the *des-diwan* and *pargana hakim.*[18] The assignment entitled the grantee to collect the revenue of his assigned portion of the land and keep it to himself, and as such it did not disturb the rights of the peasants in that land. If the grantee himself happened to be a peasant he was not required to pay the revenue of his *sasan* land. The grantee could mortgage his *sasan* right.[19] He could even give a portion of the *sasan* grant by way of dowry. To quote an example, one Barhat Chatra gave half of his *sasan* village (Ratnawas in *pargana* Merta) in dowry to Dana Gangawat at the time of his sister's marriage. The portion given by way of dowry was enjoyed by the sons of Dana Gangawat after his death.[20] It seems usually the inheritance of *sasan* grants was allowed, specially in case of those granted through copper plate.[21] Such grants could be made in favour of more then one person in the same village, the shares of the grantees were well defined and also often allowed to continue in the line of the grantee accordingly.[22] A portion of a village could be given by way of *sasan,* keeping the remaining part in the *khalisa* or giving it to some *pattawat.* Nainsi's *Vigat* also contains a reference to a *sasan* grant made in favour of a woman. The wife of one Asio Yera Karamsgot was given a *sasan* village in *pargana* Sojhat by Prince Gaj Singh, son of Raja Suraj Singh.[23]

It seems that the land alienated through *sasan* was generally a less productive or partly deserted village (*viran, suna khet*). Often some fields situated on the fringe of the cultivable land of a village were assigned by way of *sasan* grant, where due to efforts of the grantees or otherwise a new village (*naya khera*) would settle in due course of time. To quote an example, a Rathor *sardar,* Dungarsi Udawat, is said to have given some fields in *sasan* to one Mehadu Jodha on the fringe of the agricultural land of Hunawas village in *pargana* Jaitaran where a new village, Jodhwas was founded. Nainsi's *Vigat* contains a number of such examples.[24] Obviously actual collection or income from such lands might have been erratic, far less than the expected amount or the *rekh.*[25] Thus one important aspect of these grants was that they helped in extending the land under cultivation and resettling the *viran* villages.

Generally, the *sasan* grants were not resumed and allowed to continue with the holder and even his sons after his death. A Sanskrit *shloka* contained in the text of a copper-plate grant declares that if a grantor of the charity resumes or takes it back, he thereby commits an eternal sin (see Appendix). In fact, charity grants made even by former rulers of the conquered territory were usually not disregarded.[26] However, the grants of temporary nature or those granted by a *pattawat* were subject to renewal and as such in the process such grants were made over to some person other than the original holder or even at times could be resumed to the *khalisa*, partly or in full.[27]

There is a reference to a *sasan* village of *pargana* Jaitaran being resumed to the *khalisa* by Raja Suraj Singh. The grant, however, was restored after a year.[28] After the conquest of a territory, the charity grants of the previous rulers also sometimes required confirmation by a new ruler and in the course such grants could either be bestowed on a new person or resumed to the *khalisa.* Following his conquest of Nagore, Rao Maldev refused to honour the charity grants of the Charans, which their ancestors had got from the Khan of Nogore. He offered to give new villages in lieu of those grants. The Charans opposed the move and even threatened mass suicide, but were eventually pacified by the queen, Bhatiyani Umade.[29] Subsequently, when Nagore was granted to Prince Jagat Singh, these grants were restored.[30] Mota Raja Udai Singh too resumed a number of *sasan* grants after the re-establishment of Jodhpur State in 1583. During the period of succession dispute over the Jodhpur throne, Rao Ram Maldevot and his son Kala had made several *sasan* grants to Charans and Brahmins. After Mota Raja's enthronement, these grants were resumed and this resulted in annoyance of the Charans. Consequently, when Mota Raja was encamped at Sojhat on his way to Gujarat, Aadha Dursa and Barhat Aakha along with several Charans gathered at the temple of Kajesar Mahadev and threatened to commit suicide in protest. Barhat Aakha, along with several Charans, even committed suicide, while Aadha Dursa injured his neck but was saved. However, undeterred, Mota Raja resumed their grants in 1586.[31] If the holder of a *sasan* grant left no heir, his grant could be confiscated or given to his brother.[32] Desertion of a *sasan* village or bad conduct on the part of the grantee could also result in the resumption of the grant.[33] A village held in *sasan* could also be transferred somewhere else on the request of the grantee, or on the part of the grantor himself.[34]

Only a modest portion of the total revenue of the principality was alienated through *sasan* grants. On the basis of the data available in Nainsi's *Vigat*, I have worked out the percentage of the amount of *rekh* of the *sasan* villages as well as the percentage of the *sasan* villages against the totals of the *rekh* amount and the number of villages of the various *parganas* of Marwar held by Maharaja Jaswant Singh (see Table 1). Unfortunately, Nainsi does not provide us with *rekh* figures for the *parganas* of Jodhpur and Phalodi. However, considering the figures for the *tappa* Mehwah, of *pargana* Jodhpur, for which *rekh* figure are given, and also the percentage of villages alienated through *sasan*, these *parganas* might not have represented any remarkable difference in terms of the *rekh* of the villages held in *sasan* grants. Thus, the percentage of the *rekh* of *sasan* grants out of the totals of *rekh* of various *parganas* ranges from 4 to 5.29 per cent. Considering the entire principality, the quantum of revenue alienated by way of *sasan* grants was at best a mere 4.35 per cent (excluding the *parganas* of Jodhpur and Phalodi). Thus, broadly it comes near to the percentage of the revenue alienated through charity grants by the Mughal emperors. For the twelve *subas* of Akbar's empire, for which *suyurghal* figures are recorded in the *Ain-i-Akbari*, the proportion of revenue alienated through this category was a little over 3 per cent of the total revenue.[35] The modest percentage of the *sasan* villages against the total number of villages in various *parganas* show that grants could have covered only a small area of the total cultivable land of the principality. However, compared with the percentage of *sasan* revenue alienated through *sasan* grants, the higher percentage of villages tends to show that these grants were generally located in areas of cultivable waste or insignificant land.

While giving details about the *sasan* villages given by various Rathor rajas and their *sardars*, Nainsi has also recorded the names of the *sasan* grantees along with their castes, holding the grants at the time of his survey of various *parganas*. I have set this caste-wise data in Table 2. It is evident from this table that the Charans were the most favoured among the grantees and accounted for more than half of the revenue assigned by way of *sasan* grants. Found mostly in Rajasthan, Gujarat and Malwa, the Charans were intimately associated with the Rajput rajas throughout the history of their rule. They have preserved the memory of the brave deeds of the Rajput rulers and their warriors through their ballads and other writings and thus have not only

TABLE 1: PERCENTAGE OF *REKH* ALIENATED IN *SASAN* GRANTS, AND OF THE VILLAGES HELD IN *SASAN*

Sr. No.	*Parganas*	A Total *rekh* (in Rs.)	B *Rekh* alienated in *Sasan* (in Rs.)	B as % of A	C Total no. of villages	D Vill. held in *sasan*	D as % of C	Reference
1.	Jodhpur	–	–	–	1,167	144		
	Tappa Mehwah	43,300	1,730	4%	128	18	14%	*Vigat*, I, 203-4, 367
2.	Sojhat	3,02,500	16,000	5.29%	244	33	13.52%	*Vigat*, I, 424, 489
3.	Jaitaran	2,07,200	10,200	4.92%	152	18	11.84%	*Vigat*, I, 507-8, 497-8
4.	Phalodi	–	2,450	–	67	9	13.46%	*Vigat*, II, 12, 31
5.	Siwana	89,270	4,550	5.09%	144	30	20.83%	*Vigat*, II, 223, 286
6.	Merta	6,80,001	24,700	3.63%	384	46	12%	*Vigat*, II, 115, 213
7.	Pohkaran (Satalmer)	33,860	1,700	5.02%	86	15	17.44%	*Vigat*, II, 355, 357
	Total (excluding *parganas* of Jodhpur and Phalodi)	13,12,831	57,150	4.35%				

TABLE 2: CASTE-WISE DISTRIBUTION OF *SASAN* GRANTS

Sr. No.	*Parganas*	Charans *Rekh* in Rs./No. of Villages	Brahmins *Rekh* in Rs./No. of Villages	Jogis *Rekh* in Rs./No. of Villages	Bhats *Rekh* in Rs./No. of Villages	Leds *Rekh* in Rs./No. of Villages	Pirzadas *Rekh* in Rs./No. of Villages	Temples/ Priests/ Bhopas *Rekh in* Rs./No. of Villages	Total *Rekh* of *Sasan* villages (in Rs.)
1.	Jodhpur	13,820 (75)	12,800 (63)		...(1)			750 (60)	27,370
2.	Sojhat	8,750 (17)	7,150 (15)	100(1)					16,000
3.	Jaitaran	3,900 (8½)	16,100 (8½)	200(1)					10,200
4.	Phalodi	200 (1)	850 (4)			400(1)		1,000 (3)	2,450
5.	Siwana	1,250 (13)	3,300 (17)						4,550
6.	Merta	15,000 (27)	7,700 (15)		200(1)		500(1)	1,300 (2)	24,700
7.	Pohkaran (Satalmer)	1,200 (11)	500 (4)						1,700
	Total	44,120 (152½)	38,400 (126½)	300(2)	200(2)	400(1)	500(1)	3,050 (11)	86,970
	Percentage of *Sasan* share in total *rekh*	50.73%	44.15%	.34%	.23%	.46%	.57%	3.50%	

kindled their chivalrous spirit but also enriched the Dingle and Pingle literature of Rajasthan. Another reason for the special treatment of the Charans is said to be that the Rajput rajas had deep faith and veneration for the Charan-born goddesses.[36] Next to the Charans were the Brahmin recipients of the charity grants who accounted for 40.50 per cent of the revenue alienated for the purpose. A sense of piety and religiosity seems to be the obvious reason for the favour shown to them. Benevolence shown to the Jogis and Bhats was quite negligible, a mere 1.30 per cent of the total charity grants. And though the Rathor rajas spent a lot on the construction of temples, the *sasan* land grants created for the purpose of the maintenance of temples and the priests and Bhopas attached to these was just 3.50 per cent of the total revenue alienated in charity grants. It is not worthy that Muslim religious establishments were also considered for giving *sasan* grants by Maharaja Jaswant Singh. He created a *sasan* grant, in 1652, of 5,046 *bighas* of land with the *rekh* amount of Rs. 500 (village Khatolai near Merta) for Pirzada Nizarbali Nizam Khwaja Mahmud, associated with the Chishti shrine of Khwaja Muin-ud Din of Ajmer.[37] Viewed in the context of Aurangzeb's religious bigotry and the fact that during the occupation of the territory of Jodhpur principality after Jaswant Singh's death, the imperial revenue officials, following emperor's order, disregarded the remissions (*sasan* grants) granted to the Charans by the raja,[38] this grant is of special interest.

NOTES

1. Cf. R.S. Sharma, *Indian Feudalism c.* AD *300–1200*, Madras: 1980, pp. 3–6, 126–69. Sharma ascribes the rise of local magnates with feudal features to this system of land grants. For reference to *sasan* grants made by Chauhan and Parihar rulers, see Muhnot Nainsi, *Marwar Ra Pargana Ri Vigat*, vols. I, II, ed. Narayan Singh Bhati, Jodhpur, 1968–9, vol. I, p. 241, vol. II, pp. 266–7 (hereafter cited as *Vigat*).
2. Muhnot Nainsi served as *hakim* of various *parganas* of Jodhpur principality for nearly 20 years before he was appointed *desh-diwan* of Jodhpur from 1658–62 and during this period he compiled his *Vigat*. Manohar Singh Ranawat, *Itihaskar Muhnot Nainsi or Usake Itihas Granth*, Jodhpur, 1981, pp. 36, 50.

3. For a discussion of the revenue grants of the Mughal empire, see Irfan Habib, *Agrarian System of the Mughal Empire,* Oxford, revd. edn., 1999, pp. 342–63; Shireen Moosvi, *Economy of the Mughal Empire,* Oxford, 1987, pp. 153–73; also I.H. Siddiqui, 'Wajh-i Ma'as Grants Under the Afghan kings (1451–1555)', *Medieval India—A Miscellany,* vol. II, Aligarh, 1972, pp. 19–44; Iqtidar Alam Khan, 'The State Patronage in Medieval India', *Proceedings of Indian History Congress,* 61st Session, Kolkata, 2001, pp. 276–84.
4. *Vigat,* II, pp. 51, 106–12.
5. *Vigat,* I, pp. 78, 238, 242, 254–5.
6. Cf. B.L. Bhadani, 'The Ruler and the Nobility in Marwar during the Reign of Jaswant Singh', *Medieval India,* vol. I, ed. Irfan Habib, Delhi, 1992, p. 189; also R.S. Sangwan, *Jodhpur and the Later Mughals: A.D. 1707–52,* Delhi, 2006, p. XX.
7. *Vigat,* II, p. 267, also Manohar Singh Ranawat, op. cit., p. 198.
8. *Vigat,* II, pp. 495, 547–49.
9. Ibid., II, p. 275.
10. B.L. Bhadani, op. cit., p. 193; G.D. Sharma, *Rajput Polity,* Delhi, 1977, Appendix 7.1, p. 217.
11. *Vigat,* I, pp. 488; II, 349–50.
12. Ibid., I, pp. 334, 486, also pp. 478–9.
13. Ibid., I, pp. 482, 547.
14. Ibid., I, pp. 479, 486.
15. Ibid., I, p. 37.
16. Ibid., I, pp. 481, 548.
17. Ibid., I, pp. 481, 489, 548.
18. Ibid., II, p. 351.
19. Ibid., II, p. 119.
20. Ibid., II, p. 185.
21. Ibid., II, p. 489, also see Appendix I.
22. Ibid., II; pp. 106, 138, 185, 270, 351.
23. Ibid., I, pp. 487–8.
24. Ibid., I, pp. 549–51, 547.
25. After securing *jagir* from the Mughal emperors, the Rathor chiefs used to predetermine the *rekh* (official estimate of revenue) of the *jagir* in order to sub-assign it to their subordinate *sardars.* For a discussion of *rekh,* see B.L. Bhadani, 'Revenue estimation and realization in the Mughal Empire', in Muhammad Taher (ed.), *Mughal India,* Delhi, 1997, pp. 128–37.
26. *Vigat,* I, p. 241; II, pp. 266–7.
27. Ibid., I, pp. 480, 488, 548; II, pp. 269–76.
28. Ibid., I, p. 544.
29. Ibid., I, pp. 53–4.

30. Ibid.
31. Ibid., I, pp. 78–9, 81–2, 480, 484.
32. Ibid., I, pp. 243, 483, 520, 546.
33. Ibid., I, p. 335; II, p. 243.
34. Ibid., I, p. 488; II, p.107.
35. Shireen Moosvi, *The Economy of The Mughal Empire,* Oxford, 1987. pp. 158–9.
36. *Vigat,* I, Introduction, p. 24.
37. Ibid., II, pp. 114, 166.
38. *Waqa'i-i Ajmir* (p. 318) quoted by Irfan Habib, *Agrarian System of Mughal India,* p. 363, fn. 93.

APPENDIX

Copy of the text of a copper plate issued by Maharaja Ajit Singh in 1702 granting the village Hirabus of *pargana* Sojhat. It was issued owing to the loss of an earlier copper plate issued by Maharaja Suraj Singh, during the Mughal-Rajput conflicts in 1699/v.s. 1947. This *sasan* grant is also mentioned in Muhnot Nainsi's *Vigat* (vol. I, p. 489). The copper-plate was found at *saran,* a village of Pali district in Rajasthan. Text of the plate quoted from an article by Mangilal Vyas entitled 'Maharaja Ajit Singh Ke Abhilekh', *Sodh-Patrika,* vol. III, Udaipur, 1967, p. 34.

Copy of the Text

।। श्री परमे वरजी सत्य छै ।।

श्री कृष्णजी (तलवार का चिन्ह) सही

१ ।। : ।। सिधि (ध) श्री महाराजाधिराज श्री अजीतसिंहजी
१ महाराज कुंवार श्री उद्योतसिंघजी वचनात तथा परगने
३ सोझत रो गांव १ हीरावस कदींम सांसण महाराज श्री
४ सुरजसिंघजी आयस सांवतवनजी ने षेचरवनजी नै
५ तांबापत्र करनै दीयो थो सो आगलो तांबा पत्र संवत १७४७
६ रै बरस तुरकलसकरीषां गांव मारीयो आसण लुटियो लठै गयो सो कदीम सांसण छै सो आगला दसतुर माफक ही मैं ही
७ षैरायत दाखल ओ गांव आयस सीतलवनजी ने दयानवन नु तांबा पत्र
८ कराय दीयो छै सो गांव रो हासल सदामद माफक धरम अरथ
६ षैरायत बांटबी (टियो) गांव आसण षेरायत दाषल छै कोई उथापव न पावे
१० सीलोक आपदतं परदतं जे लोपतं बसंधरा ते नरा नरकां जांते
११ जालग चन्द्र दीवाकरा।।१।। संवत् १७५६ रा असाढ़ वद १ मु। जालोर
१२ दुवै श्री मुष परवानगी राठोड़ उदसिंघजी लिषतं पंचोली
१३ बेणीरांम गंगारांमोत ... ...

Baburvani: A Historical Perspective

M.S. AHLUWALIA

Baburvani or Babur's command or sway refers to the four hymns of Guru Nanak containing description of the first Mughal Emperor Babur's invasions (1483–1530) of India. Three of these find mention in *Asa di Var* (pp. 360 and 417–18) and the fourth is in *Tilang* measure on pages 722–3 in the standard versions of *Srì Guru Granth Sahib.*[1]

Baburvani hymns are reflective of the contemporary events in a larger social and historical perspective. Historically they deal with Babur's invasion of Saidpur (now Eminabad, 15 km south-east of Gujranwala in Pakistan) in 1520 and socially they are the outpourings of a compassionate soul touched by the scene of human misery and cruelty perpetuated by the invading hordes of Babur. It will be appropriate here to discuss the *Baburvani* in historical as well as social context, though the present paper deals only with the historical context of *Baburvani.*

HISTORICAL CONTEXT

Zahiruddin Muhammad Babur (1483–1530), apart from being a soldier of fortune, a diarist and a poet, was the founder of the Mughal dynasty in India. Descending from the fifth generation of Amir Timur, Babur succeeded his father, Umar Shaikh, as ruler of Farghana and spent most of his time in the struggle for power in his native place. After the conquest of Kabul in 1504, Babur began to consider himself as the rightful heir to all the Timurid dominions in India. With a view to conquering the remnant of the Timurid possessions in India, Babur left Kabul for his first Indian expedition in January 1505.[2] The cause of Babur's second inroad into India was Shaibani Khan's attack and investment of Kandahar in 1507, whereas the third invasion was in 1519. Babur writes in his memoirs: 'As it was always in my heart to possess

Hindustan, and as these several countries, Bhera, Khushab, Chenab, Chiniot, had once been held by the Turks, I pictured them as my own and was resolved to get them into my hands whether peacefully or by force.'[3]

The occasion of the third expedition was a very opportune one. Torn by the open hostility of the nobles caused by the high-handed policy of Ibrahim Lodi, the empire was not in a position to oppose the invader seizing its distant territories. On the Ist Muharram, 4 January 1519, Babur turned towards Bajaur,[4] stormed it with gunpowder and artillery and conquered it on 7 January. A general massacre was ordered till 3,000 heads, according to Babur's estimate, had fallen on account of the Bajauris 'being rebels and at enmity with the people of Islam'.

On the invitation of Daulat Khan Lodi, the governor of Punjab and Alam Khan, an uncle of Ibrahim Lodi, the Delhi sultan, Babur entered Punjab in 1523. However, the Uzbeg pressure at home compelled Babur to return and his final invasion could not begin until November 1525.

Although there is no mention of any meeting between Babur and Guru Nanak in Babur's autobiography (*Tuzuk-i-Baburi*), the Sikh tradition (*Janam Sakhis*) strongly subscribes to Babur's contact with Guru Nanak around 1520 during his invasion of Saidpur when the town was taken by assault, the garrison put to sword and the inhabitants carried into captivity.[5] Thus only the *Janam Sakhis* give a detailed description about the only recognizable and dated event of the history of medieval Punjab.

Babur's attack on Saidpur *vis-à-vis* Guru Nanak's references in the *Baburvani* have posed three serious questions:

1. Which of Babur's invasions is referred to in the account of *Baburvani*?
2. Was Guru Nanak present during Babur's invasion of Saidpur?
3. Did Guru Nanak ever meet Babur?

Regarding the first question Mrs A.S. Beveridge, the learned translator of *Tuzuk-i-Baburi* or *Baburnama*[6] puts the above event in the year 1520, The description follows as under:

The march out from Kabul may have been as soon as muster and equipment allowed after the return from Lamghan chronicled in the diary. It was made through Bajaur where refractory tribesmen were bought to order. Bhera was traversed . . . advance was made beyond lands yet occupied, to Sialkot, 72 miles north of Lahore . . . it was occupied without resistance, and a further move was made to what the manuscripts call Sayyidpur; this attempted defence was taken by assault and put to sword . . . whatever he may have planned to do beyond Sidhpur was frustrated by the news which took him leads to Kabul and thence to Quandhar, that an incursion into his territory had been made by Shah Beg.[7]

Let us now turn to the Sikh accounts as preserved in the *Janam Sakhis.*

According to the Sikh traditional accounts, Guru Nanak arrived at Saidpur and visited his devotee, Bhai Lalo. When the latter complained to the Guru of the oppression of the Pathan rulers, the Guru replied, 'When goodness departs from men and nations, they invariably come to grief. The end of the Pathan regime is at hand'. On this occasion, he uttered a prophetic hymn pointing to the advent of Babur who was soon to occupy the throne of Delhi after bitter fighting in the Punjab.

O Lalo, I utter as is revealed unto me the Word of God;
With the marriage procession of sin, Babur is marching upon us from Kabul and asks for the hand (of the bride, our motherland) at the point of sword. . . .

It is related that Guru Nanak and Mardana happened to reach Saidpur at a time when the Pathan inhabitants were celebrating numerous marriages. The *faqirs* who were accompanying the Guru were weak with hunger and thirst and asked for food, but everywhere they were refused.[8] One of the Brahmins of the town happened to hear the Guru's verses and recognized it as a summons to Babur to punish the uncharitable town, and begged him (the Guru) to retreat his course. The Guru was unable to do, but promised the Brahmin, the safety of his life.[9] Babur then descended upon Saidpur, reached it, put all its inhabitants to the sword and ravaged the surrounding countryside. All this happened because the inhabitants of the town failed to show proper consideration to the *faqirs.*[10] The *Janam Sakhis* then refer to an interview of the Guru with Babur.[11]

A good deal of the above account however, is open to suspicion and may be outrightly rejected. It has been reasonably argued that firstly the destruction of the town can be dismissed on rational grounds and secondly it is completely out of character in so far as Guru Nanak is concerned. That Guru Nanak was capable of such vindictive behaviour is not known from his works, including the verse which is interpreted as curse.[12]

A close study of Guru Nanak's verses however, indicate that the above account do not tally with Mrs Beveridge's date, who puts the date of the event to in the year 1520.[13] According to the verses: 'Now [that] Babur's authority has been established, the princes starve. . . .'[14]

Again,

Thousands of *pirs* tried to stop Mir [Babur] when they heard of his invasion. Places were burnt, rock-like temples [were destroyed], princes were hacked into pieces and trampled in dust. . . .[15]

The events mentioned in the above passages indicate that it concerns some latter invasion of Babur probably between 1524 and 1526. The first verse refers that Lodi rule had come to an end prior to the composition of the *Ashtapadi* in which it occurs.

Again:

The wealth and sensuality which had intoxicated them became their enemies. To the messengers (of death) the command was given to strip them off their honour and carry them off. . . . But the rulers paid no heed, passing their time in revelry, and now that Babur's authority has been established, the princes starve.[16]

It seems certain that the reference here must be to the Lodis, as there are no 'rulers' and 'princes' to whom it could conceivably apply. That the Lodis had acted in a manner contrary to the divine intention and they paid the inevitable for having done so. This must refer to the ultimate overthrow of the Lodi dynasty and not to the invasion of 1520, which was by all means a decisive defeat for the contemporary Lodi sultan. Again, the description of the battle and devastation caused by the Mughals, was something more than a comparatively small invasion of 1520 as mentioned by Mrs Beveridge. The description goes as follows:

The Mughals and the Pathans fought each other, wielding swords in the battlefield. One side took aim and fired guns, others urged on (its) elephant . . . Hindu, Muslim, Bhati and Thakur women (suffered), some having their *burqas* torn from head to toe. . . .[17]

It is obvious that the reference is to an important battle in which the presence of elephants further suggests that it was not a skirmish but a full-scale battle and the sack of the town. This might refer to the invasion of 1524 when Babur defeated Bihar Khan Lodi who was sent by Ibrahim Lodi at Lahore.[18] That Talwandi of Kartarpur is not far away from Lahore, the presence of Guru Nanak seems to be certain. The presence of the Guru subsequently found outlet in a graphic description of the event.

It is also possible that the fall of the Lodi dynasty and the description of warfare, written positively after AD 1526 (final defeat of Ibrahim Lodi and the establishment of the Mughal rule in India) refer not to a single event but to a series of events which culminated in the overthrow of the Lodis.

Two conclusions may be drawn from the *Baburvani* verses:

1. That Guru Nanak must have personally witnessed the devastation caused by Babur's troops. The vivid description of the death, agony, destruction, etc., given an expression of personal experience.
2. The four verses were probably composed after 1526, after completion of the series of invasions. As *Ashtapadi* 12, with its battle scene refers to a specific event, but the nature of references points to the year AD 1524, capture of Lahore and not to the sack of Saidpur in 1520.[19]

Thus it may be safely concluded that the account of Guru Nanak's presence as an eye-witness during the sack of Saidpur, as presented in the *Janam Sakhis,* is accurate and is also supported by several references in the *Adi Granth.*

The *Janam Sakhis* also agree on the Saidpur sack and there is a measure of accuracy in their accounts. Had this not been a fact, the narrators would have chosen the description of Lahore or Panipat battle rather than the sack of an obscure town.[20]

Nothing however can be said regarding the meeting of the Guru with Babur as the *Janam Sakhis* also differ regarding their account of the event.

NOTES

1. The free translation of the *Baburvani* passage runs as follows:

Khurasan was protected and Hindustan terrorized. The Creator does not take the blame upon Himself. Didst Thou feel no compassion when the people wailed after much destruction? Thou art the same for all, O creator, if a powerful man attacks an equally powerful man then no one feels sad. But if a strong lion attacks a herd of cattle its master is to answer. The dogs (Lodi kings) spoiled their jewel (of Hindustan), none will remember them after death. Thou Thyself separatist, lo, this is Thy greatness. If a man calls himself great and indulges in pleasures dear to his heart, in the eyes of the Lord, He is but a worm nibbling corn.

The ladies whose heads were adorned with tresses, with vermilion in the partings, are being shaved with shears and are dust-laden up to the neck. They lived in palaces, but now they are not getting a seat in public. Hail, Hail, to Thee, O Master, none knoweth Thy limits, O Primeval Being. Thou watchest in various guises. When they were married, their charming grooms sat by their side. They were carried in palanquins inset with ivory (the mother-in-law drank), water waved over their heads and fans studded with glass-pieces were in their hands. Lacs of congratulations were offered when they sat and lacs of congratulations when they got up. Eating coconuts and dates they shared beds with their grooms. Nooses are now round their necks, their pearl necklaces are snapped. Beauty and wealth, which were the harbingers of their enjoyments, have now turned into enemies. Orders have been given to the soldiers, who are talking them along in dishonour. When it pleases Him, He bestows greatness. He punishes when He so desires. Had they thought of Him beforehand there would have been no cause for punishment. The kings lost themselves in luxury and revelry. Now that the wrist of Babur prevails even princes do not get bread to eat. Some are losing the time of their prayers, other are missing their Punjab. How can Hindu women bathe and anoint their foreheads with saffron marks without a plastered square. They never thought of Rama, now they cannot call Khuda even. Some are returning to their homes and are getting together to sit and weep over their misery. Whatever He wills, happens, Nanak, What is man.

Where are those sports, stables and horses, where those drums and trumpets? Where are the sword belts made of wool, where the red togas? Where are those mirrors and foppish faces? They are not seen here. This world is Thine, and Thou art its master. . . . Thou canst establish and destroy and distribute wealth, as Thou likest. Where are those beautiful rest-houses. Where is the beauty losing in bed, seeing whom sleep departed. Where are the betel leaves, betel-sellers and harems, all vanished. For this wealth many people got ruined, this wealth led many a man astray. Without sins it cannot be accumulated and it does not accompany the dead. Whom the Creator leads astray, he is deprived of all goodness. When they heard that Babur was rushing on, millions of Pirs tried to restrain him by their spells, sacred places of Hindus and Muslims were set on fire and princes cut into pieces rolled in dust. No Mughal was struck blind, no charm had its effect. Battle took place between the Mughals and Pathans and swords were piled in that fight. They took aim and fired guns and the Indians attacked with elephants. Those whose letters were torn in His court must die. Of Hindu and Muslim women, Bhatti and Thakur girls, some had their robes torn from head to foot, others lay in crematoriums. How did those whose husbands did not return home pass their night? To whom should we complain when the Creator Himself does this or makes others do it. Joys and sorrows come as Thou willest. There is none other to whom we may go wailing. The Commander manages all this under His order and is pleased. Nanak, everyone gathers his portion according to his lot.

2. The first *Indian expedition* is the subject of much controversy. This is partly due to the gaps in *Baburnama* and partly due to the omission of the medieval historians to mention the expeditions which Babur undertook prior to that of 1523, i.e. the one undertaken at the invitation of Daulat Khan. Abdul Halim, *History of the Lodi Sultans of Delhi and Agra,* Delhi, 1974, p. 167, fn. 2.
3. *Baburnama,* tr. Mrs A.S. Beveridge, vol. I, Delhi, 1989, pp. 345–6.
4. Bajaur is the chief town of the Bajur valley in old NWFP.
5. According to the *Puratan Janam Sakhi,* Guru Nanak and Mardana were also captured and taken to prison as slaves along with other inhabitants during Babur's invasion of Saidpur in 1520. The Guru was given a lad to carry and Mardana a horse to lead. The *Janam Sakhi* further recounts that the Guru's bundle was carried without any support and Mardana's horse followed him without reins. When Mir Khan reported this to Babur, the latter remarked, 'If there was such a holy man here, the town should not have been destroyed'. The *Janam Sakhi* continues'. Babur kissed his (Guru Nanak's) feet and said, 'On the face of this *faqir* one sees God himself'. Babur is further stated to have spoken, 'O dervish, accept something'. The Guru answered, 'I take nothing, but you must release all the prisoners of Saidpur and restore their property to them.' The king thereupon instantly ordered the release of all the prisoners of Saidpur. Guru Nanak's visit to Saidpur is also supported by the *Janam Sakhi* accounts. For details see Kirpal Singh, *Janam Sakhi Parampara—Itihasik Drishtikon Ton,* Patiala, 1969, pp. 149–51; Gopal Singh, *Guru Nanak,* Delhi, 1992, pp. 32–3.
6. *Tuzuk-i-Baburi* or *Baburnama,* English Mrs A.S. Beveridge, op. cit.

7. Ibid., vol. I, pp. 428–9.
8. *Janam Sakhi,* p. 58.
9. Compare the traditional account of Chadha (a Khatri sub-caste) whose forefathers fought with Babur at Eminabad and all fell, save one, who hid himself under an *aak* bush. His descendants still perform the miracles at Eminabad and worship the *aak* tree. It seems that this tradition and the *Janam Sakhis* have a common origin. Ibbetson, *A Glossary of the Tribes and Castes of the Punjab,* Lahore: Punjab Govt. Press, 1936, p. 518.
10. *Janam Sakhi,* p. 59.
11. Ibid., pp. 62–3.
12. MacLeod, *Life of Guru Nanak,* London: Oxford University Press, p. 134.
13. *Babur Nama,* vol. I, p. 429.
14. Ibid., vol. I.
15. *Asa Ashtapadi* 11 (5); *Adi Granth* (Standard Edition), Amritsar: SGPC, p. 417.
16. Ibid., 11 (4–5); *Adi Granth,* p. 417.
17. *Asa Ashtapadi,* 12 (5–6); *Adi Granth,* p. 418.
18. *Baburnama,* vol. I, p. 441.
19. MacLeod, op. cit., pp. 137–8.
20. Ibid., p. 138.

The House of Asad Khan

MOHD. AFZAL KHAN

During the reigns of Akbar and Jahangir a number of Iranian families migrated to India.[1] In this paper an attempt is made to trace the antecedents of one immigrant Iranian family with an account of its pre-emigration position in Iran, which has not been discussed so far in modern works.[2] Efforts will also be made to analyse the power exercised by the members of this family in the Mughal empire, for which lists showing the *mansabs* and offices held by them have been appended to the paper.

ANTECEDENTS

Asad Khan belonged to a reputed Turkmen family of the Qaramanlu tribe.[3] His ancestors had served under the Safavid rulers from Shah Ismail's time. Bairam Beg (or Bahram Beg)[4] was the governor (*hakim*) of Balkh during Shah Ismail's reign and it was he who, along with other Iranian generals, helped Babur against the Uzbek sultan in the battle of Khurasan. Subsequently, he lost his life fighting against the Uzbeks in the battle of Ghajdwan.[5] His son Husam Beg Qaramanlu was raised to the status of *amir* and was appointed to Ashkur,[6] a district near Gilan, during the reign of Shah Tahmasp.[7] His sons, Rustam Khan, Farhad Khan, Zulfiqar Khan and Alwand Sultan, were also men of rank under Shah Abbas I. Rustam Khan, the eldest among them, probably held some important post at Talish (also his native place) where on account of the enmity with the nobles he was forced to settle in Shirwan, then under the Ottoman Turks. However, hostility with the Ottoman authorities soon broke out, and the Turks killed Rustam Khan along with his one or two brothers (names not known) and followers. Farhad Khan and his younger brothers, Zulfiqar Khan and Alwand Sultan escaped with their lives leaving behind one sister, two daughters of Rustam Khan and other servants and followers. They arrived in Azerbaijan in the beginning of Shah Abbas' reign and joined the service of Shah Abbas I.[8] Farhad Khan was appointed governor of Mazandran with Alwand Sultan as his deputy in 1596–7.[9] In 1598–9 he was also appointed the governor of Astarabad,[10] Herat and the *amir-ul umara* of Khurasan.[11] But in the same year he was assassinated on account of a suspicion of rebellion.[12] Zulfiqar Khan's younger brother Alwand Sultan was first appointed as governor of Langar Kanan, a city (*ulka*) near Ardbil, in 1591–2.[13] In 1596–7 he acted as deputy for his brother Farhad Khan in Mazandran,[14] where in 1597–8 he joined the conspiracy of Alwand Dev, the rebel *qiladar* of Aulad.[15] But the rebellion was soon suppressed by Farhad Khan and Alwand Sultan was sent to the court where he was pardoned and made free (*mutlaq-ul inan*).[16] Nothing more is known about him.

Asad Khan's grandfather Zulfiqar Khan Qaramanlu also appears to have held several appointments during Shah Abbas I's reign. He was first appointed governor (*beglarbegi*) of Azerbaijan in 1591–2.[17] As it was customary in the Safavid empire that *beglarbegis* alone were sent on diplomatic missions, Zulfiqar Khan was sent as an envoy to the Ottoman empire in 1595–6[18] and returned in 1597–8.[19] In 1603–4 he was appointed governor (*hakim*) of Ardbil, and the same year, after the recapture of Tabriz, he was made its governor.[20] In 1606–7 the governorship (*ayalat wa darai*) of Shumakhi and the *amir-ul umarai* of the entire Shirwan was also conferred on him.[21] During his stay in Shirwan he defeated Ma'sum Khan, the governor (*wali*) of Tabar *saran* in 1607–8 on account of his not allowing Zulfiqar Khan to construct a fortress at Shabran near his territory to which the Khan had been deputed. However, the fortress was built and equipped with necessary provisions, and castellans (*harisan*) were posted.[22] But the next year (1608–9) some of the officers of Daghistan and Tabaristan became agitated over the construction of the fortress. Consequently Qarchaqai Beg, a confidential officer of the Shah, was sent to Shirwan with orders to join Zulfiqar Khan in suppressing the turbulence at Shabran. In the meanwhile Qarchaqai Beg received a second order from the Shah by which Zulfiqar Khan put to death by the attendants of the Beg.[23] The author of *Alam Ara-i Abbasi* explains that Zulfiqar Khan on account of his being an important and powerful noble had become very proud of his position and perhaps had developed a kind of turbulent tendency, the signs of which were noticed by the king. The other reason, which he feels was that by killing Zulfiqar Khan the Shah wanted to reconcile with the officers of Daghistan.[24]

The author of *Masir-ul Umara* says that after Zulfiqar Khan's murder his family members faced hard times as the Shah did not show them any kindness.[25] It might be true because none of the family members is found to have been taken into the royal service; even Khanlar, the only known son of Zulfiqar Khan, does not find any mention in the *Alam Ara-i Abbasi.* Khanlar appears to have arrived in India, as a fugitive towards the close of Jahangir's reign (i.e. 1627).[26] This suggests that after his father's death Khanlar still remained in Iran for about twenty-five years. The information of the *Masir-ul Umara* therefore can not be fully accepted.

THE FAMILY IN INDIA

In India Khanlar married the daughter of Sadiq Khan, *mir bakhshi*, brother-in-law and a cousin of Nurjahan's brother Asaf Khan.[27] He thus established matrimonial relations with the most important family in the Mughal nobility. Subsequently his children and grandchildren also married in this and some other important Iranian families. Muhammad Ibrahim Asad Khan, his son, was married to the daughter of Asaf Khan[28] whose granddaughter (Shaista Khan's daughter) was married to Muhammad Ismail Zulfiqar Khan, son of Asad Khan.[29] A daughter of Khanlar (later entitled Zulfiqar Khan Qaramanlu) was married to Namdar Khan, son of Jafar Khan[30] and another to Prince Zainuddin, a son of Prince Shah Shuja.[31] Another of Asad Khan's sons Inayat Khan (by Nawal Bai) was married to a daughter of Abul Hasan, the ruler of Hyderabad.[32] Asad Khan's four daughters were respectively married to Azizuddin Bahramand Khan;[33] Iftikhar Khan Mufakhir Khan, son of Fakhir Khan Najm-i Sani;[34] Khuda Banda Khan, son of Shaista Khan;[35] and Tarbiyat Khan.[36] Asad Khan's two grand daughters (by his daughter and the wife of Bahramand Khan) were married to Muhammad Taqi Khan, the son of Darab Khan Bani Mukhtar,[37] a reputed family of Mukhtar Khan Sabzwari. The other granddaughter was married to Mir

Muhammad Mahdi entitled Mir Khan, son of famous Amir Khan Mir Miran Yazdi.[38] Thus Asad Khan's family was well connected with the four important Iranian families of I'timad-ud Daula, Baqir Khan Najm Sani, Mukhtar Khan Sabzwari and Mir Miran Yazdi on the one hand and with the ruling families of Mughals and Abdul Hasan of Hyderabad on the other.[39]

Being such a well connected family the rapid rise of its members under Shahjahan and Aurangzeb becomes easier to explain. Further, the marriage pattern of the family in the successive generations shows that the Qaramanlus were quite adroit in living up to their status by establishing matrimonial relations with aristocratic families. Their closest links were with the house of I'timad-ud Daula as it appears from the genealogical chart that most of their children were married in this house. Their other known marriage, were strictly with those few Iranian families which had already established such relations with I'timad-ud Daula. It is significant that they always married their daughters into Iranian families. The only exception was the daughter (no. 14) of Zulfiqar Khan Qaramanlu (no. 12) who was married to a Mughal prince (no. 18), and this was a practically forced marriage.[40]

Two male members of the family were married to the daughters of non-Iranian families. Asad Khan's son Muhammad Ishaq (no. 27) by a Hindu wife Nawal Bai (no. 17) was married to a daughter of Abul Hasan, the Golkunda ruler and another son Zulfiqar Khan (no. 20) was married to Tahira Bagum (no. 31), daughter of a Turani noble Islam Khan Rumi.[41]

On his arrival in India, after Jahangir's death, Khanlar appears to have been appointed to the Central Command (*qaul*) along with Asad Khan against Shahryar, Nurjahan's candidate for the throne.[42] In 1631 in the battle of Balaghat, against Khan-i Jahan Lodi and Nizamul Mulk, Khanlar rendered good services in the left wing of the imperial forces.[43] In 1632 he was granted the rank of 1000/600 and the next year his ancestral title of Zulfiqar Khan.[44] In 1634 he received his first independent appointment as *faujdar* of *miyan-i doab* being promoted to the rank of 1500/ 800.[45] In course of time he held many important offices like *darogha-i topkhana*, *qiladar* (keeper of arsenal) of Lahore fort, *faujdar* of Mandsor and finally attained the office of *subedar* of Bihar and the rank of 3000/3000 in the 30th R.Y. of Shahjahan (i.e. 1656).[46] Later, when struck with paralysis, he took to retirement and settled in Patna where he died in 1660.[47]

His eldest son Muhammad Ibrahim entitled Asad Khan (Asaf-ud Daula Jumla-ul Mulk) started his career under Shahjahan being first appointed as *akhtabegi* (master of horse) in 1653 with the rank of 1500/600.[48] In 1657 he was appointed to the more important position of second *bakhshi*[49] which he relinquished in the 13th R.Y. of Aurangzeb (1671) being further promoted to the office of deputy *diwan*.[50] Subsequently the office of *mir bakhshi*[51] was added to it. In 1676 he was exalted to the highest post of *wazir*[52] which he held for the longest tenure in the Mughal empire, right to the end of Aurangzeb's reign. He also then held the highest rank assignable to a noble, namely, of 7000/7000.[53]

Muhammad Ismail entitled I'tiqad Khan later Zulfiqar Khan (no. 20), the son of Asad Khan, also held several posts during Aurangzeb's reign. Starting his career at the age of eleven with the rank of 3000 *zat* in 1668,[54] Zulfiqar Khan occupied the most important central post, that of *mir bakhshi*,[55] and attained the high rank of 6000/6000[56] towards the close of Aurangzeb's reign. Besides holding so many important offices both Asad Khan and Zulfiqar Khan are found to have been successfully engaged in a number of battles.[57]

Muhammad Ishaq (no. 27) entitled Inayat Khan[58] was another son of Asad Khan by Nawal Bai, popularly known as 'Rani'. He was an expert calligraphist and for a time held the office of the *darogha* of jewel house.[59] In 1689 he is known to have been reinstated to his previous *mansab* of 700/150.[60] He was married to a daughter of Abul Hasan, the ruler of Golkunda.[61] His sons were named Muhammad Salih and Mirza Kazim. The former held a moderately high *mansab* and the titles of I'tiqad Khan and Inayat Khan during the reign of Jahandar Shah.[62] In the 29th R.Y. of Shahjahan (1656), a third son of Asad Khan named Darab (no. 21) is noticed for the first time, being granted an *inam* of Rs. 2,000.[63] He was perhaps a younger brother of Zulfiqar Khan (their mother being Mihr-un Nisa, a daughter of Asaf Khan). Nothing more could be traced about him.

According to the *Masir-ul Umara*, Zulfiqar Khan Nusrat Jang was childless (*aulad nadasht*),[64] but curiously enough in 1686 one Yusuf, the son of Zulfiqar Khan, appears to have been sent, along with other generals, as a special officer (*sazawali*) under Lutfullah Khan in the campaign of Hyderabad.[65] That Zulfiqar Khan was not childless is further corroborated by the account of William Norris, an English ambassador visiting Aurangzeb's court towards the close of his reign. During his stay at Brahmapuri (or Islampuri) in 1701, William Norris' surgeon, on the request of one of Zulfiqar Khan's wives, treated her child who was only 'one of 10 surviving and ye hopes of ye family, all dyinge of ye same fitts this child labours under'.[66]

We may in the end mark the fact that, all in all, Asad Khan's was a very small family with only three male members who could attain rank and power in the Mughal nobility. Their sons-in-law and grandsons-in-law have not been taken into account as members of this family, because almost all of them were related or belonged to the great house of I'timad-ud Daula.[67]

An analysis of the appendices showing the careers (in tabulated form) of the Qaramanlus in India reveals that the two Zulfiqar Khans, one the father of Asad Khan and the other his son, were military generals by virtue of their profession. They are found to have been deputed, most of the time, on important military expeditions or entrusted with assignments pertaining to the maintenance of law and order, such as *subedar, faujdar, qiladar*, etc. Asad Khan, on the other hand, held mostly administrative offices like *akhtabeqi, arz qaqai subajat*, deputy *diwan* and *wazir*.[68] As second *bakhshi* and *mir bakhshi* too he is not found to have accompanied any military expedition.[69] Perhaps an independent command was never given to him, though for this he once expressed his desire among his friends. 'I have never been appointed on outside expeditions, if per chance appointed people will acknowledge my organizing capacity and administrative efforts.[70] This conversation was reported verbatim to the emperor who accordingly sent him in 1693 to reinforce his son Zulfiqar Khan in the siege of Jinji. It was for the first time in 1701 that he was given full command of the imperial force besieging Khelna and was granted the title of *amir-ul umara*.[71]

From our table it is clear that the military career of Asad Khan started with his arrival in the Deccan in 1684 (second time), and he is found to have been continuously engaged there till 1702. After that due to his old age and ill health he remained in constant attendance of Aurangzeb.

Zulfiqar Khan Nusrat Jang provides an example of a full-time military commander who was, throughout his life, engaged in campaigning. If Asad Khan was a successful civil administrator, Zulfiqar Khan was equally good on the military front. His matchless generalship may be judged by the fact that in 1705 during the siege of Wagingera fort, at a time when the Mughal commanders like Chin Qulich Khan, Muhammad Amin Khan, Tarbiyat Khan, etc., had failed, Aurangzeb recalled Zulfiqar Khan from Burhanpur, writing to him with his own hands to take the command of the imperial army. Zulfiqar Khan ultimately captured the fort.[72]

Our tables also reveal that the family of Asad Khan enjoyed considerable power throughout the reigns of Shahjahan and Aurangzeb as some of the very important and confidential posts were held by the members of the family. Rankwise too, they enjoyed a high position especially under Aurangzeb. Asad Khan held the rank of 7000/7000 and titles like *amir-ul umara, jumdat-ul mulk, madar-ul muhami* while his son Zulfiqar Khan those of *nusrat jang* and *bahadur* and held the rank of 6000/6000. The latter was also granted the most dignified insignia of *mahi-maratib.*[73]

Lastly, it may be noted that notwithstanding their doubtless loyalty[74] and sincerity to the empire, sometimes they appear to have become the target of Aurangzeb's displeasure.[75] Moreover, Asad Khan seems to have misused his position of *wazir* and benefited by his close association[76] with the emperor. In 1679 Asad Khan appears to have been promised a bribe of Rs. 20,000 by the English Factors for procuring a custom-free *farman* from the emperor. But the latter refused saying that he could not grant it even for Rs. 22 lakh.[77] However, there are a number of *parwanas* issued by the grand *wazir*, Asad Khan, proclaiming and ensuring the desired concessions to the English merchants from time to time.[78] William Norris writes:

In dealing with officials at the Mughal Court—as, indeed, at any other court in the world—there was the problem of appeasing the underlings, who always took undue advantage of their privileged position. It was equally impossible to determine whether they had been genuinely commissioned by their superiors to do a certain thing, and how far they represented affairs to their masters as they really were.[79]

Elsewhere he criticizes the great nobles like deputy *wazir*, Arshad Khan, second Bakhshi Ruhullah Khan, and Mir Bakhshi Bahramand Khan for their illegal exactions[80] but never, however, complains against Asad Khan and Zulfiqar Khan with whom he was on friendly terms and the two had been instrumental in procuring and sending for him *dastaks* to Masulipatnam and Surat.[81]

NOTES

1. For such immigrant families from Iran see Afzal Husain 'Growth of Irani Elements in Akbar's Nobility', *Proceedings of Indian History Congress,* Aligarh Session, 1975, pp. 166–79.
2. Cf. Thomas William Beale, *An Oriental Biographical Dictionary,* ed. H.G. Keene, Delhi: Manohar, 1971, pp. 79–80, 430; Satish Chandra, *Parties and Politics at the Mughal Court,* 2nd edn., Delhi: People's Publishing House, 1972, pp. 1–5; Laiq Ahmad, *The Prime Ministers of Aurangzeb,* Allahabad: Chugh Publications, 1976, Chapter 4 (Asad Khan); also cf. Shahnawaz Khan, *Ma'sir-ul Umara,* ed. Molvi Abdur Rahim, Calcutta: Bib. Ind. Asiatic Society of Bengal, 1888, vol. I, 310–21; vol. II, pp. 85–9.
3. Apparently a very small and insignificant tribe.
4. He was the grandfather of Zulfiqar Khan Qaramanlu (no. 5), the grandfather of Asad Khan (no. 13). See the Genealogical Chart in Appendix A.
5. Iskandar Beg Turkman, *Tarikh-i-Alam Ara-i Abbasi* (hereafter see *A.A.A.*, Tehran: Chaap Khana Gulshan, AH 1350, vol. I, p. 40; also *Baburnama,* Eng. tr. A.S. Beveridge, rpt., Delhi: Oriental Books Reprint Corporation, 1979, p. 359.
6. Hamd-ullah Mustaufi, *Nuzhat-ul Qulub,* tr. G. LE Strange, London: Luzac, 1919, pp. 65–6, *Hudud-al Alam,* tr. V. Minorsky, London: Oxford University Press, 1937, p. 388.
7. *A.A.A.*, vol. I, p. 113.
8. Ibid., vol. II, p. 752.
9. Ibid., vol. I, pp. 520, 542, 565; earlier he appears to have served in several battles, ibid., pp. 404, 427–8, 433–4, 436–7, 442–5, 449–51, etc.

10. Ibid., p. 565.
11. Ibid. p. 574.
12. Ibid., p. 575.
13. Ibid., p. 442.
14. Ibid., 520.
15. One of the strongest forts of Tabaristan.
16. *A.A.A.*, vol. I, pp. 542–3.
17. Ibid., pp. 442, 492, 588.
18. Ibid., pp. 512–13.
19. Ibid., p. 543.
20. Ibid., vol. II, pp. 638, 640, 642–3.
21. Ibid., p. 733.
22. Ibid., pp. 786–7.
23. Ibid., p. 806.
24. Ibid., p. 807; also *M.U.*, vol. II, pp. 86–7.
25. *M.U.*, vol. II, p. 88.
26. Abdul Hamid Lahori, *Badshahnama* (hereafter Lahori), Calcutta: Bib. Ind. Asiatic Society of Bengal, 1867, vol. I (a), p. 73; also *M.U.*, op. cit.
27. Shaikh Farid Bhakkari, *Zakhirat-ul Khawanin* (hereafter *Z. Kh.*), ed. S. Moinul Haq, Karachi: Pakistan Historical Society, 1961, vol. II, p. 411; *M.U.*, II, p. 88. For Asaf Khan's family see Irfan Habib's article, 'The Family of Nurjahan during Jahangir's Reign—A Political Study', *Medieval India: A Miscellany*, Bombay: Asia Publishing House, 1969, vol. I. pp. 74–95.
28. *M.U.*, II, p. 93.
29. *Akhbarat-i Darbar-i Mu'alla* (hereafter cited as *Akhbarat*): Newsletters from the imperial court, Aurangzeb's reign. I have used microfilms of the National Library transcripts as the CAS in History, Aligarh, 32 R.Y./ 3 October 1688. *M.U.*, II, 93.
30. Muhammad Kazim, *Alamgirnama*, Calcutta: Asiatic Society of Bengal, 1968, p. 439 (hereafter See *Al. N.*); Saqi Mustaid Khan, *Masir-i Alamgiri*, Calcutta: Asiatic Society of Bengal, 1871, p. 27 (hereafter *M.A.*); Mirza Muhammad Mutamad Khan, *Tarikh-i Muhammadi*, ed. Imtiaz Ali Arshi, Deptt. of History, Aligarh Muslim University, Aligarh, 1960, vol. II, p. 8 (hereafter *T.M.*).
31. *Al. N.*, p. 493; *M.U.*, II, p. 89.
32. *M.A.*, pp. 312–13; *M.U.*, I (a), pp. 320–1; *T.M.*, p. 74.
33. *M.A.* 461; *M.U.*, I, 454–7; *T.M.*, p. 16.
34. *Al. N.*, p. 858.
35. *Akhbarat*, 33rd R.Y./11 July 1689; Cf. *M.A.*, p. 374.
36. Akhbarat, 39th R.Y./18 January 1696. He was perhaps Tarbiyat Khan *Mir Atish*, son of Darab Khan.
37. *M.A.*, p. 221; *T.M.*, p. 90.

38. Ibid., p., 473; Ibid., 66; *M.U.* I, pp. 454–7.
39. See Genealogical Chart in Appendix A.
40. *Al.N.*, p. 493; *M.U.*, II, p. 89.
41. *T.M.*, p. 72.
42. Lahori, vol. I (a), pp. 72–3.
43. Ibid., pp. 405–6.
44. Ibid., p. 476; Cf. Laiq Ahmad, op. cit., pp. 100–1 says that the title was given by Jahangir. He has confused him with Muhammad Beg who was given the same title in 1614. See *Tuzuk-i Jahangiri,* ed. Sir Syed Ahmad (printed at his private press), Aligarh, 1864, pp. 134–5.
45. Lahori I (b), p, 101.
46. Muhammad Waris, *Badshahnama,* transcript of the Raza Library MS of Rampur in the Deptt. of History, Aligarh, pp. 347–8, (hereafter Waris).
47. *Al. N.*, p. 439; *M.A.*, p. 27; *M.U.,* II, pp. 88–9.
48. Waris, pp. 208, 211.
49. Muhammad Salih Kanboh, *'Amal-i Salih,* ed. G. Yazdani, Calcutta: Asiatic Society of Bengal, 1932, vol. III, p. 244.
50. *M.A.*, p. 103.
51. Ibid., p. 108.
52. Ibid., pp. 152, 281; *M.U.,* I (a), p. 311; Cf. Abul Fazl Mamuri, *Tarikh-i Aurangzeb,* OR. MS. 1671, I.144 (b) gives the year as 16th R.Y., i.e. 1673. (I have used the Rotograph Copy in the Department of History, AMU, Aligarh) (hereafter see Mamuri).
53. *M.A.*, p. 302; *M.U.*, I (a), p. 312.
54. *M.A.*, p. 71; *M.U.*, II, p. 93, Satish Chandra, op. cit., p. 2, makes a slip when he gives the date of his first *mansab* as 1660 and the date of his birth as 1649 (11 years). The date of his birth in 1657 has been supported with a chronogram, *Ze Burj Asad ru namud Aftab,* by *Masir-ul Umara.*
55. *M.A.*, p. 461; *M.U.*, II, p. 96; Kewal Ram, *Tazkirat-ul Umara,* tr. Azizuddin Husain, Delhi, 1985, p. 72 (hereafter see *T.U.*) (in 1702).
56. *M.U.* II, p. 97; *T.U.*, p. 72 (in 1705).
57. See their respective biographies in *M.U.*
58. The title was conferred on him in the 32nd R.Y. of Aurangzeb, *T.U.*, p. 115.
59. *M.U.,* I (a), pp. 320–1.
60. *Akhbarat,* 33 R.Y., 30 July and 3 November 1689.
61. *M.A.*, pp. 312–13; Mamuri, f, 185 (a); *M.U.,* I (a), pp. 320–1.
62. *M.U.,* I (a), pp. 320–1; *T.U.*, p. 74.
63. Waris, p. 313.
64. *M.U.*, II, p. 105.
65. Mamuri, f. 164 (b).
66. Harihar Das, *The Norris Embassy to Aurangzeb* (*1699–1702*), Calcutta: K.L. Mukhopadhyay, 1959, p. 264.

67. See Irfan Habib's article, op. cit., also my article, 'Position of I'timad-ud-Daula's Family During the Reign of Shah Jahan', in the *Proceedings of Indian History Congress*, Hyderabad Session, 1978, pp. 437–57.
68. See Appendix B.
69. In 1674 he was first sent to Kabul together with Prince Akbar, *M.A.*, pp. 133, 136; then after about nine years in 1682 he served along with Prince Azimuddin to check Rathor activities in Ajmer, *M.A.*, p. 213.
70. Muhammad Abdul Wahid (ed.), *Ruqat-i Alamgiri,* Mustafai Press Lucknow AH 1294, letter no. 153, pp. 41–2. This letter has also been translated by J.H. Bilimoria, *Ruka'at-i Alamgiri* tr. Idarah-i Adabiyat Delhi, 1972, 147. For a slightly different version also see *M.A.*, pp. 352–3.
71. *Ruqat-i Alamgri,* p. 42; *M.A.*, p. 450.
72. *M.A.*, pp. 502–5; *M.U.*, II, pp. 96–7.
73. *Ruqat-i Alamgiri, Ruqa* no. 16, p. 7; also see Isar Das Nagar, *Futuhat-i Alamgiri* (hereafter *Futuhat*), B.M. MS. Add. 23884, f. 160. Cf. Tasneem Ahmad, *Ishwar Das Nagar's Futuhat-i Alamgiri* (Eng. tr.), Delhi: Idarah-i Adabiyat, 1978, p. 269. For *Mahi-O-Maratib* see William Irvine, *The Army of the Indian Moghuls,* Delhi: Eurasia Publishing House, 1969, p. 33.
74. Manucci writes that after his accession to the throne Aurangzeb wrote to Shahjahan asking for a gift of the jewels under his possession. But Shahjahan, in place of the required jewels, sent him the loyal Asad Khan, a person whom he strongly recommended, declaring that he might be more safely trusted than any other living being. See *Storia Do Mogor (1653–1708),* tr. William Irvine, vol. II, London: John Murray, 1907, 20–1; also vol. IV, p. 241 for Asad Khan reply to Prince Kam Bakhsh for not handing over the imperial treasures as long as the emperor was alive. In his last will Aurangzeb mentioned that 'There is not, nor will there (ever) be any *wazir* better than Asad Khan', the letter has been quoted by J.N. Sarkar in *History of Aurangzeb,* Calcutta: M.C. Sarkar & Sons, 1930, vol. V, p. 262. In his letters to Asad Khan and Zulfiqar Khan, Aurangzeb always addressed them by using the phrase 'My sincere and devoted (servant)', see relevant letters in *Ruqat-i Alamgiri.*
75. During the siege of Jinji Asad Khan was ordered to hasten to Zulfiqar Khan's help. As he delayed in going the emperor remarked 'It is easy to make a boast but it is quite different to make it true', and also read the verse 'Don't boast any more of yourself (being a Turk) because your Turkship has ended', *Ruqat-i Alamgiri,* pp. 41–2; *M.A.*, 352–3. In 1705 after the conquest of Wakinkhera Zulfiqar Khan was not given due rewards on account of some reasons. *M.U.*, II, p. 97.
76. He enjoyed the privilege of visiting the emperor in *Gulalbar* (enclosure) riding on his *palki* which was forbidden to all the nobles and princes

except those who had been granted *palkis* by the emperor. Multafat Khan, another intimate servant, was also allowed. See *M.A.*, p. 354.

77. R.C. Temple (ed.), *The Diaries of Streyansham Master, 1675–1680*, vol. II, London: John Murray, 1911, p. 292.
78. *Farmans, Nishans and Parwanas*, Dept. of History, AMU, Rotograph no. 229, pp. 48–9, 58–9. These *parwanas* belonged to the 21st and 23rd R.Y. of Aurangzeb.
79. *The Norris Embassy to Aurangzeb*, p. 271.
80. Ibid., pp. 276–7.
81. *Norris Embassy*, pp. 275–6.

APPENDIX A

Genealogical Chart

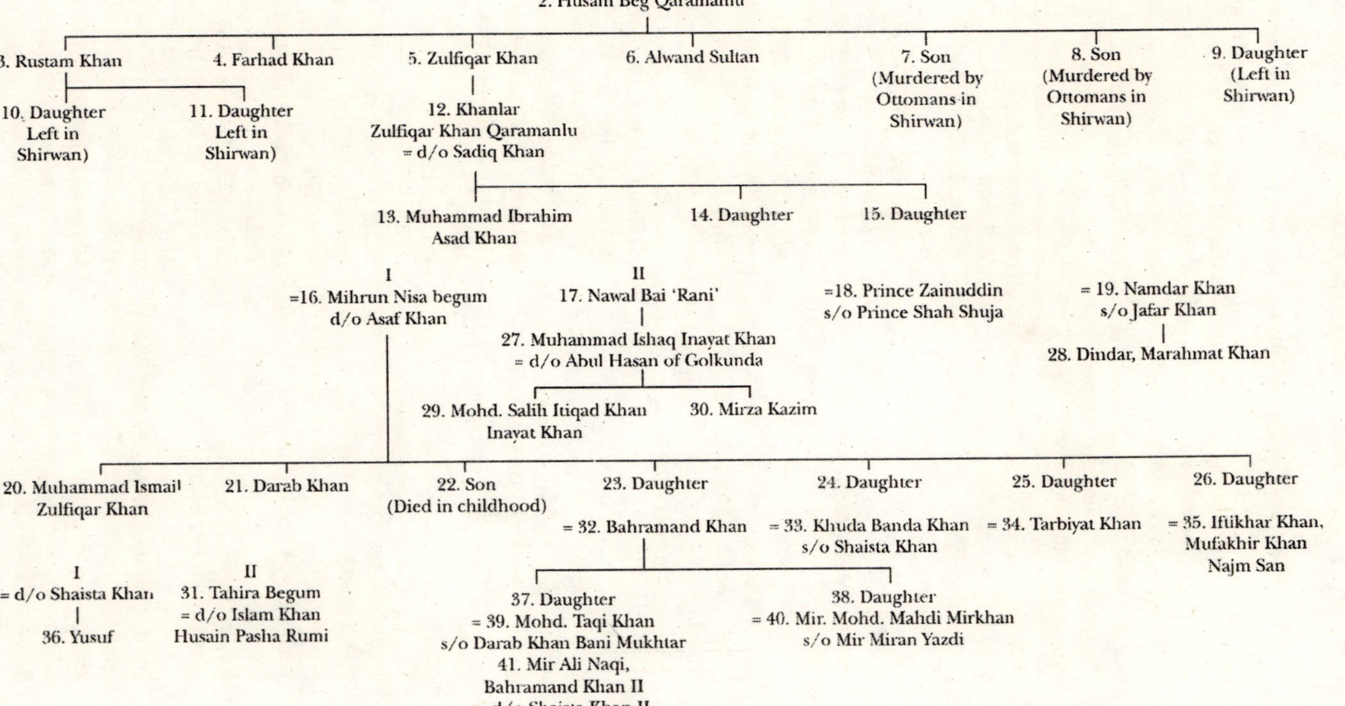

References to the Genelogical Chart

:	Indicates	Father of
+	Indicates	Brother/Sister of
=	Indicates	Husband/Wife of
–	Indicates	Grandson of
%	Indicates	Son-in-law of

Number prefacing the names of persons in the Chart	Sources
1:2	*A.A.A.*, I, 112
2:3, 4, 5, 6,	*A.A.A.*, I, 443
3+4, 5, 6, 7, 8, 9	*A.A.A.*, II, 752
3:10, 11	Ibid.
4+5, 6	Ibid. I, 442, 449, 520, 542, 575, 588
5:12	*M.U.* II, 85
12=d/o Sadiq Khan	*Z.Kh.* II, 411; *M.U.* II, 88.
12:13	Sadiq Khan, f. 89 (b); *Al.N.* 439; *M.U.* I, 310; *T.M.*, 35, 74.
12:14, 14=18	*Al.N.*, 493; *M.U.* II, 89
12:15, 15+13, 15=19:28	*T.M.* 8
19%12	*Al.N.*, 439; *M.A.*, 27.
13=16, 13% Asaf Khan	*M.U.* II, 93; *T.M.*, 35
13=17, 13:27	*Akhbarat*, 25 R.Y. 10 Sept. 1681; Mamuri, f. 185 (a) *M.A.*, 312; *M.U.* I (a), 320–1.
13:27, 27:29, 29+30	*T.M.* 74; *M.U.* I (a), 320–1
27=d/o Abul Hasan of Hyderabad	*Akhbarat*, 32 R.Y., 4 Oct. 1688; Ma'muri, f. 185 (a); *M.A.*, 312–13.
13:20	*M.U.* I (a), 320–1; *T.M.*, 72.
13:21	Waris, 313
13:22 (22 died in childhood)	*Al.N.*, 757–8
13:23, 23=32, 32%13	*M.A.*, 461; *M.U.* I, 454–7; *T.M.*, 16.
13:24,24=33	*Akhbarat*, 33 R.Y., 11 July 1689; *M.A.*, 374.
13:25, 25=34	*Akhbarat*, 39 R.Y. 18 January 1696; *T.M.*, 22.
13:26, 26=35	*Al.N.*, 858; *Akhbarat*, 4 R.Y. 1662.
20=d/o Shaista Khan	*Akhbarat*, 32 R.Y. 3 Oct. 1688; *M.A.*, 158; *M.U.* II, 93.
20=d/o Shaista Khan, 20-Asaf Khan	*T.M.*, 31.
20=31	*T.M.*, 72.
20:36	Mamuri, f. 164 (b)
32:37, 38	*M.U.* I, 454–7.
37=38:41%32&23	Ibid.; *T.M.*, 90.
38=40	Ibid.; Ibid., 66; *M.A.*, 473.

APPENDIX B

Mansabs and Appointments Held by Asad Khan's Family

1. Khanlar, Zulfiqar Khan

S.N.	Year	Rank	Title	Appointment	Source
1.	1627			In the central command with Asaf Khan in the battle against Shahryar.	Lahori I (a) 73.
2.	1631			In the left wing command of the imperial army in	Lahori I (a), 406; *Z. Kh.* II, 411; *T.U.*, 71.
3.	1632	1000/600			Lahori I (a), 432.
4.	1633		Zulfiqar Khan		Lahori I (a), 476.
5.	1634	1500/800		*Faujdar of Miyan-i Doab*	Lahori, I (b) 101; *T.U.* 71.
6.	1638			*Bakhshi* of Dara's contin-gent in the Qandahar expedition.	Lahori, II, 140–1; Sadiq Khan, ff. 50 (a) 51(a)
7.	1639		*Topkhana.*	*Darogha-i-* 154.	Lahori, II,
8.	1640	2000/800		*Qiladar* of Lahore fort.	Lahori II, 198, 223; *T.U.*, 71.
9.	1642	2000/1,200		*Faujdar* of Mandsor.	Lahori II, 306; *T.U.*, 71.
10.	1644	2000/1500 (500X2-3h)		Tuyuldar of *Pargana* Bhojpur (Bihar)	Lahori II, 380; *T.U.*, 71.
11.	1653	3000/2000		296.	Waris, 208,
12.	1656	3000/3000		*Subedar* of Bihar.	Waris, 347–8; *T.U.*, 71.

2. Muhammad Ibrahim, Asad Khan

S.N.	Year	Rank	Title	Appointment	Source
			(A) Under Shahjahan		
1.	1651	1000 *zat*			*T.U.*, 196
2.	1653	1500/600	Asad Khan	*Akhtabegi*	Waris, 208, 211, 237; Sadiq Khan f. 89(b); *T.U.*, 196.
3.	1655	2000/600		*Arz Waqai* Subject	Waris, 289, 296, *T.U.*, 196.
4.	1657	2000/800			Waris, 361.
5.	1658			Second *Bakhshi*	Salih, III, 244; Cf. *T.U.*, 196.
		(B) Under Aurangzeb			
6.	1658	3000/1500		Second *Bakhshi* (H)	*Al.N.*, 119, 157; *T.U.*, 196.
7.	1659	3500/2500			*Al.N.*, 395–6.
8.	1663	4000/2500			*Al.N.*, 762.
9.	1664	4000/3800			*Al.N.*, 843.
10.	1670			*Dy. Diwan*	*M.A.*, 103.
11.	1671			*Mir Bakhshi*	*M.A.*, 108; *M.U.* I(a), 311.
12.	1673			*Dy. Diwan* (Resigned)	*M.A.*, 125–6.
13.	1673			Sent to Kabul along with Prince Akbar to suppress the Afghans.	*M.A.*, 133, 136.
14.	1676			*Wazir*	*M.U.* I(a), 311; *T.U.*, 196.
15.	1677			Deputed in the Deccan.	*M.A.*, 161; Maruri, f. 149(b); *M.U.* I(a), 312.
16.	1681–2			Deputed with Prince Azimuddin to check Rathor activities.	*M.A.*, 213; Futuhat, ff. 83(b) 84(a).
17.	1684			Visited Aurangzeb at Ahmednagar.	*M.A.*, 241; *M.U.* I, (a), 312.

S.N.	Year	Rank	Title	Appointment	Source
18.	1687			Granted *Masnad-i-Wizarat.*	*M.A.*, 281; *M.U.* (a), 312.
19.	1688	7000/7000			*M.A.*, 302; *M.U.* I(a), 312.
20.	1690			In the conquest of Nandial fort	*M.A.*, 354
21.	1691–2			In the siege of Wakankhera, etc.	*M.A.*, 354–9.
22.	1693			In the siege of Jinji fort.	*M.A.*, 356.
23.	1698	7000/7000			*M.A.*, 391–2.
24.	1699			Appointment at Brahmapuri (Islampuri) to guard imperial harem.	*M.A.*, 408; *M.U.* I(a), 314.
25.	1701		Amir-ul Umara	Commanded Mughal troops besieging the fort of Khelna.	*M.A.*, 445, 450; *T.U.*, 196.

(*c*) *Muhammad Ismail Zulfiqar Khan*

S.N.	Year	Rank	Title	Appointment	Source
1.	1668	300/*zat*			*M.A.*, 71.
2.	1673–4			Appointed in Kabul.	*T.U.*, 71.
3.	1677		I'tiqad Khan		*M.A.*, 158.
4.	1679			Bakhshi of Andis	*M.A.*, 176.
5.	1681–2	1500/300		Appointed in Ajmer; defeated Rathors in Merta.	*M.A.*, 213; 214–5; *Akhbarat,* 25th R.Y. December, 1681, *M.U.*, II, 93–4; *T.U.*, 72.
6.	1684			Sent towards (Bidar) with a strong force.	*M.A.*, 243.
7.	1684	2000/400		Qurbegi, conquered Chanda.	*M.A.*, 250–1; *T.U.*, 72.

S.N.	Year	Rank	Title	Appointment	Source
8.	1684-5			Sent towards Sangamnir, and Bidar.	*M.A.*, 252, 259.
9.	1685			*Thanedar* of Indi	*M.A.*, 266.
10.	1686			Punished Marathas near Mangalbeda.	*M.A.*, 283.
11.	1687			*Darogha-i Ghusal Khana.*	*M.A.*, 297; *M.U.*, II, 84.
12.	1688			Sent to conquer Bangalore fort	*Futuhat*, ff. 127(b)–131(a).
13.	1689	3000/2000	Zulfiqar Khan	Sent to conquer the fort of Raheri.	*Akhbarat*, 33 R.Y., 4 Nov. 1689; *M.A.*, 331, 332; *M.U.*, II, 94.
14.	1691	4000/2500		Conquered the fort of Nirmal (Trino-mali).	*M.A.*, 345; *M.U.* II, 94.
15.	1692–3	4000/3000		Appointed to conquer fort of Jinji.	*M.A.*, 351, 352–3, 354–9, *M.U.* II, 94.
16.	1694	5000/3000			*M.A.*, 369.
17.	1695	5000/4000	Nusratjang		*M.A.*, 374; *M.U.*, II, 95.
18.	1698	5000/5000		Conquered fort of Jinji (renamed Nusratgarh after his name).	*M.A.*, 392; *M.U.* II, 95–6.
19.	1699			Darogha-i-Jilau (A.C.)	*M.A.*, 406.
20.	1700			Sent towards Par-nala under Prince Bedar Bakht, crushed Dhanna Jadav.	*M.A.*, 430, 432, Mamuri, f. 197(a)
21.	1702			*Mir Bakhshi*	*M.A.*, 461; *M.U.*, II, 96, 97.
22.	1703			Sent towards Bur-hanpur to punish Marathas.	*M.A.*, 470.

S.N.	Year	Rank	Title	Appointment	Source
23.	1705			Deputed in the siege of Wakan-khera fort.	*M.A.*, 502–3; Mamuri, f. 205 (b), *M.U.*, II, 96–7; *T.U.*, 72.
24.	1706	6000/6000		Sent towards Aurangabad to punish Marathas; receptured Kondana (Bakh-shanda Bakhsh)	*M.A.*, 511–12; *M.U.*, II, 97.

Udai Sagar: A Sixteenth-Century Dam in Rajasthan

B.L. BHADANI

The tradition of construction of waterworks appears to have become a symbol of cultural ethos for the rulers of Mewar (Rajasthan). Inumerable extant structures are witness to it.[1] This is reflected also in the literature and inscriptions composed in the early and late medieval times.[2] In fact, they are the true memorials of the builders. Undoubtedly, the role of geography and ecology of the Aravalli range in the Mewar region had been quite crucial in the building of dams, tanks, wells and step wells as components of their value system. In the absence of any perennial river system, it became more prudent for the masters of the region to search out other alternatives to make water available throughout the year for drinking as well as irrigation. Their endeavours were based on two objectives: first, to achieve the mythological status of Bhagirath, who is said to have brought the Ganga on the earth; and secondly, the more earthly utilitarian purpose as mentioned above. The latter was interlinked with the economic necessity of the state.

Following the family tradition, Maharana Udai Singh (AD 1540–72) planned a big project encompassing the founding of a new capital city and the erection of a dyke (*pal*) for irrigating the surrounding vast agricultural tract.[3] The site selected for it was located to the east of the city. The existence of a deep gorge between the hills was fancied by the Maharana as an ideal location for the construction of the weir there. He successfully achieved his aim by creating a big lake (*sagar*) by joining the two isolated hills with a wall of rubbles, which attracted both contemporary and modern writers.[4]

For our study, we made an extensive survey of the sixteenth-century water structure and took detailed measurements of each and every part of it. On the basis of this survey we have been able to draw its ground plan which is appended at the end of this paper.[5] The aim of this paper however is to study the structure in its entirety. An attempt has been made to determine its date of construction to explore the canals by which the vast tract was irrigated, and which furnished a substantial income to the state.

II

The Udai Sagar dyke is located about 8 miles east of Udaipur (south of Rajasthan) near the valley of Debari.[6] There was a cluster of hills (*dungar*) which were surrounded by villages owned by the Devra Rajputs, the *bhumias* of the area.[7] The maximum height of the hills around the area reaches to 770 ft. A deep gorge is formed by the mountain.

Here at one point on embankment wall was erected between the two hills and a lake of enormous magnitude was created. The dyke was named after its builder Udai Singh, the ruler of Mewar. It is said that it was a part of a broader plan which included the foundation of a new city, later known as Udaipur.[8]

The mountains around Mewar are the originator of major rivers. The deep gorge near the Debari receives water from the mountains (*magra*) of Gogunda and Kumbhalmer.[9] The spring that flows from the hills north of Udaipur carries two names; Ahar and Berach. When it passes through the village Ahar, it is given the name of the village and finally falls into the Udai Sagar.[10] The water which flows out of the lake is first known as *Udai Sagar-ka nala.* When it reaches the open area it takes the name Berach.[11] Nainsi does not use the name Ahar for the river but instead designates the spring as the river Berach which falls into the lake.[12] A chart of the catchment of Udai Sagar prepared by the Department of Irrigation, Rajasthan, shows the mountains to the north of the city of Udaipur. Here water originates from the place known as *Gorana ki nal,* first falling into the Pichhola lake and from their it reaches Udai Sagar. The channels from the Bari tank and Madar tank also contribute water to the lake. Though both the tanks were built in later times, presumably the springs from the hills of this direction might have merged into the lake.[13]

III

The water works of Mewar constructed during the seventeenth century ordinarily have official or non-official inscriptions on the structure itself giving details about the name of the builder, date of initiation and completion of the work, names of the engineer (*sutradhara*) and masons and sometimes the cost incurred on the structure. [14] But, unfortunately, the Udai Sagar dyke does not have the official inscription by its builder. This led to speculations about its date and time of its completion. There is no unanimity among the historians about its date of construction. The uncertainty is reflected in Nainsi when he gives two dates vs 1620/AD 1563 and vs 1621/AD 1564—for the building of the structure.[15] Ranchhod Bhatt composed two epics—*Rajprashasti Mahakavyam* (composed in vs 1718/AD 1661) and *Amarkavyam* (vs 1748/AD 1691, vs 1750/AD 1693). In the former, he does not oblige us by giving the date of construction while in the latter, the year vs 1600/AD 1543 as the beginning of the building and vs 1618/AD 1561 as the completion of the dyke is recorded.[16] Another seventeenth-century source offers the year vs 1618/AD 1561 as the year of completion of the dam.[17]

The celebrated historian of Mewar, Shyamal Das records the year vs 1616/AD 1559 as the inauguration of the work and vs 1619/AD 1562 as its completion year.[18] G.H. Ojha agrees with Shyamal Das on the date of the beginning of the work while he gives the year vs 1621/AD 1564 for its completion.[19] James Tod merely writes that the lake was formed 'several years previous to the catastrophe', i.e. before 1568.[20] This kind of uncertainty prevails in other sources too.[21]

This uncertainty is, however removed by the recently discovered contemporary source—the *Chittor Udaipur Patnama.* It records the year vs 1615/AD 1558 as the initiation of the work,[22] which means that the dyke was constructed well before the fall of Chittor.

It gets further support from the date discovered on the structure. We noticed the stonecutters, marks and signatures of the masons, sometimes with date, on the temples erected at the top of the dam. On one of the temples, the year vs 1623/AD 1566 is inscribed by one mason with his signature.[23] This date assumes significance. The temples were built after the completion of the water structure. It shows, then, that the weir was ready at least six or seven years prior to this date, i.e. in 1559 and not 1560. At least this date confirms the time of the completion of the structure.

IV

The Udai Sagar is a huge tank with enormous capacity to contain water. High hills along the four sides created a deep depression. The river enters into this valley from the western side near the village Lakadwas. The passage of water is blocked by erecting a masonry wall between the two hills which runs north to south. On the opposite side facing the wall, there is a continuous range of hills which make this gorge like a deep melting pot.

Abul Fazl was the first chronicler who noticed the existence of a large lake at Udaipur with a circumference of 16 *kos* (40 miles). Wheat crops were being grown by the waters of the tank.[24] Our celebrated historians and the statistician of seventeenth-century Rajasthan, Nainsi, too, gives the circumference of the tank which comes to 10 *kos* (25 miles).[25] At another place he writes that when the water from the hills of the Gogunda and Kumbhalmer forms the river Berach and water gushes into the tank, its circumference expands and reaches up to 20 *kos* (about 50 miles).[26]

The information provided both by Abul Fazl and Nainsi corresponds strikingly. From this, it becomes clear that the structure identified in the *Ain* is certainly that of the Udai Sagar and not the Jai Samand as erroneously recognized by one historian.[27] because the dyke noticed by the Mughal chronicler was located at Udaipur, while the Jai Samand was in the *pargana* of Tana.[28] It is located in the south-east and 32 miles away from the city of Udaipur.[29]

Nainsi further records the measurements of different sections. He gives the length and breadth of the *pal* which is 500 *gaz* (1,250 ft) and 250 *gaz* (625 ft) respectively.[30] The total height recorded comes to 70 *gaz* (175 ft). Seventy *gaz* wall was in water while 12 *gaz* (30 ft) is exposed. Then, he gives the size of the canal (*nala*). Its depth is recorded as 50 *gaz* (125 ft) and the breadth as 12 *gaz*

(30 ft) which was cut out of the hill (*Bhakhar*).[31]

The measurements provided by Nainsi require verification. No one has compiled the data in so much detail. After a gap of 350 years or so, Erskine records only the breadth of the structure which came to 180 ft.[32] G.H. Ojha reiterates it while Raj Shekhar Vyas gives both the length and the breadth as 100 and 180 ft respectively.[33] But none matches with Nainsi.

We have taken up an extensive physicial survey of the structure. The detailed measurements of each of the section was carried out. On this basis, a ground plan has been prepared. Detailed photographs from different direction were also taken (Figs. 3–6).

The wall erected between the two hills runs north to south. The obvious aim was to hold back water or to conserve water to channellize it in the desired direction. The length measured comes to 303 m. The engineers took extra care about the safety and long life of the dyke. This necessitated the building of the back or retaining wall to muster additional strength to the embankment wall. The distance between the two walls comes to 97 m which is the width of the weir. Even the width of 1.20 m was given to the retaining wall. The space or gap between the front or back wall was filled with lime and mortar.

Protection and safety appear to have been of utmost necessity to the civil engineers. The danger of washing away of the structure in the rainy season was always looming. In an attempt to obviate this eventuality the embankment wall was imparted strength by additional projections. The maximum breadth in the north comes to 28 m and decreases as we move towards the south. Possibly the northern side wall faced the violent thrust of water gushes from the south-eastern directions. Interestingly, the projections were in the descending order.

In the north, there is a pathway adjoining the hill that goes towards the other side of the dam. The embankment wall starts from here. On this a rectangular bastion was erected and a temple, circular in shape, was built up. Adjoining the bastion, a wall of the first section extends towards the south and joins the semi-circular projection towards the lake. The section has seven projections in the descending order. The stairs are provided on both sides to reach up to the fourth floor. Then a second section starts in the form of a semi-circular projection. Its width from the embankment wall to water comes to 28 m. It has ten platforms. The access up to the sixth platform is provided by constructing the steps.

The embankment wall from the semi-circular bastion towards the south is further divided into six sections by constructing a solid platform of 4.80 × 4.00 m. The water-lifting place also served as the seventh platform. This is located on the north near the semi-circular projection. Its size is 6.50 × 2.40 m. Five stairs of 1 m in length joins the two platforms. The division of the projections into sections was certainly meant for the solid strength of the embankment wall.

Towards the southern corner of the dyke, a temple similar to that at the north was built. In the same direction, a guard's chamber was constructed near the outlet. Two objectives seem to have been in operation behind erecting this structure at this point: first, to control the supply of water in the canal, and secondly, to look after the safety and protection of the dyke and take necessary steps in the time of danger, particularly from torrential rains.

An important component part of the water structure is the outlet located at the end of the embankment in the south. Nainsi rightly observed that the channel (*nala*) was cut out of the mountain. He records its size which is 50 *gaz* (125 ft) deep and 12 *gaz* (30 ft) in breadth.[34] The round figures perhaps indicate that these were conjectures. Our measurement of the outlet comes to 4 m in width.

At the end of the outlet, a rectangular cistern was constructed to store water to release in the canal. At both ends of the outlet, there were devices to control the supply of water into the cistern. Two canals were dug out to supply water in different directions towards the south-west and the north. The former first goes towards the west then turns south, while another flows towards the north and goes parallel adjoining the back wall and then takes a turn towards the west. Two flood gates were erected to regulate water supply to the canals. Both the channels were of masonry nature that irrigated a large area where, as the *Ain* notices, wheat cultivation was done. Its width measures 1.15 m. Its length could not be measured, but it appears to have been quite long in size. It is noteworthy that at regular intervals. Square or rectangular outlets of 2 × 2 ft size were cut out to drain the agricultural fields.

Near the backwall, a sloping passage was meant to go to the backside of the dam. Along the pathway a masonry wall was constructed. The passage at the end of the slope trifurcates. Right and left directions lead towards the canals on both the sides. The straight path goes towards a residential complex meant probably for the officer-in-charge of the dyke.

Niches are carved out on half of the embankment wall towards the southern direction. The stone slabs are on the four sides of them. One of the slab is signed by a certain artisan named Parsa. The reason for carving out the niches is not clear. Was there any techinical point behind it, or simply a design pattern?

V

The study of the Udai Sagar Dam demonstrates that the site chosen by its builders and civil engineers was ideal and perfect. It was surrounded by hills with only one opening. That was closed by a huge masonry structure in length and breadth. Both dimensions increased its weight which was considered as the strength of the dam. This was the exclusive technique employed against the forceful pressure of water. It is the weight of the structure which enables it to remain standing for 450 years coping with the vagaries of weather. No damage has been done to this date.

The hydrological factor was the dominating element. The exclusive purpose behind the construction of this barrage was irrigation. The builder wanted to create a vast fertile tract to feed the residence of the newly founded city. He got tremendous success in his mission by increasing wheat cultivation. This embankment is still active, irrigating the surrounding fields. The report of the Department of Irrigation, Rajasthan, shows that 6,070 acres of land was being irrigated during 1992–3. One can conclude on this basis that it was an excellent example of a 'gravity' dam constructed during the middle of the sixteenth century. The refinement and improvement in the indigenous dam technology could be inferred from this study.

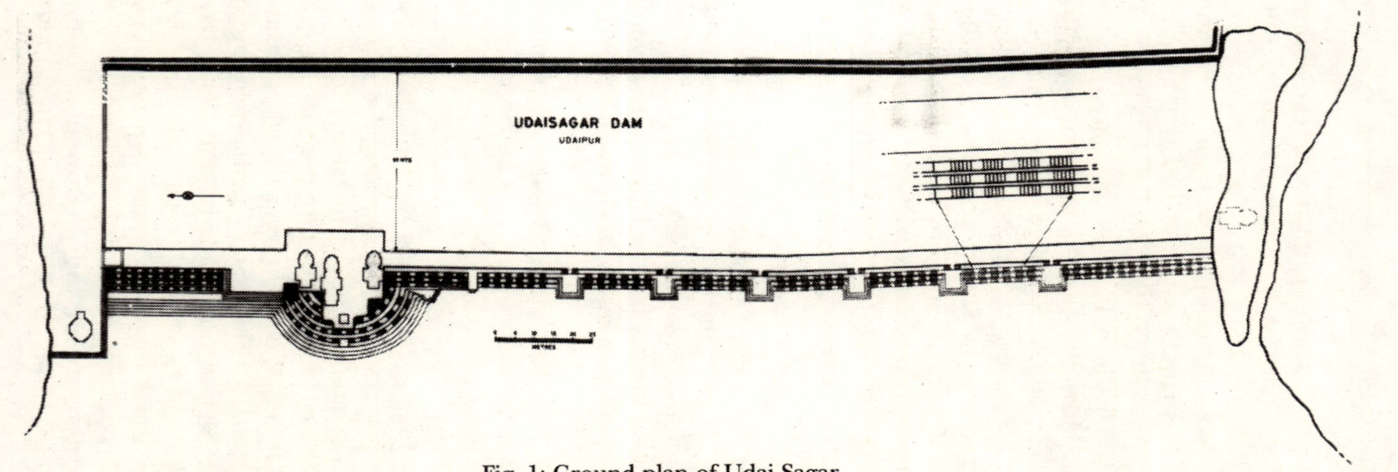

Fig. 1: Ground plan of Udai Sagar.

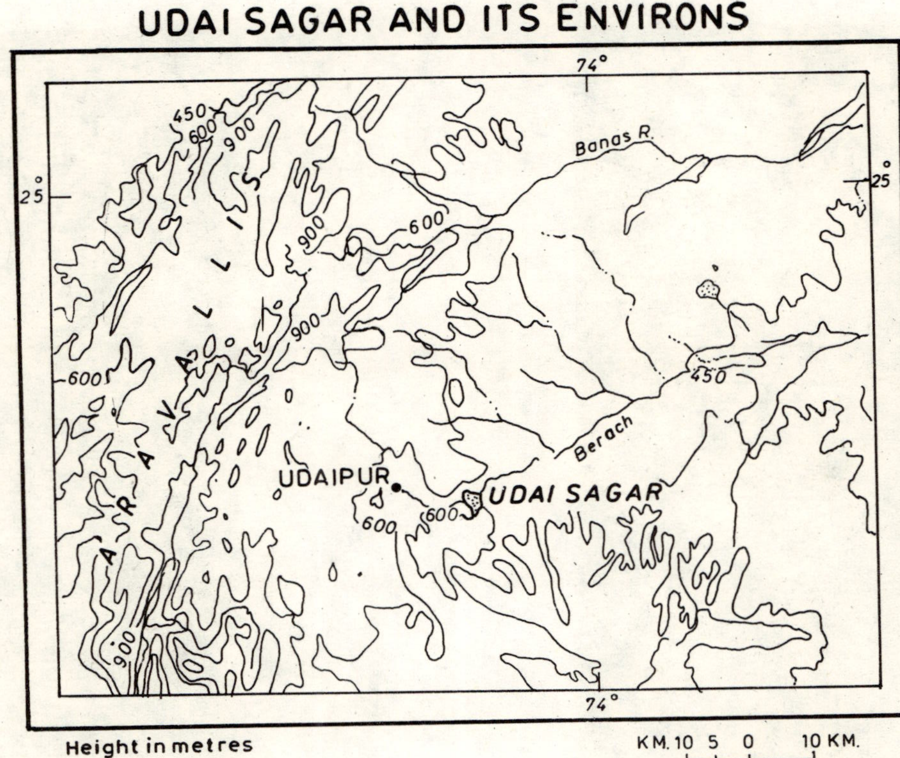

Fig. 2: Udai Sagar and its Environs.

Fig. 3: Front view of the dyke.

Fig. 4: Side view and bastion of the dam.

Fig. 5: Canal.

Fig. 6: Water tank connected with canal and passage.

NOTES

1. In the source, it is mentioned that the Udai Sagar is the eighth lake, which denotes the existence of seven more lakes previous to its construction by Maharana Udai Singh. (See 'Sisod Vanshavali Evam Rajasthan ke Rajwaron ki Vansavaliyan', in *Majjhamika*, vol. 23, Udaipur: Pratap Shodh Sansthan, 1995, p. 55). Raj Samand, *Jana Sagar or Bari ka Talao*, Dhebar or Jai Samand, Pichhola and Fateh Sagar are the well-known names (see Ranchhod Bhatt, *Rajprashasti Mahakavyam*, ed. Motilal Menaria, Udaipur: Sahitya Sansthan, Rajasthan Vidyapeeth, (hereafter SSRV, Udaipur) 1973; Munhot Nainsi, *Khyat*, ed. Badari Prasad Sakariya, I, Jodhpur: Rajasthan Oriental Research Institute, 1960, pp. 32–3; *Chittor-Udaipur ka Patnama*, f. 217(a); A photocopy of the manuscript is preserved at the Natnagar Shodh Sansthan, Sitamau; K.D. Erskine, *Rajputana Gazetteers—The Mewar Residency*, vol. II, Gurgaon: Vintage Books, rpt., 1998, pp. 8–9).
2. The first stanza of the *Rajprashasti Mahakavyan* makes it clear that the rulers of Mewar took inspiration of bridge or dyke construction from Lord Rama. This bridge erection brought popularity for him in this world (p. 1). Besides this, the Sisodia rulers also had deep faith in the theory of salvation (*moksha*). The construction of tank could bring *moksha* to the ancestors of the builders or the builder himself. Gradually, this assumed the status of cultural ethos for the rulers. That is why almost all the Maharanas endeavoured to erect water structures in their life time (cf. *Rajprashasti Mahakavyam*, pp. 40–1. References are scattered all over the text).
3. *Chittor-Udaipur ka Patnama*, ff. 217 a–b.
4. Abul Fazl, *Ain-i Akbari*, vol. II, tr. H.G Jarret and 2nd edn. corrected and annoted by Sir Jadunath Sarkar, Calcutta: Orient Books Reprint Corporation, 3rd edn., 1978, p. 278 Nainsi, *Khyat*, vol. I, pp. 32–3; James Tod, *Annals and Antiquities of Rajasthan*, vol. I, London: Routledge and Kegan Paul, 1960, p. 263.
5. Zameer Ahmad, Technical Assistant (draftsman) and Ghulam Mujtaba (photographer) of the archaeology section, accompanied me in the survey work.
6. Nainsi, *Khyat*, vol. I, p. 35; one *kos* is tentatively equivalent to $2^1/_2$ miles. Erskine too gives the location of the Udai Sagar 8 miles east of Udaipur, *The Mewar Residency*, op. cit., p. 9.
7. *Chittor-Udaipur ka Patnama*, f. 217 (a).
8. Ibid.
9. Nainsi, *Khyat*, vol. I, p. 35.
10. Erskine, op. cit., pp. 7–8.
11. Ibid., The river Berach is the tributary of the river Banas, the biggest river of Mewar.

12. Nainsi, *Khyat*, vol. I, p. 35.
13. See Figs. 3–6.
14. Raj Samand has perhaps the longest inscription in India runing into 25 block stone slabs of 3 × 2½ ft, giving each and every detail about the dyke. The first slab contains the prayers to gods and goddesses. The remaining 24 slabs have one section of the 'epic' engraved on each of it. It was composed by Ranchhod Bhatt and published under the title *Rajprashasti Mahakavyam*, ed. Motilal Menarija, Udaipur, 1973. Similarly, the Jana Sagar or Bari ka Talao possess inscription (see Appendix 2 in *Rajprashasti*, pp. 272–7). The Jai Samand or Dhebar also carries inscription .
15. Nainsi, *Khyat*, vol. I, p. 34.
16. Ranchhod Bhatt, *Rajprashasti*, p. 41; Ranchhod Bhatt, *Amar Kavyam*, ed. Shakti Kumar Sharma 'Shankunt' and Rajendra Prakash Bhatnagar, SSRV, Udaipur, 1985, pp. 213-14.
17. 'Sisod Vanshavali Evam Rajasthan ke Rajwaron ki Vansavaliyan', in *Majjhamika*, p. 55.
18. Shyamal Das, *Vir Vinod*, vol. II, part I, Delhi: B.R. Publishing Corporation, rpt., 1986, p. 73.
19. G.H. Ojha, *Udaipur Rajya ka Itihas*, vol. I, Jodhpur: Rajasthani Granthagar, 2nd edn., 1999, p. 421.
20. James Tod, *Annals and Antiquities*, vol. I, p. 63.
21. Erskine says that the embankment was built between 1559 and 1565 (see *Rajputana Gazetteers—The Mewar Residency*, vol. II, p. 9. Raj Shekhar Vyas follows Erskine (see *Mewar ki Kala aur Sthapatya*, Jaipur: Rajasthan Prakashan, 1988. p. 128).
22. *Chittor-Udaipur ka Patnama*, p. 220 (b).
23. The date is engraved on the stairs of the temple in the north. This slab is signed by one Shri Balaji. On another site, the words inscribed are 'Shri Likhtam Patel Kachra Jamburan' (Patel Kachra writes in honour of God). Similarly, two masons named Bhat Mohan and Vachali Ramo Viko also inscribed their names.
24. Abul Fazl, *Ain-i-Akbari*, vol. II, p. 278.
25. Nainsi, *Khyat*, vol. I, p. 34.
26. Ibid., p. 35.
27. Irfan Habib in the first edn. of his book (*The Agrarian System of Mughal India*, Delhi: Asia Publishing House, 1963, p. 28 and note) rightly identified the structure in the *Ain* with the Udai Sagar. But in his *An Atlas of the Mughal Empire*, Delhi: Oxford University Press, 1982, p. 19, notes, he changed his earlier view and recognized it with the Jai Samand, basing his argument on the size of the lake. He writes that the size of the dam shown in the *Ain* is only that of the Dhebar Lake. Again, he asserts this view in the second (revised) edition of his book (*Agrarian System*, Delhi: Oxford University Press, 1999, pp. 30–1). His

entire argument is based on James Tod's description (James Tod, *Annals and Antiquities of Rajasthan,* vol. I, p. 619). But he has failed to notice two evidences; Nainsi's two statements about the circumference of the Udai Sagar, and, secondly, the location of the Jai Samand which was 32 miles away from Udaipur.

28. *Maharana Raj Singh Paragana Bahi,* ed. Hukum Singh Bhati, Udaipur: Himanshu Publications, 1995, p. 10.
29. Ojha, *Udaipur Rajya ka Itihas,* pp. 309–10.
30. Nansi, *Khyat,* vol. I, p. 34.
31. Ibid.
32. Erskine, op. cit., pp. 8–9.
33. G.H. Ojha records the measurement of the structure. According to him it is 2½ miles in length and 2 miles in breadth. Its catchment area is in 185 sq miles. The river Ahar falls from it. The embankment wall is constructed between the two hills which is quite high and 180 ft in breadth (Cf. *Uday Rajya ka Itihas,* vol. II, p. 7). Raj Shekhar Vyas, *Mewar ki Kala aur Sthapatya,* p. 128.
34. Nainsi, *Khyat,* vol. I, p. 34.

PART IV

BOOK REVIEWS

Ziauddin Barani's *Tarikh-i-Firuz Shahi*

IQTIDAR HUSAIN SIDDIQUI

Ziauddin Barani is one of those Indo-Persian historians of the middle ages whose works rest on certain theoretical foundations, for they reflected thoughtfully on the method and purpose of history. The variety of changing research methodology and critical perspectives that have been brought to bear upon Ziauddin Barani's *Fatava-i Jahandari* and *Tarikh-i-Firuz Shahi* reflect their wide range of reference and the strata of significance. It is noteworthy that the early thirteenth-century Indo-Persian historians were emigrant writers who were forced by the political upheavals in their homelands to seek refuge in India. They suffered from nostalgia and had little knowledge of the life and conditions of India. In order to gain patronage of the Sultan and the members of the ruling elite they wrote about their achievements in the political and military fields. Unlike them, Ziauddin Barani was an Indian-born historian and therefore, his *Tarikh-i-Firuz Shahi* was composed from an Indian perspective. His *Tarikh* covers the period of the history of the Delhi Sultanate from the reign of Sultan Ghiyasuddin Balban up to the sixth regnal year of Sultan Firuz Shah's reign. It was brought to completion in 1357.

The importance of Barani's contribution to historical literature lies in the fact that he widened the scope of history, writing through the inclusion of socio-economic changes that took place in each reign. For example, his account of the price-control introduced by Sultan Alauddin Khalji (r. AD 1296–1316) is fulsome in that we are provided with insights into the measures

* Edited by Sir Syed Ahmad Khan, Sir Syed Academy, 2005, 602 pp., Rs. 720.

that made it a success. Barani not only mentions the prices of essential commodities such as food grains but also of all the commodities in demand, including, cattle, war-horses slaves, cotton textiles, silk, fabric, etc. This casts light on Barani's grasp over the market phenomena and his competence in economic analysis. Likewise, the importance of the process of urbanization that served as a catalyst in socio-economic life has been duly emphasized. The reigns of Sultan Alauddin Khalji and the Tughluq sultans, which witnessed the emergence of new towns, metropolitan cities, the construction of ports, along with beautiful palaces and laying out of gardens, besides, the construction of canals and waterworks in the regions which suffered from the scarcity of rainwater has been described along with the progress of agriculture that resulted from them. According to Barani, no reign could be compared with that of Sultan Alauddin as the construction of innumerable buildings, 'the fortification walls of the city (of Delhi), Jami' Mosque, the fortification of Siri (the capital founded by the Sultan near Delhi), mosques, his own tomb, and several cities and towns were founded and completed during his reign. The construction of a new *minar* (Qutb tower) was begun and the sea-like Nawzi-i-Khas was built (pp. 325–6).

Also interesting is the mention by Barani of the efflorescence of the intellectual culture during the Khalji period (pp. 348–60). It was during this period that people began to question the accepted truth and discarded what did not appeal to reason. Describing Sultan Muhammad bin Tughlaq's interest in rationalist sciences and also his fondness for the company of philosophers and rationalist thinkers, Barani mentions the thinkers who influenced him by their radical views. Barani says that Sa'd Mantaqi (logician) who was a misguided person, Uabaid Shah'ir (the poet), an atheist, and Najam Intishar had become Tughlaq's associates before his accession to the throne. Another person, Maulana Alim Uddin, the most learned of the philosophers, spent much time with him in discussing philosophy. These scholars believed in rationalism and under their influence the Sultan had discarded traditional sciences and became a great supporter of reason.

In Firuz Shah's account, the sixth chapter, relating to the construction of a network of canals is invaluable. The details of the canals, cut-off from big as well as small rivers, are more insightful than their account furnished by the anonymous author of the *Sirat-i-Firuz Shahi* or Shams Siraj Afif. Barani implies that these canals would go a long way towards creating conditions favourable for socio-economic growth in the areas through which they flowed. That these canals, besides irrigation facilities also provided travel and transport facilities.

In fact, the publication by Barani of his *Tarikh-i-Firuz Shahi* was epoch-making. Influenced by him, the later writers followed him in devoting space to the description of socio-economic development along with political events in their respective histories. It widened the scope of historiography in medieval India.

It was really its higher standard from the point of view of historiography that Sir Syed Ahmad Khan, who was a pioneer in writing history, selected it for a critical edition of its text, some time after 1857. He edited his text on the basis of five manuscript copies acquired from different places. After several years' labour, his text was published by the Asiatic Society of Bengal, Calcutta, in 1862 without any introduction or index. For long this text was out of print and the scholars of medieval Indian history could not have easy access to it, as it was available only in a few old libraries.

The copies available were also not in good condition, their paper has become brittle and many pages are missing. We are grateful to the learned director of Sir Syed Academy, Aligarh for making its reprint available. It is also to his credit that he found out the original introduction written by Sir Syed in Urdu and appended it to the Persian text. Besides, a table of contents and index, added to the text, make it easy for the scholars to utilize the text. Sir Syed's introduction casts interesting light about his views on history writing demonstrating how modern he was in his approach to history. Again very many thanks to Professor Asghar Abbas, the Director of Sir Syed Academy, Aligarh.

Sunil Kumar's *The Emergence of the Delhi Sultanate* (*1192–1286*)

SHAHABUDDIN IRAQI

The second-half of the twentieth century witnessed a multitude of studies on medieval Indian history and culture. Besides the political history, other aspects of life and culture also began to engage attention. In surveying the modern literature, much of it is found related to the history of the Mughal Empire and little to the Delhi Sultanate period. Therefore, the publication of a work on any aspect of the history of pre-Mughal period is taken as a welcome addition to the existing literature.

As usual Sunil Kumar's recent publication is certain to attract the scholars of Indian history. The reader would, however, be disappointed at finding each of the six chapters full of factual errors, confusion, misinterpretation and unwarranted theorization. The explanations that have been offered of the patterns of behaviour of rulers are speculative and not evidence-based. Let us point out some glaring errors.

The very opening sentence of the book is misleading. Sultan Muizuddin Muhammad bin Sam, the conqueror of North India is called an Afghan and his country Afghanistan (p. 1). Sultan Muizuddin Muhammad bin Sam (hereafter mentioned as Sultan Muizuddin) was a Tajik and neither a Turk nor an Afghan. The contemporary historians, Fakhr-i-Mudabbir and Minhaj-i Siraj Juzjani incorporate genealogical table of the Shansabani dynasty to which Sultan Muizuddin Muhammad belonged. According to both the writers, the Shansabani rulers traced their genealogy to Zuhak, the legendary king of Iran and the so-called ancestor of the Tajiks. The Tajiks lived in different parts of Iran, Khurasan and Central Asia and spoke dialects of Persian language. The

* Permanent Black, 2007, 422 pp., Rs. 795.

mountainous region of Ghur and the area around it was a part of Khurasan. The medieval Indo-Persian writers' Khurasan is identified with the present-day country of Afghanistan. The name of Afghanistan was given to the region by Ahmad Shah Abdali in the eighteenth century. This change of name caused much resentment among the Tajiks and other non-Afghans who still constitute the majority of people there.

In this introductory chapter, the criticism by the author of Peter Jackson and Irfan Habib, regarding their assessment of the Sultanate polity under Sultan Muizuddin Muhammad cannot be substantiated by the evidence (p. 49). As a matter of fact, the two models of Sultanate polity had developed in Central Asia under the Ghaznavids and the Saljuqs. Unlike the centralized polity of the Ghaznavid Sultanate, the Saljuq Empire had collective sovereignty because each prince of the dynasty got an appanage with complete autonomy. The rulers of the succeeding dynasties in Central Asia adopted either one or the other model. Sultan Muizuddin Muhammad, being the Sultan of Ghazna, was inspired by the tradition set by Sultan Mahmud of Ghazna and he centralized all political and financial powers in Ghazna and India as well (cf. Iqtidar Husain Siddiqui, *Authority and Kingship under the Sultans of Delhi*, New Delhi: Manohar, 2006, pp. 18–43.

The author has also failed to escape the pitfalls in describing the conquests made by the lieutenants of the Sultan in India after his return to Ghazna in 1192. The credit of the conquests of Delhi, Meerut, Baran and Kol is given to Sultan Muizuddin Muhammad instead of Qutbuddin Aibak. The latter seized these territories in 1192–3 when the Sultan was in Ghazna. The date of the conquest of Nadia by Muhammad Bakhtyar Khalji is, according to the author, 1197 which is incorrect. Even Bihar was occupied some time in 1198, as Bakhtiyar Khalji's visit to Qutbuddin Aibak in Badaun tends to suggest. Nadia, the capital of Bengal, was attacked in 1201. Even Raverty's translation of the *Tubaqat-i-Nasiri* has not been consulted carefully.

Likewise, the analysis of the composition of the ruling elite under the Ghurid Sultan, given in the first chapter, is not only misleading but also demonstrates his inability to use the sources in original. The author blames the senior scholars for not giving an adequate attention to the ethnic background of different groups of the nobles (p. 64). He himself is not able to identify the ethnicity of the leading nobles. He would have the reader believe that the Tajiks in the nobility were immigrants from eastern Iran, while they were actually the local people of Ghur and Ghazna.

The narrative of the campaigns led by Sultan Muizuddin Muhammad against different rulers in India is full of confusion, their dates are also incorrect. For instance, the author mentions the appointment of Malik Izzuddin Kharmail in Sialkot after the conquest of Lahore in 1186. According to Juzjani, Sultan Muizuddin attacked Lahore in 1184 but he had to raise the siege and return unsuccessful, because the fort was well defended. He left Kharmail in Sialkot with the orders to have a fort constructed there for its defence. Soon, Kharmail was besieged by Khusrau Malik and his ally, the Khokkar chief. Kharmail defended Sialkot successfully and Khusrau Malik had to retreat. It was in 1186 that Lahore was seized by the Ghurid Sultan (*Tabaqat-i-Nasiri*, p. 398).

The use of the term *bandagan-i khass* not only in the first chapter but throughout the work is impertinent. The slaves were not divided into *bandagan* and *bandagan-i khass*. The slaves purchased by the Sultan were given training to serve the royal household and made progress from below. The trained and senior slaves were given high ranks and posts in the army and the administration of the Sultanate.

Like the first chapter, the second chapter is also marred by factual errors and confusion. Malik Bahauddin Tughril, a senior Turkish slave, was entrusted with the charge of Bayana territory after its conquest in 1196. Minhaj says that he died in Bayana a few years after his posting and then the Sultan allowed Malik Qutbuddin to bring it also under his control (cf. *Tabaqat-i-Nasiri*, vol. 1, p. 421). But Sunil Kumar says that he outlived the Sultan (p. 105) and assumed the title of Sultan after the assassination of Sultan Muizuddin in 1206 (p. 106). The source of information is a damaged inscription having no date. As much of its text has been lost it cannot be taken as a reliable source. Moreover, the remaining portion clearly mentions Bahauddin with the suffix Sultani which was used for the royal slave. Some other nobles have also been described differently. Hussamuddin Ughalbak has been mentioned as Aibak's rival (p. 122), though he was one of his most trusted men. He served as *naib sipahsalar* under him during the reign of Sultan Muizuddin Muhammad. After his accession to the throne, Aibak elevated him to the rank of *sipahsalar* with the charge of Awadh and Benaras territories.

The third chapter is not different from the preceding one in so far as the factual errors, confusion and misinterpretation is concerned. Nasiruddin Qubacha is said to be in rebellion against Iltutmish as if the latter's succession to the throne of Aibak was peaceful and in accordance with the will of his master. The fact is otherwise, Nasiruddin Qubacha was the son-in-law of Aibak and he is reported to have declared himself the Sultan just after the accidental death of Aibak in Lahore. At the same time, the senior nobles in Delhi placed Aibak's son Aram Shah (probably a minor) on the throne in order to maintain law and order. The *amir-i dad* Ismail secretly invited Iltutmish from Badaun to Delhi, concealed him for some time, had Aram Shah removed from the scene in mysterious circumstances and then declared him the Sultan, Iltutmish married the daughter of Aibak to legitimize his claim to the throne. The modern scholars have failed to take notice of this fact narrated by Juzjani. Nasiruddin Qubacha also had a grown-up son born of Aibak's daughter whom he had nominated heir apparent with the grant of the regal title of Alauddin Bahrain Shah. Qubacha declared himself Sultan, seized Multan, Lahore and the region of present-day Haryana up to Sirsuti (modern Sirsa) before Iltutmish left Badaun for Delhi (*Tabaqat-i Nasiri*, vol. 1, pp. 419–20). Sunil Kumar is also incorrect when he says that Iltutmish lost Lahore and the western wing of the Lahore–Delhi, appanage (p. 140). In fact, Iltutmish started an aggressive war against Qubacha after the latter's power was considerably weakened by Sultan Jalaluddin Khwarazm Shah and the Mongol invasions.

The use of the term of appanage for the Sultanate under Qutbuddin Aibak is also impertinent because Aibak had already founded an independent Sultanate in India that came to be known as the Delhi Sultanate under Iltutmish.

Besides, the translation of the terms is also erroneous. The term *turkan-i chihalgani* has been wrongly translated as forty Turkish slaves. Its correct translation is forty Turkish families. According to Ziauddin Barani, forty Turkish families (*turkan-i chihalgani*) got into prominence during the post-Iltutmish period and the heads of these families monopolized the key positions and the Sultan was reduced to a figurehead on the throne. Therefore, the inclusion of Bahauddin Balban among the senior nobles of Iltutmish whom the Sultan is said to have manumitted cannot be substantiated (p. 152). The Sultan is never reported by any contemporary writer to have granted the manumition letter to him during his reign.

It is worth noting that the biographical details provided by Juzjani in his *Tabaqat-i-Nasiri* devoted to the nobles of Iltutmish mention Balban as a junior slave who served at a low post during the reign of Iltutmish. He began to rise since the reign of Sultana Razia.

The fourth chapter, entitled 'The Ulama and the Emergence of Delhi as the Sanctuary of Islam in North India' begins with the repetition of political events, discussed in the preceding chapters. The heading gives the impression that it would have an argument on the social and cultural role that the scholars and men of talents performed under the patronage of the Sultans and the ruling elite. It is disappointing that there is nothing about cultural orientation of the Sultanate polity. In this chapter also is repeated Fakhr-i Mudabbir's statement about the migration of Turks from their ancestral Turkistan and again it is wrongly applied to India (pp. 195–6). The fact is that there was never a large-scale exodus of Turks to India during the thirteenth century. Only the Turkish slaves were brought by the merchants to India for sale. The Turks in Turkistan were still non-Muslims like the Tatars. The slaves were bought when very young, educated and trained in various arts and Persianized. That is why we find their names Persianized. The poets who composed panegyrics in their praise, address them with their Persianized names. It is, therefore, incorrect to transliterate them in conformity with Turkish syntax.

The attack by the Qaramitahs (Ismailis) on the congregational mosque of Delhi on Friday is repeated over and over again (pp. 204–8, 211, 222–3 and 237). Juzjani mentions it as an event that could be tragic but was averted by the timely action taken by the people. Juzjani blames Maulana Nur Turk for instigating people to attack the mosque at the time of congregational prayer. But Shaikh Nizamuddin Auliya refutes this allegation and calls

Nur Turk a pious Sunni Mussalman. It is not known on what ground Sunil Kumar calls Nur Turk a Shi'i.

Chapter five, entitled 'Social and Political Changes and a Disintegrating Shamsi Dispensation (1236–66)' also contains repetition of political details and no important social change is mentioned. Again, the role of so-called *bandagan-i khass* finds mention in detail. The most important event of the reign of Sultan Nasiruddin Mahmud was the destruction of Mongol vassals by Balban (Ulugh Khan Azam) before his accession to the throne in 1266 in the provinces of Sind, Multan and Lahore. It has been left out from discussion.

As regards the last chapter, it may be pointed out that in its preparation even the modern scholar's works have not been used carefully. It is marred by misquotes. For instance, Wahid Mirza quotes in his celebrated work on the life and literary works of Amir Khusrau a passage from the *Debacha* of Khusrau's first *Diwan Tuhfal-ul sighar* that contains the caricature of the Afghan soldiers belonging to the army of Multan under the command of Prince Muhammad. Khusrau had served the prince in Multan. He did not feel at ease there because he missed the charm of Delhi's social life. He found the residents of Multan crude. The Afghan soldiers residing in the fort of Multan seem to have been an eyesore for him for their rusticity. Strangely enough Sunil Kumar acknowledges Wahid Mirza's work as his source and yet he states that the Afghans described by Khusrau resided in a fort near Delhi. Moreover, the preface of the Diwan has been confused with a letter said to be written to Malik Bektars in Delhi (p. 315).This chapter also contains repetition of the Turks mentioned by Fakhr-i Mudabbir, Bahauddin Tughril of Bayana and the assumption by him of the regal title. He is mentioned alive and in opposition to Aibak and Iltutmish both, whereas he had died before Aibak's accession to the throne in 1206.

The author misquotes the celebrated medieval writers and their famous works. For example, he refers to the *Maktubat-i Sadi* (collection of one hundred letters) written by the fourteenth-century Firdausi Sufi, Shaikh Sharafuddin Firdausi. He confuses Shaikh Sharafuddin with his father Yahya Maneri, who was neither a Sufi nor is said to have written any book. Sunil Kumar writes about the *Maktubat-i Sadi*: 'We only need to peruse the quality of

Shaikh Yahya Maneri's letters sent from Maner in Bihar to his disciples and acquaintances all over north India to appreciate the rigour of scholarship and attention to detail present in the pedagogy of these matters' (p. 343). It needs to be pointed out that Yahya Maneri was the father of Shaikh Sharafuddin Firdausi. The latter having finished his education in Sonargaon (Bengal) went to Delhi in search of a *pir* (Sufi preceptor) and entered the circle of the *murids* (disciples) of Shaikh Najibuddin Firdausi. On his return from Delhi, he settled down in Bihar as the representative of the Firdausi *Silsilah.* The letters were written in a Bihar town (present-day Bihar Sharif). These hundred letters were not addressed to different persons. All of them are addressed to one *murid,* Qazi Shamsuddin, the *hakim* of Chausa. These letters are available in English translation done by Paul Jackson. Its American edition was brought out in 1980 and an Indian edition in 1990.

It is also worth noting that had the author gone through Raverty's translation of the *Tabaqat-i Nasiri* and Bruce Lawrence's translation of the *Fawaid ul-Fuad,* he would not have made this misleading remark: 'Unlike the Saljuqid Iran, no large network of madrasas of religious instruction like the Nizamia were developed under the patronage of the Sultans or Amirs (in India)' (p. 343). Juzjani himself served as the principal of the grand Madrasa-i Firuzi in Uchh and Madrasa-i Nasirya in Delhi. There were *madrasas* maintained by the state in Badaun, Sunam, Hansi, etc.

The analysis of Sultan Ghiyasuddin Balban's state policy, presented in the last (sixth) chapter is not evidence based. It is absolutely contrary to what the contemporary sources in general and Barani's *Tarikh-i Firoz Shahi* in particular suggest. The author's statement that Sultan Balban tried to keep the core areas of the Sultanate free of Sufi *khanqahs* but he could not achieve everlasting success is incorrect. Sultan Balban maintained friendly relations with the leading *ulama* of Delhi and never interfered with the Sufi shaikhs in their *khanqahs.* The leading Sufi saints who resided in Delhi were Shaikh Najibuddin Mutwakil, Malik Yar Paran, Shaikh Abu Bakr Tusi and Shaikh Badruddin Samarqandi, besides Shaikh Nizamuddin Auliya. Another fallacy marked here is the portrayal of Shaikh Nizamuddin Auliya as an ambitious worldly-minded man. He translates the honorific title of *Sultan-ul Mashaikh* as the Sultan of Shaikhs and thinks that it was adopted by the Shaikh himself, in order to rival the reigning Sultan Alauddin Khalji. He does not know that this title was given by posterity centuries after his death. The image of the Shaikh underwent change in the eyes of the coming generations and with each generation his popularity increased. He was mentioned by his disciples and the followers of his *Silsilah* neither as Khidmat-i Shaikh or Shaikh-ul Islam, as the *Malfuzat* of Shaikh Nasiruddin Chiragh, Shaikh Burhanuddin Gharib and Gesudaraz show. Shaikh Nizamuddin was a popular saint and not a political man. He was really an exemplar of piety and *tsurk* (renunciation) and believed in the service of man as the means to please God.

An Eighteenth Century History of North India

IQBAL SABIR

The decline of the Mughal Empire during the eighteenth century finally resulted in the emergence of various independent kingdoms. Like different other provincial chiefs, the Rohillas too established their rule over the fertile region of Katehar. Two Rohilla principalities were founded. One, under the Bangash nawab at Farrukhabad and the other under Ali Muhammad Khan in the north-western part of the Katehar region. They made Bareilly their capital.

Though the Rohillas had no pretensions to learning and aristocratic culture, they adopted the best of the Mughal culture and polity within a short time. Ali Muhammad and later on Hafiz Rahmat Khan evinced interest in founding educational institutions in towns, patronized men of learning and arts, and instituted welfare measures for the benefit of their people. Unlike the other rulers of northern India, the Rohillas evinced a keen interest in the economic development of their territory. It was the prosperity and resourcefulness of their territory that enticed the Nawab of Awadh to destroy the Rohilla chiefs. Safdar Jung suffered a humiliating defeat and died a frustrated man. His successor, Shuja-ud-Daula first established friendly relations with the Rohilla chief Hafiz Rahmat Khan and then destroyed his power with the help of the British army and annexed Katehar to Awadh. Shuja-ud-Daula also utilized the resources of the British army officers stationed at Katehar to keep the people of the region under control.

Several works, containing the account of the Rohilla chiefs of Katehar, are reported to have been compiled by different

* Edited by Iqtidar Husain Siddiqui, New Delhi: Manohar, 2005, 124 pp., Rs. 350.

contemporary historians. These include the *Siyar ul-Mutakhirin* of Ghulam Husain Tabatabai, the *Tarikh-i-Ahmad Khani* of Hussamuddin Gwaliori, the *Gulistan-i Rahmat* of Nawab Mustijab, Khan, etc. However, the *Qissa wa Ahwal-i Rohila* (An Account of the Rise and Fall of Rohilla Chiefs) of Rustam Ali Bijnori is the earliest one as it was compiled in 1776, just two years after the murder of Hafiz Rahamat Khan.

Nothing is exactly known about the early life of Rustam Ali Bijnori. What appears from his work is that he belonged to an elite (Ashraf) family of the city of Bijnor in Katehar later known as Rohilkhand, now in modern Uttar Pradesh. He seems to have been jobless and it was two years after the collapse of the Rohillas that Rustam Ali Bijnori was employed by an officer in the British army posted as commanding officer at Daranagar, one John Hours Ford, who was popularly called by Indians as Spot Saheb Bahadur, to teach him Urdu/Hindi. The British officer seems to have been impressed by the prosperity of the region under the Rohillas. He, therefore, desired Rustam Ali to compile the history of the Rohillas in local dialect called Urdu or Hindawi. Hence the compilation of this work took place.

A careful study of the *Qissa wa Ahwal-i Rohila* shows that Rustam Ali Bijnori must have been instructed by the British officer to narrate the historical facts in an objective manner. Every one who played a historically important role has been portrayed impartially. Unlike Rustam Ali's compilation, the other works mentioned above were written in accordance with the likes and dislikes of their patrons, portraying the Rohillas in a poor light. The writers of these works failed to write objectively. Bijnori's account, marked by objectivity in his approach, is a non-official history and contains only relevant details of historical significance. The rejection of unnecessary details makes his work unique in the history of history writing in pre-modern India.

As there was friendly relation between the British rulers and the nawabs of Awadh, Rustam Ali Bijnori gives these events objectively. At some places he seems to have been constant to write between the lines. For example, the ill treatment by Safdar Jung of the mother of Nawab Qaim Khan Bangash and confiscation of his (Qaim Khan's) wealth by Emperor Ahmad Shah at the instance of Safdar Jung is narrated objectively. The reader of the work finds a hidden critique of the emperor and the Wazir Safdar Jung in the narrative.

The *Qissa Wa Ahwal-i Rohila* is not only an important source of history but is the first attempt of history writing in Urdu language. In view of the importance of the work, Professor Iqtidar Husain Siddiqui edited it critically and published it with introductions both in Urdu and English. He has evaluated Rustam Ali Bijnori's account scientifically in the light of the methodology of both medieval and modern historiography. Really, the critical editions of such histories, particularly comprising the history of regional kingdoms, is an important academic need of our time.

S. Liyaqat Husain Moini's *The Chishti Shrine of Ajmer: Pirs, Pilgrims and Practices*

S.M. AZIZUDDIN HUSAIN

Sufism and Sufi practices have been a popular subject of study and research among scholars in both the West and East since the later half of the twentieth century. Since the literature relating to the historical role played by the Sufis in Medieval times is either in Arabic or Persian, the Western scholars had to work hard to acquire proficiency in these languages.

In the Indian subcontinent, too, the Sufis played an important role during the medieval times; in fact they influenced the life and thought of people irrespective of religion and birth. It is, however, sad to note that the works published by the South Asian as well as Western scholars on Sufism in recent years are generally based on secondary sources. There is a lack of desire on the part of young scholars to learn Persian and a correct perception of the subject cannot be had without their study in original. The work under review is an exception.

The author, Dr. Moini comes of a family, the members of which were associated with the *dargah* (shrine) of Shaikh Moinuddin Chishti for generations. He is not only well-versed in Persian but also possesses inside knowledge of the working of the shrine and its people. Not only his understanding of Sufism and familiarly with primary sources of information but also the objectivity in his approach makes this work a useful contribution to modern literature on Sufism in India. The scholars interested in Sufism and visitors to the shrine from all over the world will find *The Chishti Shrine of Ajmer: Pirs, Pilgrims and Practices* a breakthrough.

* Jaipur, 2004, 258 pp., Rs. 800.

The book is a collection of his five articles (all related to Khwaja Sahib and his shrine) presented at various international/national seminars/conferences. Two of the articles were later published in edited books on Sufism, and has been well received and assessed by scholars of repute in India and abroad. It is a significant scholarly and pioneering study on the history of Sufism in South Asia, especially of the Chishti order, and its doyen Khwaja Moinuddin Chishti and his shrine. It is due to his vigorous efforts that minor, and minute, that valuable scattered references from earliest important sources and original works has come to light, including hundreds of rare (unutilized) documents unearthed and discovered at Ajmer from private collections. They are related to the life, teachings and philosophy of Khwaja Sahib, and the inner working and influence of his shrine. On the basis of these references, royal decrees, *Vikalatnamahas, Fathmanias Dar-Jawab*, etc., mainly of seventeenth/eighteenth centuries, combined with the archival records available at Ajmer, Jaipur, Bikaner, Pune, etc., that Dr. Moini was able to produce such a masterly work.

Dr. Moini writes in his introduction that the Khwaja advocated the love of God, His Prophet, and mankind and will continue to bless his benedictions to the people for centuries to come, despite the occasional 'Curries' and 'Suvorovas' of the Christiandom of European world, and the *wahabis* of the Muslim world. History is not a haven of Rationalizers, but a 'portal' of 'Reasonables'.

The first chapter deals with the affairs and activities at the shrine and the role of its *khuddam* during the Sultanate era (1236–1562). The theory that the shrine of Khawaja Sahib was not a popular pilgrimage centre during this period, and therefore did not come up on the map of India, has been well argued, and contested scholarly and refuted solidly in this chapter. Dr. Moini has furnished several evidences from the early and contemporary sources which established that the Sultans of Delhi, Mandu, Gujarat, local Rajput chieftains, Sufism of Chishti, and other important *silsilahas,* and even the general masses were regular visitors to the shrine, and that some of the notable Sufis stayed here for years on end in the fulfilment of their spiritual quest. However, details of these are not available simply because during the period under review the city of Ajmer witnessed regular warfares among these rulers, creating chaotic conditions and turmoil in the region. It is interesting to note that a visit on foot to the *dargah* has been practised by these Sultans and other common people (devotees) centuries before Akbar did. Monarchs' grant of *madad-i-maash* land for the upkeep of the *dargah* and *khuddam*, was also made, and that the presence of a group of hereditary *khuddam* (*mujaviran, sidana*) maintaining affairs of the *dargah* and performing all the rituals and looking after pilgrims has also been highlighted. The popularity of the Khwaja and his shrine even in the remote rural areas is evident from the incident of Midhakur/Mindhakar (near Fatehpur Sikri) which promoted Akbar's first visit to the shrine in 1562, as has been recorded by Abul Fazl.

The second and third chapters of the book deals with the rituals, customs, practices performed (by *khadims* only) daily, weekly, monthly, and annually and on *Urs*—at the shrine, and the devotion, respect, veneration, contribution, and services of Hindus towards the shrine and *khuddam* as well. Both these chapters are of great value and importance in the present social context and milieu, in which communal tension is increasing day by day. In fact, none other than Dr. Moini, could have dealt with such a sensitive aspect of the shrine so brilliantly, simply because in the words of Prof. C.W. Troll:

> That Syed (Liyaqat) Moini combines the privilege of an intimate knowledge of devotional life at Khwaja Moinuddin Chishti's shrine . . . he belongs to one of the leading Khadim families there, with the skills of a trained scholar of Indian History.
>
> (*Muslim Shrines in India*, Delhi, 1989, p. xii)

As these rituals, etc., are not recorded or referred to anywhere else but practised regularly and transmitted only within the family generation after generation, this chapter (second) is of course a novel contribution on South Asian Sufism.

In fact, the rituals that are performed at the shrine round the year are the outcome and mixture of the Sufi traditions, local customs, court etiquettes (specially of the Mughals), which led to the development of the shrine as a great centre of spiritual, liberal, tolerant trends, and a symbol of communal harmony, and of course of composite culture. It should also be noted that for the third chapter, i.e. *The Hindus and the Dargah of Ajmer*

Dr. Moini has utilized rare documents for the first time, as has been rightly observed by Prof. Harbans Mukhia:

> He (Dr. Moini) has at his disposal what appears to be a dream of a collection of documents . . . and his is the attempt to establish the non-sectarian attitude of both the Sufi saint and his devotees, cutting across communal divide, which is fair if not novel.
>
> (*Indian Historical Review*, vol. XVIII, nos. 1/2 July 1991–January 1992, pp. 47/51)

In creating such an atmosphere of goodwill, mutual trust, the centuries old role of *khuddam* cannot be underestimated or ignored. In the fourth chapter, Dr. Moini, specially deals with that community, his own family, which holds the distinction of maintaining their eight centuries-old relations with the shrine of their master, in a most loyal and devotional manner in all odds and circumstances besides also keeping their family records intact. Their ancestor or founder of the family Khwaja Fakhruddin was a *Girdizi Sadat*, a cousin-cum-*pir-bhai* and *Khadim-i-Khas* (personal secretary) of Khwaja Sahib, managing the affairs of his *khanqah* during his lifetime. His descendants known in history as *Khadims* are the sole custodians of this shrine till date, uninterruptedly and hereditarily, for the last eight centuries performing all kinds of rituals, duties, services besides guiding pilgrims in performing *ziarat* at the holy place and in other religious matters, as well as looking after their comforts and needs. For centuries they have been treated by devotees as the sole representatives of the Khwaja at his shrine, and perform the twin duties of *farzand-i-jani* and *farzand-i-nani.* In that capacity they were/are always treated with respect, devotion and full attention and were/are the sole receiver of all kinds of *nazr* (cash or kind), *madad-i-maash* and other privileges and facilities bestowed by the ruling elite as well as by the common man, and spiritual heads, Hindus and Muslim alike. They are instrumental in preaching the true doctrine and lofty message of 'Chishti ideals' from a place where lakhs of people visit throughout the year. Their contribution and role cannot be overlooked, under-estimated or easily dismissed by those vested interest groups who are bent upon to malign and disrepute them. According to Dr. Moini they maintained their self-respect, dignity, loyalty, and the sanctity of the shrine at all odds and circumstances, and in the most turbulent periods of history, and emerged as one of the well-reputed Syed family of Indian soil, ever playing a vital role in creating an atmosphere of *sulh-i-kul*, and in the process of Indianization, well followed by the ruling class, specially by the Mughals and mainly by Emperor Akbar.

The last chapter is a detailed but thought provoking critique and a brilliant scholarly review of an Oxford awarded D.Phil. to P.M. Currie under the guidance of Simon Digby, later published in the form of a book entitled *The Cult and Shrine of Moin-al-Din-Chishti of Ajmer*, Oxford University Press, New Delhi in 1989. It is really a pity rather than astonishment, that a degree holder from such a renowned, reputed, world famous academic institution like the Oxford University miserably failed and was unable to understand the simplest of the simple difference between *namaz* (daily prayer) and *qul* (last day ceremony of an *Urs*), also ignorantly claiming that Shaikh Moinuddin Chishti was a saint of fourteenth century (1300–1400) and to add insult to injury a portrait of Shah Daula of Punjab is depicted as the portrait of Moinuddin Chishti, on the jacket of the book.

Dr. Moini rightly observes that the blunders with regard to the names of persons, places, buildings, books, officials, poor understanding of Sufi terminologies, philosophy, teachings, specially of *Chishti silsilah* and Khwaja Sahib combined with his negative and biased approach with regard to *malfuzat*, biographies and other Sufi literary sources and historical works, makes one feel that it is a deliberate attempt to malign the great historical personality, and to portray him as an unknown, wandering, doubtful *darvesh*. Dr. Moini's lengthy review of 87 pages of the book suggests that he has done a great job by doing a micro-study of the work and pointing out unbelievable blunders, mistakes, and shortcomings which a scholar under Simon Digby could do, and above all Oxford University could be so generous to bestow a D.Phil. degree upon such a patchy and dodgy work full of glaring blunders. It appears that all the endeavour taken by Currie is either an outcome of a well planned scheme, or preconceived notions, under the scheme or influence of either 'crusade' or 'clash' of cultures. The painstaking corrective that has been well pointed out by Dr. Moini, in the words of learned scholar and authority on Indian/South Asian Sufism Bruce B. Lawrence (Chair, Department of Religious, Duke University, Durham, North Carolina, who had also written the preface of Moini's book), should be of great value and an eye opener for those who study Currie. Bruce Lawrence sums up his findings in these words:

> The extraordinary details of his (Liyaqat Moini's) investigation is not matched in any other extant source in English, 'and', Prior . . . to this book no one has examined the nature and extent of Hindu as well as Muslim visitors' use of *Vikalat Namahs* as the lynchpin of pilgrims' observations.

On Currie's review, Bruce further suggests that

> Both the content and the tone of this major, but flawed monograph (of Currie) are examined. . . . With the result that no one should hereafter cite Currie's study without also noting correctives of Dr. S. Liyaqat Moini's thoughtful and detailed critique . . . as Currie's 184 page monograph underscores how diminished is scholarship bereft of limnolity.

In short, the work of Dr. Moini is a breakthrough in understanding the true face of Indian Sufism, mainly of Chishti *silsilah* and Shaikh Moinuddin and his shrine, and is of great value and remarkable importance for those working on Indian *tasawwuf.* Based on authentic sources and rare documents, it is a scholarly endeavour undertaken by the one who is also closely linked and associated with the shrine at Ajmer for generations. Many misconceptions with regard to the early life of Khwaja, his teachings, descendants, inner working of the shrine, *khuddam*, have been cleared and new facts and dimension have been added for the benefit of the scholars interested in the study of this great spiritualist and his place from a historical perspective.

Unfortunately the publisher has not done justice and by their callous attitude, has in fact let down the author by using poor quality paper in the book, and printing too is substandard, making the book less attractive. We hope Dr. Moini in his next endeavour will take care of these shortcomings.

Muzaffar Alam's *The Languages of Political Islam in India, c. 1200–1800*

SYED BASHIR HASAN

The author claims that his aim is to present an analysis of the politico-cultural orientation of the Indo-Persian literature produced in Persian since the beginning of the Delhi Sultanate period up to the end of the eighteenth century. The author further states: 'This book is focused on materials from premodern history of India's Islamic past. Yet, though my discussions and illustrations are from such relatively distant times, they are relevant to an understanding of the trajectory of Islam in our own time' (p. 15). At the end of the introductory chapter the author further says: 'I believe this book of history speaks as much to historians as to serious readers who, like myself, are worried by both the "threat of Islam" and the "threat to Islam"'. However, to this reviewer, the study of the book makes it clear that it has been written with preconceived notions as the author appears in each of the six chapters to search material that could be misinterpreted and help in showing that the so-called Islamic *Sharia* (canon law) was overlaid by un-Islamic accretions in the conquered lands from the very beginning of Islam. Moreover, the motive behind the publication is to prove the superiority of Western culture and thus please the Zionists and their supporters in the USA.

In this review an effort has been made to evaluate the work in the light of contemporary sources and offer some criticism.

The title of the book is so attractive that every scholar who is interested in the history and culture of India is certain to pay attention to it. But simplifications and factual errors found in each chapter are disappointing. The parts related to the Delhi

* Permanent Black, Delhi, 2004, 244 pp., Rs. 575.

Sultanate period are weak in conception and also betray the author's ignorance of some important contemporary sources that have been discovered and introduced by modern writers. Most of it seems to be written on the basis of modern works, no attempt has been made to check source material afresh. Let us begin our comment from the first introductory chapter.

The author says about Lahore: 'Though Lahore was only the capital of a Mughal province, it has almost invariably been mentioned in Mughal chronicles as *Darul-Sultanate*. Yet the governor of this province would never go so far as to assume the title of "Sultan", not even in the days when he has acquired a measure of authority' (pp. 2–3). It may be noted that since Akbar's reign Lahore served as one of the metropolitan cities like Delhi and Agra. Akbar and his successors stayed in Lahore and ruled over the Empire from there as they did from other metropolitan cities from time to time. The same status was accorded to Burhanpur after its annexation. Bijapur also enjoyed the same status after it had been conquered by Aurangzeb. They were called as *Darul-Khilafa, Darul-Sultanate, Darul-Aman*, etc. Bhimsen states that the empire would last as long as these five cities, the names of which have been prefixed with Darul exist.

In the same chapter generalization is made about Sufi's involvement in politics of the State. They are blamed for intervening and shaping the course of politics since the beginning of the Sultanate period (pp. 6–7). No evidence is cited to substantiate this statement. As a matter of fact, neither any sultan is reported to have sought guidance from any Sufi in formulating his state policy nor any Sufi tried to influence the state policy. Unlike the Sufis, the Ulama could advise the Sultan with regard to the system of governance. It is, however, true that the Suhrawardi and the Firdausi Sufis were entrusted with the charge of government of *khanqahs* (rest-houses), built outside the large cities and along the highways to provide necessary help to the wayfarers and distribute money among the poor on behalf of the Sultan. The officer-in-charge of the state-maintained *khanqah* was designated as Shaikh-ul Islam. The great Chishti Sufis neither accepted any land grant nor *shughl* (state job) because they considered a permanent source of income as the negation of *tawakkul* (trust in divine help). They could accept *futuh* (gift in cash and kind both) sent by the ruler. It may also be added that there is no shred of evidence to show that any Suhrawardi or Firdausi Sufi was ever consulted by any Sultan in state matters.

The second chapter entitled, 'Sharia, Akhlaq and Governance' begins with the discussion of *Sharia* explained in early Arab writings. The entire discussion seems to be based on the works of orientalists showing that *Sharia* (Islamic canon law) underwent change in the conquered non-Arab lands because the converts to Islam valued their old social practices and retained them. This is not the whole truth. The conversion to Islam requires the convert to repudiate the former religious allegiance and membership. After his conversion, the convert acquires a new identity and becomes part of the Muslim community. The same is the case with Christians. It is worth noting that in northern Mekran, the Turks maintained their ethnic identity from ancient time till its Arab conquest towards the close of the seventh century. Their region was called Turan. After its conquest by the Arabs, the Turks embraced Islam and intermingled with the Arabs. They merged completely with the Muslim community in due course of time (cf. Iqtidar Husain Siddiqui, 'The Process of Acculturation in Regional Historiography: The Case of Delhi Sultanate', in *Art and Culture: Endeavours in Interpretation,* ed. A.J. Qaisar and S.P. Verma, New Delhi, 1996, pp. 1–8, fns. 3 and 13). The same happened in Sind after its conquest in AD 712–13. The Sindhi converts to Islam not only changed in their customs but also mixed with the Arabs in the urban centres. They had their children educated in Islamic tradition. Some of them distinguished themselves as the leading scholars of *hadith* (Prophetic tradition). These Sindhi scholars of *hadith* belonged to the second and third generation of the converts (Bukhari and Yaqut as cited by N.B. Baloch, commentary on *Fathnama-i-Sind,* known as *Chachnama,* Islamabad, 1988, p. 104).

It is also to be pointed out that the works produced during the Sultanate period do not seem to be paid due attention and discussed on the basis of other scholars' assessment. The author's comment on Fakhr-i-Mudabbir's *Adab ul Harb wa Shuja,* dedicated to Sultan Iltutmish, 'the first sovereign Sultan of India, was compiled outside India, although it has a strong bearing on the Sultanate' is fallacious. How can the contemporary historians,

Hasan Nizami, Sadiduddin Awfi and Minhaj-i-Siraj Juzjani be ignored or refuted. They mention Qutbuddin Aibak as the founder of the independent Sultanate in India and also as an ideal Sultan who had gained fame for the invincibility of his arms. Lahore was the capital of Qutbuddin Aibak. As regards the work *Adab ul Harb wa Shuja*, it could not be written because its author was four or five years old when his father migrated with his family to Lahore after the city of Ghazna had been seized by the Ghuzz Turks in AD 1161. Fakhr-i-Mudabbir describes his father's migration from Ghazna in the *muqadima* of *Shejra-i-Ansab.* The family was associated with the Ghaznavid court for generations. He was brought up in Lahore and completed his works there. The *muqadima* added by him to the *Shejra-i-Ansab* describes the career and the reign of Sultan Qutbuddin Aibak and in view of its importance E. Denison Ross edited and published it in 1927 under the title *Tarikh-i-Fakhruddin Mubarak Shah.* It may also be added that Lahore was a prestigious city as it had served the capital of the last Ghaznavid Sultans and also been made the winter capital by Sultan Muizuddin Muhammad bin Sam (cf. *Minhaj Juzjani, Tabaqat-i-Nasiri*, vol. 1, Kabul, 1963, p. 405). Delhi was at that time a mere *pargana* headquarters of no historical importance (cf. Isami, *Futuh-us Salatin*, Madras University, 1948, p. 108). It was made the capital by Iltutmish in 1211 after he had seized power by removing Aram Shah from the scene. In his account of the Sultans who occupied the throne in Delhi, Ibn Battuta mentions Iltutmish as the first Sultan. Mention is made by him of Aibak also who declared his independence in India. Had the author checked the sources carefully he would not have failed to escape pitfalls.

Likewise, the author's analysis of the role of *Sharia* is misleading, herein the fact has been distorted. No study of the nature of *Sharia* and its impact on the life of people is complete without a reference to the *fatwa* literature produced in medieval India from time to time. The author does not seem to have had any knowledge of the corpus produced during the Delhi Sultanate period. The works on jurisprudence were many and written on the basis of classical literature. Yet, we find some relevant information about the problems that arose in changed circumstances and how the jurists found solution to them interpreting law within the framework of Hanafi law. Since students were imparted instruction in different sciences without charging any fee or wage in the past, and considered it a work of religious merit, the question arose whether the payment of salary to the teacher was lawful from the point of view of *Sharia*. The *Fatwa-i-Ghiyasia*, compiled by Yusuf al-Khatib al-Baghdadi and named after the reigning Sultan Ghiyasuddin Balban (1266–87), calls the profession of teaching noble and the payment of wages to the teachers lawful. Sometimes the use of those things or practices was allowed, in case it was not found at variance with the teachings of the Quran. Similarly, we find interesting queries made by people and the answers to them in another work *Fatawa-i-Firuzshahi*. Once it was asked whether the use of *hundi* (a draft effecting the transfer of money from one place to another) was permissible for the Muslims. The *Fatawa-i-Firuzshahi* calls it the equivalent to *Suftajah* prevalent in the Arab lands and declares its use as lawful (cf. Zafarul Islam, 'The *Fatawa-i-Firuzshahi* as a source for the Socio-Economic History of the Sultanate Period', *Islamic Culture*, Quarterly, Hyderabad, vol. LX, no. 2, April 1986, pp. 97–117, 113; idem, *Fatawa Literature of the Sultanate Period*, New Delhi: Kanishka Publishers, 2005).

The fact is that the Islamic orthodoxy preached complete adherence to *Sharia* and were opposed to un-Islamic accretions. They commanded respect in the society and the rulers also showed consideration to them. A compromise seems to have been made between the ruler and the Ulama with regard to the division of power. The Ulama were given freedom to exercise judicial and legislative powers, the Sultan was allowed discretionary power only to deal with the offenders against the State. As regards the executive and financial powers, they were exercised by the Sultan or his officer to whom he could delegate it. The discussion between Sultan Alauddin Khalji and Qazi Mughis on this matter provides us with insight into the problem. The Sultan had the grievance that he never interfered with the Ulama in matters concerning their province, yet they were critical of his state policy. The Sultan did not show any regard to the *Sharia* in dealing out punishment to the rebels or other offenders against the State (Barani, *Tarikh-i-Firuzshahi*, pp. 289–95). It is sad to mark that the entire discussion of *Sharia* is based on the works of orientalists who did not have correct perception and also presented a distorted picture to establish the superiority of Western culture.

As for the assessment by Muzaffar Alam of works on history, it is also not based on a careful and serious study. His disagreement with Irfan Habib over Ziauddin Barani's theory of aristocratic or noble birth as a requirement for the maintenance of social equilibrium in society and the longevity of the Sultanate is indicative of the fact that he did not go through his (Barani's) writings seriously. According to Muzaffar Alam, 'The principal aim is not, as has been suggested, to build legitimacy for a class state. Rather, the interests of the Muslim community define the contours of his ideas on the heredity question' (p. 41). This is to be repudiated absolutely. A person who has looked up Barani's works knows how prejudiced he is against the recruitment of the Muslims in the government service who belonged to the lower strata and were the descendants of the low-caste converts to Islam. In Barani's and his contemporaries' works we find the names of people who came from non-aristocratic families but attained to important positions in the administration and the army of the Sultanate. There was social mobility since the advent of the Khaljis to power (cf. Iqtidar Husain Siddiqui, 'Social Mobility in the Delhi Sultanate', in *Medieval India,* ed. Irfan Habib, Delhi: Oxford University Press, 1992, pp. 22–48 for details).

Further, there are incorrect reference to the secondary works in this chapter. In referring to Sultan Sikandar Lodi's *farman* that banned the use of any language other than Persian in the State offices and that led the Hindus to learn Persian, the works of K.A. Nizami and A.B.M. Habibullah have been cited (p. 42, fn. 45). Both the works, *Some Aspects of Religion and Politics in India during the Thirteenth Century* (Nizami) and the *Foundation of Muslim Rule in India* (Habibullah) exclusively deal with the history of the thirteenth-century Sultans and contain nothing about the following centuries.

The third chapter, entitled 'The Sufi Intervention', is marred by simplifications and factual errors. No distinction has been made between the approaches and styles of the Sufis belonging to different orders, the elitist and popular ones. Also no mention has been made of the existence of *Maghrabi* and *Ajmi* traditions of Sufism. The work would have us believe that 'they (Sufis) shunned ritual and ceremony, they spoke the language of the common people, they gave an impetus to linguistic and cultural assimilation' (p. 82). This statement, though based on a popular legend, is partly correct. It may be pointed out that the representative Sufis, no matter whether Suhrawadi, Chishti or Firdausi, ever shunned rituals or ceremony, they strictly followed *Sharia.* The Qalandars were exception. Secondly, the early Chishti and other Sufis who migrated to India during the thirteenth century in the wake of Mongol irruption in Central Asia and Khurasan were Persian-speaking people. There was communication gap between them and the local people. These emigrant Sufis settled down in the cities and towns where military garrisons composed of armymen of foreign origin who spoke Persian were installed. Of the early Sufis of eminence, only Shaikh Bahauddin Zakarya was an Indian-born Shaikh and his mother tongue was Saraiki. Therefore, he was the most popular Sufi, in spite of the fact that his Suhrawardi order was elitist in the sense that only educated persons found with genuine concern to spirituality were admitted as *murids* and trained in esoteric sciences to provide religious guidance afterwards. Among the early Chishtis, Shaikh Fariduddin Ganj-i-Shakar was an Indian-born Shaikh and his verses in the local dialect show that his mother tongue was also Saraiki. He and his Indian born *murids* made the Chishti order a popular order. They spoke in people's language (cf. Iqtidar H. Siddiqui, 'The Pir and Murid', *The Indian Historical Review*, vol. XXI, nos. 1–2, 1997).

In describing the relationship between the Sultan and the Sufis, the impression is given that the Sufis generally dangle around the royal Court in the hope of getting favour. There is no shred of evidence to show that any representative Sufi visited the court of his own accord to gain favour. Nor we find any evidence of the visit paid by any Sultan to the *khanqah* of a living Shaikh before the reign of Sultan Firuz Shah (1351–88). The popular legend of Iltutmish contained in the nineteenth-century *tazkira*, '*Khazinat ul Asfia,* tells us that Shaikh Qutbuddin Bakhtiyar Kaki left the will that his funeral prayer would be led by the man who neither had ever been guilty of committing adultery nor missed late night supererogatory prayer, etc. Sultan Iltutmish also joined his funeral procession. In the graveyard people were told about the Shaikh's will. Nobody came out but after some time Iltutmish himself came out and led the prayer. It has been accepted by the author uncritically even though it is not corroborated by any earlier source. The dates and times of the Sufis have been described wrongly like the medieval Sufi *tazkira* writers who had no sense of time. For instance, the early fifteenth-century Sufi saints, Shaikh Abdul Haq of Radauli and Shaikh Ashraf Jahangir Simnani are mentioned as sixteenth- century Sufis (p. 92). Shaikh Nizamuddin Auliya is portrayed as a political man and in rivalry against the reigning Sultan. The author's source of information is Simon Digby's misleading article, 'The Sufi Shaykh and the Sultan: a Conflict of Claims to Authority in India' (p. 112). Simon Digby's argument is not supported by the sources but its acceptance by Muzaffar Alam betrays his ignorance of the contemporary sources of information.

The fourth chapter, 'Language and Power', begins with the description of India's contact with Persian-speaking lands of Iran and Central Asia since the third quarter of the ninth century. No authority is cited by the author in support of his argument. This chapter also abounds in factual errors. The region of Sind is said to be the part of the Saffarid kingdom (p. 115). This is incorrect because the regions of Sind and Multan were under the occupation of the Carmathians during the period of the short-lived Saffarid dynasty. The Carmathian rulers were connected with the Fatimids whose language was Arabic. Sultan Mahmud of Ghazna is wrongly credited with the creation of the post of *Malik ul-Shuara* but there is no source of information to support it. The post as such and with this nomenclature does not seem to have existed during the Ghaznavid period. The Samanids and the Ghaznavids were great patrons of scholars and poets and the association of leading poets and men of learning became a permanent feature of royal culture in consequence but none is reported to have been made the *Malik-ul-Shuara*. However, the chapter is also marred by self-contradictory statements and confusion. Earlier the author rightly called Sultan Sikandar Lodi (r. 1489–1517) the first ruler of the Sultanate of Delhi who banned the use of any language other than Persian in the State departments. Since Hindus manned the revenue department, they learnt Persian, in order to maintain their position. Soon, the author states in this same chapter that Akbar was 'the first among the Indo-Islamic Kings of north India to formally declare Persian as the language of administration at all levels' (p. 128).

Similarly, the last chapter is full of errors and misleading statements and simplifications. The author differs from modern scholars without any sustainable reason. For example, from Iqtidar Alam Khan regarding Shaikh Abdul Quddus Gangohi's relations with Babur and Humayun as well as his hostile attitude towards the Hindu revenue officials. That the Hindus should not be employed in the revenue department. Iqtidar Alam Khan rightly points out that since the Hindu revenue officials did not show any consideration to the land grant holders in collecting state dues, the Shaikh wanted them to be replaced by Muslims and wrote to Babur about it. The author refutes Khan and states that the Shaikh had been a supporter of the Lodi Sultans and, for that reason, Babur and Humayun did not trust him. In an attempt to please Babur and win over his favour, the Shaikh started correspondence with the Timurid conquerers of India. But the fact is that Babur and Humayun made all possible efforts to please the Sufis and Ulama, in order to consolidate their power with their support. It may also be pointed out that Shaikh Samauddin Kambo Suhrawardi was the patron saint of the Lodi dynasty and not Shaikh Abdul Quddus Gangohi. Shaikh Jamali Kambo, the son-in-law, joined the court of Babur after the fall of the Lodi King (cf. Iqtidar Husain Siddiqui, *Mughal Relations with the Indian Ruling Elite*, New Delhi: Munshiram Manoharlal, 1986 for details).

To conclude, it seems that the work has been written in a hurry without any serious search for data even in the conventional sources. Much of the part of the book is not found in tune with the attractive title of the work. If the works Andre Wink, Peter Jackson and Iqtidar Husain Siddiqui had been consulted, the author would have been able to save himself from several errors.

Contributors

ALI ATHAR: Reader, Department of History, Aligarh Muslim University, Aligarh

AMAL KUMAR MISHRA: Utkal University, Bhubaneswar, Orissa

ASHOK KUMAR SRIVASTAVA: Department of History, Deen Dayal Upadhyaya University, Gorakhpur

AZIZUDDIN HUSAIN: Jamia Millia Islamia, New Delhi

B.L. BHADANI: Professor, Department of History, Aligarh Muslim University, Aligarh

GULFISHAN KHAN: Reader, Department of History, Aligarh Muslim University, Aligarh

IQBAL SABIR: Lecturer, Department of History, Aligarh Muslim University, Aligarh

IQTIDAR HUSAIN SIDDIQUI: Professor (Retired), Department of History, Aligarh Muslim University, Aligarh

JIGAR MOHAMMED: Department of History, University of Jammu, Jammu

K.L. MATHUR: Department of History, Dungar College, Bikaner (Rajasthan)

M. EHSAN AKHTAR: Lecturer, University Polytechnic, Aligarh Muslim University, Aligarh

M.S. AHLUWALIA: H.P. University, Shimla

MOHD. AFZAL KHAN: Reader, Department of History, Aligarh Muslim University, Aligarh

PARWEEZ NAZIR: Lecturer, Department of History, Aligarh Muslim University, Aligarh

R.S. SANGWAN: Reader, Department of History, Kurukshetra University, Kurukshetra

RASHMI UPADHYAYA: Lecturer, Department of History, Aligarh Muslim University, Aligarh

S. CHANDNI BI: Lecturer, Department of History, Aligarh Muslim University, Aligarh

SHAHABUDDIN IRAQI: Chairman and Coordinator, Department of History, Aligarh Muslim University, Aligarh

SURENDRA GOPAL: Department of History, Patna University, Patna

SYED BASHIR HASAN: Senior Research Assistant, Department of History, Aligarh Muslim University, Aligarh

Z.U. MALIK: Professor (Retired), Department of History, Aligarh Muslim University, Aligarh